DATE DUE

DEMCO 38-296

Above the Clouds

Above the Clouds

*Status Culture of the
Modern Japanese Nobility*

TAKIE SUGIYAMA LEBRA

University of California Press

BERKELEY   LOS ANGELES   OXFORD

University of California Press
Berkeley and Los Angeles, California

University of California Press, Ltd.
Oxford, England

© 1993 by
The Regents of the University of California

Library of Congress Cataloging-in-Publication Data

Lebra, Takie Sugiyama, 1930–
    Above the clouds : status culture of the modern Japanese nobility /
Takie Sugiyama Lebra.
        p.   cm.
    Includes bibliographical references and index.
    ISBN 0-520-07600-1 (alk. paper)
    1. Japan—Social life and customs—20th century.   2. Nobility—
Japan.   I. Title.
DS822.3.L42   1992
306.4′0952—dc20   91-28488

Printed in the United States of America
9 8 7 6 5 4 3 2 1

The paper used in this publication meets the minimum requirements
of American National Standard for Information Sciences—
Permanence of Paper for Printed Library Materials,
ANSI Z39.48-1984. ∞

To the memory of William P. Lebra

Contents

Tables

Illustrations

Plates follow page 195

Orthographic Note
on Japanese Words

Japanese names appear with the family name first, unless the authors of cited publications identify themselves using English name order. Japanese words are italicized only on their first appearance. A compound noun may be rendered as separate words (e.g., *bekkaku kanpeisha*), as one word (*kōbugattai*), or hyphenated (*ikan-sokutai*), to signify different degrees of discreteness or connectedness and somewhat depending on the word's length. The honorific prefix *o-* or *go-* is treated as part of the stem (e.g., *otsuki*) if it is inseparable from the latter in informants' speech (this is particularly true in imperial reference, e.g., *gogakuyū, gokashikin*) and thus appears under *o-* or *go-* in the glossary and index. Otherwise the honorific prefix is connected with the stem by a hyphen (*go-sanke, o-atotori*) and the stem alone is indexed.

Acknowledgments

In the long years taken up by this study, I have come into debt to countless people. Foremost, I am grateful to the former aristocrats and those around them who allowed me to share their experiences as an interviewer, guest, or semiparticipant observer of their rituals and other activities. Without their willing cooperation this project could not have been undertaken. Alas, these individuals must remain nameless, as they were promised. Many of my Japanese colleagues and friends, including my Gakushuin classmates, assisted me as introducers of informants or as informants themselves. Special thanks are due to Ms. Inukai Tomoko for her continuous generosity with time and knowledge. Gakushuin University was a host institution twice, providing me with an office and library privileges, as well as an opportunity to present a working paper at a seminar of its Oriental Culture Research Institute. I want to thank Hayashi Tomoharu and Tanaka Yasumasa for these arrangements. Among other helpers are Hashimoto Akira, Ishimoto Noriko, Matsumoto Masako, Ide Sachiko, Kuno Susumu, and the late Hara Tadahiko.

Back in the United States, my work on this book was supplemented by paper presentations at the annual meetings of the Association for Asian Studies and the American Anthropological Association. I was also an invited speaker on the subject at the University of Toronto, the University of Pittsburgh, the University of California, Berkeley, Stanford University, the College of William and Mary, and Pepperdine University. More than once, I spoke at seminars of the Center for Japanese Studies, University of Hawaii. Responses from my audience on each occasion inspired and guided my further writing.

It was my honor and good fortune to have two eminent scholars, in history and anthropology respectively, read an earlier draft of this book.

The erudite Marius Jansen alerted me to some errors in my historical presentations and interpretations and offered suggestions to improve the manuscript. William Kelly made invaluable comments that will help the book appeal not merely to Japan specialists but to other social science readers outside the Japan area. I am grateful not only for the critical suggestions but also for the warm encouragement that both gave me. I did my best to assimilate their suggestions; nevertheless, any inevitably remaining flaws are entirely my responsibility.

To be mentioned are a number of students who assisted me with library search, photocopying, filing, and coding, among them Usui Hiroko, Watanabe Eri, Suzuki Nobue, Yoshino Junko, and Frances Yuasa. James Roberson, a doctoral candidate, helped me as more than a student assistant, by exercising his professional judgment in collecting and abstracting relevant literature for me.

During the lengthy period of research I received several grants, which I gratefully acknowledge. Benefactors were the Joint Committee on Japanese Studies of the American Council of Learned Societies and the Social Science Research Council, the Japan Foundation, Wenner-Gren Foundation, and the University of Hawaii (through the Japan Studies Endowment Fund and the Presidential Scholar Award).

Some chapters partly overlap previously published journal articles. Portions of chapter 4 appeared in "Adoption Among the Hereditary Elite of Japan: Status Preservation Through Mobility," *Ethnology* 28 (1989): 185–218. The first part of chapter 7 is from "The Socialization of Aristocratic Children by Commoners: Recalled Experiences of the Hereditary Elite in Modern Japan," *Cultural Anthropology* 5 (1990): 78–100. The last section of chapter 8 repeats the content of "Resurrecting Ancestral Charisma: Aristocratic Descendants in Contemporary Japan," *Journal of Japanese Studies* 17 (1991): 59–78. And part of chapter 5 appeared as "The Spatial Layout of Hierarchy: Residential Style of the Modern Japanese Nobility," in a collection of essays edited by myself, *Japanese Social Organization* (Honolulu: University of Hawaii Press, 1992). Thanks go to these publishers for permitting reproduction.

The late William P. Lebra inspired this study initially: he was excited by the subject matter, convinced me of its worthiness, and wrote me faithful responses to my "reports" from the field. As a token of my heartfelt appreciation, this book is dedicated to the memory of Bill.

For various phases of processing the manuscript into publishable form, I owe much to the University of California Press staff, particularly Jeanne Sugiyama, Sheila Levine, Monica McCormick, Betsey Scheiner, and Dore

Brown. Special thanks are due to Anne Canright for her painstaking and thorough copyediting.

The photographs in this book are from family albums, except a few which were taken by me during fieldwork. I thank the subjects of these pictures, or their surviving families, for kindly allowing me to reproduce them here. With their permission, names are given, while anonymity is maintained in the text throughout except for historical figures and published materials.

ONE

Studying the Aristocracy

Why, What, and How?

On May 15, 1947, some two hundred titled noblemen gathered in the imperial palace to hear words of farewell from His Majesty, who in the previous year had already renounced his "divine" status and assumed a human role. Twelve days before, the new constitution had come into effect, designed to ensure universal equality under the law. The titles and prerogatives of the nobility were thus revoked, and the former elite became commoners like everybody else: the word *commoner* was now obsolete. This abolished aristocracy of modern Japan is the subject of the present book.[1] My aim is to reconstruct the experience of the former nobility both before and after this constitutional change, as recalled and depicted by its surviving members and descendants. More precisely, I have undertaken a double reconstruction: narration by the insider informants, and interpretive rearrangement by this outsider researcher.

RATIONALES AND GOALS

What is the sense, one might wonder, of studying this seemingly anachronistic segment of the population? Was I being merely a curio collector? Or, more seriously, was I following in the footsteps of those anthropologists who prepared the memory ethnographies of dying tribes? I cannot deny that the latter was an initial motive, for I did wish to be a salvage ethnographer of a rapidly vanishing culture. In this respect my interest coincided with that of my informants: the main impetus behind their collaboration was their desire to document for posterity what was now beginning to appear illusionary even to themselves. Without this common interest, the research would have been impossible or futile, and I do intend to meet the expectations of my informants by recapturing part of that world which has been lost for good.

1

There are more important rationales, however, and they will be discussed below at some length. It will be shown that the aristocracy, rather than being an antiquated phenomenon, carries a present-day significance. Although legally fossilized and socially diminished, the aristocratic status survives, or is reviving, as a *cultural* configuration. Further, the aristocracy mirrors the rest of society; in that sense the present study is about outsiders as much as insiders of this small group, about commoners as well as the elite. More generally, this study is intended to contribute to the existing literature on hierarchy and stratification. I therefore proceed from the more to less obvious layers of significance, from what motivated and prepared me when I began this research, and move on to what evolved only after I had become deeply involved in fieldwork and post-field thinking and writing.

Four levels or dimensions of significance are delineated. The first concerns the need to fill the gaps in research on social elites. The second connects the Japanese aristocracy to the emperor- and ancestor-cult complex. The third locates the hereditary elite in relation to the nonhereditary elite and pursues the contemporary relevance of studying the former. The fourth analyzes the "traditional" prewar aristocracy from a modern vantage point, as seen against the massive changes taking place in Japan and the rest of the world, in an attempt to answer why this seemingly archaic social group warrants an ethnographic study *now*. The last two levels, which are closely interlinked, are intended to address theoretical concerns.

Let us first consider the dearth of research on elites. In studying complex societies, anthropologists and sociologists have traditionally (except in the case of caste societies) paid more attention to the lower or middle than the upper strata of the society, more to peasant or folk culture than to elite culture. This is certainly true of Japanese studies. Substantial knowledge has been accumulated on rural peasants since John Embree's (1939) pioneering work on Suye Mura, and on the lower to middle classes in cities. Yet no research is available on upper-class Japanese, with one recent exception dealing with the business family (Hamabata 1990)—not the same substratum of the upper class as I describe, but connected with it. To be sure, historians have a magnitude of historical and biographical documentations of the hereditary elite, but no study has yet been done in ethnographic perspective.

As a possible reason for why Western ethnographers have avoided the elite, Marcus (1979, 136) mentions the researchers' moral and ideological sympathies with common people: "As a result, the cultural conditions of typical subjects of ethnography in complex societies are humanly portrayed while those of elites in the background appear more as caricatures, created from the ideological biases of the ethnographer combined with inferences drawn from non-ethnographic data on elites." Indeed, as if to confirm this viewpoint, one of my Japanese colleagues characterized a former aristocrat he had met as a "clown." Fuse (1972, 125–26), too, mentioned a similar ideological "hostility" toward the elite among sociologists. Whatever the reasons for the paucity of research on elites generally, that gap in our understanding of Japanese culture and society certainly needs to be filled. This book, then, is intended to reveal some ways in which elite culture is different from that of commoners, and at the same time to dispel some of the stereotypes of the people "above the clouds."

With this emphasis on status, might similarities between Japanese and non-Japanese elites lead us beyond the national border? After all, even the United States, generally considered a foremost representative of egalitarian, mobile, achievement-oriented, and capitalistic societies, has "dynastic" families that have accumulated capital over generations and thus form a hereditary class (Hansen and Parrish 1983; Marcus 1983). Sinclair flatly states: "That a genuine American aristocracy now exists is incontestable. The Cabots and the Lodges and the Biddles and the Whitneys have far longer and more distinguished pedigrees, not to mention greater wealth, than most Europeans who bear titles, for most titles in Europe date from no more than the nineteenth century" (1969, 267). More comparable to the Japanese elite may be the British nobility, which, according to my informants, offered a primary model for many aristocrats of Westernizing post-Meiji Japan. What similarities or differences do we find? In this book, although I do make comparative references to other societies (mainly the British) through occasional insertions and footnotes, I necessarily concentrate on the Japanese case as a step toward understanding human universals with regard to elite status or hierarchy in general.

This first level of significance assumes that the nobility formed a status group with institutional or social boundaries that inhibited, if not precluded, crossover between nobles and commoners. One of my goals was to locate such boundaries and to delineate the culture of this upper crust of society. This does not, however, mean that commoners were set apart from the nobility, or that the latter has lost its significance in democratic Japan. Which leads us to the second dimension.

In prewar Japan, the nobility was closely allied with the royalty, and in fact the emperor was a focal point of aristocratic life, as every chapter of the present volume will make clear. This historical memory has not vanished in the mind of the populace, but is kept kindled by the presence of the emperor and his family, the only hereditary elites today who survived constitutional democratization. The emperor, though no longer divine or sovereign, remains a viable center of contemporary Japan. In fact, in this age of mass media, the "humanized" emperor plays a more visible role than ever before in authenticating, dignifying, dramatizing, or otherwise highlighting political decisions, high-level state appointments, and social events. As Japan's role in international politics expands, the emperor's presence is conspicuous on television screens as the ceremonial host of foreign dignitaries. Indeed, Japan seems to share an "inverted relation between spectacular pageantry and de facto royal power," a situation attributed to the Swedish court as well by Rundquist (1987, 2). The emperor has not ceased to be a dominant symbol although he is no longer politically dominant. An emperor amounts to no less than what Ortner (1973) calls "a summarizing symbol," arousing reverence and catalyzing emotions, as occurred during the last phase of the illness that ended Emperor Shōwa's sixty-two-year reign on January 7, 1989. It is also understandable that left-wing activists target the emperor as the most central embodiment of the Establishment, whereas right-wing extremists rally around the emperor for the very same reason.

As long as the emperor or royalty remains vital, the former nobility retains its symbolic weight because of the halo effect. There continues to be real or presumed intimacy between the royal family and the former aristocracy, for the latter serves as a buffer to protect the royal life space from public intrusions. Indeed, the impenetrability of the imperial private sphere is the very source of a mystique that envelops the nobility as well.

Anticipations of a royal marriage have always stimulated speculations regarding sons and daughters of the former aristocracy as possible candidates, and the media have never missed any opportunity to play up such associations. According to a veteran journalist specializing in imperial household affairs (Togashi 1977, 73), the list of bridal candidates for then Crown Prince Akihito (the present emperor) was first compiled from among former noble families only, with no question being raised regarding this limited scope of choice. The nationwide sensation caused by the surprising nomination of a commoner businessman's daughter merely underscored the continuing role presumably played by the former nobility in royal affairs. Nor did this break with the imperial tradition, drastic as it was, bring to an end the royalty-nobility matrimonial alliance: subsequent royal marriages (of the crown prince's younger brother and sister) were with descendants of noble families.

Nevertheless, the remnant of matrimonial or social affinity between the royalty and nobility is probably destined to vanish entirely. Prince Aya, the younger son of Emperor Akihito, personally chose Kawashima Kiko, the daughter of a commoner scholar, as his bride, an "unexpected" announcement that the whole nation hailed with feverish enthusiasm. The hereditary status of former nobility seems to have lost its relevance in the selection of a future empress, a bride for the crown prince.

The resiliency of the emperor cult, and the resonance between the royals and nobles or between these hereditary elites and the Japanese populace as a whole, is deeply embedded in the cultural legacy of ancestor worship. Japanese people in general, resisting the monotheistic idea of a single, transcendental deity, continue to derive their mental security and spiritual salvation from a sense of connection with their ancestors. Their overall identity and self-esteem are, in my view, ultimately linked to their images of ancestors. The ancestral shrine is the center of the household, and parents continue to call on the authority of family ancestors in disciplining their children and themselves. For the majority of Japanese, memorial services are the most important religious rite. One survey (NHK Yoron Chōsabu 1984, 6–11) suggests a persistent and widespread sense of attachment to dead ancestors: 57 percent of the survey sample prayed at the household ancestor altar at least occasionally, and 28 percent every day; 89 percent visited the cemetery on the days of major annual rites for the dead at least occasionally, and 69 percent did so regularly; and 59 percent felt "connected with ancestors at the depth of heart." To this extent, Japanese remain ancestor worshipers.

It is all too natural that a commoner Japanese will elevate his or her "original" ancestor to the status of village headman, samurai, warlord, feudal domain lord, court noble, royal prince, or emperor. Stories of subsequent family downfall (to explain one's present commoner status) are heard more often than those of ascension from bottom to top.[2] Given the ancestor cult, the individual bases his or her self-esteem in part on aristocratized ancestors. There is nothing surprising in the Japanese tendency to trace genealogies upward to prominent ancestors rather than downward to obscurity. If one's own ancestry is found to be not so lofty, vicarious identity may be drawn from a borrowed genealogy. In the *iemoto*, for example—traditional schools of arts such as the tea ceremony, flower arrangement, dance, and music—the grand master (himself called iemoto as well) is worshiped by his disciples as embodying the essential formula of the art created by his "original" ancestor and perpetuated by more recent ancestors. By becoming attached to the iemoto master, a disciple takes part in the long line of distinguished descent of the iemoto family and thereby elevates his or her identity. In the same vein, the nobility has popular appeal as a model for identity construction. The nobility, like the iemoto, represents the "other" for the commoner "self"; via ancestors, however, the noble other becomes accessible and absorbable into self.

It is against this general background of genealogical aristocratization—whether direct or vicarious—that we can understand the persistent idiom of *kishu,* "noble species" or "of noble origin," as a category of people. How often we hear such phrases as *yuisho tadashii, rekki to shita, o-iegara no yoi, kakushiki no takai* (all meaning "of proper origin" or "of good birth") in asserting a person's unequivocal reputation. Bridal candidates for royal princes, including those of commoner origin, are characterized in these terms by the approving media. In a TV show featuring Crown Prince Hiro's speculated marriage choice, the emcee was carried away in endorsing one potential candidate: "Miss —— is fully qualified in every respect. First of all, she is from the right kind of family [*rippana o-iegara*]." A Gakushuin University student, "she has been the best friend of Princess Nori since primary school at Gakushuin." Even though her family does not belong to the nobility, still "her great-grandmother is said to have mothered Emperor Taishō." In other words, "Miss ——" virtually "came from the former nobility [*kazoku shusshin de irassharu*]." The speaker was saying what the popular audience wanted to hear.[3]

Ancestor worship and the emperor cult are wrapped in a single package. The emperor's legitimacy as a key symbol of the nation has been largely unquestioned because of his genetic connection with a supposedly "unbroken" line of imperial ancestors whose origin fades into the mythical space of heaven. In other words the emperor cult is inseparable from the ancestor cult. It is no coincidence that Robert Smith (1974) begins his discussion on Japanese ancestor worship with a historical account of the imperial house. To the extent that the emperor cult and ancestor worship are alive, the hereditary charisma of the nobility remains untarnished. (Aristocratic ancestry occupies a prominent place throughout this book, but especially in chapters 3 and 4.)

The general sense, however ungrounded objectively, of national homogeneity and kinship, of the Japanese as a single race, follows from genealogical aristocratization, which ultimately can end up with all Japanese ancestors converging in one common stock. This feeling of shared ancestry has significant repercussions for minorities, who cannot claim to partake of such noble heritage. I return below to this issue of dominant versus marginal groups in Japan; for the moment, suffice it to say that the significance of research on elites extends far beyond the tiny anachronistic segment of nobles per se and to the general population, in terms of self-other interchange via the emperor/ancestor cultural package. The people "above the clouds" are thus viewed through a double lens by those down below: as an inaccessible other sharing the imperial mystique, and as an accessible other to be assimilated for self-elevation. Such bipolarity is inherent in the kishu consciousness.

I have argued for the contemporary and societal significance of the present study by linking the aristocracy to the still-viable cultural legacy of the emperor/ancestor complex. Underlying this argument is the assumption that the past survives in the present. This survival premise is then stretched or qualified by the third and fourth levels of significance. At the third level, we consider the nonhereditary elites who dominate modern Japan, beginning with the educational elite.

It is a national educational obsession to exact rigorous standards in the school life of Japanese children, from preschool through high school and to the "hell" of entrance examinations. Policymakers, seeking to unwind this national frenzy, are trying to overhaul the educational program, but without success. Children continue to crowd the ever-proliferating cram schools—commercial establishments that supplement the regular school curriculum—thus relinquishing play hours and cutting sleep time. This educational obsession on the part of both children and their parents reflects a very realistic perception: Japan's dominant career structure is interlocked with the eminence of its universities.

Commitment to educational attainment as the primary determinant of one's career placement is itself a sign that the prewar hereditary elite is obsolete and the ancestor market bankrupt. Takane (1976) demonstrates the crucial role played by the University of Tokyo, from the Meiji period on, in siphoning commoners into the political elite, thus eventually driving the hereditary aristocrats out of political leadership. At issue, in fact, is not simply the old versus the new. Japanese have long been education-minded, reaching back at least to the samurai class in the Tokugawa period (Dore 1965). More broadly, too, the political and social history of Japan is well marked by dynamic leaders and rulers of humble origin—as best represented by Hideyoshi (detailed in chapter 2 below). "Achievement" is among the most frequently cited attributes of Japanese.

The record of successful entrance into a prominent university translates into a pedigree that is carried as an inalienable asset and, when appropriate, displayed throughout the career of its possessor. Conversely, those who lack a proper educational pedigree feel doomed for good. Hence, two paths are open to the average Japanese: either one takes an "elite course" backed by one's educational pedigree, or one must make do with the mediocre back-alley course open to educational "common-ers." It is in this context that the ferocity of educational monomania be-comes understandable. The composition of the elite has changed radically, but I discern a conversion of achievement into ascription, mobility into rigidity. Status here is not derived from birth, but acquired in adolescence at the time of passage through entrance examinations into university. In a similar vein, Galtung (1971, 357) draws an analogy between aristocracy and "degreeocracy," or between biological birth and social birth:

> It (the system) is essentially an ascriptive system in the sense that once one is allocated to a group it is very difficult to change one's class. It is like being born into a class, only that *in a degreeocracy social birth takes place later than biological birth*. More precisely it takes place at the time of the various entrance examinations, and like all births it has its pains. There is the pregnancy period with some element of social isolation (preparation for the exam); the labor (the exam itself); and there are miscarriages and infant mor-tality. . . . It is traumatic and dramatic. . . . The entrance exami-nation is to be born again. (emphasis in original)

The candidate's success arouses extraordinary excitement among fam-ily and friends because success means a huge step of sublimation from achievement to ascribed status. Precisely because educational or profes-sional aristocracy is an oxymoron, virtual aristocratization through edu-cational performance magnifies liminal grandeur. In short, ascription serves as a cultural template for achievement. The educational aristocracy, born thus in youth, forms the career elite in various fields—economic, political, administrative, professional. This is demonstrated every time a top leader in any particular field is introduced with his educational back-ground (see Rohlen 1983, 88–91).

There is nothing new about a nonhereditary elite: indeed, Japan's aris-tocracy created in the modern period (1868–)—the subject of this book—itself was an amalgam of old, hereditary nobles and hereditarily lightweight upstarts (see chapter 2). What is new is an enormous prolif-eration of fields for placement of nonhereditary elites, along with the predominance of the educational route for the attainment of elite status, which amounts to an aristocratization of the educational elite. Further, the unprecedented affluence of Japan since the 1960s corresponds with the rise of a massive economic elite topped by high-technology multi-national businesses. Among the most recent economic aristocrats are young people, including unmarried "office ladies," who with insatiable appetite consume the latest fashions, whether of commodities like brand-name dresses, accessories, perfumes, luxury cars, boats, and art objects, or of services like those of trendy beauty salons, well-known French restaurants, and foreign travel. These parvenu compete in joining prestigious sports clubs—tennis, golf, horseback riding—whose fees are often double or triple a salaried worker's annual income.

This instant aristocratization of the affluent class, entailing a gaudy commodification of status, while despised and abhorred by old-time aristocrats as a wild version of nouveau riche status grabbing, is not totally anomalous; rather, it is indexical, however crudely, of the fundamental nature of a social hierarchy. Just as educational achievers are aristocratized, so are the moneyed classes. This juxtaposition of hereditary and nonhereditary elites brings us to the heart of stratification in general, and Japanese stratification in particular.

Involved here are basic polarities such as ascription versus achievement, prestige versus power, status (of honor) versus class (of wealth) in the Weberian sense, and rigidity versus mobility. The main issue is how one side relates to the other, how the two are reconciled with each other in a shared status system. The present study addresses this theoretical question from the point of view of the hereditary elite—the issue being how deeply the first of each pair entangles with the second.

It is likely that some compromise, collaboration, exchange, collusion, complicity, or conversion occurs, that the two sides in fact enhance each other through the mechanism of "agglutination" (Lasswell and Kaplan 1950, 58) whereby one's position in an ascribed hierarchy, for example, correlates with that in an achieved one, status of honor with economic class, prestige with power, and so on. When a discrepancy exists, exchange or "complicity" between the "symbolic capital" of the hereditary status and the "economic capital" of the bourgeoisie, to appropriate Bourdieu's (1984) terms, is a possible solution. But even so, it is unlikely that perfect fusion is possible: dissonance, ambivalence, tension, guilt, or resentment may always be involved, and outright repulsion, confrontation, or inverse correlation is conceivable. An alternate solution may therefore be found in the coexistence of both as formal and informal, structure and practice, front and rear, public and private, as sanctioned in Japanese idiom. Whether and how an alliance or exchange between the hereditary and nonhereditary elite took place may be inferred from instances of marriage (the topic of chapter 6) and from the occupational careers of aristocrats (chapter 8).

The polar types, in short, make sense only if they are taken together as a dynamic interchange having mutual implications, as Parsons (1954) has demonstrated with regard to ascription and achievement, or "quality" and "performance." We must therefore ask again, Is the ancestor market really bankrupt? Has there been a complete turnover in the composition of the elite from the old to the new? If one glances at recent popular publications on the old aristocracy, the answer would be a strong no. These publications indicate clearly and consistently that the old nobility and the royal family are closely connected with individuals prominent in the governmental, political, financial, industrial, and professional domains (Shin Jinbutsu Ōraisha 1988a, b, 1987; Satō 1987; Hayakawa 1983). The Japanese popular press seems never to tire of printing genealogies showing networks of alliance between ancestry and money, name and power, heredity and talent. The Shōda, the commoner natal family of Empress Michiko, has often appeared in these published genealogies. Whether such a genealogy is faithful to "reality" is less important than the fact that it conveys the "cultural" survival of the old elite as assimilated by the rising elite.

The marketability of the old aristocracy can be seen in the appropriation by a number of professional actors and actresses of the names of prominent court nobles, such as Konoe, Ichijō, Nijō, Kujō, Tokudaiji, and Saga (Shūkan Yomiuri Henshūbu 1987, 325)—a telling sign that the aristocracy has been reincarnated in popular culture. If translated as snobbery, aristocracy is indeed a universal, timeless phenomenon. And indeed, the old, supposedly nonexistent elite is being recycled in contemporary Japan. In the following chapters, hence, I will explore how the hereditary elite and nonhereditary elite, status and class, honor and power, symbolic capital and economic capital, have entered into alliance, conflict, or any other relationship.

The foregoing does not imply that the hereditary elite has been free from criticism, animosity, or ridicule in the post–World War II era. On the contrary, negative views have been expressed not only by outsiders but by members of the hereditary elite themselves. Such criticism may reflect universal ambivalence toward power, authority, and the social order as being at once desirable and oppressive (Sangren 1988). Here we are facing another set of polar types of stratification: hierarchy versus equality, verticality versus horizontality.

Nakane (1967) has labeled Japan a "vertical society," though this view has been challenged by many who see more "horizontality" in Japan, whether of village organization or business management. Indeed, common sense tells us that no society is either exclusively vertical or horizontal, and Nakane's book itself reveals an extremely egalitarian aspect of Japanese society. Even the Tokugawa social structure, which is regarded as the most rigidly stratified system in Japanese history, was not simply vertical. Irokawa (1975), like folklorists led by Yanagita Kunio, sees equality as having its genesis in the rural, "natural" community of the *buraku* (hamlet), uncontaminated by external administrative authority; in his view, that ideal is being recaptured as a model for citizens' protest movements in Japan today.

I think, though, that it is naive to dichotomize equality and hierarchy in this manner. It would be more productive to look at how one links to the other within the same system. John Whitney Hall (1974b), for example, synthesizes the two sides of Tokugawa society into one package: rule by status. Dore (1973), in comparing British and Japanese factories, perceives in the latter *both* a more elaborate hierarchy *and* greater equality. And Bestor (1989) traces the subtle but dynamic coexistence and interchange of horizontal and vertical relationships in a Tokyo neighborhood.

Solidarity or even intimacy goes with hierarchy as much as with equality. Hierarchy, far from being a solid pyramid, is rather a fluid, multiple, vulnerable organization. This book reveals the contacts that the nobility had with lower strata of society. The elite can exist only if there are nonelites who sustain the status boundary: paradoxically, status distinction is maintained by having commoners cross the boundary, freely enter the aristocratic life space, and control their aristocratic masters. Such a cross-class relationship may, however, be a social logic rather than a paradox. In the high society of nineteenth-century England, too, as depicted in Jane Austen's novels, superiors maintained their independence by being dependent on inferiors (Handler 1985). A superior's dependency may have been even greater in Japan, where individual autonomy was not as prized as in England. It will be shown in chapters 5 and 7 that the two layers commingled, sometimes to an astonishing degree.

I have presented three levels of significance (and goals) of this research. Now we come to the fourth and last. This has to do with the twofold change that is engulfing not only Japan but other postindustrial societies as well, one that goes hand in hand with high technology and economic prosperity. One aspect of this change is "informationalization" through audio-visual mass media and computerized communication. Japan seems irreversibly trapped by the information industry, which not only codes, represents, and thus produces reality, but also sensitizes its clients to the newest information, along with the newest equipment—information and equipment that, however, are destined to become outmoded by whatever comes next. Updating is only an instant ahead of outdating; newly gained information quickly ends up in a trash can. Thus, an informationally precocious younger generation rises to outmode the older generation in increasingly shorter and more rapid cycles. Even the so-called *shinjinrui* (new human being) is said to have become obsolete. The information kick seems to intensify the Japanese cultural drive not to be left behind.

The second aspect of the ongoing change is internationalization or globalization, which presses Japan to lower or even remove its national or ethnic walls. While trade-barrier issues seem never to be resolved, goods and personnel *are* crossing the national borders in unprecedented magnitude, bringing ordinary Japanese into direct encounter with foreigners. Japan, having risen as an economic elite that stands out among economic commoners of the world, is a target of resentment, but at the same time it is solicited, not as a workaholic producer, but as a prodigal consumer in foreign markets—a true aristocrat. As a result, overseas tourism (including sex tours) has become routine for average citizens of Japan; studying at foreign schools, instead of being subjected to the rigid examination system, is a widely accepted option; and multinational businesses send native employees to overseas subsidiaries to maintain long-term contact with foreign locals. The host-guest relationship is also reversed. Japan hosts an increasing number of foreigners as travelers, investors, employees, teachers, students, stage and media performers, conferees, refugees, and so on. International schools have been set up to internationalize both Japanese and foreign enrollees. Cross-national contact results in intercultural and interracial marriages, which are no longer anomalous. Allied with the information industry, live overseas broadcasts flash instantaneously on Japanese televisions, and American movies are a standard viewing option.

Japan, then, is today confronted with a historically unparalleled situation: unrestricted access to constantly changing up-to-date information and expanding foreign contact. But no change is linear; indeed, the more sweeping and radical a change is, the more likely it is to invoke the past, tradition, and continuity (Shils 1981). Even while they adapt to the above changes, Japanese react by searching for fixed, "timeless" roots of their "indigenous" identity. This reaction seems stimulated by an ironic byproduct of internationalization: namely, the worldwide exposure of historically persistent fissures between dominant and marginal Japanese. Especially noteworthy in the "marginal" class are former *burakumin* (outcaste) and Korean Japanese, who, though physically and culturally indistinguishable from the "mainstream" Japanese (De Vos and Wagatsuma 1967; Lee and De Vos 1981), remain targets of discrimination. In this sense, their situation differs from that of American blacks (Russell 1991). Illegal immigrant workers from Southeast Asia, the latest addition to the minority list, are also widely reported as targets of Japanese abuse and exploitation.

Internationalization, together with speedy, worldwide dissemination of information, thus poses a threat to the national, ethnic identity of Japan. It should come as no surprise, then, that the double change described above coincided with a search for and recovery/discovery of Japan's ascribed, rooted self. This fact is best exemplified by domestic tourism. As Ivy (1988) shows, the Japan National Railways, tied up with Dentsū, the world's largest advertising agency, began the "Discover Japan" campaign in 1970. Nostalgic appeals, radicalized paradoxically under the subsequent slogan of the 1980s, "Exotic Japan," were readily accepted by prosperous masses of clients.

The mass media, even as they circulate constantly renewed information and present an elusive, boundless, chameleonic, chaotic world, are playing a significant role in promoting the "retro" boom. Television programs highlight the buried, hidden, or vanishing legacies of the past, such as folk crafts carried on by a handful of people, local performing arts, and centuries-old houses, temples, and shrines. Historical dramas depict the morally disciplined, socially ordered cosmos (which includes a rigidly structured gender hierarchy) of old Japan. The national government, through the Cultural Agency (established in 1968), launched a systematic cultural-property preservation policy, which has transformed a multitude of symbols of local and national "traditions" into public museums of sorts, which in turn serve as major tourist attractions. It is this backdrop of nostalgic yearning that makes the former elite worth studying.

Nostalgia is, according to Lasch, an inclination to evoke the past not so much in order to restore it as "to bury it alive" by "lock[ing] it up in museums," not to establish a continuity with the past but to dramatize a discontinuity from it (1989, 69–70). Lasch's definition may reflect the future-oriented American resistance to being dominated by the past, but if it contains any universal validity—and I believe it does—then nostalgia is better aimed toward the archaic, not the recent, past.[4] Understandable, then, is the spate of popularized archeology that has accompanied the construction boom. This fever for things prehistoric was foreshadowed in the late 1940s by the Toro site excavation and the sensational disclosure of a well-preserved farming village of the Yayoi period (300 B.C.– A.D. 300). This discovery allowed Japanese, precisely when defeated and stripped of their identity, to reemerge with a repaired national identity: they found their roots in a rice-growing culture that had lasted for two millennia (Edwards 1991). Again, the aristocracy, along with the imperial lineage, is rooted in its ancient origin—the symbol of a fossilized past well suited for nostalgic consumption. I show in what follows, particularly in chapter 8, what part surviving aristocrats play in nostalgic dramas and the retro kick, how, in other words, they contribute to contemporary *popular culture*. Unlike Ivy (1988), who finds in remote, rural, and marginal space and people sources for the "cultural recuperation" of Japan, I see a recuperative asset in the centrally located, urban elite. If these two spheres have anything in common, it is that both are vanishing. (For dialectics of change and nostalgia, see also Kelly 1986; Robertson 1991.)

It goes without saying that nostalgia ties in with the second point made above, namely, the ancestor/emperor cult. Ancestry translates into "blood," which may be pure, not so pure, or downright polluted. That the fear of contamination by "impure" blood has not diminished in urban Japan is demonstrated by the thriving detective agencies that undertake premarital or preemployment investigations of a candidate's family background. As Japan faces the inevitable inflow of aliens as part of internationalization, the Japanese "blood ideology" (Hayashida 1976) may be restimulated and revitalized. The purity of one's blood tends to be measured by the nobility of one's ancestors, the emperor's being the purest. Nostalgia for an immutable, native identity is interlocked with the idiom of kishu (noble species), as discussed above. This study thus explores the vulnerable point of Japanese self-identity as it is reflected in life experiences codified and recalled by the nobility.

CULTURE AND STATUS: THEORETICAL DIRECTION

Having presented the rationales and objectives of this book, I turn to its overall theoretical direction. As indicated by the subtitle, this study attempts to delineate the status "culture" of the aristocracy. Culture is generally understood as that which orders a universe that would otherwise be chaotic and absurd. The vast literature in contemporary anthropology provides multiple definitions of culture; I have decided to focus on the following delineation because of its relevance to my purpose.

Culture can be distinguished from what it is not in two ways. It is defined, first, in opposition to nature—biological and ecological—in that culture is designed and created by human ingenuity and work. As such, culture functions to extend or control, accommodate or disturb, or in some way modify nature. This definition covers both the adaptive and repressive function of culture relative to nature. Culture in this sense is an artificial construct; it is technology in a broad sense, in opposition to the world of givens. Second, and more narrowly, culture refers to the symbolic realm of human action, which is tapped for signification and representation of "reality" and is thus distinguished from the thing signified or represented. Culture here stands for meaning, conceptual scheme, code, cognition, ideation. This semiotic focus tends to capitalize on the operation of the "mind," thereby allying culture with the philosophical tradition of idealism in opposition to materialism (Sahlins 1976). Paradoxically, however, the same focus draws attention to communication among members of a cultural community and the sociological emphasis on collective sharing as an essential part of culture. This communicative dimension takes culture beyond the subjective mind over to the intersubjective plane: culture is not in a mind, but between minds; not private, but public (Geertz 1973).

These two definitions of culture are not necessarily distinct from each other. All symbols are indeed products of human construction (or technology), while the nature-culture boundary is made, and nature becomes recognizable, only through the semiotic application of culture. Nevertheless, difference in perspective and emphasis is significant. In the following discussion, I attempt to relate culture thus defined to nature and the "real" world insofar as it is relevant to the status of aristocracy. I argue with Sahlins that culture and non-culture (nature/reality) are conceptually independent, that is, irreducible to one another. But I do not believe, unlike pure symbologists such as Sahlins, that culture can be fully dissociated from nature/reality. Here I come closer to action-theory sociologists like Parsons (1951), who is strongly opposed to reductionism and insists on the "independence" of action systems or subsystems, but whose analytical work concentrates on their "interpenetration." How independence is reconciled with interpenetration is elusive, to be sure, and in his later work (1961) Parsons does propose the idea of a hierarchy of four systems—cultural, social, psychological, and biological, with culture at the top—a formulation somewhat similar to Dumont's (1970) encompassment. Still, Parsons never did away with the notion of energy "input" from a lower to a higher level.

In analyzing status, I start with the culture-nature distinction. Status is a cultural construct par excellence, having nothing to do with the naturally given, as evidenced by the variation in status systems from society to society. Complicating the nature-culture dichotomy, however, is the fact that culture incorporates some arbitrarily selected elements of nature in its construction of status, such as race, gender, body height, energy level, and life stage. Culturally created status, moreover, is often deemed a law of nature. This culture-nature interchange (interpenetration?) assumes a special significance when applied to the status of hereditary elite.

Generally, aristocrats are distinguished from commoners by the main-tenance of a wider gap between cultural control and natural proclivities. Aristocrats, for example, are supposed to be well regulated by cultural rules of decorum, inoculated against the unpredictable outbreak of nat-ural drives, protected from "organic eruption" (Douglas 1975, 213). Aristocracy best symbolizes what Elias (1978) calls "the civilizing proc-ess," which transforms such natural vagaries as spitting and nose blowing. The result is a strict division of culture and nature, or of the public and private spheres of life, allowing nature to be concealed from public view. Hayden (1987) addresses the same situation when she discusses the two "bodies" of the British monarch—the "body politic" and the "body natural"—which must remain rigorously separate. This nature-culture segregation can be further characterized by the stereotypic irrelevance of the aristocrat's activity to his physical survival. He busies himself with ritual preoccupations and enjoyment of esthetic taste rather than pursuit of utilitarian gain, leisurely play instead of strenuous work, dilettantism rather than professionalism.

Yet significantly, all this "culturalization" (or "denaturalization") of behavior or activity should occur "naturally," as if one were born with it. What is more, the aristocratic status is deeply embedded in what is deemed as nature—blood, descent, ancestry, heredity. More correctly, these criteria are culturally defined as natural processes or states that are beyond human control (hence ascribed). The aristocrat, who is expected to denaturalize his behavior, activity, and appearance, is thus heavily dependent on nature and subject to its unpredictable course. The "natural" base of an aristocratic family—its "blood"—may run out, as when no heir is born, thus threatening the line's extinction. But status is a cultural production, after all; when "anemia" strikes the family, status will likely be reproduced through cultural "transfusion."

More generally, the rule of separation between nature and culture, or between the naked and the dressed-up body, requires special accom-modations, for aristocrats are just as embodied as commoners. I venture to propose that aristocratic subculture, if there is one, crystallizes and is elaborated around the imperative of segregating and bridging culture and nature. In the following chapters I will continually question whether this in fact occurred, and if so, in what guise.

Similar confluence occurs in the second, semiotic dimension of culture as contrasted to reality. I see two sides of reality: subjective and objective. First, I want to capture the relationship between status culture and the subjective experience of individual aristocrats. If culture is meaning that does not reside in the individual mind but moves between minds, we need to see how it relates to the inner thoughts, feeling, and selfhood of persons. Despite the Geertzian definition of culture, it goes without saying that intersubjective meaning depends on the meaning carried in each individual, approaching the world with his or her own psychological apparatus, and vice versa. This focus on personal experience is largely lacking from the elite study, and I regard it as a native ethnographer's privilege to fill this gap (a point which raises a methodological issue that I will tackle later).

More importantly, in looking more closely at personal experiences of the nobility, my account will, I hope, contribute to revising the stereotype held of the aristocracy, which amounts to an exaggerated uniformity produced by viewing things from a distance. Only revising, not demolishing, is my aim, for I do not surf on the waves of contemporary Western academia, which compel one to attack the previously accepted or opponent's view as a stereotype or myth and so dismiss it as entirely false.[5] I concede that the stereotype of the Japanese nobility is not entirely false; my contribution therefore lies in providing the nobility's subjective view of themselves, which may or may not be consistent with the outsiders' stereotype.

The other, objective side of reality has to do with political economy. Involved here are material, coercive means of production, hegemony, and oppression. In opposition to the culturalist, symbologist, or semiotic views of social phenomena, Keesing (1987, 166) warns us against (over- and mis-)reading cultural meanings and metaphors with no attention to the political reality behind them: "Where feminists and Marxists find oppression, symbologists find meaning." In the area of stratification, Dumont (1980) represents the culturalist position in explaining the Indian caste system in terms of the ideological opposition of pure and impure. He is counterposed by Marxists (see Cancian 1976 for a review) and criticized by those who see in the caste system the injustice of political domination and economic exploitation as well as class antagonism (Mencher 1974; Apparadurai 1986).[6]

The Japanese nobility can certainly be considered a political elite. Indeed, its creation in modern Japan was without question politically motivated (see chapter 2). The top positions of the new government were monopolized by the nobility in the beginning, and later, new political leaders were ennobled. The new, bicameral Imperial Parliament, established in 1889, offered them a directly political opportunity as members of the House of Peers. The nobility, therefore, could be defined as having "political status" (Iwai 1980) and characterized in terms of its political function as a bulwark around the emperor and the "absolute imperial domination" (Suzuki 1979).[7]

Political and economic factors will enter into the picture I am going to draw, but only as they affect or are affected by status *culture*. In this limited sense, I go along with Cohen's (1974) idea of "two-dimensional man" being political and symbolist. My choice here is dictated by my own interests, but also by my informants, who were more willing to release or more ready to recall the cultural, rather than the political and economic, aspects of their experience. Moreover, cultural data, in addition to personal data, are significantly lacking in studies of the elite.

Basically, my approach is eclectic. "Capital" varies from economic to political to social to cultural, and the boundaries of these categories are far from fixed or closed. To reiterate the argument made above, there can be complicity (as Bourdieu [1984] demonstrates with regard to French society) between the "cultural" and "economic" currencies, between a nobility of taste and the bourgeoisie. Conversely, it would be preposterous to obliterate the distinction, or even the contradiction, between these categories, in view of the notion of "genteel poverty"— a state that is not necessarily resented, but on occasion is even played up as a matter of pride by the nobility, which identifies itself as a cultural elite. While I agree with Keesing (1987) about the danger of over-reading hidden meanings, I think the same warning can be addressed to the Marxian overinterpretation, however coated in cultural terms, of the economic, coercive, exploitive, and conspiratory nature of social structure.

Generally, the economic basis of nobility is land, but this formula does not apply to the Japanese modern nobility, which was created after the feudalistic estate system had been dismantled. As will be shown in chapter 2, the modern nobility was an anomaly, devoid of the land base otherwise essential to an estate hierarchy, as in the case of the British nobility. On the one hand, this historical situation created among the Japanese nobility an extreme case of symbolic status, one not buttressed by economic reality. On the other hand, this upper crust of population had, along with the rest of the country, to make the best of whatever legacy it could claim in order to adapt and survive in a modern, rapidly westernizing, industrializing society. The aristocracy, as a single symbolic-status group, was broken up into different "classes" depending on success and failure in the capitalist market. This historical accident makes it difficult to apply a universal theory of stratification to the particular case of the Japanese aristocracy. Thus this investigation, in which we will delve into the subtle, fluid interchange between symbol and reality, culture and political economy, status and class, prestige and power, ascription and achievement, hierarchy and equality, becomes all the more vital. We have come full circle to the earlier discussion on the hereditary and nonhereditary elite.

RESEARCH, METHOD, INFORMANTS

I now turn to the method I used in gathering information and the kind of information gathered. Instead of drawing on the remote, indirect information to be gleaned from archives and historical documents, I had intimate contact with my informants. The bulk of my data derives from what they said to me spontaneously or in response to my questions or comments. Informants talked about their lives generally, as well as about particular experiences, including their memories of their parents and grandparents. By narrating, it seemed, they were reexperiencing their memories and recalling what they had forgotten. By listening to them and watching their facial expressions, I was empathetically constructing my own version of their experiences.

This approach was necessary in view of the above-stated emphasis on subjective reality—"lived experience"—but at the same time it raises the question of epistemological dubiousness, a problem inherent in the life history approach, as highlighted in the recent anthropological literature, notably by Crapanzano (1980, 1984). Forgetfulness, selectivity, distortion, and illusion are inevitable concomitants of human memories, as Bartlett (1967) argued in general and Langness and Frank (1981, 109) warned with respect to the life history study in particular. Some "fabrication" (Plath 1980) is inevitable. In this, one of my oldest and now deceased informants is a good example. A granddaughter of Tokugawa Yoshinobu, the fifteenth and last shogun of the Tokugawa regime (1603–1867), was recalling her childhood in detail, while I listened with fascination. She remembered, she said (without firm conviction, though), having met Princess Kazu, the widow of the fourteenth shogun, Tokugawa Iemochi, and sister of Emperor Kōmei (r. 1847–66). She went on to describe the widowed princess's short "malelike" hairdo. I could not believe the princess lived that long and checked the chronology. She had died eleven years before the informant's birth!

This episode, which demonstrates the recaller's innocent illusion about her remote past, reminds us of a major contemporary influence reshaping our memories. Among the most popular TV programs in Japan are historical drama series depicting the rulers of premodern days, such as shogun, feudal lords, vassals, and imperial courtiers, as well as the heroes of modern Japan. Likewise, historical novels sell wildly, feeding readers with historical "knowledge." As I pointed out above, the media give Japanese the information needed to identify their "roots." Japanese history is reconstructed on a massive scale by television producers and novelists, to be stamped on the minds of viewers and readers. For my informants, such reconstruction of the past involves their own experiences and identities: they encounter *their* ancestors in those TV series and best-sellers. It is therefore understandable that their personal memories become tangled with what they see in the popular media. In fact, it may well be, as we will see below, that their interest in and identification with their ancestors were kindled by media exposure.

This problem is nothing new. History and tradition, as well as personal memories, have always been a reconstruction, transformation, or even "invention" (Hobsbawm and Ranger 1983) of the past from a present point of view and under present conditions. If there is any difference between today and yesterday in this respect, it is that reconstruction today can be achieved much faster than ever before, thanks to electronic reproduction and circulation of information. Yanagisako (1985) sees in the kinship of Japanese-Americans a reformulation of their "Japanese past" in the eyes of their "American present," a symbolically polarized pairing.

Conversely, but within the same logic, something new may be created and justified in the name of the past and tradition. As we know, modern Japan (a term associated with the Meiji era, 1868–1912) was created in the name of "restoring" Japan's antiquity, which amounted to "the creation of tradition" (R. Smith 1983, chap. 1) itself. "Archaic" rituals, along with modern ones, were created in Meiji Japan (Fujitani 1986). In the same vein, Bestor (1989) analyzes an urban neighborhood organization, arguing that, rather than being a remnant of historical "tradition" itself, it was a creation of a new system justified by "traditionalistic" ideology.

The "present" is affected by many factors, including one's personal preferences and exposure to the media and other stimuli. Underlying these is the dominant ideology in a given society. In anthropology, this point brings into question the "objectivity" of ethnographies that deal particularly with politically sensitive areas. As Bruner (1986) demonstrates, anthropological studies of Amerindian culture change have shifted from the acculturation theme of the 1930s and 1940s to a subsequent emphasis on ethnic resurgence. Apparently, such thematic change mirrors the contemporary political ideology of anthropologists who sympathize with the subjugated and exploited native Americans and advocate their retrieval of what was lost to European colonialists.

The contemporary zeitgeist of Japan is characterized by democracy and egalitarianism, as proclaimed in the postwar constitution, taught in postwar schools, and expressed in the current media. Although these public enunciations are not necessarily practiced in fact, Japanese have generally been influenced by the postwar ideology in one way or another. Democratic ideology affects the kind of research I have undertaken in several ways. First, it explains the academic prejudice against the elite as a focus of research and hence the absence of studies in this area. Second, my informants, also influenced by postwar egalitarianism, had refused to discuss their prewar experiences until recently, when their memories had hazed over into something like a fairy tale. I hit the time when they showed themselves willing to talk about their past. In other words, the passage of time after the war was the necessary price for access to their personal lives. Third, and ironically, the same postwar ideology that inhibited both research into and self-disclosure on the part of the former elite made my own study possible. That is, under the prewar ideological taboos concerning the imperial establishment, my research program would have been utterly inconceivable. Finally, democratic ideology, I expect, will be projected by my informants into the narratives of their prewar experiences. It is interesting that, although many were critical of what has happened since the war, few expressed any serious nostalgia for the "good old days."

I have belabored the epistemological vulnerability inherent in the life history approach (or, for that matter, of interviews in general). Still, I must add one more important dimension to the issue. As underscored in recent reflexive anthropology literature (Clifford 1980; Crapanzano 1980, 1984; Keesing 1985; Langness and Frank 1981, 96–105), an informant's autobiography is a product of interaction, negotiation, and reciprocal exchange between the informant/narrator and the researcher/listener. The narrator may highlight something in order to influence, teach, or otherwise send some particular message to the listener. A few of my informants, particularly businessmen, drifted away from their autobiographies to blame the U.S. trade deficits on the ethos of American workers: "Let them produce quality goods we want and we will buy them"; "As long as unions keep striking, they cannot compete with us." They were criticizing Americans through me, a naturalized American.

The researcher/listener, conversely, betrays her expectations of what she wants to hear through questions, comments, or nonverbal responses to what the informant says. These expectations in turn influence what the informant, empathizing with the researcher, chooses to disclose. Many of my informants had no trouble in meeting my expectations.

Some, zealous to satisfy my wants, tended to exaggerate, I felt, the difference between their prewar aristocratic life-style and their degraded present way of life. One informant was embarrassed at finding nothing to say along the line I was pursuing, and apologized. Insofar as the researcher succeeds in obtaining the information she has expected, the gained information may turn out to be a projection of the researcher's own self more than the narrator's. Furthermore, the final product of research involves the author's cut-and-paste reediting addressed to a publisher and audience. To say the least, what finally results is a set of collaborative biographies.

What do such problems concerning the veracity of information amount to? One way of escaping this epistemological trap might be to present life histories as "stories," not "histories" (Kendall 1988); to label the information "narrative" rather than "data," thus divesting it of its empiricist burden; or to "write culture" like fiction (Clifford and Marcus 1986). In this case, what matters is "experiential" plausibility, not "empirical" validity, a position that might be justified anthropologically in that stories and narratives provide sources for *cultural* interpretations.

I will go along with this line of thinking as a matter of inevitability, paying attention to the multilayered, reflexive meaning of an informant's utterance. But I have the following reservations also. First, I do not believe that my informants are as naive and self-deceptive as such epistemological skeptics assume informants to be. Many of my informants are too intelligent to confuse their life experiences with TV dramas, for example; if confusion does take place, it is only with one or two episodes, not an entire life. If one person is naive enough to paint his past following the outlines of what is seen today on television, there is always another who disparages such media vulnerability. One woman, another Tokugawa descendant, berated a popular TV production on her ancestors as having "no speck of truth." The old woman cited above with reference to her confused memory wished to tell the producer of a popular series on Mito Kōmon that Mito-sama had never traveled so extensively and that the family crest shown on the program was not that of the Mito house. Similarly, while many described to me life experiences that I expected, there were others who insisted that their way of life had been no different from that of any ordinary Japanese. One informant, an aristocratic descendant and professor at Tokyo University, kept warning me that people might say what I wanted to hear. Story-making appeared side by side with story-unmaking.

Second, the status group under investigation is so small, and has been relatively so closed, that one person's social network tends to overlap another's, one's life history to be coupled with another's. This internal density among my autobiographers thus provides an abundance of bases on which to cross-check the information given.

Third, even though the current ideology of a democratic Japan tends to get projected into the past, this does not seem to occur following a uniform pattern. One man, embracing egalitarianism, may claim that he has been always egalitarian and did not change after the war, while another man, equally committed to equality, may paint his life in terms of a 180-degree change, with the war's end as a watershed in his ideological career. And of course, there are those in this group, as elsewhere in Japan, who resent *American* democracy as it was imposed by the Occupation authorities.

Fourth, although the present-day perspective may determine the construction of the past, the opposite is true as well. Experiences of the remote past such as childhood very likely do stay in conscious or unconscious memory, affecting one's life course or view of life. The concept of a "cohort" or "generation" is not at all meaningless. The difference between the Depression-era generation and the hippie generation does not disappear under the influence of the yuppie life-style.[8] Just as the present contaminates the past, so does the past influence the present. In other words, we can in fact infer much of what really happened from what informants say about their past. After all, tradition cannot be invented entirely out of "nothing."

Fifth, the projection of myself into an informant's autobiography may not be as serious a problem as in the case of a typical anthropological encounter between two mutual aliens. The self-other interchange within a common cultural background is less likely, I hope, to lead to gross distortions of "cultural reality." I do not share the Western ethnocentrism that Western anthropologists attack as leading to misrepresentation of the "Other."

It should be further noted that writing life histories is not my goal. I use autobiographies only as a data base for an ethnography of the status culture of the nobility. For this purpose I collected more than one hundred autobiographies, of varying degrees of completeness and various emphases. Given the situational variability and constraints of fieldwork, some persons count more than others; some are more central, others more peripheral. Moreover, as will be shown below, the selection of informants was far from random. I use these sources of information as a "sample" only in a loose sense, not as a statistical representation. Rather, I tried to cover a wide range of variation (except in age: the bias for older informants is strong), a scope that, I hope, will help defend the present ethnography from the epistemological bankruptcy associated with the life history approach: life histories are sufficiently diverse to have one bias, one memory distortion, one fantasy counteracted by another.

Strictly speaking, what is said to a researcher is always retrospective, even when it refers to the present, and thus deemed unreliable by behaviorists. In this sense, my data are largely retrospective. But I also tried to capture nonretrospective "behavior," "performance," and "activity" to supplement the verbal data. I participated by invitation or permission in events such as ancestral rites, local festivals, adult education classes, and social gatherings where my informants, their kin, or peers played a central role. Again, I am aware that my presence may have made a difference and that, in a small gathering particularly, performance was often addressed to me. Nevertheless, these semiparticipant observations were significant in that they not only reinforced the verbal information but also revealed what went unsaid.

I have said enough about my epistemological/methodological ambivalence. On the one hand, the subjectivity of my informants and, for that matter, of myself is taken as "reality." The empathetic "understanding" of their feeling and thinking constitutes my major methodology. On the other hand, I do not abandon the positivistic view of reality, at least in the sense of anthropological, if not exactly scientific, empiricism. For the reasons already stated, I believe this ethnography contains reliable information. My ambivalence will therefore be expressed in zigzag fashion in my presentation and interpretation of data.

Earlier, I argued that a study of the former nobility has relevance to contemporary Japan owing to its association with persistent and salient cultural values held by all Japanese. This does not mean that the old elite has stood still, immune from change. In fact, this group may be said to have undergone the most drastic changes of all the social strata of postwar Japan. To make this book relevant to contemporary Japan, then, it is necessary to explore how the former elite has transformed itself and adjusted to national and worldwide change, and what role the old values that this class embodied has played in the course of transformation and readjustment.

Many people ask how I was able to meet the people under study. Indeed, Marcus (1979, 136) refers to "the formidable task of gaining . . . access" as one reason for avoiding the elite as a study subject. A native researcher might be considered advantaged in this respect, but not necessarily so. Although culturally Japanese, I am a status outsider to the nobility or upper class. It was therefore mandatory that I have a proper go-between to gain my first entry into this group. Fortunately, a good friend of mine had been closely affiliated with some members of the nobility through kinship and, more importantly, through her alumni network. A graduate from Gakushuin, the school system originally created for sons and daughters of the nobility and royalty, this woman secured for me positive responses to my interview requests: "I could not turn down Mrs. ——'s request," said one informant; "The request from a *senpai* [senior graduate] is a command," said another. (My friend and mediator also told them that I was her close Gakushuin classmate. I was only a graduate from Gakushuin University, which was a postwar creation open to everyone, having nothing to do with aristocracy. Yet this piece of information did help.) Once I achieved the initial entry, I could ask informants to introduce me to their friends and relatives. Nevertheless, in each and every case I needed an introducer who was familiar to and trusted by a new informant. How I presented myself was inconsequential. I learned this lesson when, unable to find an introducer, I approached a descendant of a top Meiji leader directly by phone. The response at the other end of the line was a polite but firm "no." The need for personal introductions, needless to say, threw statistical sampling out the window. Only at the end of the fieldwork did I risk the impersonal method of mailing questionnaires, and I later learned that some of the recipients were upset and angry.

Establishing rapport was less difficult than finding informants—not so much because I shared the Japanese culture or because of my Gakushuin connection, but because I was a status outsider. I could act like an alien anthropologist by assuming the role of a culture learner from a native teacher-informant. To create such a relationship I always introduced myself as a person of peasant origin and stressed the status irrelevance of my Gakushuin background. This, I think, motivated my informants to talk about themselves; I also felt that I stimulated their sense of noblesse oblige.

It was not just status otherness that helped me. For Japanese, the sense of cultural affinity is inseparable from continual social contact; thus, being out of the country for a lengthy period of time makes one a cultural other as well. Even though I had left Japan at the relatively late age of twenty-eight and had returned to my home country several times as a fieldworker, I was, in the eyes of Japanese informants, a cultural stranger who had shed Japanese culture and identity. They found it surprising that I still spoke Japanese so well (!); they asked simple questions that even a five-year-old would know the answers to, such as the location of the city of Numazu. I was thereby encouraged to play dumb in order to take advantage of the situation. Indeed, this sense of cultural distance between informants and myself proved quite beneficial to my research. Not only did my informants feel disposed to teach me Japanese culture, but they also disclosed personal information and secrets, all because I was merely a sojourner in Japan. They felt safe with me. Many of my Gakushuin friends were surprised that I established such rapport with members of this closed group; they concurred that I could not have received cooperation if I were a "real" Japanese, and even less if I were a member of the group. It was thus to my benefit that I found myself marginal, neither fully foreign nor truly native.

My professional status, which I knew would not impress this group of people, was nonetheless important in making my claim of "academic" interest credible. What repelled my informants most was journalistic sensationalism, of which many members of this group are said to have been victims. I managed to dispel their apprehensions with ease.

Scholarly commitment, however, creates its own problem, one that was truly formidable in this writing: that is, how to maintain true anonymity. Given the small size of the population I studied, as well as its public conspicuousness, it is difficult to conceal the identities of my subjects in all cases, even under pseudonyms. How, for example, can I disguise a daughter of Emperor Shōwa, one of only three (and now two) surviving daughters? Members of the group would know whom I am talking about, in any case. At times, therefore, I have had to fictionalize some details or pluralize a single case in order to protect confidentiality, but only insofar as such disguise does not distort the message I want to get across.

This research topic began to interest me in 1976 while I was conducting fieldwork on the life cycles of ordinary Japanese women in a provincial town (Lebra 1984). When I learned that many of the older women had gone through premarital apprenticeships as maids in middle- and upper-class urban households, it occurred to me that the other side of this interclass social complex required closer examination. At the same time, I met a famous actress of aristocratic origin whose fascinating story prompted me to conceive a study of the vanishing aristocracy and to begin to contact more people of this background. This stimulus later developed into a primary project involving intensive fieldwork for five months in 1982 and ten months in 1984–85, mainly in Tokyo and environs, with occasional trips to other parts of Japan. While engaged in writing, I returned a few more times for short trips through 1991 to recontact key informants. Contact dates thus involved a fifteen-year span, during which time several of my informants, sadly, passed away. When I identify an informant's age in the text, my reference point will be the time of our first contact. The earliest birth year among my informants was 1888; the oldest age at the time of our interview was ninety-one (a woman), and the youngest, twenty-five (a man).

While men's reminiscences and opinions were essential, given that the aristocracy was decidedly male-dominated, women were equally or perhaps even more significant informants, knowledgeable and often able to cover both natal and postmarital households. In addition, I tried to maximize variation, rather than representativeness, in the selection of informants, such as in their ancestral backgrounds, ranks, careers. More detail on the interview sample will be given at the end of chapter 2, where my selections will make more sense against the historical background. (Specifically, the reader is referred to chapter 2, note 27.) To supplement the field data of interviews and participant-observations, a questionnaire was mailed to a sample of contemporary househeads to generate quantitative data. Wherever relevant, the questionnaire responses will be cited to support or qualify my arguments.

A historian, emerging with a totally different picture of the subject, might not agree with my conclusions. In fact, one of the several historians who also belong to the former nobility broke my heart by disapproving of my approach and refusing to cooperate as an informant. Fortunately, other historian informants encouraged and helped me enthusiastically. Indeed, I believe that the historical and ethnographic approaches are mutually complementary. Because the subject matter is deeply rooted in the long history of Japan, the following chapter provides a historical sketch of the nobility in which my debt to historians is self-evident. Here the nobility is described primarily as part of the political system. The bulk of my field data will appear in subsequent chapters. Those readers who are well versed in Japanese political history are therefore advised to proceed directly to chapter 3.

TWO

Creating
the Modern Nobility

The Historical Legacy

The basic structure of the nobility under study came into formal existence in 1884 as the result of an imperial ordinance called the *kazokurei*.[1]
The embryo had taken shape fifteen years before, which calls us back to
the dawn of Japan's modern era, the Meiji Restoration.

The Meiji Restoration, launched in 1868, was a turmoil of sociopolitical events and transitions. When the Tokugawa shogunate, which had
endured for over two and a half centuries, was defeated in the civil war
of 1868–69, it collapsed, together with its feudal system of control. The
winning camp thrust the thus-far marginalized imperial throne, then
occupied by the sixteen-year-old Emperor Mutsuhito (known posthumously as Emperor Meiji), onto center stage of the political theater as
the supreme symbol of legitimacy for the newly emerging order. Tokyo
became the sole capital of the national government when the shogunal
castle of Edo was commandeered by the anti-Tokugawa forces and later
turned into the new imperial palace.[2] Thus began the Meiji Period
(1868–1912, coterminous with the reign of Emperor Meiji), the period
regarded by many Japanese as the most glorious of Japan's recent history.

All this was the culmination of a series of attempts to terminate the
dual-authority system (the shogunal-military and imperial-civil) that had
existed since 1192 when Minamoto Yoritomo established the military
government, or *bakufu* (shogunate), in Kamakura. With regard to foreign
relations, the Meiji Restoration involved a turnabout of the new leadership in favor of the open door policy, accompanied by a commitment to
replace native traditions by the Western model of "Civilization and
Enlightenment."

There is no question about who were the losers. The military elite of
the old feudal system lost the bulk of the privileges they had enjoyed as

28

birthrights. Included here were the shogun, as feudal overlord; domain lords called daimyo (also known as *shokō* or *hanshu,* lords of *han,* the feudal domain); and these men's vassals, *hanshi* or samurai.[3] All these also fall under the umbrella term *buke,* warriors, indicating their common profession and expertise. (The term *samurai,* though usually understood to mean warriors in general also, will here refer only to the vassals of the shogun or daimyo. In the following discussion, moreover, the shogun will be included in the category of daimyo, since he was a supreme daimyo, unless the context requires that he be singled out as the shogun. Roughly, then, the buke comprised two major strata, daimyo and samurai, the latter being its large majority.)

The new regime—which ironically was led by samurai—was determined to centralize the sociopolitical system of the nation, and the buke as a whole bore the brunt of the reforms. The new leaders, initially uncertain as to just what form of government should be built, first revived the emperor-centered features of the ancient Nara court with its system of *daijōkan* (the state council), then later decided to assimilate the Western model. The capitulation of the buke to the emerging regime was marked by three major events: the *taisei hōkan* of 1867 (the "reverential" return of the shogunal government to the imperial court); the *hanseki hōkan* of 1869 (the reverential return of domains to the court); and *haihan chiken,* in 1871, replacing the domains (*han*) by prefectures (*ken*).

One might wonder why the buke relinquished their power and privileges voluntarily (that is, reverentially). Evidently, the first two events involved more (or less) than what their names indicate: the shogun expected to survive his taisei hōkan as a daimyo under the court government, and for similar reasons "few saw *hanseki hōkan* as any kind of death blow to daimyo rule" (Umegaki 1986, 98): that is, the daimyo, too, hoped to retain their local hegemony under the new government. These "volunteers" were clearly not aware of the consequences of their actions; indeed, some expected the emperor to reauthorize their feudal prerogatives (Kasumi Kaikan [hereafter cited as KK] 1966, 74). Although the court did reappoint the former daimyo, or hanshu, to governorship of their respective domains, it was under a less dignified title, *han-chiji* or *chihanji* (domainal governor).

In the third event, haihan chiken, many daimyo voluntarily surrendered local hegemony, largely because of their near bankruptcy (Umegaki 1986; KK 1966, 113); in the end, though, the reordering struck the daimyo like a "thunderbolt" or a "political earthquake" (Griffis, quoted in Craig 1986, 57). The three hundred–plus han were abolished and reorganized into larger and fewer prefectural units (seventy-five as of

1871, to be further reduced later on), with new prefectural governors from the samurai class recruited from outside. This development coincided with the withdrawal of the old elite (except a few) from the basically symbolic top positions of the central government, leaving all decision making to a handful of samurai. The haihan chiken thus formally completed the process of dislocating daimyo and vassals from the land-based provincial power structure and economy. This and subsequent events, which were not necessarily foreseen even by those who fought for the Restoration, produced much discontent and demoralization among the buke, whose energy was channeled into a host of rebellions, climaxing in the Satsuma Rebellion of 1877.

Apart from the feudal institution staffed by the buke, there was another pre-Restoration aristocracy, consisting of the nobles around the emperor. They had been grouped together as *kuge*, in distinction to the buke, but more formally and metaphorically were designated as *tōshō*, "in-palace," meaning the people who were allowed into the emperor's living quarters (*seiryōden*) in the imperial palace, and thus set clearly apart from *jige* ("on the ground" or "down below"), non-noble retainers at the palace. Just as the buke were concentrated around the Edo castle of their overlord or the provincial castles of their respective domains, the kuge resided within or near the imperial palace of Kyoto so as better to serve their emperor.

To understand the kuge life, we must turn our historical clock far back, to the times prior to the rise of the buke. The entry of the earliest nobles into history (or rather protohistory) coincides with the emergence of the kingly (not yet imperial) court in the Kinai region, around which the Yamato state was unfolding between the fourth and mid-seventh centuries. Known as the Tomb Period, this era has left us gigantic tombs and burial accessories indicating a well-developed social stratification. The early aristocracy was embedded in the sociopolitical organization called the *uji-kabane* system. *Uji* is translated as clan, lineage, "lineage group" (Miller 1974), "familial system" (Hall 1966, 6), or "a corporate group of households considered a single extended kin group, carrying a common uji name" (Kiley 1983, 131); *kabane* is understood as a hereditary aristocratic title attached to an uji name. These terms are used variously and confusingly (Sakamaki 1987, 27–29), in reflection of their ambiguity;[4] my understanding relies on Kiley (1983) and Miller (1974, 1976).

What is known is that the term *uji* referred to elite kin groups who exercised control over commoners organized into various occupational work groups identified as *be*. The origin of this stratification system may be surmised from the linguistic fact that both *kabane* (meaning bone) and *be* were Korean words (see note 5). Kabane titles were awarded uji chiefs by the paramount chief, the king, to mark their submission in exchange for the privilege of partaking in royal prestige and power. Miller (1974, 1) estimates that there were about thirty different kabane titles in the sixth and seventh centuries prior to Emperor Tenmu's reign (673–86), topmost among them being *kimi, muraji,* and *omi.* Kimi were kabane for uji of royal descent; and Kiley (1983, 132) distinguishes muraji and omi as two classes of high nobles characterized in relation to the king: holders of muraji "originated as the king's clients and received their *be* from him," in return serving the king in ritual and military functions; the regionally based omi holders, in contrast, submitted and dedicated be to the king, supplied consorts to him, and took ministerial offices in his court. The chieftains of the most powerful uji with the title of omi or muraji were identified as *ō-omi* and *ō-muraji,* respectively (*ō* meaning grand: the king was called *ō-kimi*). The coalition among such chieftains was brought to an end by the ascendancy of the Soga family, whose chieftain, *Soga no ō-omi,* became a dictatorial power figure in court politics.

The next stage of ancient aristocratic history opened with the Taika Reform. This event, prefaced by a successful palace coup d'état in 645 that overthrew the Soga, inaugurated drastic steps to compel kabane holders further to uphold the imperial authority. Politicization of kabane titles reached a peak during the reign of Emperor Tenmu, when a new system of eight cap-color ranks (*yakusa no kabane*) was superimposed on the earlier system, relegating the titles of omi and muraji to the lower ranks (sixth and seventh, respectively). Allocation of the eight ranks was based on the threefold classification of uji in terms of descent: *kōbetsu* ("imperial uji," those who claimed descent from emperors); *shinbetsu* ("deity uji," those whose ancestors were gods of the mythological ages, implying ancestral status parallel with the imperial "sun line"); and *shōban* (uji of foreign origin).[5] The kōbetsu group was clearly favored at the expense of the other two: in 684, of the new kabane titles granted by Tenmu, all recipients of the first rank, *mahito,* were of kōbetsu clans, as were 85 percent of the second-rank (*asomi*) grantees; shinbetsu clans appear as a majority (74 percent) only in the third rank, *sukune* (Miller 1976, 168).

This was one of the earliest post-Taika attempts to reorganize ranks under a formal, centralized system, one that was to be revised and perfected during the late seventh and early eighth centuries by means of imperially issued codes reflecting a steady flow of Chinese influence. The formalization process culminated in the Taihō Code, completed in 701, which assimilated the nobility into one central bureaucracy adapted from the T'ang model, thus antiquating the kinship-based uji-kabane system. Ancient aristocrats were transformed into "officials" holding high-ranking offices in support of the "emperor," who capped the pyramidal bureaucracy as the sovereign. Between the emperor and the nobility were formalized princely ranks called *hon*. The Taihō Code was further revised by the Yōrō Code, the only extant early legal code, from which prior codes are inferred.

Taken all together, the reforms of this period are called the *ritsuryō* system, a cumulative body of penal (*ritsu*) and administrative (*ryō*) codes. This system—which survived until the Meiji Restoration (if only symbolically) and was temporarily revived for a brief period of the early Meiji—transformed the nature of uji chieftainship. Before the Taika Reform, the uji "chieftain had held a hereditary post at the Yamato court by virtue of the fact that he was leader of a powerful uji. Now the situation was reversed: a man became uji chieftain because he, of all the uji members, held the highest governmental position" (Hurst 1974a, 42). Significantly, however, the hereditary status of the aristocracy did not lose its importance; in fact, the terms *uji* and *kabane* survived for a long time in varied functions.[6]

The administrative hierarchy was based on the conjunction of two rank systems: office ranks (*kan*) and court ranks (*i*). The latter comprised thirty ranks designated by ordinal level, together with senior versus junior and upper versus lower scaling: for example, the fourth, senior, upper rank, which is seventh on the thirty-step scale. In practice, the ordinal-number designation (from first through eighth plus one nonnumerical bottom rank, for a total of nine) was the primary rank marker. For the nobility, fifth was the lowest, and the "genuine" nobility, classified as *kugyō*, occupied only the third rank and above. There were clear promotion barriers from the sixth to the fifth rank, and from the fourth to the third. The term *jige*, mentioned above, referred to the sixth rank and below.

A rule of correspondence (*kan'i sōtō*) linked the office and court ranks, such that a particular kan (office) could not be held by a person whose i (court rank) was too low or too high. The topmost office, for example, that immediately below the emperor, called *daijōdaijin* (chancellor), required the first court rank; the next highest offices, *sadaijin* (minister of the left) and *udaijin* (minister of the right), required the second court rank (Tōkyō Daigaku Shiryō Hensanjo [hereafter cited as TDSH] 1966, 536–37). When a gross imbalance existed that could not be avoided, readjustment was made by promotion on one of the two rank scales. (The court women who staffed the *kōkyū* [the "rear palace," that is, the imperial harem], which was also part of the ritsuryō bureaucracy, were not bound to this rule of correspondence [Nomura 1978]; the kōkyū and imperial consorts, however, will be dealt with separately in chapter 6.)

Rank acquisition and promotion was based partly on an individual's performance in official examinations, following the Chinese example. But in contrast to the Chinese system, the Japanese bureaucracy paid considerable attention to family status as a determinant of ranking. Side by side with the examination system, for example was the "shadow-rank" (*on'i*) system, whereby the sons of a fifth or higher rank holder were granted a court rank as a birthright: "For example, if an official enjoyed the first court rank, his son at age twenty-one automatically was given the fifth court rank and his grandson the sixth." The shadow rank thus obtained could, depending on one's father's status, be higher than the rank one might attain by passing qualifying examinations (Miller 1978, 108–9). Furthermore, the Daigakuryō (Bureau of Great Learning), which trained the examination candidates, was open only to certain professional families and to families of the fifth rank or higher (KK 1966, 18).

The privileges that noble families enjoyed in terms of court and office rank acquisition and promotion were coupled with enormous revenues derived from their control of tax-producing land and farmers and other stipends in consumer goods—an important point in light of the prestige-power-wealth agglutination. These incomes again corresponded with court ranks, as indicated by such names as *ifū* (rank fief), *iden* (rank land), and *iroku* (rank stipend) (Wada 1983, 275–76, 409). The economic benefits were compounded by privileged exemption, upon the holder's death, from the tax obligations and land redistribution to which every subject was theoretically liable under the post-Taika land reform.

The irony is that the significance of the hereditary elite was in fact magnified under the ritsuryō system, which absorbed a large number of noblemen into public offices. Reflective of the rigorous attention then given to ancestry, descent, and genealogy was the early-ninth-century compilation *Shinsen shōjiroku* (The newly codified register of uji-kabane), which reclassified the noble lineages, giving as well a list of "the original progenitors of 1,182 clans" (Miller 1976, 166). Earlier, the compilation of the *Kojiki* and *Nihon shoki* in 712 and 720, respectively, could also be interpreted in terms of the need for genealogical validation of the noble as well as the imperial lineages. Miller (1978, 15–18) interprets the mythic component of these mythohistorical chronicles as a retrospective creation of the past such that the contemporary stratification of noblemen was projected into the hierarchy of the gods, their claimed progenitors. The emperor's sovereignty was thus mythologically traced to the supremacy of Amaterasu (the Sun Goddess), the progenitor of the imperial lineage, over all other deities. Put another way, the purely symbolic hierarchy of the gods, as constructed in myths, was superimposed upon, and genealogically linked to, the politico-economic hierarchy of men. The result was a deification of the top echelon of humans—a gross example of "cultural hegemony" indeed.

The genealogical legitimacy of the imperial dynasty was further constructed by *lineally* threading separate dynasties and separate provincial rulers who could have been contemporaries into a single continuous succession. As Mizuno Yu (cited in Barnes 1988, 11) demonstrates, the Yamato court consisted of three dynasties, the Sujin, Ōjin, and Keitai lines, which were localized in different areas of the Kinai region, namely Miwa, Kawachi, and Asuka. Through this connection in contrived kinship, each appeared as legitimate heir to the previous line. Here, too, we see a point of contrast with the Chinese dynasty, which had a limited tenure according to heaven's mandate, whereby one dynasty might justifiably be replaced by another. The nature of monarchy thus finds its parallel in the nature of government offices.

Assimilation of lineage status into the officialdom, as illustrated by the shadow-rank system, eventually led to the ascendancy of one lineage in the world of court aristocracy. Establishment of the "impersonal" bureaucracy resulted in the increasing monopoly of higher offices by the Fujiwara, who replicated on a larger scale what the Soga had done earlier. The Fujiwara's progenitor was Nakatomi-no-Kamatari, who on his deathbed (669) was granted the kabane of Fujiwara Ason (a title derived from *asomi*, which was to become the second in Emperor Tenmu's eight-rank system) by Emperor Tenchi in reward for his contribution to the Taika Reform. The Nakatomi clan had been muraji in charge of rites and rituals of the Yamato court, their original progenitor having been identified as Ame-no-koyane-no-mikoto, one of the heavenly gods of myth (hence the Fujiwara were classified as a shinbetsu, or deity uji).

The Fujiwara's later triumph in the Heian court meant not only external struggles against non-Fujiwaras, but also the selective survival of one or another branch family to the exclusion of all other branches among Kamatari's descendants. The Fujiwara name was inherited by only one of Kamatari's sons, Fuhito—another famous name in the history of court politics—who is credited with a major role in compiling the Taihō and Yōrō codes. Fuhito's sons established four separate houses, one of which—called Hokke, the Northern House—rose at the expense of the other houses, with such struggles continuing among that house's descendants. At this point of history we can no longer discuss the uji as a unified kin group but must focus on a smaller segment.

The Fujiwara hegemony was facilitated by the creation of extralegal positions of regency, *sesshō* and later *kanpaku*, above and outside the formal ritsuryō bureaucracy. These positions enabled a top Fujiwara leader, winning over other Fujiwara and non-Fujiwara contenders, privately and virtually to take over the authority of the reigning emperor— the sesshō for a minor emperor, the kanpaku for an adult one.[7] Initially extralegal and private, the sesshō and kanpaku together evolved into a regular institution, to culminate in the Fujiwara-led "*sekkan* government" of the late tenth and eleventh centuries (the subperiod known as Sekkan within the Heian period, 794–1185). The Fujiwara power climaxed with Michinaga, who entered the political limelight early in the eleventh century and whose descendants won over other Fujiwara men.

The sekkan institution was based on the Fujiwara's economic affluence derived from the manor (*shō* or *shōen*) system, which privatized the flow of tax revenues and was eventually to undermine its beneficiary, the sekkan government, as well as the ritsuryō system as a whole.[8] Even as it gained political prominence, the affluent Fujiwara court became the center of an esthetic culture with native taste (apart from the Chinese influence), as exemplified by the Heian literature of court ladies. What later came to be called kuge culture can be traced directly to the culture developed by the court nobility of the Heian period.

Although Fujiwara supremacy came to an end as the power base shifted to the warriors and their allies, the Fujiwara lineage did not become extinct. Strikingly—and in the same manner as the imperial dynasty managed to outlast its efficacy—the offices of sesshō and kanpaku survived the loss of their political viability and continued, with only one exception, to be held by Fujiwara men. (Toyotomi Hideyoshi and his successor, Hidetsugu, assumed the kanpaku office for ten years toward the end of the sixteenth century; see below.) Thus, not only is the Japanese monarchy unique in having been a single dynasty since the 507– 31 reign of Emperor Keitai (except the anomalous period 1331–90, when two imperial collaterals, the southern and northern courts, ruled simultaneously; Kiley 1973, 30–31), but so too was the Japanese court nobility singular, with only one lineage predominating for over a thousand years (KK 1966, 12).

By the mid–thirteenth century the dominant Michinaga-derived Fujiwara branch had split further into five houses under different names— Konoe, Kujō, Nijō, Ichijō, and Takatsukasa—though the sense of common Fujiwara ancestry was preserved. The heads of these five houses, ever at the mercy of warrior rulers, took turns filling the positions of sesshō and kanpaku; indeed, this they continued to do for six centuries up until the Meiji Restoration, when these offices were finally abolished. These houses, therefore, known as *sekke* (sesshō houses), *gosekke* (five sesshō houses), or *sekkanke* (sesshō-kanpaku houses), enjoyed special honor and prestige among the kuge, albeit under the patronage of or in alliance with the shogunal government or powerful warlords. Even as late as the end of the Tokugawa era, members of the sekke were treated like lords by lower-ranking noblemen, whose servile demeanor and comportment was delightfully described by Shimohashi Yukiosa, a former retainer of the Ichijō house, in his personal recollections (Shimohashi and Hagura 1979, 249).

The lasting preeminence of the Fujiwara in the civil aristocracy was rooted in the clan's matrimonial alliance with the imperial house. Because consorts to emperors and crown princes were selected primarily from a pool of Fujiwara women, Fujiwara men enjoyed the privilege of being brothers-in-law, maternal uncles, and—best of all—maternal grandfathers of emperors. Six daughters and seven granddaughters of Michinaga, for example, were imperial consorts or empresses, and he was the grandfather of three emperors (Takayanagi and Takeuchi 1974, 1036). The emperor, in fact, could not hope to see a son of his choice assume the throne who was not sponsored by the top Fujiwara man. Facilitating this Fujiwara control of emperors was the residential pattern that then prevailed. According to "the common practice whereby husbands occupied residences provided by the in-law family, imperial princes frequently resided in the residences of their Fujiwara wives" (Hall 1974, 19). Future emperors were thus likely to be both born and raised in Fujiwara houses.

The sekke retained their predominant if not exclusive right to supply principal consorts to emperors throughout the warrior-dominant era as well.[9] Nor did the tradition come to an end with the Meiji reforms, which did away with kuge and sesshō/kanpaku altogether. Empress Meiji (Shōken) was an Ichijō daughter, and Empress Taishō (Teimei) was from the Kujō house. The late emperor Hirohito, however, married Princess Nagako, a daughter of the collateral royal house of Kuni. When the betrothal was being arranged, both political and nonpolitical objections were raised. One objection, according to one of my informants who shares the royal blood, was that the princess was not from a sekke—a comment revealing not only the importance of tradition but also the fact that sekke outranked other members of the royal lineage in matrimonial privileges.

The emperors were not all weak and contented with their symbolic, empty status, of course. In the late eleventh century, an attempt was made to recapture the imperial authority from the Fujiwara regency, ironically through another extralegal agency that also superseded the authority of the reigning emperors. In 1086, Shirakawa, the retired and tonsured emperor, created the *insei,* a cloister government that was "in essence an imperial mandokoro [domestic government], very much like that of the Fujiwara regent" (Hurst 1974b, 79). In the end, the cloister government, which survived for only three reigns of retired emperors, in effect (though it lasted much longer symbolically), turned out to open up opportunities for warriors to rise.[10]

This new tide culminated, first, in the takeover of the central government by Kiyomori, the chieftain of the Taira clan. Kiyomori operated within the existing imperial court hierarchy, became chancellor (1167), and mimicked the Fujiwara by marrying his daughter to an emperor. He was the first kuge of warrior origin. The next military dictator, Minamoto Yoritomo, opened a new era (1192) by establishing in Kamakura, away from and in parallel with the imperial court of Heian (Kyoto), a warrior government, the bakufu—an institution that would also be perpetuated until the Meiji Restoration, though under different families.

The Minamoto (or Genji) and the Taira (Heishi or Heike), the two clans around which warriors rallied, were of noble background.[11] These names were kabane conferred by earlier emperors on some of their (the emperors') children or grandchildren in order to make them nonroyal nobles. In other words, the practice of granting kabane functioned in two directions: either to promote or to demote (in the case of a royal prince) a person to aristocratic rank.[12] This practice is, by the way, a reminder of the clear-cut boundary that separated royalty from nobility as ruler and subject (*shinka*). (Hence the Fujiwara, despite their marital alliance with the imperial family, their surrogate exercise of imperial authority, and their outranking of royalty in some ways, never crossed that boundary. In the end, Fujiwara men could become no more than *gaisofu,* "outer" or affinal grandfathers of emperors.)

The kabane of Genji, in particular, was generously awarded by various emperors, which necessitated categorizing Genji descendants by the posthumous names of the emperors who had granted the title. Thus history recognizes a number of Saga Genji families, descendants of the princes who received the Genji name from Emperor Saga (r. 809–23), their father. Saga is known as the first grand-scale grantor of the Genji name upon his sons and daughters for the divestiture of royal status: he had twenty-nine known consorts, who gave birth to twenty-three princes and twenty-seven princesses, of whom seventeen and fifteen, respectively, became noble "subjects" (Kodama 1978, 173). Among other Genji were Seiwa Genji, Murakami Genji, and so on, similarly named after emperors. Yoritomo belonged to the Seiwa Genji, the group that emerged as a prominent warrior clan and rose to claim supreme chieftainship over all Genji groups. Kiyomori, in contrast, descended from the Kanmu Heishi, founded by Emperor Kanmu's son. The Genpei (Genji versus Heishi) war was fought by respective branches of Seiwa Genji and Kanmu Heishi.

The familiar pattern then repeated itself. The Genji represented by Yoritomo as the first full-fledged warrior ruler became recognized as the only legitimate lineage to head the shogunal government, just as the Fujiwara had been sanctioned as the only legitimate ruling clan in the imperial court. Thus the two succeeding shogunal dynasties subsequent to the downfall of the Kamakura regime were both of Genji descent. Although the Ashikaga dynasty (1338–1573) apparently had solid credentials of Genji ancestry, the same claim for the Tokugawa (1603–1867) was dubious. The suspected genealogical fabrication by the Tokugawa is all the more telling of the cultural mandate that shogunal authority be legitimized through Minamoto ancestry.

Anomalous intervals did occur between one shogunal dynasty and the next. When the Yoritomo line ran out, the Hōjō, originating from a provincial Taira family, did not step directly into the shogunal post but instead reduced the shogunate to nominal authority and staffed the shogunal office first with Fujiwara men of the Kujō branch, and then royal princes, inducted from Kyoto, as figureheads. In the meantime, the Hōjō exercised dictatorial power through the office of shogunal regency (*shikken*), created in 1203. The latter office thus amounted to a virtual shogunate, and the Hōjō dynasty lasted over 130 years. The Kamakura Period (1192–1333), then, is identified by two families: the Genji as the founder of the Kamakura shogunate, and the Hōjō as its regent and expropriator.

The next interval was marked by the ascension of two warlords in succession, Oda Nobunaga (r. 1573–82) and Toyotomi Hideyoshi (r. 1582–98), to restore order following the chaos of warfare that had marked the last hundred years of the Ashikaga regime. Nobunaga had at first claimed Fujiwara descent and so obtained ministerial positions in the imperial court, but he soon switched to a Taira identity, probably influenced by the contemporary ideology that the succession of shogunal dynasties should be based on the Minamoto-Taira alternation (Hayashiya 1966, 59–60), counting the Taira hegemony prior to Yoritomo and the Hōjō regency as equivalent to the shogunate.

Nobunaga's vassal and successor, Toyotomi Hideyoshi, presents a most interesting case, of which Berry (1982) provides an illuminating account. Hideyoshi, who was to complete the project of national unification, was the son of a footsoldier father and a peasant mother, too lowly to claim any genealogical legitimacy. And yet he needed more than lofty predecessors to legitimize his power, not only because he was handicapped by his humble origins but also because he now emerged as a "national" leader, no longer just a feudal lord leading his men. Hideyoshi chose, therefore, to seek legitimacy in the imperial throne rather than to take over the virtually dead shogunate. He patronized the imperial family, court nobles, and religious establishments by means of conspicuous gifts and awards of land, rice, money, and other valuables, as well as by restoring the run-down imperial palaces to their former dignity: "Between 1589 and 1591, Hideyoshi had eleven structures rebuilt, from the *shishinden* (official ceremonial hall) to the bath" (Berry 1982, 182).

In admission of his dictatorial power, and as a reward for his "dedication," the court accepted Hideyoshi into its tradition-loaded hierarchy, eventually promoting him from the initial fifth rank to the first junior rank, the highest that any living man could attain. Hideyoshi was elevated quickly in the office ranks (kan) as well as the court ranks (i): from *sangi* (advisor), to *gondainagon* (deputy senior counselor), to *naidaijin* (minister of the interior to manage State Council affairs, an office created outside the ritsuryō bureaucracy, like sesshō and kanpaku),[13] to kanpaku (!), and later to *taikō* (ex-kanpaku), the next step up. "Thus he became the first regent in Japan's history to rule without benefit of a blood tie to Michinaga" (Berry 1982, 179). The highest ritsuryō position, the chancellorship, was also awarded him. Granted that these offices had long served merely as empty titles of honor, Hideyoshi's climb in the court hierarchy is nevertheless remarkable. Here we see a stark example of complicity between hereditary honor and the new political power, between symbolic asset and material resources.

It might sound as if Japan had by then transcended the principle of descent to legitimize militarily acquired power. Berry enlightens us on this matter. At court, Hideyoshi was formally addressed as Taira-no-ason as well as Fujiwara Ason ("Ason" had by then evolved into a general title attached to holders of rank among the court nobility) and so in effect could claim the proper ancestry consonant with his court rank and office. To effect Fujiwara membership, he was nominally adopted by the Konoe. The court must have felt all this genealogical juggling necessary, "as much to excuse itself of affiliating with a peasant as to flatter Hideyoshi" (Berry 1982, 178).[14] It might be added that Hideyoshi also adopted an imperial prince as a son and successor—an arrangement that was later nullified. Berry demonstrates how Hideyoshi played down his warrior background, presenting himself instead as a full-fledged court noble, adopting the aristocratic life-style, sponsoring tea parties and noh plays, and the like.

Hideyoshi's success story epitomizes a double message regarding Japan's historical legacy of aristocracy. On the one hand, Hideyoshi made a mockery of the hereditary aristocracy, exposing its pliability and vulnerability in the face of rising plebeian power. On the other hand, Hideyoshi's self-aristocratization was a forceful testimony of the rigid interlocking of the aristocracy and state governance. Although these two sides of the Hideyoshi legacy might appear paradoxical and contradictory, in fact they were functionally complementary, as we shall see below.

I have argued the cultural importance of the fact that tradition, precedents, and especially ancestry or genealogical orthodoxy served as the principal sources of legitimacy for state authority. The prestige of such dynastic families or lineages as the Fujiwara, the Minamoto, and, above all, the imperial family thus remained unchallenged. Even Hideyoshi kept this traditional hierarchy intact—or rather, dramatized it into a caricature.

Nevertheless, dynastic continuity alone would not be able to sustain a political order, keep the political machine in operation, or, least of all, cope with sociopolitical change. Alongside dynastic traditionalism we therefore find the persistent recurrence of what may be called dyarchy. During the Fujiwara period, the emperor and the Fujiwara regent shared hegemony, as the author of *The Tale of the Heike* testifies through Taira Shigemori, who refers to the rule of the country by "the descendants of the Sun Goddess and Ame-no-Koyane-no-Mikoto" (Kitagawa and Tsunoda 1975, 110). Such joint rule was not unique to this period; indeed, dyarchies had existed on a smaller scale before and multiplied after the Fujiwara period, as if they were a fixed feature of Japanese political history inherent in Japan's monarchy. Earlier, the Soga and the imperial family had held "a hegemony which was to be the prototype of the dyarchy that was to characterize Japanese rulership for centuries to come" (Miller 1974, 5). Later, the establishment of the shogunate in juxtaposition to the imperial court represented the most clear-cut case of dyarchy.

Webb (1968, 26) attributes this phenomenon to the native tradition (as distinct from the Chinese model) of dividing the sacerdotal from the secular function of government, and claims that the only emperors who in fact can be said to have ruled—from Tenchi (r. 668–71) to Kanmu (r. 781–806)—were under Chinese influence. "In addition," Hall

(1973, 21) argues, "in almost every instance [the monarchs with administrative vigor] found sources of influence outside of the institution of monarchy itself," a fact best exemplified by the first cloistered emperor, Shirakawa (who retired from the throne in 1086 but maintained power until his death in 1129).

Most likely, the separation of administration from authority was intrinsic to the consecration (or tabooing) of imperial descent—as opposed to individual emperors—as possessing hereditary charisma. It might be argued that the two recurrent patterns mentioned here—namely, the rigid adherence to lineal authenticity and the cycles of dyarchy—were but two sides of the same coin. The persistence of the first necessitated the second; or the practice of the latter enabled the former to perpetuate itself.

This argument presupposes the functional difference, rather than equality, of the two heads. Although the emperor was the sovereign, the Fujiwara regent executed sovereign authority as his surrogate; if the emperor symbolized civil authority, the shogun personified military authority. Implied here is not only functional complementarity, but a hierarchical order with the emperor at the top. Even a military dictator like Minamoto Yoritomo, instead of creating a new title for himself, revived an old and seldom used military office, *seii-tai-shōgun* (the shogun's formal title), whose purpose in the imperial government had been to subjugate rebellious "barbarians." Theoretically, then, the shogun was to serve and assist the emperor militarily. Indeed, for several centuries after the establishment of the shogunal government, "the Japanese polity was held together by the remnants of the imperial bureaucracy or at least the idea of an imperial state to which both the court aristocracy and the warrior aristocracy subscribed" (Hall 1966, 8). The dyarchy, hence, was asymmetric, not competitive.[15]

The asymmetric dyarchy was duplicated at many levels of hierarchy, as if it were the dominant cultural model, one that all super-subordinate relations were compelled to follow. The Hōjō regency for the puppet shogun was one such example, the hierarchy involved in the *shōen* (manor) system another. As for the latter, Kiley (1974, 109–10) presents a clear picture of what generally appears quite confusing:

> The title to authority and the power to administer [the shōen]
> were permanently separated and kept within distinct lines of succession. This was a typical feature of land ownership in the eleventh and twelfth centuries, when ownership and possession were
> separated on many levels. A lord, or *ryōke*, belonging to the capital nobility might be represented on his holdings by a custodian,

often called *azukari dokoro,* who held all administrative powers and whose office often amounted to a perpetual, irrevocable, hereditary agency.

The central absentee proprietor, whether a member of the royal, noble, or religious establishment, and the local resident manager thus formed an asymmetric dyarchy. "As the dynasty legitimized the power of the regents, the lord legitimated the authority of the local custodian. In this arrangement, disparity of status was crucial. The lord and the custodian functioned cooperatively because neither could fundamentally challenge the other's prerogatives" (Kiley 1974, 110).

Likewise, status disparity made possible the formation and maintenance of the feudal bond between the shogun and daimyo, and between the daimyo lord and his samurai vassals. The system worked and order was maintained only as long as the disparity was recognized and the two parties respected each other's jurisdiction and prerogatives. The equilibrium of asymmetric dyarchy thus lasted well into the early fifteenth century under the alliance of the Ashikaga shogun and *shugo* daimyo (provincial military governors), which was in turn authorized by the imperial sovereign. It was during the fifteenth and sixteenth centuries—the *sengoku,* or warfare, period—that asymmetric dyarchy gave way to competitive polyarchy among rising and falling sengoku daimyo, with the above disparity losing ground and anarchy coming to prevail.

After the short interval of Nobunaga and Hideyoshi, the Tokugawa reestablished an elaborate system of dyarchy in which the symbol of authority and its administration ruled jointly. The Tokugawa, while ruthlessly depriving the emperor and his court of political and economic autonomy, adhered to the precedent established by Yoritomo of having the emperor authorize the appointment of each new shogun (*shōgun senge*). The shogun, in turn, was elevated (?) to the position of a symbol who did not govern; and the same pattern was repeated by each daimyo, who held symbolic hegemony over his han (feudal domain) and left its governance to his administrator-vassals.

Nevertheless, the symbol was not empty: "The daimyo might not actually govern, but the men who did govern did not try to displace him or undercut his prestige" (Strayer 1968, 10). The same was true of the relationship between the shogun and daimyo: the daimyo was lord and master of his domain, yet he accepted the shogun's authority to alienate him from the domain by transferring him (*kunigae*), even confiscating his territory, and forcing him to reside every other year or so in Edo, the shogunal capital. The daimyo, in short, was what Strayer (1968, 9) calls "an autonomous but obedient prince." It seems that the equilibrium of asymmetric dyarchy at various levels of the total hierarchy was maximized under Tokugawa feudalism, which may explain the survival of the Tokugawa shogunate for 260 years.

The dyarchy did not come to an end with the Meiji Restoration, but was re-formed by the imperial sovereign and a group of upstart leaders of samurai origin who were to become part of the modern nobility. The dyarchical order went out of control in the 1930s and into the war period, when military officers resorted to violent attacks on the civilian arm of the dyarchy.

To return to the medieval era, we find the weight of history also felt in the aristocratic life-style. Despite the royal origins of the Taira and the Minamoto, the warrior class was culturally unrefined, associated with provincial vulgarity and readiness for homicide, a distasteful tendency indeed to the court nobility.[16] Thus, this class began to aristocratize by copying the life-style of the court nobles. The Hōjō's invitation to the Kujō sons and royal princes, accompanied by court retainers, to assume the shogunal post might have had something to do with this aristocratization process of warriors, considering that court nobles, thus imported, did teach kuge life-style to their buke host (KK 1966, 44). The kuge's tutorial role in this process remained significant even in the Tokugawa period, as exemplified by the *ō-oku*, the shogunal harem, where kuge manners prevailed and kuge women served as *jōrō*, the top female administrators of palace women (KK 1966, 24). The assimilation of court culture by the Tokugawa was inseparable from the shoguns' political practice of marrying women of the court. In this sphere, the imperial family and court were an almost exclusive field, particularly from the third shogun on: among shogunal principal wives were seven royal princesses, five sekke (Fujiwara) daughters, one other kuge woman, and two daimyo daughters adopted by sekke (Saiki 1946, 420).

It should also be noted that the military elite sought and were granted ranks and offices of the imperial court, as stipulated by the ritsuryō; they were also identified by these, though they were empty titles of honor. Nobunaga, for example, was known as the minister of the right (udaijin), Hideyoshi as *taikō*, Ieyasu as *naifu* (the office of naidaijin). Lesser warriors also carried court ranks and offices, including the title of "governor" (*kami*) of provinces, which had nothing to do with actual jurisdiction.

The parallel existence of two categories of aristocracy—courtiers and warriors—reflects a similar phenomenon in European history, if I may digress from Japan for a moment. And there, too, according to Elias (1982), wild, impulsive, barbaric warriors were subjected to the "civilizing process" of self-restraint and courtly manners. The difference, however, is that in the European case, the two categories of nobility represented two sequential historical eras, marked by the dawn of the modern age in about the sixteenth century. The warrior nobility (knights), whose status was based on territorial divisions, belonged to the medieval age; they were then "replaced" or assimilated by the courtly nobility, a product of the centralized monopoly of force by monarchs. Warriors, in short, were "transformed" into "courtiers," their impulses "muted" by courtly protocol and gentility. This was the most decisive "transition" for the civilizing process: the courtly aristocracy evolved from the warrior aristocracy as a matter of need, to bring about societal integration in the course of differentiation (Elias 1982, 259).

Thus in Europe, the warrior aristocracy predated the courtiers. In Japan, by contrast, the emperor's court existed and developed its culture (or "civilization") long before the rise of warriors; the "courtization" of the latter was far from a "transition," but rather a sign of veneration for the older, "true" aristocracy and its culture. This historical accident may account for the parallel survival of the two aristocracies as distinct social categories, instead of the replacement of one by the other.

For while emulating and replicating kuge culture in many ways, the buke did evolve into a new type of aristocracy. These men's aristocratic self-esteem derived from their profession as warriors, their honor symbolized best by the sword. True, the Tokugawa shogunate did suppress belligerence, promoting self-control, etiquette, and learning instead, and in this sense it played a role similar to that of the European monarchy in civilizing the fighting class. Nonetheless, the military ethos was not entirely stifled. Pride in military expertise and prowess accompanied the sense of rectitude vested in valor and loyalty. The ethos of the military elite was masculine, whereas the civil aristocracy in its seclusion represented the esthetic taste of femininity. And in the world of arts, too, the buke developed their own Zen-inspired repertoire and styles, notably under the sponsorship of the Ashikaga shogun, in certain genres such as noh and *kyōgen* theater, black-ink painting (*sumi-e*), tea ceremony (*chan-oyu*), *shoin*-style domestic architecture, and gardening (Varley 1984). (However, see Wakita 1990 for a refutation of the commonly held association between noh and buke culture.)

The most important difference between the courtly and warrior aristocracies stemmed from the political economy, which, controlled exclusively by the military elite, was institutionally elaborated and sanctioned under the Tokugawa shogunate. Although feudal lords had existed before, as we have seen, it was during the Tokugawa period that the terms *daimyo* and *hanshu* came into regular usage; thus, *daimyo* used alone conventionally refers to those of this period only—that is, *kinsei* (early-modern) daimyo—as distinct from the earlier *shugo* and *sengoku* daimyo (KK 1966, 42). A daimyo's prestige was measured by the land he commanded, his hegemonic power symbolized by the amount of rice levied from his territorial peasants.[17] The amount of rice tax was assessed in *koku* (one koku approximating 180 liters or 164 quarts), and a warrior lord was awarded the title of daimyo if his reported revenue (*omote-daka*, usually lower than the true revenue, *jitsu-daka*) was ten thousand or more koku of rice.

The koku amount (*koku-daka*) varied enormously from one daimyo to the next. According to one extant record (cited in KK 1966, 48–61), in the mid–seventeenth century there were 271 daimyo, with revenues ranging from ten thousand all the way up to over one million koku.[18] This variation was due in part to the fact that, contrary to the stereotype, not all daimyo were *kunimochi* (or *kokushu*), domain proprietors, or *shiro-mochi* (*jōshu*), castle proprietors (KK 1966, 46)—possession of provinces and castles being the most basic criterion of power and autonomy for daimyo.

Another indicator of daimyo ranking was house status (*kakaku*), determined by proximity to the Tokugawa family in kinship and allegiance. First, Tokugawa kinsmen were set apart from the rest and then further broken down into three classes: the three original branches of the Tokugawa main house (*sanke*), the three secondary branches (*sankyō*), and all other kin (*shinpan*). In the last category, the family name Matsudaira—Tokugawa Ieyasu's earlier name—predominated. Below the daimyo of Tokugawa descent were two categories of nonkin daimyo: the *fudai*, "hereditary vassals," namely those who had been Tokugawa loyalists since before the Sekigahara war, the major war between the Toyotomi and the Tokugawa, which ended with the latter's victory; and the *tozama*, or "outsiders," so named because they had submitted to their Tokugawa opponents only after the war.

House status determined appointment to offices of the shogunal government; receipt of imperial court ranks and office titles (which were under shogunal control); assignment to one of the seven halls within the shogunal castle, where each daimyo was required to remain in attendance during his obligatory residency in Edo; and the like.[19] Fudai daimyo dominated in shogunal decision making.

There was a gross discrepancy, however, between house status and land-based revenues. The daimyo with half a million or more koku of rice were all tozama, the lowest rank in the kakaku hierarchy. To adjust this inconsistency the Tokugawa resorted to marriage politics, giving their women to some of these powerful tozama families and granting the name Matsudaira to eleven such daimyo (KK 1966, 46). This compromise on the part of the Tokugawa reveals that what counted most was the daimyo's political and economic power over his domain, measured by koku of rice assessed in taxes. House status, by comparison, meant much less, unless bolstered by affluence.

In sharp contrast were the circumstances of the kuge, a pitiful lot indeed if we apply the daimyo standard of koku to assess their status. In the late Tokugawa period, the total revenue of the imperial family and court as a whole (as allocated by the shogunal government) amounted at most to 130,000 koku. Of this amount, the kuge families altogether received less than 50,000 koku—an amount corresponding to the revenue of one small daimyo (KK 1966, 37). According to the 1865 record, the Kujō house, as top earner, received a little over 3,000 koku, while most kuge collected but a few hundred koku, and some no more than thirty (KK 1966, 28–37). To be sure, the kuge household had to feed only a small number of retainers, whereas the daimyo had a vast vassalage. Still, the difference is stunning. The kuge, in other words, had nothing but the traditional house status (kakaku) as its ranking criterion, which was determined by ancestry and succession bound to hereditary court ranks and offices. Economically, however, the kuge embodied destitution.

After a short excursion into earlier history, we are now back at the point where we left off, the Meiji Restoration. It might seem that the kuge, unlike the buke, could have hoped as the emperor's allies to return to their ancient glory through the "restoration." Yet as it turned out, although some small favors were extended to them by the new government, their fate was no better than that of their warrior counterparts. The ritsuryō-based functions of the kuge in the imperial court bureaucracy were simply too outdated to find a place in the Meiji government. Thus the kuge status, together with the buke status, was rendered obsolete.

Nevertheless, Japan had a long way to go to transform into an egalitarian society, and in any case, no such radical outcome was desired by the new leaders. The former elite could not be eradicated overnight but had to be reorganized in a simplified form to supersede the elaborate hierarchy that had prevailed under feudalism. In 1869, the second year of the Meiji period, simultaneous with the decision for hanseki hōkan (the return of domains), the daimyo and kuge were merged as *kazoku* (meaning the flowery lineage),[20] a rank considered necessary for daimyo governors, or *han-chiji* (Jansen 1986, 77). Below the kazoku were the samurai vassals, now designated simply *shizoku* in equal disregard of their internal rank variation, who in turn were placed above the commoners, or *heimin,* representing the largest majority of the population. The kazoku and shizoku (whom Japanese historians often condense as *kashizoku*) may be understood as the nobility and gentry, respectively. This renaming presignified a later reorganization and consolidation of the Meiji elite.

For centuries, the kuge and daimyo, except at the top level and despite the latter's assimilation of the courtly way of life, had lived in two separate worlds, so much so that they regarded themselves as different "races" (KK 1966, 4). Now the two "races" came under a single name: kazoku. Nor was a name all that they shared: as Ōkubo (1979, 43; 1982, 2) points out, both the kuge kazoku and daimyo kazoku (as they came to be categorized in the vernacular) were in the losing camp together. The kuge kazoku, losers under the previous regime, now saw the daimyo kazoku coming down to their level as "unemployed." Furthermore, following the replacement of the feudal domains (han) with the prefectural system, the daimyo kazoku were ordered to leave their provinces and resettle in Tokyo; the kuge kazoku, for their part, were strongly urged as well to move from the ancient capital to the new one. Thus the two groups "came to meet face to face in Tokyo for the first time." By sharing the same predicament, the two "races" began to develop "a sense of kinship" (Ōkubo 1982, 2).

What numbers constituted kazoku membership at this stage? Initially, kazoku households totaled 427, comprising 136 former kuge, 248 daimyo, 28 kuge equivalents, and 15 daimyo equivalents. Kuge equivalents referred to branches of some of the higher-ranking main kuge houses, whereas daimyo equivalents were a mixture of various subcategories, including the Tokugawa secondary branches and the chief retainer-administrators of daimyo (*karō*) (KK 1985, 88–97). Later, more households—76 altogether—were cumulatively added. The multifarious backgrounds of these and "equivalent" households, needless to say, pose a problem in drawing the kazoku boundary. Two major subcategories are indicated for these additional houses (listed in KK 1985, 27–31): branch houses of selected kuge and daimyo; and the houses of head priests of prominent Shinto shrines and Buddhist temples, including the twenty-six houses known collectively as "Nara Kazoku" (the houses of chief priests of the Kōfukuji temple complex at Nara, which consisted of the Fujiwara-uji main temple and its satellite temples).

Selective inclusion of the priesthood in the kazoku ranks throws an interesting sidelight on the historical alliance between religious institutions and the secular elite. Both Shinto and Buddhism (which were often mixed as *shinbutsu konkō*) enjoyed special status in the state hierarchy from the ancient era on. In fact, many major shrines and temples were openly allied with imperial and noble families, who acted as the religious sites' proprietors, patrons, sponsors, devotees, and hereditary ritualists or might even claim to be descended from the gods enshrined. The very terms *ujigami* (tutelary god or shrine) and *ujidera* (lineage temple) suggest the aristocratic origin of Shinto shrines and Buddhist temples.

There was a hierarchy of religious institutions, and in medieval times high-ranking temples and shrines were proprietors of vast shōen like the imperial and noble families, and they had armed priests to protect their interests. In the Tokugawa period, certain temples and shrines were authorized by the military government to receive rice revenues from their respective territories; the Ise Shrine, for example, was entitled to forty-two thousand koku (Ōkada 1977, 88). In many ways, then, the highest stratum of the religious establishment was on a par with the secular aristocracy. Prominent temples received royal princes, princesses, or sekke children as their abbots and abbotesses, noble headship that in turn elevated or maintained the temple status (*jikaku*). These royal and noble temples came to be known as *monzeki* (the aforementioned Nara Kazoku being among them).[21] It was in these monzeki establishments that politically inept royals and high court nobles remained influential. Note, too, that the Rinnōji temples within the Kan'eiji of Ueno and in Nikkō, built for and under the Tokugawa family, were headed by the highest-ranking imperial princes as chief priests to symbolize the Tokugawa's unequaled power and prestige (Urai 1983).

An "aristocratic temple" was in fact an oxymoron as far as Buddhism was concerned: Buddhist priests (with some exceptions, such as the Honganji group, founded by a successor to Shinran, Japan's Luther) were supposed prior to the Meiji reform to have renounced family life and thus had no chance to become hereditary nobles. Instead the secular elite families exercised their hereditary right to place their children in their own temples over successive generations. Indeed, it is said that the priest-supplying families, both imperial and noble, used these temples as a dumping ground for their unwanted sons and daughters. The Meiji Restoration put an end to the monzeki institution and recalled the royal and noble priests to their secular status (*genzoku*), allowing them to establish personal "houses." The houses thus established by the noble laicized priests were added to the kazoku list, whereas royal former priests became heads of the newly created *miyake*, collateral branches of the main imperial house (see below).

Quite another scenario characterized the situation of Shinto priests, who took no vow of celibacy. Indeed, Shinto shrines could derive their prestige from the "unbroken line" in the blood of their abbots. Religious aristocracy, both Buddhist and Shinto, will be detailed in later chapters as revealed by my informants.

The incipient kazoku discussed thus far was to be formally reestablished in a new form under the kazoku ordinance of 1884. The intervening fifteen years had been a period of trial and error in the attempt to define the kazoku's role in new Japan. Arguments were exchanged and competing proposals drafted by leaders both within and outside the kazoku group, including Iwakura Tomomi, Kido Takayoshi, Itō Hirobumi, and Inoue Kaoru. The European aristocracies, along with the Chinese tradition, were studied as models.

In this debate, two points of view—one represented by Iwakura, minister of the right and of kuge background, the other by Itō—collided, with the conservatism of Iwakura temporarily overwhelming Itō's more progressive view. In 1874, the central clubhouse of nobles, called Kazoku Kaikan, was installed in Tokyo, with Imperial Prince Arisugawa Taruhito as its first president. Iwakura, upon becoming the second president, "was endowed with dictatorial power to control the whole group of kazoku" (Ōkubo 1982, 11). Led by Iwakura, the kazoku was brought under the jurisdiction of the Kunaishō (Ministry of the Imperial Household), a move that amounted to the institutionalization of the kazoku into the *hanpei* (literally, "fence," meaning guard or bulwark) for the imperial house, a commitment that was not to be reversed throughout kazoku history.

Another important and interesting sign of Iwakura's conservatism was his attempt to reorganize kazoku under a lineage system (*sōzoku*) reminiscent of the ninth-century *Shinsen shōjiroku* (see above). All the kazoku families were grouped into three *betsu* categories: kōbetsu (imperial descent), shinbetsu (godly descent), and *gaibetsu* (foreign descent). These betsu were further broken down into *rui* (also called sōzoku), equivalent to uji or sub-uji; and under the rui came individual *ie*, the elementary stem family unit. This Meiji version of *Shinsen shōjiroku* was compiled by Iwakura, with his preface, in 1878 as *Kazoku ruibetsu roku* (*KRR*). Under the three betsu, seventy-six rui were recognized: thirty-six kōbetsu, thirty-four shinbetsu, and six gaibetsu and others. Interestingly, Iwakura included two samurai families of the topmost Meiji leaders, Ōkubo and Kido, in this otherwise unblemished list of old aristocracy, revealing his concession to the real power in the government. Each rui was identified by the ancient uji-kabane title plus the name of the founder of the particular lineage. Thus one rui was described, for example, as "Shinbetsu, Fujiwara Ason, descent from Muchimaro, minister of the left, grandson of Kamatari, Naidaijin." This particular rui comprised twelve kazoku households. As might be expected, two kabane were predominant: twenty-two kōbetsu rui assumed the title of Minamoto Ason, and twenty-two shinbetsu rui carried Fujiwara Ason as their kabane (KK 1985, 166–84). Table 1 clarifies this rui-betsu system and certain lineage biases. The thirty-six rui of kōbetsu, comprising 229 houses altogether, are subgrouped into twenty-two Minamoto (Genji) rui with 170 houses and fourteen non-Minamoto rui with 59 houses. The former group is further divided into Seiwa versus other Genji. The same three-level classification applies to the shinbetsu as well. Predominant is the Seiwa Genji descent for the kōbetsu, and the Fujiwara descent from Kamatari for the shinbetsu.

This ultratraditionalism seems to have been more metaphorical than literal, intended to dramatize the status distinction of kazoku from the rest of the population and the kinship solidarity of kazoku groups within single rui, as well as to remove the old division between kuge and buke (inasmuch as the two could belong to the same rui [Ōkubo 1982]).

The Iwakura scheme was challenged by other leaders of the Meiji government, who had risen from the modest status of vassal (shizoku) and found it necessary to elevate shizoku ranks to the level of nobility. Two arguments seemed to underlie their objection: the need to compensate for the economic plight of the former samurai, and the prospect of revitalizing the kazoku with new blood. Kido Takayoshi, for example, upon returning from Europe, proposed a single three-rank system to replace the current system separating kazoku and shizoku: shizoku were to occupy the third rank but within one noble grouping; they were also selectively to be entitled to the second and first ranks as well on the basis of meritorious contributions to the Restoration (KK 1966, 155–56).

The idea of mixing kazoku and shizoku into one class horrified Iwakura. Yet whereas the kuge in Iwakura disdained the rustic origins of shizoku, the shizoku in new leaders, led by Itō Hirobumi and his Chōshū colleagues, scorned the mentally and physically debilitated kazoku. The conflict between the Iwakura and Itō lines came to end with Iwakura's death in 1883. The following year witnessed the issuance of the kazo-kurei, the final product of compromise but one that definitely reflected the voice of shizoku leaders, particularly of Chōshū and Satsuma, the han that had engineered the civil war against the Tokugawa forces and come to dominate the Meiji government. Ōkubo (1982), noting a marked dis-

Table 1. The Rui-Betsu Classification of Nobles,
1878

	NO. RUI	NO. HOUSES
Kōbetsu		
Minamoto Ason	22	170
Seiwa Genji	(17)	(126)
Other Genji	(5)	(44)
Non-Minamoto	14	59
Total	36	229
Shinbetsu		
Fujiwara Ason	22	201
From Kamatari	(19)	(198)
Other Fujiwara	(3)	(3)
Non-Fujiwara	12	39
Total	34	240
Gaibetsu and misc.[a]	6	7
Grand total	76	476

[a]This category includes four gaibetsu (three Chinese and one Korean) and two unclassed rui (the Toyotomi and Shō, the Ryūkyūan king).

continuity between the earlier kazoku of 1869 and the new kazoku created under the 1884 kazokurei, calls the two "traditional kazoku" and "Meiji kazoku," respectively.

The kazokurei stipulated a system of five *shaku* ranks, equivalent to the European prince (or duke), marquis, count, viscount, and baron: *kōshaku, kōshaku, hakushaku, shishaku,* and *danshaku* (abbreviated as *kō-kō-haku-shi-dan*). (Because the homophonic titles of the first two ranks were distinguished only by their Chinese characters, the Japanese speaker would specify each character to avoid confusion in conversation. We shall use the English titles for the sake of simplicity.) The old nobility all assumed the fourth rank or above, except a small number of marginal aristocrats, such as the priestly houses, which were awarded the title of baron. The criteria for rank allocation reflected the difference between kuge and daimyo.

What determined ranks for the kuge was the traditional family status (kakaku), defined primarily by the highest possible office (*sendo*) to which its ancestors had been entitled in the imperial court. Thus the five sekke, whose sendo were the sesshō and kanpaku, all received the rank of prince. The families just below the sekke, categorized as *seiga,* whose highest attainable office was daijōdaijin, the top ministerial position in the State Council, became marquises. The *daijinke,* the families with sendo up to the ministers of the left and right, and those middle-ranking kuge entitled to positions up to *dainagon* (senior counselor) received the rank of count. All other kuge became viscounts. The gap between count and viscount suggests the survival of the barrier between the third and fourth court ranks in the ancient hierarchy of nobility. By and large, this rank distribution for the kuge articulates the conservative side of the Restoration, and in it the Iwakura obsession was vindicated.

Rank distribution for the daimyo was based primarily on rice revenue: the rank of marquis went to those with 150,000 koku or more, that of count to those with 50,000 koku or more, and that of viscount to those with less. The only exception concerned the shogunal lineage, where the kakaku concept was applied: the Tokugawa main house was granted the rank of prince, its primary branches (sanke) marquis, and secondary branches (sankyō) count.

In view of the pre-Meiji political supremacy of the military aristocracy over the imperial court, the above shaku distribution indicates a favoritism for the court nobility. This may be interpreted as a symbolic reversal of hierarchy, penalizing the military as usurpers of the imperial sovereignty and rewarding the civil elite as an imperial ally—even though the division was in fact not that clear. But some military houses were penalized more than others. The Tokugawa loyalists, concentrated in the northeastern region (Tōhoku), who had fought against the imperial army, recruited primarily from the southwest and led in the Boshin War (1868) by Satsuma and Chōshū, experienced the partial loss or transfer of their territories, ending up one or two ranks below what their original koku amounts would have dictated. For instance, the Date (of the Sendai-han), Nanbu, and Matsudaira (of Aizu) families were ranked count, count, and viscount respectively, instead of marquis for all.

Turning from penalties to rewards at the time of the Restoration, we encounter what made the Meiji kazoku truly new. It is here that Itō's input was revealed most clearly. As one of the qualifications for rank entitlement, the kazokurei specified "meritorious contributions to the state" for each and every rank. At this point, "merit" referred primarily to Restoration-related accomplishments. Some kuge received a "merit increase" in rank for this reason, as exemplified by Sanjō Sanetomi, known as a Restoration leader, who became a prince.

Much more direct was the contribution of the buke who had fought the Boshin War on the side of the imperial camp or provisioned the imperial army. First, the daimyo of those han that supplied the core of the imperial army were raised one step to the top rank; hence, the Shimazu of Satsuma and the Mōri of Chōshū were made princes. More remarkable was the following outcome.

The above provision of the kazokurei enabled some shizoku to cross the traditional barrier between kazoku and shizoku, making what in nonlegal vernacular would become known as *kunkō* (merit) or *shin* (new) *kazoku*, a third major category next to kuge kazoku and daimyo kazoku. Again, it was largely shizoku from Satsuma and Chōshū, and to a lesser degree from Tosa and Hizen, who would appear in the cumulative roster of new kazoku. Indeed, of the ninety kunkō-kazoku ennobled between 1884 and 1888 (KK 1966, 220–22), fully fifty-four (60 percent) were from Satsuma and Chōshū, and sixteen (18 percent) were from Tosa and Hizen.

If the recognized meritorious achiever was dead by the time of the kazokurei promulgation, his contemporary successor was entitled to the kazoku rank he had earned, as occurred, for example, with the Iwakura. Iwakura Tomosada received the princely rank credited to his late father, Tomomi, even though the Iwakura by the traditional standard should have been viscounts. Ōkubo Toshikazu was made marquis by virtue of the meritorious distinction of his father, Toshimichi, who had led the early Meiji government to the point of alleged "despotism"; the elder Ōkubo was assassinated in 1878.

Moreover, a kazoku could attain promotion to a higher rank through further recognition. Many Meiji statesmen, such as Itō Hirobumi, Yamagata Aritomo, Matsukata Masayoshi, Ōyama Iwao, and Katsura Tarō, were promoted from count to marquis and eventually to prince. Significantly, these and some others, who were to become *genrō* (senior counselors for the emperor, extralegal nominees) after retirement from government offices, all had started their careers as samurai, especially those from Satsuma and Chōshū. Prince Saionji Kinmochi, the last genrō, was the only exception in having no samurai background but coming from a prominent kuge family. As in the case of rank bestowal (*jushaku*), rank promotion (*shōshaku*), too, was applied to the successor of the deceased person to whom promotion was credited.

The shizoku as a class continued to exist, with the majority of shizoku remaining as such. But their prestige lessened: the shizoku-heimin distinction became almost unrecognizable, while the kazoku stood out as the elite. Further, once shizoku-to-kazoku mobility was sanctioned, the opportunity to join the kazoku ranks was increasingly widened, eventually to include heimin and a diversity of professionals (e.g., physicians, lawyers, educators) and businessmen, in addition to government officials and military officers in the modern army and navy. The kunkō kazoku, a minority in the beginning, thus expanded into a large majority: indeed, by 1928 the initial total had nearly doubled, an increase due chiefly to the sharp rise in the number of barons (table 2).[22] One might ask how the ancestor statuses from before the Meiji Restoration correlate with the five ranks (table 3). Here, "kuge" and "daimyo" ancestors require no explanation; the majority of their descendants were awarded the rank of viscount. "Other" (of which 356, or 73 percent, are barons) refers predominantly, though not exclusively, to kunkō kazoku whose ancestors were samurai or commoners.[23]

The category "imperial" in table 3 calls for an explanation. These nobles of royal origin were analogous to those princes "deroyalized" to nobility status and given kabane names, already familiar to us. But to understand this modern version of the ancient practice we must again digress into a brief historical account of royal children. There have been two categories of imperial princes: *shinnō* and *ō*. (Princesses were correspondingly *naishinnō* and *nyoō,* but here for the sake of simplicity we focus on the male royalty only. But see note 25.) The two differed in terms of closeness to the reigning emperor in descent, the shinnō being closer and thus of much greater institutional significance.

Under the ritsuryō, shinnō were ranked in hon, from the first hon (*ippon,* designated *ippon no miya*) down to the fourth, while ō fell under the i-rank system like the nobility. Nevertheless, no fixed standard existed by which a prince might be designated a shinnō. According to the ritsuryō, shinnō status was given to the emperor's sons and brothers only, and their offspring down to the third generation (that is, the fifth generation in absolute terms, counting the emperor as the first) were designated ō; further generations were thus destined to lose the status of imperial kin. Princes, like the nobility, were integrated into the high echelon of ritsuryō bureaucracy, including the office of daijōdaijin (chancellor).

In practice, the shinnō status was given arbitrarily to other, remoter imperial kin as well. At the same time, for economic and political reasons it became necessary occasionally to reduce the overall number of shinnō by denying some imperial sons the title. By the early Heian period these opposite practices—expansion and contraction of the shinnō population—came to be institutionally sanctioned by what was called *shinnō senge,* in which an imperial decree was required for a prince to be designated a shinnō (recall shōgun senge). Without this authentication, even

Table 2. Number of Kazoku by Rank, 1884–1928

YEAR	PRINCE	MARQUIS	COUNT	VISCOUNT	BARON	TOTAL
1884	11	24	76	324	74	509
1887	11	25	81	355	93	565
1899	11	34	89	363	221	718
1907	15	36	100	376	376	903
1916	17	38	100	380	398	933
1928	18	40	108	379	409	954

Source: Adapted from KK 1985, 292–93.

Table 3. Rank Distribution of Kazoku by Pre-Meiji Status, 1928

	KAZOKU RANK					
STATUS	*Prince*	*Marquis*	*Count*	*Viscount*	*Baron*	*Total*
Imperial	0	5	4	0	0	9
Kuge	9	10	29	85	43	176
Daimyo	3	16	33	220	12	284
Other	6	9	42	74	356	487
Total	18	40	108	379	411	956

Source: Ishinshi Shiryō Hensankai [1929] 1976, 720.

the emperor's blood son could not become a shinnō, while with it even a remote (third- or fourth-generation) prince could be recruited into shinnō status, thereby becoming the emperor's "son." The shinnō designation, needless to say, was of political importance, for a shinnō was by definition a potential heir to the throne and therefore was often the object of political intrigues and bloody fights among competing court factions.

In the medieval era, the shinnō institution was further developed with the creation of *shinnōke* (shinnō houses). Logically, of course, the idea of a shinnō "house" was contradictory, in that a shinnō was theoretically, if not actually, an emperor's son and thus a member of the imperial family. If he married and raised his own family, his successor son would not be a shinnō unless so designated by the emperor, whereupon the new successor "son" would become another member of the imperial family. And so on. Practically speaking, however, establishment of a shinnō house (of which there were four in the Tokugawa period: Fushimi, Katsura, Arisugawa, and Kan'in) meant that each successor to the house could become a shinnō under shinnō senge, regardless of his genetic distance from the imperial designator; in this manner shinnōke were perpetuated as collaterals to the core imperial house, making of imperial kinship a more or less *dōzoku*-like organization (*dōzoku* referring to the Japanese version of lineage, which consists minimally of the main house [*honke*] and its branch houses [*bunke*], linked hierarchically).[24]

If the main house failed to produce an heir, one of the branch houses would provide the future emperor. For instance, Emperor Gohanazono (r. 1429–64) was recruited from the Fushimi house. When the seventeen-generation imperial line of Fushimi origin came to an end, the Kan'in house took over, supplying imperial "blood" through one of its sons, Emperor Kōkaku (r. 1780–1817), the lineal ancestor of all the subsequent emperors. The sun line could thus remain "unbroken" thanks to blood replenishment by the adoption of sons from the shinnō houses. But blood flowed in a reverse direction as well: an emperor's blood son or grandson could be called upon to succeed the headship of a sonless shinnōke. Intralineage adoption, then, together with a certain amount of lineage endogamy, preserved a pool of imperial blood.

What happened to nonheir shinnō? The establishment of another shinnō house being prohibited, only two career options remained: to "descend" to a nonroyal status with a nobility title like Genji, or to embark on a priestly career as the head of a monzeki temple. The latter course absorbed the majority of excess shinnō, sons of both the imperial house and the shinnōke, who were then designated *hōshinnō*, priest shinnō.[25]

From time to time, however, shinnō priests were recalled to secular shinnō status, essentially as political pawns. In the late Tokugawa period, for instance, some new shinnō houses were established by former hō-shinnō at shogunal request, the military government wishing to take advantage of a loyalty split within the imperial house. The Meiji government, too, had reasons quickly to increase the number of miyake (collateral branches, a term that covered both the shinnōke and ōke), which constituted the closest satellite to the imperial throne. And there was a religious reason for recall as well: removal of royal kin from Buddhist temples dramatized the post-Restoration policy of separating Shinto from Buddhism and dissociated the imperial family from Buddhism (Sakamoto 1983, 480–82).

In 1871, all the priest shinnō were recalled and further entry of shinnō into the Buddhist priesthood was banned. Including the four shinnō houses of the Tokugawa period, then, there were by early Meiji ten miyake. With the further addition of several more houses through branching and the dying out of some old ones, as of 1928 there were thirteen miyake, the majority of which had descended from the Fushimi house.

The national hierarchy of houses was now complete (figure 1): at the very apex was the *kōshitsu*—the imperial family, consisting of the emperor, the empress, the crown prince, other dependent sons who would eventually branch out and establish their own miyake, and daughters who would marry out—surrounded by the miyake. This group as a whole was called *kōzoku*. Next came the kazoku, the shizoku, and finally, the heimin, forming the overwhelming majority. (At the bottom of the heimin category, it might be added, was a legally no longer recognized but socially

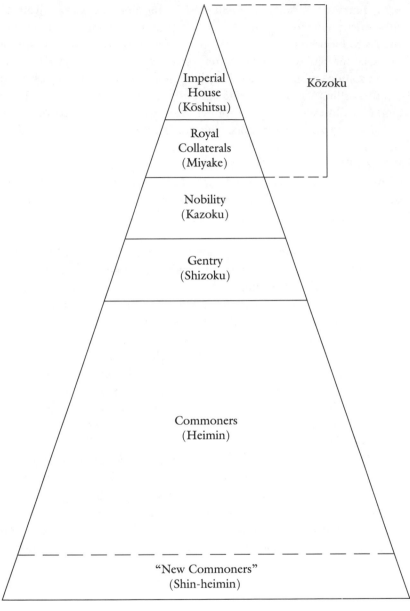

Figure 1.   The Hereditary Hierarchy

persistent layer, the outcastes, called *shin-heimin* [new commoner] and other various local names.)

In the meantime, the old practices of shinnō senge and imperial-line adoption were put to an end by the Imperial House Law of 1889, and the assignment of shinnō or ō status was legally standardized following (patrilineal) consanguineal proximity to the reigning emperor. If the earlier option to create and delete a shinnō could be called the preponderance of "culture" (arbitrary choice) over "nature" (biological destiny), this modern reform was a restoration of the "natural" principle of blood. The result was the extinction of heirless miyake and, in turn, the eventual termination of every miyake house *except* the imperial house, which was to last forever. The law thus provided a long list of imperial heirs, including miyake, in hierarchical order of succession rights. In other words, the imperial group was organized by a double principle. On the one hand, it was a collection of semi-independent stem families, each of which would last only as long as its male blood supply was replenished every generation. On the other hand, the group collectively formed a single lineage (kōzoku) with the emperor as its chieftain; if the incumbent had no offspring, an imperial heir would be secured from the lineage without resorting to "adoption." In both the stem-family and lineage principles, male primogeniture was mandatory.

What would happen to the nonsuccessor royal children, particularly in the case of ō? Following the early period of the Meiji era when miyake proliferation through branching was deemed politically necessary, the rule of succession by one son (preferably the eldest) required a measure to address the perennial problem of surplus sons. A 1907 amendment to the Imperial House Law thus allowed nonheir ō to descend to subject status (*shinseki kōka*), a reactivation of the old tradition. These subroyal branch houses therefore joined the kazoku, receiving the ranks of marquis (for the oldest nonheir) and count (for younger sons), together with their created family names. For example, the four nonheir sons of Prince Kikumaro of the Yamashina house (the miyake established by a son of Prince Fushimi) were allowed to shed royalty and assume kazoku status with different family names: Yamashina (marquis, distinct from Prince Yamashina main house), Tsukuba (marquis), Kashima (count), and Katsuragi (count).[26]

As table 3 indicates, there were nine kazoku of royal origin as of 1928. Shinnō remained such, which meant possibly both a proliferation of shinnō houses and the eventual loss of shinnō status or house extinction. Among all the shinnō, the reigning emperor's brothers were called *jikimiya* (closest princes). In 1928, the thirteen miyake included two jikimiya houses—the Chichibu and the Takamatsu, Emperor Hirohito's brothers' (the youngest brother, Prince Mikasa, was then still too young to establish a house). Like the kazoku, all the miyake except the then three jikimiya houses lost their royal status in 1947.

The complete list of former kazoku and kōzoku reminds us of the colonial history of the Japanese empire. When the Kingdom of the Ryūkyūs, after having been subjected to the local daimyo of Satsuma, came under the hegemony of Japan's central government, its deposed king, Shō Tai, was made a kazoku, and after the kazokurei he was granted the rank of marquis (W. Lebra 1966). Further, as a result of the Russo-Japanese War, Japan took control of Korea, a circumstance that culminated in the 1910 "annexation." This colonial past involved Japan's dethronement of Korea's king, demotion of his successor to the status of Japanese royalty (equivalent to miyake), and thus coercive termination of the Yi dynasty, which had existed since 1392.

The history of Japan's elite, as we have seen (albeit in brief) is filled with instances of dynamic interrelationship between order and disorder, ascription and achievement, traditions and reversals with respect to hierarchy, a declining elite and a rising commoner class—in short, the status complex and the power complex. This relationship, though manifested in various forms at various levels, was maintained in cycles of dyarchy. The two complexes, split into one form of dyarchy or another, not only challenged each other but also on occasion came into open or collusive alliance, reciprocal appropriation, or transmutation of one into the other (remember the aristocratization of Hideyoshi) in order to reproduce the dyarchical structure.

The remarkable resiliency of asymmetric dyarchy both explains and is explained by the resiliency of the sun-line dynasty, which proved to be the single uncontestable apex of the ascribed-status hierarchy. While representing one side of the dyarchy, the imperial institution provided upper limits to the fluctuating relations between the two complexes and at the same time prevented their excessive agglutination on a lasting basis. The unique status of the emperor in the dyarchical structure may be partly explained in terms of culture as defined in chapter 1. The emperor, in my view, was culturalized to an extreme degree by his genealogical linkage with the supernatural ancestors as it was irreversibly documented in the public record. The cultural—that is, mythological—construction of his status amounted to its dissociation from nature and sublimation into a pure symbol divested of real power. The cultural purity of imperial status was then preserved by relegating the management of its noncultural—natural and real—basis to holders of lower status. The natural basis of the imperial heredity, for instance, was managed and controlled by regent families that offered their women to mother imperial successors. Similarly, the reality of political economy was taken over and handled by the less "cultural" elite. As a culturally constructed, symbolically pure status, emperorship could perpetuate itself only as long as it was ritually enacted. This is an oversimplified picture, of course, but it does show how far cultural construction can go.

The Meiji Restoration, which at first glance appeared to put an end to cycles of dyarchy, in fact turned out to utilize the dyarchical legacy to maximal limits to ensure success. Although the kazoku played a role in the Meiji dyarchy, its diverse composition made its role and identity much more complex than was the case with the previous elite.

In the following chapters, further history will appear through the "lived" and recalled experiences of my informants. Yet because the "modern" creation of the Meiji kazoku was deeply embedded in the long pre-Meiji history, historical return trips will be necessary now and then to clarify where the informants stood. Let us now listen to what the survivors of kazoku had to say.[27]

THREE

Ancestors

Constructing Inherited Charisma

Members of the hereditary elite, by definition, owe their status to their ancestors. Kazoku life histories are indeed shaped by the weight of ancestors, which is still felt in one way or another. It is fitting, therefore, to begin our analysis with images of ancestors held by descendants. By linking the living generation to bygone generations, this chapter exhibits the continuous aspect of life experience, keeping it more or less separate from wartime and postwar events that dislocated all Japanese, including the kazoku. Discontinuity and transformation are thus reserved for the following chapters.

We have already met kazoku ancestors in chapter 2 as they emerged out of historical accounts. The present chapter takes a more "emic" point of view, biased by what my informants said about their ancestors, in contrast to the more "etic" overview presented earlier. I use *more* deliberately here, because the emic-etic distinction is relative; the two viewpoints, that is, influence each other, as will be illustrated below.

Another point requires clarification at this juncture as well. The aristocracy, as we have seen, was transformed in the Meiji period and entirely abolished after World War II. My informants have thus never encountered a kuge or a daimyo. But to use chronological markers like "descendant of" for each informant would subvert presentational economy. Hence, if I simply designate an informant as a kuge, he should be understood to be a grandson or great-grandson of a last kuge forefather. The same parsimony dictates the designation of an informant by a kazoku title: a baron may be the abbreviation of "a former baron" or "a baron's son." This follows the emic principle as well, because my informants also abbreviated their status identity by saying, for example, "I am (we are) a kuge."

CULTURAL AND PERSONAL CONSTRUCTIONS
OF ANCESTORS

The ancestor cult, as noted in chapter 1, is shared by Japanese in general, but ancestral charisma is likely more irresistible for the hereditary elite because of the "public" stature of their forebears. These ancestors were national figures—holders of the highest offices of government, famous warlords, eminent civil leaders. Ancestors of the hereditary elite, then, belong not just to particular families but to the public.

Aware of the public status of their ancestors, kazoku informants referred to them with honorifics (*keigo*), adding *sama* to a personal name, using such expressions as "this honorable person" (*kono kata*), and employing polite forms of verbs, such as *irasshatta* instead of the simple *kita* (came) or *itta* (went). Ordinarily, in speaking to an outsider the use of honorifics for one's own ancestors would be as inappropriate as using them for one's contemporary family members, since humility should prevail, whether in reference to the speaker's self or to his or her extension in kinship, living or dead. Similarly, purely public figures who appear in history texts would also be referred to without honorifics, however great they were—not for reasons of humility, but in accordance with the rule of impersonal objectivity. The kazoku deviation from the dominant speech rule, I came to realize, is a product of psychological compromise: honorific terminology at once distances ancestors as public figures and personalizes them as the speaker's own forebears.

Ordinary Japanese, too, tend to include renowned persons among their ancestors or trace their utmost ancestry to an illustrious lineage, as noted earlier. Their claims, however, are considered, with skepticism, as fantasy. Most kazoku informants do not even bother to argue their distinguished ancestry: they assume it to be common knowledge or at least on public record. "Open any history book," said the sixty-six-year-old head of a sekke family, instead of detailing his ancestral background; "you will find my ancestors as having served emperors from generation to generation as sesshō and kanpaku."

The public availability of ancestor histories may explain why a surprisingly large number of parents have neglected to teach their children about their forebears. A Tokugawa daughter said that until a certain Gakushuin history class, she had not known that it was her grandfather who returned the government to the emperor (*taisei hōkan*). Nor was a student's self-esteem necessarily enhanced by an encounter with family history in the context of national history: it might be that a humiliating experience in connection with one's ancestors was more vividly recalled. One descendant of a Kyushu daimyo claimed that she first became conscious of her ancestors as a sixth-grader at Gakushuin when the history teacher called class attention to her in reference to one of the first three Christian daimyo, Ōmura Sumitada (1533–87). Christianity was banned during the Tokugawa period, and it was again stigmatized as an enemy religion in the prewar Shōwa period, when the informant was a schoolgirl. The Christian ancestors were a taboo topic in the family, which had since converted to Nichiren Buddhism and then Shinto. With the eyes of the whole class directed at her, she felt deeply humiliated. Similar experiences were related by many other former students of Gakushuin, some of which will appear later.

The "public" status of ancestors thus derives not only from their prominence but also from the knowledge shared by or accessible to the public. In this sense, ancestors of the elite are more *culturally* constructed and articulated than are those of commoners. As outlined in chapter 1, the double-edged function of culture is self-evident in relation to the "reality" that it represents. On the one hand, culture as symbolic representation is capable of creating a world of its own or of distorting the real world; divergence between reality and culture, then, can become magnified when dealing with intangible, otherworldly objects like ancestors. On the other hand, culture is the necessary means whereby reality becomes recognizable, intangible ancestors become tangible, the dead come back to this world. Because kazoku ancestors are more culturally constructed and represented, they look more real, though they are also more liable to be mythologized.

The cultural representation of ancestors takes various forms in addition to historical accounts: genealogies; family crests and other emblems; family treasures including letters, diaries, calligraphic and painted scrolls, tea bowls, and other art objects handed down from remote ancestors; awesome mausolea, shrines, and castle ruins; the periodically conducted rites to memorialize ancestors or reenact family "traditions." Many legacies have been lost, burned down, sold, or simply forgotten, but some have survived even against the wish of a descendant now too impoverished to maintain the family legacy. Rows of extraordinarily huge tombstones representing generations of daimyo lords would simply be impossible to remove, confessed the wife of a daimyo descendant. The weight of an immovable gravestone, indeed, is symbolic of the "real" weight of ancestors, which cannot be lifted from the descendant's back.

As Japan recovered from the ruins of the war and began to pay attention to cultural preservation, many of these family legacies came under public possession and protection, designated as national or local "cultural treasures," "historical sites," and the like. Thus ancestors have become even more public, more dissociated from the personal ownership of the family.

The cultural preservation policy went hand in hand with the local economy's interest in appealing to the rapidly growing mass of sightseeing travelers as a means of revitalization. Thus castles and daimyo estates, shrines, temples, and mausolea have been restored; museums housing family treasures built; and daimyo processions replicated—all as tourist attractions. Some kazoku informants resent this commercialization as a desecration of their ancestors and refuse to heed the demands of local politicians and business leaders. Many, however, have become more sharply aware of their ancestors and of a descendant's responsibility as a result of the mass exposure of their family heritages.

The public sharing of kazoku ancestors, albeit in various degrees of distortion, is thus expanding through preservation policies, the tourism industry, and media transmission. Nor are kazoku descendants themselves entirely immune from the popular versions of their ancestors carried by the media. Two informants of kuge descent, for example, included as a notable ancestor one of the imperial envoys (*chokushi*) in *Chūshingura,* the story of forty-seven vassals loyal to a daimyo of the Tokugawa period—and the most popular TV and stage drama year after year. Another woman singled out an "interesting daimyo" who is described in a best-seller of Shiba Ryōtarō, a widely read historical novelist. The televised serial production of *Shin Heike monogatari* (The new tale of the Heike) stimulated the surviving Heike descendants to form a club for a periodical reunion and travel together to historical Heike sites. In the questionnaire, I asked whether informants' ancestors had appeared in historical novels or television dramas; sixty-eight respondents, 79 percent of the total, gave affirmative answers. Their reactions to such semifictional representations varied widely from aloofness ("Not impressed at all") to disapproval ("The author's subjective viewpoint is shown considerably") to involvement ("I am deeply moved when I see, for example, the banners [of my ancestors]"). Whether detached or involved, whether in agreement or disagreement with the producers, these descendants are reminded of their ancestors by such popular media.

Clearly, the culturally constructed and manifested existence and weight of ancestors has occupied the minds of kazoku descendants, as either a source of honor or an unremovable burden. Yet kazoku individuals and families, as private actors, have personally reacted to the culturally created or perpetuated images of their ancestors as well, both to reinforce and to rectify them. Indeed, in characterizing ancestors, informants tended to project their own selves, their own experiences, and contemporary life conditions. Ancestors, in other words, are not only culturally constructed, but they often mirror the descendant's selfhood. (Coincidentally, deified ancestors in Shinto are symbolized by mirrors.) What was said about ancestors was often indistinguishable from what was said about the speaker. Several responses in the questionnaire revealed strong identifications with ancestors: "I realize I had great ancestors, and am determined not to disgrace their name"; "[The ancestors'] thinking and looks ring bells somehow. . . . I was surprised that the figure depicted by Shiba Ryōtarō resembles me so much"; "I felt the same blood running in myself."

Informants encoded ancestors either explicitly or implicitly by opposing or juxtaposing one set of ancestors to another—an indication of a great variety of ancestor categories within this small group of kazoku— and then tended consciously or unconsciously to cross the boundary between the two sets. A host of such oppositions or juxtapositions emerged around several themes, of which I select five: genealogy, performance, allegiance and animosity, wealth, and style. Genealogy as the primary theme and groundwork for the rest of the discussion throughout the volume will take up the most space; the other, secondary themes are meant to counteract, qualify, or complement the genealogical argument.

GENEALOGY

Genealogical orthodoxy, a popular topic among elites and nonelites alike, is measured by a combination of generational depth, ancestral origin, and hereditary house rank, among other factors. "True" kazoku are thus often equated with the old, pre-Meiji aristocracy (typically, kuge and daimyo), while the new Meiji kazoku are dismissed as a sort of fake nobility. For this reason, I encountered greater resistance to my interview request among the new kazoku, and those who did cooperate tended to denigrate themselves as "not true kazoku," "unable to provide the kind of information" I was looking for, and so forth.

Genealogy is one of the most important factors entailing "vertical opposition" (Schwartz 1981) in a more or less clear-cut manner as "high" and "low," "above" and "below," "up" and "down," "noble" and "base." Even within the old aristocracy, invidious comparison was frequently made on the basis of genealogical prestige. The kuge's superiority to the daimyo on this score went unquestioned. Cynical daimyo descendants exaggerated the obscurity of their origins, even hinting at their earliest ancestors having been "mountain bandits" or "sea pirates," in contrast to the urban, sedentary, cultured kuge at the court.

Baroness Shidzue Ishimoto, in her autobiography (originally published in 1935), describes the ancestor games played by her classmates at Gakushuin, games that manifested their genealogical rank consciousness:

> Girls from the houses of smaller feudal lords would be humble enough to take the part of ladies-in-waiting, or subjects to the great lady, but the daughters of court nobles who were mostly counts or viscounts . . . would not dare to take the part of subjects to the girls from the great feudal families, as they believed that their own families made up the most refined circle around the imperial court. They had the habit of looking down even on the daimyo class as one engaged only in barbarous fighting. These feudal traditions affected the innocent minds of these young girls so deeply that they could not think of a person apart from house and rank.
>
> (Ishimoto 1984, 46)

It is not entirely clear, however, just who kept tabs on such rank distinctions, and whether genealogical superiors really looked down on their inferiors. Many Gakushuin graduates, including those of Ishimoto's generation, strongly repudiated the above passage as "absolutely untrue" and declared that no place was less rank conscious than Gakushuin. Some suggested that certain people, bound by an inferiority complex, may have projected their own feelings onto others (*katte ni omoikomu*). Male informants tended to attribute such rank discrimination to feminine sensitivity, "because among us boys the family rank didn't count at all." My observation confirms both arguments.

Whatever did or did not happen at Gakushuin, these views suggest something essential to social hierarchy in general. I am sure that rank inferiors are more conscious than superiors of hierarchy simply because they are more bound by the rules of hierarchical behavior. The distinction between the old and new kazoku as "true" and "false" nobles was stressed much more by the latter, whether for self-belittlement or in attribution of prejudice to the former. The inferior (daimyo) saw the superior (kuge) as "looking down"—though the latter did not admit such behavior. This seemingly simple discrepancy in rank consciousness has a double implication: first, the inferior or outsider, encountering rank discrimination more often, is "objectively" more perceptive of the hierarchy (hence a better informant to a researcher), whereas the superior or insider is more blind; second, however, this situation induces the inferior "subjectively" to read prejudice into the superior's behavior over and beyond the superior's awareness. Such asymmetry and discrepancy in rank awareness caught my attention in various contexts and will reappear throughout. Suffice it to say for the moment that the question of hierarchy versus equality is not a simple matter psychologically: disagreement over rank prejudice is therefore inevitable.

The importance of genealogical orthodoxy was tellingly revealed on one occasion when a man, the grandson of a prominent Meiji statesman of samurai background who had been awarded the rank of prince, introduced a kuge count to me with utmost reverence. Equal deference was betrayed when the same man talked about the lord of the domain where his grandfather was a samurai. He confessed that he could not raise his head before the "great lord." I protested, "But how about your grandfather!" The real nobility had ceased to exist, he contended, paying no attention to my interruption, with the Meiji creation of the kazoku, which was a hybrid of all sorts including nouveaux riches. "No longer pure." He talked nostalgically about pre-Meiji nobles "who had the kind of dignity [*fūkaku*] that you cannot pin down but feel as real." Contemptuous of the non-noble nobility of Japan, he admired the British for preserving the old aristocracy. The pre-Meiji status of a vassal, in short, seemed to weigh more than the achieved post-Meiji status of a prince. This attitude is mirrored by the episode in Meiji history when former domain lords were alienated from the new government, which was run by their former low-ranking vassals: the triumph of Satsuma, for example, was not enjoyed by Shimazu Hisamitsu, the virtual lord of Satsuma, who found himself unable to transcend the status barrier between himself and the upstarts.

Generational depth is indicated by the number of generations (*dai*) in a line of succession from the first ancestor (*shodai*): "I am the fourteenth-generation head of the house"; "My husband is the twenty-seventh generation." The number, of course, depends on who is picked as the first ancestor. In view of that necessarily arbitrary choice, I was amazed at the exact numbers of generations that were cited. Though there were exceptions. The ninety-one-year-old widow of a kuge marquis, for example, referred to her son as "the twenty-sixth generation . . . or was it twenty-ninth?" Another woman, age eighty-eight, the widow of a daimyo-count, carelessly identified her late husband as the 116th generation, whereupon her son-in-law, present along with his wife, snapped in disgust: "One digit too many! Even the emperor [who is supposedly unequaled in genealogical depth] is only the 124th." This exchange prompted an argument between the son-in-law and his wife over whether the correct generation was in fact the sixteenth or seventeenth. But such cases were few. The generally demonstrated precision regarding genealogical depth may indicate that it was a regular topic of family conversation. If not in the family, the topic often arose in conversation with others: "I am asked by many what generation I am; I have the answer ready." Further, almost every household had a genealogical chart, more or less updated, indicating the successive generations of househeads by name and number as well as rank and office.

Self-reported information from the questionnaire confirms the above generalization (table 4). Even though it was easier here to leave questions unanswered than in an interview, 87 out of 101 respondents specified numbers of generations, with the average number for all ancestor categories being 28.4. (The category of "Other" shows the greatest generational depth because it includes priestly houses; this will be clarified shortly.)

So far we have examined quantifiable ancestry, but this is only part of ancestral depth. When a typical genealogy traces ancestry further back, it includes remoter, unnumbered ancestors, and thus a double or triple "original" ancestry. The Reizei, a kuge-count house, for example, lists twenty-four numbered generations in succession beginning with Reizei Tamesuke; yet he in turn is connected with six ascending generations of Fujiwara forebears, whose progenitor is Fujiwara Michinaga. Inclusion of the Fujiwara portion, by the way, is very important for the Reizei, a house of poetry, since two top poets of the Heian period, Shunzei and Teika, are among the six.

Such multilayered genealogical construction is very common, as abundantly documented in *Kazoku kakei taisei* (hereafter cited as *KKT*), the most recently compiled kazoku genealogies (KK 1982–84) comprising edited versions of self-supplied family genealogies. Because of space limitations, not all the numbered ancestors of each house are listed; instead a line begins with X—who is, to take for example a kuge house, the eighteenth generation from Y (the first numbered ancestor), who in turn is the fourth son of Z. Each—X, Y, and Z—is identified by name and imperial court office. Let us now sample a daimyo house: the numbered genealogical line starts with K, who is the eighth generation from L, who is the third son of M, who is a grandson of N.

Why not simply say the nineteenth from Z, or the eleventh from N? Generally speaking, for the kuge, the line of numbered generations continuous to the living generation is identified with the house name, which is still carried, with the previous forebears being known by other name(s). Hence, the name Reizei began twenty-four generations ago when Tamesuke branched from the previous six-generation line, known as Mikohidari, and became Reizei. Presumably, the Mikohidari became such through the same process of branching from the main line of Fujiwara.

Table 4. Generational Depth, by Ancestor Categories

	NO. RESPONSES[a]	NO. GENERATIONS	RANGE
Kuge	19	27.0	2[b]–86
Daimyo	27	19.0	10–44
New Kazoku	33	7.9	2–34
Other	8	29.5	2–80

[a]Questionnaire responses, 1985.
[b]Such genealogically shallow kuge houses are post-Meiji branches of kuge main houses.

Likewise, the Kujō line begins with Kanezane, a Fujiwara son who assumed the Kujō name. Branching is not always accompanied by assumption of a new name, but knowing when a new name did begin is crucial
to the construction of a genealogy, at least for the kuge.

Why and how was a new name assumed? Most kuge houses converge
in the Fujiwara ancestry, specifically the Northern House (Hokke) of
Fujiwara, and ultimately in Fujiwara Kamatari. (Recall the Fujiwara dominance in the *KRR*.) Following the first Fujiwara ancestors, the expansion
of their offspring necessitated other names to differentiate one Fujiwara
from another. According to Hirayama (1980), in the Heian period kuge
of the same uji used *shōgō* (titles) to distinguish themselves from one
another.

The shōgō might be the name or location of the residential mansion,
or the name of a temple founded by or affiliated with the person named
(note such kuge names as Saionji, Tokudaiji, Kanroji, *ji* referring to temple). Initially, shōgō belonged to individuals, and it was customary that
father and son used different ones. As an example, Toyoda (1978, 28)
gives the five Fujiwara generations, with five different shōgō: Kan'in
(Fuyutsugu), Ichijō (Yoshifusa), Horikawa (Mototsune), Koichijō (Tada-
hira), and Kujō (Morosuke).[1] In practice, then, Fujiwara Fuyutsugu was
called Kan'in-dono, *tono* referring to a mansion or palace and thus meaning the "lord" who resides therein. (See chapter 5 for such spatial honorifics.) If the shōgō derived from one's residence, it likely changed as
one moved from one residence to another within one's lifetime, as can
be inferred from *The Tale of Genji*, where Prince Genji is known by a
sequence of different names according to his changing residence as well
as his promotion in court ranks and offices.

McCullough (1967) offers an explanation for the father-son name discontinuity in terms of the marital residence that characterized court

nobles. On the basis of Heian literature, McCullough demonstrates that before the twelfth century the rule of residence was uxorilocal, that is, the husband moved in to the wife's residence. This fact, combined with the convention (then and even now) of identifying a person by his or her residence, meant that a man was most likely known by his wife's residential name, which he could not share with his married son. McCullough shows the Fujiwara genealogy starting with Fuyutsugu (Kan'in), which indicates that "no Fujiwara heir bore the same designation as his father" (McCullough 1967, 122). There was thus a split between descent and residence or between genealogical patrilineality and residential matrilocality. This pattern began to give way in the twelfth century to patrilineal succession *and* virilocal residence, so that the originally residential name became the fixed "family name" to be passed down from father to son (Hirayama 1980; McCullough 1967). This development, in which the likelihood of father-son co-residence increased, corresponds with the incipient stage of the stem-family household known as the ie (see chapter 4).

The residence-derived family name was used without replacing the previous ancestral uji name, among which the name Fujiwara was most persistent. So the five sekke, known as Konoe, Kujō, Ichijō, Nijō, and Takatsukasa, retained Fujiwara as a residual designation to be activated when propitious. Note, for instance, that all imperial mothers, except some Minamotos and a few others, are formally named Fujiwara from the reign of Emperor Shōmu (724–49) down to that of Emperor Kōmei (1847–66), with no Konoe and no Nijō. Even in this century, the Fujiwara name is not totally dead. Konoe Fumimaro, who was prime minister three times between 1937 and 1941, used the seal "Fujiwara Fumimaro" to sign formal documents, a descendant recalled. At Gakushuin, according to my female informants, the Fujiwara name as a sort of exalted pen name superseded one's regular name when students submitted poems to the imperial court. In connection with court poetry, one kuge woman married to a daimyo said: "I still use Fujiwara," explaining her practice in terms of the Chinese custom that women keep their maiden names.

Even though they share Fujiwara ancestry, differently named houses are grouped into lineages and sublineages based on common ancestors, such as the sekke, the five houses stemming from Fujiwara Tadamichi, and Kan'inke, which stems from Fujiwara Kimizane and includes such well-known houses as Sanjō, Saionji, and Tokudaiji. A kuge, then, would typically locate his or her house in a lineage as a subcategory of the Fujiwara. The Bōjō, for example, belongs to the lineage called Kajūjike, which traces its ancestry to a son of Fujiwara Fuyutsugu. The Reizei, belonging to the lineage of Mikohidarike, has its own branches, Fujitani and Irie. Some lineage names are drawn from the names of main-line houses within the lineages, such as the Kajūjike lineage, named after its main-line house, Kajūji. Others like sekke and Kan'inke, are independent of any constituent houses (there is no single house named Sekke or Kan-'in). This difference suggests hierarchy as opposed to relative equality between constituent houses, a point we will return to.

How many lineages of Fujiwara descent existed? Toyoda (1978, 30) lists ten as of the Tokugawa period, but great variation exists among compilers, not only because of arbitrariness in determining when a sub-lineage became a lineage, but also—and more importantly—because lineages cannot be separated from the hereditary court ranks (that is, kakaku in the narrow sense of the word). But before we explore this latter point, a word is needed about the kuge outside the Fujiwara group.

Among the minority kuge of non-Fujiwara descent are Genji descendants, who are grouped into several lineages with the names of the imperial grantors of the Genji title (see chapter 2), such as the Murakami Genji, who originated from sons of Emperor Murakami. And there are also Heishi (Taira or Heike) descendants. Indeed, some kuge have Genji or Heishi ancestors, contrary to the general association of these names with buke houses. A kuge of Heike descent explained this apparent incongruity by saying that the Heike produced both civil and military court officials, but only the buke Heike perished at Dan-no-ura. His, then, is one of the six surviving kuge Heike. There are several other minor kuge houses as well, which do not belong to any of the three major uji of Fujiwara, Genji, and Heike.

In fact, all surviving houses are branches, but the Japanese genealogical conception differentiates the main lines from branch lines—or, using a river metaphor, the main/true/orthodox stream (honryū or chakuryū) from its tributaries (shiryū or shoryū).[2] The sekke houses, the Konoe above all, stand out as the most prestigious of all kuge because they are considered the utmost honryū of the whole Fujiwara clan. At lower levels, the honryū/shiryū distinction was recognized as well, older branch lines having attained a main-line status with greater prestige than that enjoyed by newer branch lines.

I have avoided using familiar terms like honke, bunke, and dōzoku that we use in reference to other classes, even though these terms appear in kuge conversation. The lineage system as inferred from kuge informants, coupled with main-versus-branch differentiation, is not like the dōzoku group unified in the honke-bunke hierarchy. It is a more purely genealogical category rather than a corporate group, intended more for name sharing than for functional cooperation. Except at the lowest level of sublineage, a kuge lineage seldom maintained *social* ties, let alone economic cooperation, among its members. When we compare a kuge lineage with a business-centered dōzoku like that of the Mitsui (which, by the way, will appear later on as a new kazoku), the contrast is remarkable. Occasionally, the latent relationship among members of a kuge lineage was reactivated, primarily when house succession was at issue: that is, the lineage was tapped for adopting heirs. This point, which will be discussed in the following chapter, reinforces the characterization of the kuge lineage as being mainly genealogical.

Cutting across and partly mixed with the lineage system is the system of kakaku, as determined by the sendo (the highest court office attainable by a house—potentially, if not necessarily in fact—as a hereditary right; see chapter 2). The sekke—a confusing name referring at once to a lineage and a kakaku—were revered not only as the utmost honryū lineage but also, and more importantly, as carrying the sendo of sesshō and kanpaku; hence they are called sekke or sekkanke. (This multiple meaning of the term *sekke* necessitates a fluctuation between upper and lower case in this writing.) Remember, this is a kakaku attached to the house, not an individual member holding the office. Shimohashi recalls how, in the late Tokugawa period, a member of the sekke was treated reverentially by a lower kuge with a deep bow, even though the latter's court rank or office was higher (as when the former happened to be much younger, only to be promoted later), to which the former responded as if to a vassal (Shimohashi and Hagura 1979, 249).

The sekke were set apart from the rest of kuge; indeed, one sekke informant considered the sekke and kuge as two distinct categories, equating sekke status with that of imperial princes (shinnō). Actually, Shimohashi's recollection illustrates that the sekke outranked princes both as exclusive holders of the highest court offices and as suppliers of imperial consorts: during ancestor rites at the court, sekke representatives preceded the shinnō in incense burning; when two vehicles met on a street, one carrying a sekke lord and the other a shinnō, it was the latter that made room. Only in the Meiji period was this order reversed (Shimohashi and Hagura 1979, 231). One of my daimyo informants repeated the stereotype of kuge as "poor and snobbish," but he hastened to add, "No, the sekke are different." Many kuge informants ranked themselves relative to the sekke.

The subordination of kuge to the sekke took the institutional form of *monryū*—similar to a daimyo-vassal hierarchy—which is said to have emerged during the Muromachi period (1336–1573). There were five monryū groups of kuge houses, each headed by a sekke. One source (cited in Shimohashi and Hagura 1979, 265) indicates that forty-eight houses belonged to the Konoe monryū, thirty-seven to the Ichijō, twenty to the Kujō, eight to the Takatsukasa, and four to the Nijō. A monryū follower owed the ritual obligations of a subordinate to his monryū lord and was supposed to secure approval from the latter for every important family transition such as a son's initiation, a marriage, or an adoption (ibid., 266–67). One of my kuge informants drew three concentric circles crosscut into five sectors, placing the emperor at the center, the five sekke in the next inner circle, and his own house in the Konoe sector of an outer circle. His ancestors, he said, served emperors in a capacity of Konoe monryū follower.

The kakaku second to the sekke was that of the Seigake, entitled to the office of daijōdaijin; and the third rank was that of the Daijinke, entitled to three ministerial offices: sadaijin, udaijin, and naidaijin. Below these were the Urinke (holding military ranks), the Meika (exclusively in civil service offices), the Hanke (going into either military or civil ranks), and so on. For some informants the kakaku was the most important identifier of the house: "Our house is one of the nine Seigake"; "We were a Meika that would start from *benkan* (controller) and could go up to dainagon (senior counselor)."

The genealogical hierarchy thus consists of a mixture of ancestral origin, generational depth, lineage status, honryū-shiryū distinction, monryū affiliation, and kakaku. Informants referred to these singly or in combinations of varying emphases. By sorting out lineage categories from kakaku categories (based on *KKT* and *Kazoku seido shiryōshū* [hereafter cited as *KSS*]), we can determine kuge genealogical status distribution, depicted in table 5. As this table shows, there was a general tendency for a single lineage to concentrate in one kakaku. The main reason for dispersal was branching to allow honryū-shiryū distinction in status. When kuge were reorganized in 1884 into the formal kazoku system, the rank of prince was given to the Sekke; that of marquis to the Seigake; that of count to the Daijinke, and some Urinke and Meika; and that of viscount to the remaining majority, in general recognition of the old genealogical hierarchy. The Sekke, Seigake, and Daijinke were considered "genuine" nobles, while the others were marked as *hirakuge* (rank-and-file kuge). The rank of baron went to post-Meiji branch houses of high-ranking kuge houses; these branch families are excluded from the Tōshō club (*tōshō* meaning nobles who were allowed to enter the emperor's living quarters, distinct from jige; see chapter 2), which exists to this day among surviving kuge kazoku.

The genealogical consideration has thus far drawn our attention entirely to the kuge. Yet daimyo houses are also contrasted to the genealogically shallow new kazoku, though to a lesser degree than are kuge houses. Here, too, ancestral origins are inseparable from the house names. Most buke ancestors derived their names from the provincial areas where they emerged as local *gōzoku* (powerful kin group) or served as local governors or shōen managers. The Shimazu, for instance, originated from Shimazu-shō (which was under Konoe proprietorship) in the late twelfth century, according to the self-compiled family chronology. Some names were the result of alliances between local powers and central lineages of distinguished ancestry (Toyoda 1978, 32–33).

Many of my daimyo informants identified still-existing villages or towns as the origins of their ancestors and family names; some have even renewed the old ties and are often invited as guests of honor at local festivals. The first numbered ancestor (shodai) is typically connected with the twofold engagement in feudal relationship: vassalage and dominion. This ancestor, namely, was the first to become a vassal to a warlord and to become a lord himself over a territorial segment assigned or granted by his lord. The first ancestor of the Nanbu, according to a descendant, originated as a gōzoku in Nanbu-shō (the present town of Nanbu in Yamanashi Prefecture), followed Minamoto Yoritomo in his expedition to subjugate the northeastern region, and was granted five counties of the region. This was in 1189, and the house has lasted forty-five generations—a remarkable number, especially considering that the generational depth of sekke houses is much less (the present heads of Konoe and Kujō, for example, are the thirty-first and thirty-third generations, respectively). Similarly, the Shimazu, whose present head is the thirty-first generation, claim that the first ancestor was appointed by Yoritomo to *jitō* (estate steward) of Shimazu-shō and then to *shugo* of three southern Kyushu provinces, including Satsuma. Named Shimazu Tadahisa, the first ancestor was supposedly Yoritomo's illegitimate son.

Such cases of generational depth with numbers extending back to Yoritomo are more the exception than the rule. As survivors from the Sengoku through the Tokugawa periods, the majority of daimyo descendants have a shallower genealogy: their first ancestors were vassals to more recent lords—Nobunaga, Hideyoshi, and the Tokugawa. When daimyo informants talked about *kuni* or *kunimoto* (provinces), they usually meant the last fiefs over which their ancestors had been *hanshu* as authorized by the Tokugawa overlords. (See table 4 for average generational depth of daimyo compared with kuge.)

As among the kuge, however, daimyo ancestry is usually extended

Table 5. Kuge Kakaku by Lineage, Tokugawa Period

	KAKAKU						
LINEAGE	Sekke	Seigake	Daijinke	Urinke	Meika	Hanke	Total
Fujiwara							
Sekke	5	1[a]	0	0	0	1[a]	7
Kan'inke	0	4	2	23	0	0	29
Kasan'inke	0	2	0	5	0	0	7
Nakamikado	0	0	0	9	0	0	9
Mikohidarike	0	0	0	4	0	0	4
Shijōke	0	0	0	7	0	0	7
Minaseke	0	0	0	5	0	0	5
Takakurake	0	0	0	2	0	1	3
Hinoke	0	0	0	0	12	0	12
Kajūjike	0	0	0	0	13	0	13

Genji (Minamoto) and Heishi (Taira)

							Total
Murakami Genji	0	0	1	8	0	0	10
Ōgimachi Genji	0	1	0	0	0	0	1
Uda Genji	0	0	0	3	0	2	5
Other Genji	0	0	0	0	0	2	2
Heishi	0	0	0	0	3	2	5
Other	0	0	0	0	0	18	18
Total	5	9	3	66	28	26	137

Sources: KKT; KSS.
[a]Refers to branches of two sekke houses.

beyond the shodai, with genealogical prestige being sought in remoter ancestors associated with notable families—shogunal (Ashikaga or Minamoto) or imperial—either in descent or vassalage. The Seiwa Genji are often claimed as primogenitors. Thus, as the kuge tended to converge in the Fujiwara ancestry, so did the daimyo in the Minamoto ancestry. A Tokugawa descendant recalled his most recent forebears replacing their family name with Minamoto in formal signature: "I wondered if I should not follow suit," he said lightly, "but decided it would be silly. So I have kept my name as it is. It should be Minamoto, however, according to the old-fashioned kabane practice." A kuge woman married to a daimyo mentioned her double identity as Fujiwara and Minamoto. I witnessed a latter-day daimyo, during an annual ancestral rite at a temple in his "province," offer *kanshajō* (formal notes of appreciation) to several "vassals." The kanshajō were signed with the seal of "Minamoto Ason" prefacing his name.

Some daimyo houses lean toward the court nobility in their search for pristine ancestry. The Maeda identify their shodai ancestor as Toshiie, who, as a top vassal to Nobunaga and then Hideyoshi, was granted the province of Kaga. But, a somewhat cynical descendant reported, the Maeda "are also said to have descended from Sugawara Michizane," one of the few non-Fujiwara distinguished court nobles of the Heian period. The Sugawara connection was exhibited by *gō*, professional names used by artists, given to and used for poetry and calligraphy by each member of the family: in association with Michizane's love of the plum (*ume*, read as *bai*), the family assumed such gō as Baidō, Baikei, Gyokubai. Another daimyo descendant linked his ancestors to the pre-Kamakura period, and attributed the "good looks" of his family and forebears to a "truly aristocratic" (that is, non-buke) origin. When daimyo claim the Fujiwara as progenitors, they tend to select branches other than the Hokke.

It is natural that, inasmuch as the Fujiwara or Minamoto identity is a source of dignity and esteem, such claims are not limited to the elite. One man confessed that to his chagrin his house was made into a mere bunke (branch house) and thus was practically reduced to a vassal house of the daimyo house, even though his line in fact goes back to the Fujiwara. Genealogically, he was trying to argue, his house should not rank lower than the main house. Indeed, genealogical obsessions on the part of the nonelite often result in group formation as exemplified by the following episode.

During a trip to Kyushu, I encountered a small group of people called the Seiwa Genji Club. The club was started by a retired school principal when his father died from cancer, a disease that the victim had attributed to his own neglect of ancestors. The son decided to actualize his father's unfulfilled wish and dedicate himself to his ancestors. His appeal through a local newspaper to "all descendants of the Seiwa Genji" for a get-together was received "enthusiastically." The first meeting brought together thirty-six, though attendance dwindled thereafter. The following is from my notes on the meeting at a restaurant, to which I invited myself:

> Today there were only nine people attending, including one woman. All the participants were pleased to hear of my research interest in "aristocratic culture," except one old man who did not hide his hostility. As he began to speak, I understood his displeasure had nothing to do with me. He said the club used to be more exclusive, admitting only those who were truly qualified to membership; he was disturbed by the presence of some unqualified attendants. His protest, however, was gently ignored.
>
> My presence stimulated the attendants to discuss their background in connection with the Seiwa Genji. One described his ancestors as hereditary holders of the office of top *karō* [chief administrator-vassal] to a daimyo, but then his honesty got in the way. "No, no, I meant *sōjōya* [chief of a village headmen's group]," he interrupted himself, blushing to his ears. A young man conspicuous in this senior group was present as a substitute for his mother, whose maiden name was Minamoto. He had had no interest in ancestors until he happened to watch a historical TV drama and heard his mother say that he carried Genji blood. Suddenly his ancestor interest was awakened.
>
> Unfortunately for the club, there is no central symbol. The daimyo descendant of the province, as the most likely symbol, has been solicited to dignify the meeting with his honorable presence, but apparently his response has been less than enthusiastic. A leading member of the club has been working hard to link the group to a shrine located at some distance which carries his family name and is believed to be the shrine of his ancestors. He had brought a tape of the shrine song and played it. His zeal to inspire the Genji group with the lively song caught nobody else, even though we went over the stanzas endlessly while the leader conducted our joint singing.

If genealogical orthodoxy meant so much to both commoners and nobles, it is indeed remarkable that the Meiji Restoration was carried out by a handful of mere samurai, who were not genealogical nobles. It is then understandable that they had to secure *gyoku* (jewel, the inner-circle word for the emperor) on their side, whose genealogical prestige was unquestioned. Hilarious but equally comprehensible is the overnight aristocratization by name of the early Meiji leaders: "Ōkubo became Fujiwara Ason Toshimichi, Ōkuma became Sugawara Ason Shigenobu, and Itō, who had begun as a lowly *ashigaru* (foot soldier), became Shu Ochi no Sukune Hirobumi" (Craig 1986, 51). These names were matched by the court robe with all its accoutrements, which these leaders were required to wear. The whole farce was dropped soon afterward.

Generational depth is an important factor but by no means the only criterion for genealogical status, a point that can be illustrated by contrasting two kinds of lineage we have not yet discussed. The imperial dynasty aside, which family or lineage has the next longest numbered genealogy? Neither a Fujiwara nor a Genji. Recall the threefold betsu categorization of descent as listed in the *KRR:* kōbetsu, shinbetsu, and gaibetsu (see chapter 2). The shinbetsu (deity descent) was theoretically traceable to gods as original ancestors. The Fujiwara's ancestral god, for instance, is Ame-no-koyane, a major deity who appears in the *Kojiki* and *Nihon shoki* and is enshrined at Kasuga Taisha, the Fujiwara's ujigami.

All twelve non-Fujiwara shinbetsu rui (comprising thirty-nine houses; see table 1) are claimed to have descended from a god, and they carry such ancient kabane titles as omi, muraji, and sukune besides ason. The "divine" connections of these houses were maintained through a hereditary priesthood attached to particular Shinto shrines; indeed, seven of the thirty-nine present househeads are in the priesthood, in charge of either their own ancestral shrines or other shrines. In *KKT,* too, we find that seven of these houses carry the title of *kokusō(ke),* the sinified rendition of *kuni-no-miyatsuko,* suggesting that they had something to do with provincial power groups (gōzoku) more or less autonomous of, or at least as old as, the Yamato court. Typically, these houses boast long genealogical continuity, longer than any other class of kazoku lineage. The present head of the Kii, kokusōke of the Kii province, for example, is identified as the eightieth generation from Ame-no-michine, a god who accompanied Ninigi, the grandson of Amaterasu, when he descended from heaven. The kokusōke of the Aso Shrine in Kumamoto Prefecture, Kyushu, claims (*KKT* 1:31) to extend back ninety generations to Hayamikadama, the ancestor god who descended from Emperor Jinmu (because of this imperial connection, the Aso are classified as a kōbetsu).

The most prominent of all the shrines controlled by kokusōke is the Izumo Shrine, second in prestige only to the Ise Shrine. The Senge, one of the two Izumo kokusōke, count eighty-three generations, beginning with Ame-no-hohi, a son of Amaterasu.[3] The eighty-second head priest writes:

> Thus, the Izumo kokusō has been succeeded by a single unbroken line (*ikkei*) of descendants of the god Ame-no-hohi since the Age of Gods, and has kept its kokusō name of ancient origin to this day. I do not want to sound self-promoting, but it would not be an exaggeration to say that this kokusōke embodies the spirit of Japan's history, that it is a pedigree of rare distinction, the oldest of all old houses, second only to the imperial house, older than the sekke in origin.
>
> (Senge 1968, 195)

Boasting and rivalry among peers came freely to the fore in interviews. To outsiders, the Izumo kokusō would seem to be beyond challenge in terms of genealogical prestige, but a descendant of another kokusō house, "A," while conceding that the A and the Senge were the "only true" kokusō, did challenge the latter. A was in fact the superior of the two, he tried to convince me, because every new successor to this kokusō position had been authorized by the imperial court immediately after a single application, whereas the Izumo kokusō had to submit a second application. More importantly, the A ancestors belonged to the celestial group of *tenson* (surrounding Amaterasu's grandson who descended from heaven), not a terrestrial group like the Senge. Meanwhile, a third kokusō house, "B," was claimed by a descendant to be among the "three oldest" houses of Japan, the other two being the imperial and the Senge. This spokesman of the B lineage did not even mention the A. Such genealogical competition may be a natural product of a hereditary hierarchy.

Despite such claims to genealogical depth and divine origin, these priestly houses were granted nothing more than baronetcies in the Meiji period, a rank hardly regarded as noble by the old aristocracy. They lacked, namely, the necessary status of secular office.

Conversely, there was another category of kazoku that did not belong to the kuge, daimyo, or new kazoku and was genealogically as shallow as the new kazoku but more esteemed than many old aristocratic houses, and that was the miyake. As we saw in chapter 2, all surviving miyake except the Fushimi and the revived Kan'in were post-Meiji, created from laicized mozeki priests or collaterals that branched from existing main houses. Contemporary miyake descendants count generations from "original" priest-princes (hōshinnō) or nonheir princes who branched out to establish new miyake under new names. The Kuni house, for instance, began with Prince Asahiko, a former monzeki, and so far has lasted four generations; the first ancestor of the Takeda house was its present head's father, who branched from the Kitashirakawa. Miyake informants thus emphasized the newness of their houses, "unlike the kuge or daimyo," instead of linking themselves to the long line of the imperial house.

With the cessation of miyake expansion began the production of new kazoku of royal origin, established by nonheir princes under new family names, with the ranks of marquis and count (see chapter 2). Between 1888 and 1943, sixteen such royal kazoku were created: seven marquises and nine counts. These royal kazoku houses, of course, were no older than any other kazoku. The Kashima line, for example, established in 1928 by Prince Hagimaro, the fourth son of Prince Yamashina Kikumaro, extends back only two generations. Nevertheless, the royal origin of these houses was often recognized as deserving special esteem second only to that accorded the miyake.

PERFORMANCE

Genealogical respectability, important as it is, is often contrasted to prominence in achievement, as if one precludes the other. Because of this oppositional categorization, informants tended to be ambivalent about genealogical prestige. The new kazoku, not surprisingly, were most vocal with regard to performance. While embarrassed about their genealogical deficiency or resentful of discrimination, descendants of *kunkō* kazoku were proud to mention their recent ancestors as distinguished national leaders to whom, or to whose heirs, kazoku titles had been awarded.

Ancestral performance was recognized as central to the Tokugawa-Meiji transition, for without strong leadership the construction and management of the Meiji polity could not have proceeded. Such ancestors thus contributed to Japan's modernization in industry and other fields along Western models, to the enhancement of the nation's standing in the international arena through both military and diplomatic leadership, to educational and professional progress, and so on. Table 6 breaks down ancestors' achievements into five categories, based on the brief narratives, following genealogies, given by descendants or the compilers in *KKT* (with multiple entry allowed). Of 1,011 households listed, 598 (almost 60 percent) mention one or more meritorious accomplishments attributed to one or more ancestors. Needless to say, this group is overrepresented by new kazoku, while the 413 households who make no such claims are largely descendants of the pre-Meiji aristocracy, but still, the figure 60 percent means that not a small number of old kazoku claim

Table 6. Repertoire of Ancestral
Performances

Achievements mentioned	598
Political/Governmental	263
Military	294
Industrial/Financial	25
Professional	35
Other	109
Not mentioned	413

Source: *KKT.*

ancestral achievements. In addition, the table shows a clear predominance of military and political/governmental contributors, a distribution that is confirmed by my informants' narratives.

The career patterns of recent forefathers will be covered in chapter 8; here, suffice it to say that grandfathers, fathers, or brothers of my informants were concentrated most densely in the military. Saneyoshi Yasuzumi, as narrated by a granddaughter, was born a *hiyameshi* (cold-rice eater; i.e., a nonheir son) in a samurai family of Satsuma; he left for Tokyo as a young man, sided with the *kangun* (imperial army) in the Satsuma Rebellion and participated in the two Meiji wars (with China and with Russia) as a military physician, to be awarded the rank of viscount. While Emperor Meiji encouraged kazoku men to follow a military career, many men were ennobled because of wartime achievements; thus every war produced new kazoku. The result was a high percentage of military officers among both the old and new kazoku.

Several informants discussed the political and governmental contributions of their forefathers. Fukuoka Takachika was a transition-time hero whose "greatest achievement was to bring about the Tokugawa's taisei hōkan." He worked hard, said his great-grandson, toward a "peaceful completion of the Meiji Restoration" but was disillusioned by the Chōshū's "betrayal" in favoring military confrontation and by its subsequent "dictatorship." In conversation the young man did not conceal his own distrust of the crafty Chōshū (the Satsuma being more tolerated) as contrasted to the honest Tosa (the origin of the Fukuoka line). Fukuoka Takachika, though "disgusted" with his excessively Westernized Meiji colleagues, was nevertheless "well versed in Mill and Spencer, and wished to establish a democracy in Japan, too far ahead of the times."

His progressive idea was culminated in the *seitaisho* (the formula for the new body politic), promulgated in 1868 soon after the *gokajō no goseimon* (the Charter Oath, which, incidentally, the informant was instructed in his childhood by the family to memorize). Two other informants referred to the Meiji constitution: "My grandfather was the 'brain' behind Prince Itō and, as his righthand man, drafted the Meiji constitution"; "My grandfather drafted the Meiji constitution, and later the Imperial Rescript on Education."

Such innovative performances required expertise in Western learning, and indeed this was a decisive factor in separating those who could make it from those who could not in Meiji Japan. A large majority of my informants related their forebears' extensive exposure to European and American education and ways of life. "Study abroad" was another motto addressed to the kazoku by Emperor Meiji in his 1871 edict; it prompted the Iwakura mission for investigatory tours to Europe and the United States, and the migration abroad of many kuge and daimyo for study (for illustrations, see Kasumi Kaikan Shiryō Tenji Iinkai 1980). Yet as in the case of the military, many nonelite Japanese, too, advanced thanks to their proficiency in Western studies, and some of them were rewarded with kazoku titles.

Among foreign teachers of ancestors who made their mark in Meiji Japan was Dr. William Clark, the legendary educator invited from Massachusetts in 1876. Satō Shosuke, then studying English, came under Clark's influence, became his "first" student at Sapporo Agricultural College, and was eventually appointed the first president of his alma mater, now expanded into Hokkaido Imperial University. He was "wholeheartedly devoted to Dr. Clark," said a descendant. Satō received a baronetcy in 1928. Another new-kazoku informant, a count, explained why his grandfather, coming from the common class (*shomin*), could rise to the top: he was the son of an interpreter in Nagasaki, "the center of civilization at that time," and studied English under a foreign tutor. "The secret of his success was his English." A woman talked about the early Meiji government admiringly, because "it ordered each han to select two promising men to study overseas." Her samurai grandfather, thus chosen, spent seven years in the United States, graduating from Massachusetts Institute of Technology with honors. He became a pioneer in the industrial and banking world, and received the rank of baron. "He kept routine notes in English"; while interested in Japanese traditional arts, "he was totally Westernized in his inner thoughts."

Extraordinary courage, diligence, and perseverance were necessary for such achievements, but more important, informants subtly conveyed, were basic intelligence and native talent—in short, "brains." Sensitive about genealogical handicaps, new kazoku tended to characterize their families as "of a scholarly line," "professionals in medicine, engineering, business, literature, and so on," "having nothing but brains." One was emphatically proud of his background, saying that his grandfather was "truly a self-made man unlike kuge and daimyo." It was precisely for this reason that he could wield real power in the government: "In those days, it was said that one glare [from my grandfather] was strong enough to crush a cabinet."

Implications could be devastating to genealogical aristocrats, who in conversation sometimes revealed profound feelings of inferiority about the caliber of their ancestors. This sensitivity was to genetic weakness, both physical and mental, of the old elite, attributed to inbreeding as well as to generations of overprotected life. Yet most kazoku survivors, it was then admitted, carried the non-noble blood of robust "womb ladies," who gave birth to lords' heirs in place of the legitimate but sterile wives. "My grandfather did not even touch his wife [who was from a high-ranking kuge]," but had many children by two womb ladies, including the informant's mother. When conversation focused on Crown Princess Michiko (the present empress), even those not entirely supportive of this marriage had to recognize the "blood" contribution she made as a commoner to the weak imperial genes. In this way, old aristocrats unwittingly released an ambivalent message about their genealogical status.

Some daimyo or kuge descendants were resigned to their destiny, even cynically accepting the label *bakatono* (Lord Stupid) instead of *wakatono* (junior lord). Others, however, strongly repudiated such ridicule. One kuge woman was incensed that historical dramas always depicted kuge as dumb and comical. Irritating to many kazoku and a royal informant, too, was the fact that they were not perceived as individuals, that their abilities were not recognized as their own. When the public comments on one's performance, "you never know whether it is because of you or only because of your family name." Despite the stereotype of bakatono, some members of the kazoku and royal lines complained that their excellent performance was taken for granted, whereas an inability to meet public expectations would quickly excite the news media. Ironically, this unfairness only reinforces the stereotype.

Nobody wants genealogical distinction without a record of performative excellence. It is only natural, therefore, that genealogical nobles also name individual ancestors as "great," "brilliant" achievers, and makers of history. Typically, such ancestors appeared during times of crisis. A Matsudaira, for example, drew my attention to his grandfather, Matsudaira Shungaku (Yoshinaga), as one of "the four wisest lords" of the Tokugawa-Meiji transition period, the other three being Date Munenari, Shimazu Hisamitsu (not Nariakira?), and Yamauchi Yōdō. "Among all the daimyo, Lord Shungaku stood out as a truly able man, not a politician but a man of learning and sincerity, who was forced into a political role during the crisis. . . . Shungaku's spirit has been inherited" by his son and grandson, the informant himself. Tokugawa informants, too, mentioned several notable shogun, including Yoshinobu, a smart shogun whose sagacity was indispensable to "the Meiji bloodless revolution"; Yoshimune, "the father of Tokugawa restoration"; Ieyasu, the *shinkun* (consecrated ruler) or *gongen-sama* (lord god) enshrined at Tōshōgū who put an end once and for all to disorder. Likewise, Shimazu descendants and the citizens of Kagoshima whom I contacted shared the legacy of Shimazu Nariakira, the "enlightened ruler" whose extraordinary foresight brought about a great renewal of the domain, in matters governmental, military, and industrial. The local museum displays the extent of Nariakira's receptivity to Western technology.

A kuge daughter called attention to a named ancestor of great stature who died as the surrogate for an emperor in the southern court (the fourteenth century). The Tokugawa-Meiji transition period produced several heroes among the kuge as well, including the seven kuge who in 1863, to escape attacks from the *kōbugattai* (court-shogunate union) faction, left Kyoto to come under Chōshū shelter, fully intending to return to central politics—an event known as *shichikyō-ochi* (seven kuge escaping from the capital). In my interviews, Shijō Takauta was named by a descendant as one of the seven. Yanagiwara Sakimitsu, an active leader in the Boshin War and a diplomat in the new government (also known as a brother of Emperor Meiji's consort and Taishō's mother), was another kuge singled out as an "extraordinary" ancestor. These kuge were deeply engaged in "real politics," far from being stereotypically aloof and featherbrained.

Among the genealogical elite, a great ancestor was sometimes praised not for what he had done, but for what he could have done. As one daimyo descendant observed about an ancestor who appeared at the Nobunaga-Hideyoshi-Ieyasu transition: "Japanese history would have been different if he had been born closer to the capital and a little earlier." This great warlord was "an atypical Japanese with his eyes wide open to the whole world," but "regrettably was born too early and too far north of the center." With better luck, he would have taken over the whole country and led it in a different direction. The same subjunctive mood was used by a royal prince when he praised his grandfather, an army general and well-informed intellectual who died prematurely: "If my grandfather had lived long enough, he would not have allowed Japan, people say, to launch the [Pacific] war."

In some cases, performance was inseparable from genealogical continuity, a point that requires a brief historical review. Many kuge houses (according to *KKT,* 66 out of 163) were associated with certain arts, crafts, and areas of scholarship as their house specialties—poetry, calligraphy, Chinese classics, Confucianism, court music, court dance, *biwa* lute, flute, flower arrangement, incense art, court kickball sport, sumo wrestling, court-costume dressing, sewing, culinary art, and the like. These houses, however, though recognized as *tsukasa* (chief—the house carrying on a certain skill or art, called *ieryū*) and likened to iemoto, did not necessarily practice the art in question. Nevertheless the Tokugawa shogunate saw in these artistic and court traditions a source of revenue for the pauperized kuge, and placed them *above* the practicing non-noble iemoto, thus enabling family members to receive fees for certification services.

This double hierarchy has survived in some quarters. "My house is the iemoto of the Ikuta school of koto music. No, nobody [in my family] teaches or plays it. [All] my father does is affix the family seal to the certificates [obtained by Ikuta trainees]." A sekke woman explained this arrangement as "a kind of *arubaito* [*Arbeit*; i.e., a side job]" for extra income. Her house has long held the seal to authenticate the highest artistic rank, called *jō,* that performing artists could obtain. This family legacy thus led her father to become involved with the *kiyomoto* music school: "Every kiyomoto practitioner who wants a jō rank must receive my family's seal." Another well-known house art is Shijō-ryū, a style of culinary art, particularly in fish slicing; indeed, the Shijō are known as the house of the slicing knife (*hōchō no ie*). "Even today, there is a sashimi-slicing style called Shijō-ryū," said a descendant, "and I can tell immediately whether a sashimi dish is prepared in Shijō-ryū or not"—although again, her family had nothing to do with the actual slicing. Such an authentication role is not limited to the kuge, however; in sumo wrestling, for example, the license for the top referee, a hereditary office of the Yoshida house, is sanctioned, I was told, by the seal of the Hosokawa, a daimyo house.

This pattern of role division between authenticator/name giver and practitioner/name receiver throws into relief the complementary opposition of genealogy and performance, exemplifying the cultural paradigm of "asymmetric dyarchy" discussed in chapter 2. But some kuge houses in fact did practice and perpetuate their house arts over generations. In all likelihood, most of these houses have recently revitalized their artistic traditions, systematically become professionalized in them, and begun to "teach" them to outsiders; in the old days, by contrast, the house arts were "secrets" not to be released beyond the house. In any event, under such circumstances, performance is inherent in genealogical succession. One kuge woman from a house of poetry argued that the house tradition could not have been perpetuated without creative talents, brains, and strenuous work by all individuals concerned.

By and large, old kazoku were more reticent than new kazoku about their ancestral performance, probably not so much because they had nothing to say as because their ancestors were more taken for granted as part of public history. To be noted, however, is the contradiction inherent in the way the hereditary elite, old and new, capitalizes on ancestral performances. When a man praises his grandfather as a self-made man, he must face the fact that he himself has been a beneficiary of this grandfather thanks to status heredity. When a recent forebear is depicted as an extraordinary talent, the question arises, "What is the descendant like by comparison?" Confronted with such a self-directed backlash, some informants prefer to remain anonymous. It may be in part for this reason that refusals to grant interviews came mostly from descendants of the best-known national leaders of the early Meiji.

I did contact the great-grandson of a famous hero from the transition time, and our conversation went as follows:

> *Do you watch TV dramas of K?*
> Yes, but fiction is fiction.
> *I suppose you are proud of him?*
> Not really proud. But people around me talk about it.
> *Do you dislike it?*
> Yes, it is very unpleasant, because it means they are comparing us, K and myself. You would feel differently if you yourself were a success, and people would say the blood still runs. In most cases, however, they look down on you.

When drafted, this count would not enter the navy, despite strong pressures to do so because his great ancestor was deified in the imperial navy as its founder. Instead he chose the army, where "I could relax," and started as a private. "I detested being compared. To surpass such a great figure would be impossible, and people would be disappointed to find K's descendant such a small fry."

Thus, there seems to be a psychological ceiling in claiming ancestors' self-made performance; in the meantime, the attraction of genealogical dignity is irresistible and persistent among elites and nonelites alike. Not surprisingly, then, many new kazoku push their genealogy back to before the original recipients of kazoku rank. Although the present househead was most likely the third or at most fourth generation from the meritorious ancestor, new-kazoku respondents located their first ancestors, on average, 7.9 generations back, ranging from two to thirty-four generations in depth (see table 4). Consider the following examples.

An informant, a businessman himself, has an impressive list of kinsmen, most being scholars, physicians, and government officials. His grandfather X studied in France and received the rank of baron for his services in codifying civil and criminal laws along the lines of the French model; but the ancestor highlighted in the family genealogy was that man's grandfather, Y, well known as a Japanese initiator of Dutch learning. The latter's forebears were domain physicians. Assisted by a team of historians who wrote a biography of the Dutch scholar, his great-great-grandfather, the informant came to learn that the really original ancestor could be located centuries back. The shodai, Z, was a Genji in command of an outpost castle, but his successors were defeated by Nobunaga. The informant, the present househead, made himself into the thirteenth-generation head of the house counting from Z, rather than the third generation from X, the kazoku-title awardee. Another example is found in a biography of Saigō Yorimichi, a new kazoku of samurai origin, written by one of his grandsons, who traces the Saigō ancestral line as far back as the Kikuchi, the famous loyalists to the southern court, whose ultimate ancestor was Fujiwara Kamatari (Saigō 1981, 19).

It seems that, just as the old nobles wanted to add a record of performance to their genealogy, the new nobles wished to add genealogical dignity to their record of performance.

ALLEGIANCE AND ANIMOSITY

The third theme refers to political roles played by ancestors involving loyalty, partisanship, oppression, betrayal, and animosity. Ancestors were often, for example, visualized in light of political opposition between kuge and buke. One kuge count, in his late forties, framed his personal hatred of militarism in terms of the kuge's collective "history of contempt for warriors." His ancestors, belonging to a meika (one of the kuge categories by kakaku; see above discussion of genealogy), had held exclusively civil offices of the imperial court until the Meiji Restoration, when his grandfather broke the family tradition by becoming an army officer. In the long history of imperial reign, he added, all emperors but two—Jinmu and Meiji—appeared in civil court dress, not in military uniform. (He could have added Emperor Shōwa.) Another kuge, a viscount, proudly boasted of the "cultural" expertise of the kuge, "developed thanks to being out of politics for eight hundred years after losing power to the buke." The kuge thus "could concentrate on creating and preserving court culture, which the buke tried hard to transplant in their domains." Japanese culture, he claimed, finds its roots in the kuge culture.

The civil-military opposition cannot be carried too far, since, from the Meiji period on, a military career was mandatory for royal princes and strongly endorsed for kazoku men regardless of their ancestry. The above-cited viscount kuge, for instance, served in the postwar self-defense ground force. Only recently retired, he began to recapture his ancestral kuge identity by serving the emperor as a palace-shrine ritualist.

For daimyo descendants, the civil-military opposition is more blurred. In reflection of the buke's assimilation of nonmilitary kuge values and probably of Japan's postwar pacifism as well, daimyo descendants tended to downplay belligerence and stress the esthetic preoccupations and cultural sophistication of their ancestors. An eighty-two-year-old Hosokawa woman emphasized the Kyoto origins and artistic fame of the Hosokawa daimyo. Powerful daimyo ancestors like the Hosokawa and Maeda were described more as practitioners and patrons of various arts—poetry, tea ceremony, noh drama, *utai* recitation, painting, calligraphy—than as warriors.

Nevertheless, kuge-buke opposition does still flavor buke characterizations of the kuge, toward whom buke informants betrayed a curious mixture of pity, inferiority, guilt of complicity, and pride. The history of the kuge, stripped of power and wealth, aroused guilt in the descendants of the expropriators ("Naturally they hold a lot of grudges against us") and at the same time reminded them of their own pathetic life-style, that of a "parasite." A daimyo daughter claimed that, while pitifully indigent and shamelessly manipulative, contemporary kuge were snobbish about their ancestry and looked down on the "obscure origins" of both daimyo and millionaire upstarts. At Gakushuin, she had few kuge friends but got along well with wealthy commoner classmates.

The kuge-buke polarity partly overlaps the imperial-versus-shogunal partisanship. Kuge informants stressed their centuries-old family traditions of loyalty and closeness to emperors. The "unbroken" lineage of the single imperial dynasty unique to Japan was credited by one informant to the loyal service of kuge courtiers. Special nostalgia was felt toward Kyoto, the site of the old imperial palace where their ancestors attended and "protected" emperors generation after generation as *denjōbito* or tōshō (both terms meaning "in-palace" nobles, in contrast to the jige, non-noble palace retainers working "on the ground"; see chapter 2 for more detail), even though most post-Meiji generations have been lifetime residents of Tokyo. Several kuge informants mentioned female ancestors who were imperial consorts and gave birth to princes and emperors. High-ranking kuge in particular stressed intimacy and kinship with the imperial family and their regard for emperors as "human, never as gods." Lower-ranking kuge, however, like many other kazoku informants, tended to deify the emperor; as one palace attendant put it, "I think the Japanese emperor is the closest to the gods in the whole world."

If kuge ancestors were imperial loyalists, were buke ancestors shogunal loyalists (here referring to the Tokugawa shogunate)? This question calls attention back to the civil war fought in 1868–69 between two groups of buke—the imperial camp and the Tokugawa camp—as a prelude to the Meiji Restoration. This was a topic of lively and emotionally charged discussion among my buke informants. In the end, the conclusion was that none of their ancestors had opposed the emperor; rather, the split occurred between the proshogunal and antishogunal camps. Hence, the kuge-buke opposition does not quite parallel the imperial-shogunal opposition.

The Boshin War, named after the Chinese calendrical term for the year (1868), came to involve all the domains, including those that were neutral or undecided, forcing them to take sides either for or against the Tokugawa. A number of informants admitted that their domains were either undecided, still hopeful that the plan of kōbugattai would be realized in one form or another, or else suffering an internal split in loyalty, until the last moment when the anti-Tokugawa tides swept them in. Led by the Satsuma-Chōshū alliance, the anti-Tokugawa camp succeeded in labeling itself the kangun (imperial army) and its enemy the *zokugun* (rebel army) or *chōteki* (the enemy of the imperial court). On the kangun side, the war was presented as a pro-imperial–anti-imperial opposition.

Quite another picture evolved for the Tokugawa loyalists concentrated in the northeast. Let us consider the poignant case of Aizu, the last citadel of the shogunal camp, governed by the Matsudaira, one of many Matsudaira lines that held status as the Tokugawa's tertiary kinsmen (shinpan). A granddaughter of Matsudaira Katamori (1835–93), the last lord of Aizu, described the tragedy of her grandfather and Aizu as vividly as if she had been on the scene—for even though Katamori died fifteen years before her birth, his widow told her the family history over and again. It was not Katamori's intention to fight against the emperor; on the contrary, he was genuinely loyal to Emperor Kōmei (r. 1847–66), who in turn trusted and relied on Katamori. Appointed *Kyōto shugoshoku* (the office created by the shogunate in 1862 to monitor the antishogunal unrest escalating around the imperial court), Katamori was there to "protect" the emperor and his palace "much as the Imperial Guards would." (Note that *shugo* means protection, which can entail confinement and control.) Nonetheless, his opponents "must have wanted to get rid of him. . . . After the Tokugawa shogun's return of the government, [Katamori] voluntarily retired (*kinshin*), when his enemy came to attack Aizu!" leaving Aizu samurai no alternative but to fight back. As soon as an imperial silk banner displayed by the enemy came into sight, the Aizu army surrendered in fear of becoming a "rebel" against the emperor. Still, Aizu ended up carrying the dishonorable name zokugun, even though, in resentful rejection of that label, the townspeople called their own army *tōgun* (eastern army). Descendants of the Aizu lord and vassals, moreover, refused to admit that their ancestors fought the kangun; their true foe, they claimed, was the deceitful *seigun* (western army) maneuvered by Satsuma and Chōshū. Yet despite these efforts, the label stuck.

Then came the day when Aizu was at last able to shake off the stigma of being called the emperor's foe. In 1928, Matsudaira Setsuko, one of Katamori's granddaughters, came into the limelight as the bride-to-be of Prince Chichibu, a younger brother of Emperor Hirohito, handpicked by the imperial mother, Empress Dowager Teimei. As narrated by a biographer of Princess Chichibu Setsuko (Ema 1983), all of Aizu was thrown into joyous revelry, proclaiming this event as the long-awaited restoration of honor to Aizu (*Aizu fukken*). Clearly, Aizu was mortified not so much by its defeat as by the disgrace of being labeled the emperor's enemy; Aizu hated the "deceitful" Satchō—the common designation for Satsuma and Chōshū together—not the emperor.

Tales of rancor and vindication against the triumphant Satsuma and Chōshū abound. The Nanbu domain, another northeastern province penalized along with Aizu, united to avenge itself on the Satchō (*Satchō o mikaesu*), according to a Nanbu descendant, by producing national leaders in the military, government, and academia. Indeed, Iwate Prefecture can boast of having generated as many as six prime ministers, including most recently Suzuki Zenkō (1980–82). The first was Prime Minister Hara Takashi (1918–21), who emerged to wrestle the government from the Satchō monopoly; he delivered a speech to the effect that the province had been "vindicated at long last from the disgraceful name of zokugun." According to a local historian and journalist (Ōta 1973, 190–91), Hara, who won the "war of vindication" (*setsujokusen*), kept turning down the offer of a kazoku title (causing him to be known as a "commoner prime minister") because the kazoku institution was created by Satchō samurai to promote themselves to aristocracy. Hara, coming from a "high-ranking" vassal family, was too proud of his "elite" background to accept a kazoku title and join the crowd of Satchō upstarts who needed such titles for reasons of status. (This interesting interpretation of Hara's rejection reminds us that alienation from the kazoku system did not always reflect egalitarian ideology.)

The phrase *kateba kangun* ("winners are called kangun [imperial army]")—meaning, essentially, "might makes right"—was mentioned by descendants of the Tokugawa and its loyalists to describe the injustice perpetrated by the self-proclaimed kangun. The Tokugawa has no treasure left, said a daughter of the Tokugawa shogunal house, repeating what she had heard her grandmother say, because everything was looted during the battle at Ueno. The phrase *kateba kangun* was stamped on her mind. Stigma was attached to the Tokugawa house not only as a rebel responsible for the Boshin War but also as a usurper of imperial power for over two and a half centuries. Tokugawa Ieyasu was no hero but a shrewd thief, and in the prewar Gakushuin history class his descendants were humiliated. One Tokugawa informant skipped the Tokugawa period in her historical study at Gakushuin, and her sister cried when a teacher called Ieyasu a *tanuki oyaji* (sly badger).

How did the kangun descendants feel about their ancestors? It turned out that, as the zokugun were abused by the kangun, so had the latter's ancestors been by Tokugawa rulers. Instead of painting his victorious kangun ancestors in glory, a descendant of Lord Shimazu, the daimyo of Satsuma, detailed the hardships that Satsuma, lords and vassals together, had endured under the Tokugawa tyranny. To begin with, the Tokugawa regime defended itself from the Satsuma threat by allocating buffer domains from Edo all the way to Satsuma. "They must have racked their brains over how to keep down the Satsuma, their strongest opponent," a Shimazu chuckled. Fearful of Satsuma's accumulation of wealth, the Tokugawa imposed costly projects on their rivals, the most severe of which was the embankment of the Kiso River in the mid–seventeenth century. The construction took one and a half years and cost the Satsuma 400,000 *ryō*, "as much as sixteen billion yen at today's rate." In fact, the Tokugawa should have done the work because they had jurisdiction over the Nōbi Plain, which was in need of flood control. "Instead, Satsuma, of all domains, hundreds of kilometers removed, was ordered to send work forces and materials all the way to do the job. How ridiculous!"

Shimazu repeated a statement I had heard many times: "The Meiji Restoration was a counterwar against the Sekigahara war." The civil war at Sekigahara in 1600 established the Tokugawa hegemony and divided daimyo into two classes: fudai (loyalists) and tozama (outsiders). The fudai, even though they monopolized offices of the shogunal government, were not necessarily better off, however (Bolitho 1974); indeed, some of my informants of fudai descent expressed strong grievances against Tokugawa despotism, including the frequent transference of domainal fiefs. Tozama descendants, for their part, seemed convinced that their ancestors were true victims of discrimination. By and large, my informants used the tozama label more generously than the fudai label for self-categorization, thus exhibiting their ancestors' anti-Tokugawa stand and subsequent predicament. The term *tozama,* in other words, was employed in opposition to the Tokugawa clan and fudai put together.

There has been a long history of alliances and intermarriages between buke and kuge, the shogunal and imperial courts, the Tokugawa and tozama, and so on. The sekke, for instance, are well known for having competed among themselves for privileged alliance with the shogunal government. One historian informant paired three sekke and three shogunal governments: the Kujō with the Kamakura, the Konoe with the Ashikaga, and the Nijō with the Tokugawa.[4] I was told, for example, that many Konoe ancestors received a character of the then Ashikaga shogun's personal name for their own (a common practice): thus the name of Konoe *Tane*ie derived from Ashikaga Yoshi*tane, Hisa*michi from Yoshi-*hisa,* and so on. The modern era only intensified such alliances, including intermarriage between the kangun and zokugun, as will be detailed in later chapters.

The loyalty and animosity that my informants attributed to their ancestors, therefore, were far from simple and monolithic, and yet at one level of consciousness I found a patterned mode for encoding buke ancestors: they were victims of one of the two major civil wars—the 1600 Sekigahara war and the 1868 Restoration war—and had suffered under the postwar regime. Nor were the kuge themselves exempt from similar hardship, for as a group they were abused (*ijimerareta*) by the buke. This situation may be in part a reflection of the fact that the old nobility in general ended as losers, first through the Meiji Restoration, then, and more devastatingly, through World War II. The cultural paradigm that Morris (1975) calls "the nobility of failure," involving moral distinction attained by losers, may have been another factor leading nobles by birth to portray their ancestors as victims. Narratives tended to focus on an ancestor's defeat, suffering, and sorrows rather than his glory in victory and triumph. Associated with his plight were his sincerity, fidelity, and proud aloofness from opportunism and corruption. The success theme was not absent, but it would come only *after* the primary theme of tragedy and misery and as a reward for perseverance.

I further discovered that residents of an erstwhile domain, regardless of ancestral rank, kept emotional ties with the domain lord through the shared memory of the province's predicament. The Aizu residents I met argued that local people were united (*kessoku ga katai*) "because Aizu was defeated and mortified. . . . If Aizu had won," they told me, "there would have been no such solidarity among us."

At a semiannual meeting of the Aizu Club at Seiyōken in Ueno (the place alone is significant because it was the last battleground for the hopeless Tokugawa defense) attended by roughly two hundred people of Aizu origin, mostly residing in Tokyo, and honored by the presence of "Lord" Matsudaira and his family, the mortifying past was replayed in a film showing. The film focused on the forced removal of Aizu loyalists northward to the blizzardy Shimokita Peninsula (Tonami-han), an act taken in 1870 by the new Meiji government to punish the "rebel" domain. The film narrator called this mass deportation nothing other than "retaliation" by the Satchō. A descendant of one resettler, interviewed in the film, declared that more anguish was caused by the Aizu defeat than by Japan's defeat in World War II. Nevertheless, in the Aizu blood ran an irresistible drive to rise again. Throughout, "the Aizu blood," "the Aizu spirit," and "the Aizu soul" appeared in the film and in speeches as key words representing a mixture of the pain felt for the abused ancestors, indignation toward the Satchō, the perseverance and resilience of local people, the determination to fight back, and pride. The ultimate symbol of local pride was the royal family, and particularly Princess Chichibu, granddaughter of the last Aizu lord.

Among the celebrities present at the meeting was a nationally known novelist and collaborator in the film production, who, seated next to me, introduced himself as an Aizu man whose ancestors three generations back had left Aizu when it was forced out of existence. He became a historical novelist in order to write about Aizu and erase the damning chōteki label. His novels infuriate Chōshū readers, he said, who often harass him.[5]

Urami (rancor or resentment) was a favorite subject for a southern informant as well. This Kagoshima business executive (non-kazoku) characterized the history of Kagoshima (Satsuma) as one of rancor and revenge against its oppressors. Parroting the apparently widespread tale of the Kiso River embankment project, which reduced Satsuma to destitution, he said the accumulated ill will finally exploded into the Meiji

Restoration (thus confirming the retaliatory motive attributed to the Restoration by northern opponents). Curiously, this informant found "rebellion" a justifiable response to the oppressive central government, and he enumerated three notable rebellions in Satsuma history: the prehistoric rebellion by the Kumaso tribe(!), the rebellion against Hideyoshi, and the Satsuma Rebellion (1877) against the Meiji government. Indeed, we know that the foremost Satsuma hero of the Restoration for locals is not Ōkubo Toshimichi, but Saigō Takamori, who was drawn into the doomed Satsuma Rebellion and killed himself. In this informant's view, however, neither the Shimazu lords nor the emperors were themselves among the oppressors.[6] Indeed, he spoke with awe about the Shimazu house and its kinship with the imperial family, pointing out that Empress Nagako was mothered by a Shimazu woman (Princess Kuni) and that one of Emperor Hirohito's daughters had married a Shimazu.

From such episodic narratives it is clear that the *culturally* encoded ancestry is enlivened and reinforced *socially* by the presence of people around the kazoku descendants, particularly in the case of daimyo. The social ties between (descendants of) lords and vassals, urban kazoku and provincial commoners, seem essential to recalling the dead to the living world of reality. This social reality will continue to be examined throughout the book.

Ironically, however, descendants of shogunal loyalists, tozama daimyo, and imperial loyalists alike, southerners and northerners alike, and, above all, kazoku elite and commoners alike all regarded their own ancestors as victims of oppression. Both kuge and daimyo descendants credited their respective ancestors with having survived centuries of trials and trepidation under oppressors—or what they called "wind and snow" (*fūsetsu*)—with great perseverance. The drama resonates still in the ever-popular Chūshingura story.

Yet not one informant considered that his or her ancestors had been victimized by emperors. The most cynical remark I heard about the imperial house came from a Tokugawa woman: while it had every reason to feel rancor toward "us," she said, the imperial line also owed its long survival to the stability of the Tokugawa regime. More strongly, Tokugawa descendants actually felt indebted to Emperor Meiji. To be sure, the Restoration government punished the Tokugawa by prohibiting Shogun Yoshinobu from continuing the main line through his son; instead it allowed a son of a branch house, Tokugawa Iesato of Tayasu, to succeed the main house. One of this man's granddaughters recalled how her grandmother, Iesato's wife, had reminded her again and again of Emperor Meiji's benevolence (*oboshimeshi*) in allowing the Tokugawa to continue even though "it had a good reason to perish." The imperial benevolence was eventually extended to Yoshinobu as well. In the thirtieth year of Meiji (1897), by which time Tokugawa Yoshinobu had been rehabilitated from his status as captain of the vanquished rebel army and had gained prominence as a great contributor to the Restoration (didn't he "return the shogunal government to the emperor" voluntarily, after all?), Yoshinobu moved from Shizuoka, where he had been confined, back to Tokyo, and five years later was permitted by Emperor Meiji to reestablish his own house as a Tokugawa branch (*bekke*) with the highest rank of nobility, that of prince (Matsuura 1975, 190–91). One of Yoshinobu's many grandchildren, at age sixty-seven, recalled what her mother used to say about him: "He was always respectful of the imperial house. He was treated kindly, cared for specially by Meiji-sama, who stood most benevolent of all" in granting him the rank of prince. Thus even the Tokugawa were able to remove the disgrace of being chōteki.

WEALTH

To the extent that one's own economic condition or a change thereof tends to affect one's image of one's ancestors, in this section I will present the informant's own experience more fully than I have thus far. Accordingly, ancestor images will fluctuate more strongly here.

People rate themselves or others as poor or rich based on a diversity of criteria. The first and most often mentioned criterion concerned the prewar/postwar opposition. As we know, the living standard has declined drastically for all kazoku since the war, primarily because of postwar reforms such as heavy taxation on estates, farmland redistribution, and the dissolution of *zaibatsu* (family-based huge financial, industrial groups). Surviving descendants thus either are totally removed from or else live in or on the proceeds of only tiny fractions of their ancestral estates. *Urigui* (sell-and-live) was a common pattern for a while; as one informant put it, her family stripped its store of goods as it would an onion, crying over every layer that had to be shed. The prewar affluence of these families can be inferred only from the visible transformations of their former estates, which now are parks, school campuses, foreign embassies, city halls, public auditoriums, sports arenas, golf courses, hospitals, hotels, condominium complexes, and so on. Only a few have established businesses utilizing portions of their old estates. Most informants called their prewar life-style "a dream."

Yet this before/after polarity is more complex than it at first appears. For not a few kazoku, poverty was not merely a postwar phenomenon, but a major feature of generations of ancestors as well. Indeed, when another criterion, the kuge/daimyo opposition, was applied, the kuge's legendary poverty in contrast to the daimyo's plenitude stood out as true for the entire history from medieval through modern times. A Seiga woman, at age ninety-one, frankly admitted that her family's poverty had nothing to do with the postwar changes: "In winter, there was nothing to keep you warm but a little charcoal brazier for the hands. We children, even daughters, were not allowed to use a floor cushion, except at the new year. Kuge kazoku were that poor, unable to afford that little." Her life turned upward only when she married a rich commoner.

Yamaguchi (1932, 22–23) tells a Meiji-dated story of kuge kazoku: because too often these individuals, when invited to the imperial palace for dinner, stole table utensils for their own kitchen use, Kunaishō (Ministry of the Imperial Household) officials were forced to invite kuge kazoku separately from other guests and to halve dinner expenses to compensate for the anticipated loss. Whether this story was but a groundless rumor, narratives by kuge informants confirm this stereotype. The frequent succession to househeadship by the incumbent's younger brother rather than a son, for example, they explained in economic terms: because a kuge was employed at the court only if he was the househead or heir, a temporary succession by a brother before a son, the permanent successor, maximized employment of the family. Kuge poverty and daimyo affluence were also discussed by those who had experienced both as a daughter and wife or as a son and adopted son. One woman of kuge origin was impressed with the enormous difference she found when she married a daimyo—even though her husband was only a small fudai daimyo (80,000 koku) with the rank of viscount, whereas her natal house stood at the marquis rank.

The kuge/daimyo economic contrast is a historical vestige of the Tokugawa period, when daimyo status was measured by rice revenues in koku. The Restoration reduced the domainal revenue to what was called *karoku,* a sort of pension allocated to daimyo houses (which by now had been removed from the domains proper) that amounted to a small fraction of the original koku revenue. Before the Restoration, a daimyo's domainal revenue (*kokudaka*) was 66,613 koku on average; after 1870 this amount was cut to the karoku of 2,906 koku, or 4.4 percent of the pre-Restoration domain revenue. Among daimyo houses, it might be noted, there was an enormous variation in karoku: from 60,000 koku (the Maeda) down to 162 koku. The kuge's income was only 299 koku on average before the Restoration, and slightly less—280 koku, 93.6 percent of the former sum—afterward (computed from KK 1985, 4–26). Clearly, the overwhelming difference between daimyo and kuge was reflected even in karoku, despite the incomparably lower reduction rate for kuge than for daimyo.[7]

Even though the economic stereotype was well grounded, exaggerations were inevitable. Given wide variation within each category, the tendency was to contrast the poorest kuge with the richest daimyo. By shifting back to the prewar/postwar opposition or comparing themselves with other kuge, some kuge descendants argued that they had been rather well off before the war, "contrary to the common image of kuge." Even prior to the Meiji period, some kuge ancestors received extra income (including bribes) from buke by occupying liaisonal offices (*buke densō*) that linked the court and the buke. After the Restoration, Emperor Meiji, in an effort to rehabilitate the impecunious kuge, benevolently granted them a money gift totaling one million yen. This imperial gift (*gokashikin*) was pooled and invested by the Kunaishō, with the proceeds then allocated to the kuge according to their kazoku ranks. For some kuge, this was an important, or even a sole, source of income that kept them alive. Furthermore, a number of kuge continued to receive rice from the tenants of former "shōen"; hence, throughout the war when rice was a scarce commodity, "we always had enough rice to eat." All these benefits were ended after the war.

Kuge privation may be further exaggerated in terms of the affluence and comfort prevailing in contemporary Japan. The kuge woman mentioned above who talked about cold winters without adequate heat also said, "We could not afford any beef." Yet at the turn of the twentieth century, who had more than charcoal braziers, and did anyone eat as much meat as Japanese do today? The perceived difference may lie more in general historical changes than in a real disparity between the kuge and daimyo or wealthy commoners. Here, clearly, contemporary experience can be seen to distort one's cognition of past reality, with the distortion being then projected onto the image of ancestors in magnified proportions.

The daimyo, too, varied greatly in economic status during the post-Restoration era. The karoku, for instance, the last economic vestige of the feudal era, was eventually liquidated through commutation to bonds (*kinroku kōsai*). The management of the capital thus made available together with its original amount determined the subsequent economic welfare of the old elite. As one woman put it, "After the [Second World] war some people took a road to success and others perished. In the same way, [after the Restoration] there was a big gap between winners and losers." This informant's grandfather, a daimyo of 100,000 koku reduced to 5,000 karoku, was so impoverished after haihan chiken that "when he married my grandmother they did not have a fish dish more than once a week. It was like right after this war, it seems." Fortunately, the grandfather had "good vassals" who made sound investments and enriched the family enormously during World War I; he was thus able to live like a true lord the rest of his life.

With financial success or failure depending largely on the ability and loyalty of vassals, it is perhaps not surprising that a significant portion of daimyo capital ended up in the hands of loan sharks. Here a word is necessary on the Fifteenth National Bank, established in 1877 entirely by kazoku shareholders out of the bonds received in exchange for their karoku. This so-called kazoku bank started as the richest of all national banks with about 17.8 million yen but after a period of successful operation went into a panic in 1927. It had to get a special loan amounting to 169 million yen from the Bank of Japan to resume business (Shōyū Kurabu 1982a, 158), which became a turning point dividing kazoku between the investor victims and those who had resisted investing and thus escaped disastrous losses. Among the top losers were the Shimazu, one of the richest daimyo kazoku, who lost three-quarters of their 30,000-*tsubo* main estate in Tokyo and the huge property in Kagoshima (Shimazu Shuppankai 1978, 345). Less affected (if at all) were large daimyo houses like the Maeda, the Hosokawa, and the Tokugawa main house, which, according to informants, owed their good luck primarily to former vassals who were now serving the lords as able financial consultants.

With few exceptions, daimyo themselves were above pecuniary matters, and their own involvement in financial management usually resulted in disaster. Indeed, many informants, in discussing their grandparents and parents, spoke of aloofness from and childish naiveté about money. In contrast to this aristocratic removal from the pecuniary world was the aggressive profiteering associated with nouveaux riches (*narikin*), viewed with contempt by all. It was new kazoku who were often labeled narikin, even though they, too, varied widely from millionaires to wage earners. The grandson of a Meiji leader admitted, "It is embarrassing to talk about money, but when I was twenty-two or so [in 1935] we had a monthly income of 10,000 yen including stock dividends—at a time when the prime minister's annual salary was 6,500." Yet when his grandfather (who would eventually be awarded a kazoku title) married, the couple had to make ends meet with a meager six yen monthly salary. Proudly, the informant talked about this astonishing rise in income; his somewhat rebellious brother, however, alluded to the grandfather's corruption.

Attention should be called here to the giants in the financial and industrial world who were ennobled in and after 1896, the year following the

Sino-Japanese War. This suggests that the kazoku title was awarded to business leaders like the Mitsui and Iwasaki (Mitsubishi) in exchange for their financial aid during the war. Nevertheless, there was resistance in the top circle of decision makers to ennobling businessmen, which, according to informants, explains why they received no more than the rank of baron. It is very likely that more negotiations and justifications were necessary to make the economic elite into kazoku. Fujita Denza-burō, for instance, who had started as a sake brewer and become an industrial tycoon, was anxious to join fellow Chōshū men with kazoku titles, and appealed to Prime Minister Katsura Tarō to expedite his wish. Katsura readily accepted Fujita's request, only to realize that the task was not as easy as he had thought, even with his stature and Chōshū ties. Later, Katsura recalled his undelivered promise as "the biggest blunder" he had ever made in his life (Andō 1927b, 53–64). Disappointed for years, Fujita was finally awarded a baronetcy for his meritorious service in 1911, a year before his death (KK 1982–84, 2:415). These zaibatsu families might be regarded as typical nouveaux riches and so looked down upon, and yet they were hardly mentioned by informants. The main reason seemed to be that some of these major families, like Mitsui, Sumitomo, and Kōnoike, were far from "nouveau" but had survived through the Tokugawa regime like other kazoku ancestors and expanded into zaibatsu in the modern period. Indeed, a Mitsui daughter described her family business as "tradition-bound"—unlike the more rational, modern Mitsubishi—and as faithfully adhering to their ancestors' creed. The business itself was run entirely by a competent managerial staff; members of the Mitsui dōzoku were thus merely passive recipients of dividends, much as the daimyo had been. Along similar lines, the Sumitomo claim Emperor Kanmu to be their ultimate ancestor. Both the Mitsui and Sumitomo, too, have intermarried with kuge and daimyo descendants. And after all, they shared with other kazoku the common fate of a post-war downfall following the zaibatsu dissolution, their abundant wealth now so reduced that all that was left was their good name—like "Mitsui"—to be "rented" to new corporations. It is likely that "traditional" respectability had thus accrued to the zaibatsu kazoku.

When the derogatory label *nariagari* (upstart) or *narikin* (nouveau riche) was attached to particular individuals, the victim was generally a postwar businessman outside the kazoku circle. The opposition here was poor (genteel) kazoku versus rich (uncouth) commoners—the equation that underlies the kazoku's exaggeration of their own poverty. Thus one kuge daughter, age thirty-four, linked her natal privation to "the blood of kuge" and presented herself as a "spiritual aristocrat" able to persevere through the utmost of hardships—a comment that moves us to the next and last theme.

STYLE

In association with poverty another virtue was stressed: disciplined austerity (*shisso*) in consumer style, in contrast to the alleged vulgar display of wealth by narikin. Shisso did not presuppose poverty; rather, it was a self-imposed abstinence from excessive and conspicuous consumption, particularly in food and clothing. The theme of austerity was shared by all categories of kazoku, old and new, kuge and daimyo, rich and poor. The Mitsui, for instance, would not have the family's nationally unequaled wealth interfere with their training of children in the virtue of shisso; indeed, a daughter claimed that the housemaids had more kimono of better quality than the master family's own girls, and that she herself had once been taken for a maid by outsiders. Because of the prewar training in shisso, many informants said it was easy to adjust to postwar economic deprivation.

In some cases, of course, aristocratic austerity went hand in hand with lordly extravagance. A viscountess berated the new rich for crudely displaying gold and went on to belittle their wealth as "no big thing compared with that of old daimyo," as her husband was. "Osano and Kodama, they say, live in magnificent mansions, but I wonder how those houses could be described as magnificent." The point is clear: the authentic aristocrats were clearly distinguished from the nouveaux riches, whether in their genteel poverty and disciplined frugality or in their lordly abundance.

Lordly composure, carriage, and bearing were mentioned as memorable characteristics of some recent ancestors. Certain ancestors, typically grandfathers, were described as "the last lord," "a truly lordlike man" (*ikanimo tonosama rashii*). A lordlike grandfather was a man "on a grand scale," his presence so awesome that his attending vassals could not help but keep their heads down, and who was aloof from the small matters of day-to-day life. He was likely to live in luxury and indifference to daily routine and to be magnanimously generous. Toda Ujitaka, the last lord of the Ōgaki-han, was eleven years old when he succeeded to lordship of 100,000 koku, though soon he lost his domainal hegemony through the haihan chiken, went to the United States to study for five years, and became the first minister to Austria. Yet despite all this experience and foreign exposure, "my grandfather remained a lord until he died at eighty-two, knowing little about worldly matters." Such lordly style was facilitated, of course, by wealth, and indeed, the Ōgaki lord had a monthly allowance of 1,000 yen, a fantastic amount at the time. Also necessary was an entourage of loyal and able vassals, an essential ingredient of lordly charisma.

The lordlike style refers to status fitness, as opposed to status transcendence. But many informants recalled their grandfathers, fathers, or fathers-in-law in terms of status transcendence, as "unlike a lord" or *heiminteki* (commonerlike). These forebears were memorable because of their "egalitarian," "democratic" style, a manner that did not belie their aristocratic status. Tokugawa Iesato, the sixteenth "shogun," was praised as heiminteki, open, and accessible not only by his children and grandchildren but even by a journalist whose object was to expose kazoku scandals (Yamaguchi 1932, 13–17). Whether one was *sabaketa* or *zakkubaran*—terms meaning frank, unreserved, open, sociable, or, in short, delightfully free from status constraint—was a main criterion for evaluating high-ranking persons, including members of the royalty.

Status transcendence and status fitness, though contrasting, have one attribute in common: both indicate freedom from status affectation and snobbishness. A person was naturally status fitted or could afford to be status transcendent because his "status personality" of lordliness had become part of him in the course of *sodachi* (upbringing). Sodachi here fuses into *umare*, birth, and reflects a value shared by most Japanese. That is, while professing to be egalitarian, not a few Japanese describe people as either *jōhin* (genteel) or *gehin* (crude), qualities that are ascribed to their sodachi; hence they conclude that one cannot dispute a person's sodachi (*sodachi wa arasoenai*), that it is impossible to make a noble of an upstart, a princess of a commoner. The "cultivated" noble style, whether in status fitness or in status transcendence, is thus "naturalized."

VALUE CONVERGENCE IN THE THRONE

In this chapter we have seen a spectrum of ancestor categories as constructed by the living descendants, whose multiple-layered narratives produce a complex world in which oppositional values and attributes intersect. Genealogical prestige is seen to collide, negotiate, or fuse with performance or wealth, the status complex with the power complex, culture with nature. The result is an ambivalent mixture of pride and shame, guilt and scorn, admiration and resentment, hierarchical discrimination and egalitarianism, felt by descendants toward their own and other categories of ancestors. Notably, ancestors were identified with more as victims of oppression and injustice than as winners and tycoons: egalitarian resentment, seemingly, has permeated the thought of contemporary descendants.

All these oppositions, accompanied by invidious comparisons and vicarious animosity, seemed to converge in the key symbol of modern Japan, the emperor, and Emperor Meiji in particular. Gratitude and loyalty to the imperial house were expressed by participants on both sides of the Restoration war, by the civil and military elites alike, by old and new kazoku, by rich and poor. As one count acknowledged, "I am what I am today thanks to my grandfather, but he was able to achieve so high a level because he was promoted by Prince Itō (Hirobumi)—we have Itō's portrait displayed in our house. But it was Emperor Meiji who produced a great man like Prince Itō." A high point in the career of another Meiji achiever, his granddaughter recalled, was when as a palace physician he attended "the lady-in-waiting of second rank" (*nii-no-tsubone,* as Yanagiwara Naruko was respectfully called), one of Meiji's consorts, in her parturition. His patient was to be the mother of Taishō. For his distinguished career and contributions, he was later awarded an "imperial-gift cane," a symbol of special privilege which the awardee was allowed to use within the imperial palace.

At the core of such emperor worship was not only the constitutional "agglutination" in the throne of ascription and political authority—the genealogically indisputable supremacy of the dynasty, together with the "sovereignty" vested in the imperial status—but also a political maneuvering in which Meiji leaders both in and out of government engaged to construct, revitalize, and manipulate the imperial sovereignty. Thus Meiji Japan created a new type of monarchy.

There was, indeed, an economic basis for the unsurpassed prestige of the imperial house. The Restoration meant a sharp rise in budgetary allocations of the national treasury to the imperial house. Most notably, the vast increase in imperial forests (*goryōrin*), as well as widespread investment in lucrative stocks and bonds, resulted in the annual proceeds skyrocketing (Titus 1974).[8] So in addition to genealogical prestige and political authority, fiscally the imperial house experienced a historically unprecedented "peak from the Meiji through the end of the war" (Togashi 1977, 184–85). It was out of this abundance that imperial "benevolence" was on occasion doled out in cash and gifts to high-ranking government officials and deserving citizens—among whom, as we have seen, the kuge kazoku were regular beneficiaries.

Only one informant discussed the prewar imperial wealth, describing it as a world high-water mark: "It was incomparable to that of American millionaires. For instance, when the Kunaishō was going to host a reception, it imported a three-ship load of wine from Bordeaux, France. One thousand dinner sets were all in gold." Contrary to my expectation, this self-labeled nonconformist kazoku who disapproved of hereditary privilege was not at all critical of such extravagance. Instead he said, "I think Meiji leaders were great indeed. They dared to do such big things. Taishō-born, I still feel nostalgic for the Meiji period."

Amid this incredible affluence, emperors were not necessarily self-indulgent. Emperor Shōwa in particular appeared in the eyes of those kazoku close to him as extremely shisso in his habits of personal consumption. In style as well as in legacy, the emperor, despite his newly acquired enormous wealth, stood in stark contrast to the nouveaux riches.

It was natural for kazoku, as opposed to commoners, to identify themselves with emperors and to partake of the imperial prestige; they were, after all, closer to emperors genealogically, physically, and socially. More important, they knew that, along with the restored emperorship, their own status was revitalized, enhanced, legitimated, or created. While they might be ambivalent, hostile, or disdainful toward certain fellow kazoku, and while some even denounced and rejected the kazoku status, they were unanimous in expressing their respect for and allegiance to the imperial house.[9]

FOUR

Successors

Immortalizing the Ancestors

Ancestor worshippers in Japan mention as a major reason for their devotion the debt they owe their forebears for their very existence. Certainly they would not have come to life without their ancestors, but neither would the ancestors have continued to exist without descendants. Essential to the ancestor cult is the interdependence of ascending and descending generations. (Ancestor worship, then, implies the worship of descendants as well.) Devotion to ancestors is demonstrated by perpetuating their legacies through a continuous line of generations of descendants. For reasons to be spelled out below, the perpetuation of ancestors is conceived as "succession," and descendants foremost as "successors."

This chapter looks at kazoku families in terms of succession: what is involved, who the successors—or descendants—were, how they related to the predecessors, and what contemporary successors did and do to keep their ancestors alive. Inevitably, too, our discussion will lead us to explore more fully the structure of the ie (stem-family household), a central element of Japanese social organization. This and the previous chapter should be taken as two sides of the ancestor cult.

The present chapter consists of two parts. Part one is concerned with succession itself, which again calls up the central issues of this book: opposition and collusion between structure and practice, or culture and nature. As defined in chapter 1, hereditary status, like any other status, is a cultural construction, and yet "heredity" is attributed to some version of nature, such as genes, blood, and birth. I focus on how the "cultural" status was sustained by replenishing the blood bank, so to speak—that is, by expanding the population of blood donors. Here we reencounter the ie, which serves as the main vehicle of hereditary status. Part two turns to rituals and symbols that memorialize and celebrate ancestors, thus perpetuating them. My perspective here extends to the post-Meiji state of religion, especially the relationship of Shinto and Buddhism, to show how that history affected the ancestor rites for the kazoku more than for commoners.

ADOPTION FOR SUCCESSION

Genealogies usually follow a patrilineal descent model as if to substantiate the assumption of blood continuity for succession. Remarkably, however, when I set out to ascertain the identities of successors of the latest generations, I discovered a high frequency of adoptions to recruit successors. Indeed, few interviews did not reveal instances involving either the informant or primary kin as a party to adoption, and in some cases it turned out that adoption had taken place over three generations in a row. For example, I spoke with a son of a daimyo viscount who was adopted by a kuge count. His deceased adoptive father had been also adopted from another kuge-count house, and his (my informant's) successor son was adopted, too, from a daimyo viscount. Occupying the middle position in this three-generation adoption series, the informant said: "In our [kazoku] circle there is no resistance to being adopted as there is in the world outside, since almost everybody here becomes adopted. My [natal] house has continued fourteen generations, but more than half of those generations were headed by adopted sons."

To put the Japanese practice of adoption in a broader perspective, we must digress briefly. Among East Asian societies, Japan is known for its indiscriminatory practice of adoption compared with China and Korea, for example, where more stringent rules and prohibitions are imposed. Even in the Tokugawa period, when law and order reached unprecedented heights, a Confucian scholar, Dazai Shundai (1680–1747), deplored Japan's lawlessness, and singled out adoption as a major example of chaos. While exalting Confucian China and ancient Japan for their alleged adherence to the "pure" family line, Dazai denounced his contemporaries for their "barbarous" custom of promiscuous adoption (Kirby 1908). In the late nineteenth century, the historian Shigeno An'eki (1827–1910) discussed the "evils" of adoption, along with those of imperial abdication (Shigeno 1887). Despite these strongly worded critiques and governmental attempts to enjoin restrictions, Japanese apparently persisted in this "barbarous" and "evil" custom. In fact, the new (1898) civil code of Meiji Japan relaxed some of the old restrictions, probably in part to come to terms with the actual situation. Unlike critics of adoption, Hozumi Nobushige endorsed flexibility in connection with ancestor worship: "From what I have stated, it may, I think, be laid down as a general rule that *adoption had its origin in Ancestor worship;* and the stronger the belief in that practice among the people, the wider is the scope allowed for adoption by the law" (1912, 164–65; emphasis in original). Regardless of which opinion is more defensible, Japan clearly stands out in the frequency, flexibility, or lawlessness of adoption.

While adoption has been undertaken more or less across all classes, upper-class Japanese seem to have resorted to adoption more than their lower-class counterparts. Both Dazai and Shigeno, for example, were referring primarily to the samurai class and above. On the basis of samurai family records gathered from four domains, moreover, Ray Moore, an academic historian, reports an increasing rate of adoption during the Tokugawa period: "The percentage rose from 26.1 percent in the seventeenth to 36.6 percent in the eighteenth and to 39.3 percent in the nineteenth century" (1970, 618–19).

My own research suggests that the upper class included a strikingly large number of adopters and adoptees. Although in earlier research I encountered instances of adoption among lower-class families, I realized that class differences exist in frequency as well as modes. As we shall see, there were good reasons why the upper class had greater recourse to adoption. At the same time, we must ask how the practice of free adoption reconciled with *hereditary* status. The answer, in part, lies in the ie, which had evolved in the ruling class from the late Heian period and been further consolidated through the Tokugawa period. In modern Japan, as a result of long debates, the ie was rehabilitated instead of meeting its demise; indeed, it was deemed a formal, legally compulsory unit in the Meiji civil code, pertaining to all classes. This codification meant, for progressive opponents, a conservative victory, a turning back of the historical clock to refeudalization (Watanabe 1963; Steiner 1987).

The Ie

The ie as a key to Japanese social structure has been recognized by many scholars as different from or more than the "family," or as not amenable to the framework of "kinship" or "descent."[1] The argument centers on two interrelated features of the ie. First, the ie is a structural unit consisting of certain roles or positions, rather than a group of persons as is the "family." Roles or positions are thus defined in the context of the ie, a corporate body with its own status, assets, career, and goal. In fact, the economic, political, occupational profile is central to the definition of the ie, and the constituent members are recognized as such by virtue of the functions they perform in contribution to the corporate status or goal of the ie. In this sense, *ie* is best translated as "house" or "household," implying a group of co-residents each occupying a particular place in it.

Even though the ie headship is likely to be held by the father, "it should be noted that his authority over the household members is validated by his *office* as the head of the household, not by his being the *father:* the authority of the head resides primarily in the office rather than the person" (Nakane 1967b, 18; emphasis in original). Such positional emphasis also entails the primacy of role fitness or competency over kinship status. Among many indications of this role fitness requirement is the practice of retirement (*inkyo*) by an aged father from the "office" of headship so that a young, vigorous successor can take over. An outsider may be adopted not only by a sonless household but also by a house with natural sons that are however not considered fit as heirs. A woman is accepted or rejected as a bride foremost on the basis of her physical and mental competence—as an additional source of labor as well as the bearer of an heir. Headship of an ie carrying a female occupation, such as a tea house or geisha house, is transmitted from mother to daughter in disregard of the "normal" father-to-son succession rule. Nakano (1968) amply demonstrates how the ie occupation takes precedence over the rule of descent and how in fact the descent rule is determined by the need for occupational continuity. Furthermore, insofar as the interest of the ie as a whole supersedes that of an individual member, the redistribution of children through marriage or adoption may be an opportunity to form politically beneficial alliances.

The second critical feature of the ie is its mandatory perpetuation through succession over generations. As Pelzel (1970, 229) puts it:

> The Japanese term *ie* has traditionally meant both the household at a given point in time and a more durable entity, the "house," which exists over time and is composed of only one household in each generation—that household headed by the male who is the legal successor to the former household head. It is this succession of households down through the generations that is the basic and ideal meaning of the term *ie;* the extant household is merely the concrete but transient form of the latter. Assets, whether tangible or not, are always the assets of the *ie,* and a current household controls them for its time as a trustee. Organizational statuses in the contemporary household are subsumed in, and secondary to, similar statuses in the durable house.

Continuous succession thus overrides all other considerations, and it is in this context that the term *stem family* is a preferred translation of *ie*.

Marriage and adoption can then be redefined as means of producing or acquiring an heir to ensure succession.

The successional well-being of the ie, for the Japanese, depends on the unity of the household as symbolized by one househead and one heir, without rivalry, fission, or dispersal of resources. The unicephalous, unigenitural structure, involving a clear status distinction between the heir and other children and the latter's exit from the ie upon marriage, is the core characteristic of the ie. This structure, while ensuring the perpetuation of the ie over generations, keeps family size relatively small (Smith 1972), with only one couple for each generation, and makes the ie look outwardly like a nuclear family. Thus Morioka defines the ie as "a vertically composite form of *nuclear* families, one from each generation" (1967, 597; my emphasis). (But of course, the ie is fundamentally different from nuclear families, whether composite or not.)

It is unigenitural succession that places Japan at the opposite pole from traditional China, where the family is embedded in the patrilineage or patriclan. Nakane (1969) proposes two "models" of family structure: a large family based on collateral, fraternal, or horizontal solidarity; and a small family based on the lineal or vertical bond between the head and his heir. China and Japan represent extremes of these two cases, and in this contrast lies an explanation for the difference in adoption practices between the two societies. In China, adoption is not as necessary as in Japan because lineage continuity is guaranteed and security for old age provided by collateral agnates when one has no son. When adoption does occur, an adopted son should come from within the lineage in the descending generation (preferably a brother's son), for two reasons: because a duly qualified candidate is easily available and because fellow members of the lineage exert pressure for intralineage selection. Yet even despite the rule of agnatic adoption, there are instances of outsider adoption. James Watson (1975), for instance, reports a case involving an infant being bought from strangers because the adopter could exert complete control over a poor outsider adoptee but not over a lineage-controlled agnatic adoptee. Nonetheless, outsider adoption involves severe penalties, such as the humiliating and costly "initiation ceremony" to which the adoptive father must submit in order to secure approval signatures from lineage elders. The Japanese model, focused as it is on unigenitural succession, makes adoption more necessary and less rule bound, since no pool of "insiders" exists for adoption. An outsider (and, historically, not necessarily a younger man) is as acceptable as a close kinsman; a sister's son or daughter's son is just as suitable as a brother's son; a brother can be adopted as a son; the house with a daughter but no son can adopt a son-in-law; a married couple can be adopted; and so on.

Both features of the ie—structural/positional and durable/successional—stress the ie entity, be it the family name, house and property, occupation, or status, as transcendent to individual persons and to "here" and "now." Involved here is a religious element, extending ie membership to ancestors (Plath 1964) as well as to posterity. By virtue of this transcendent nature, moreover, even an extinct ie is considered to carry on a latent existence, and can be "restored" by a stranger through a sort of other-worldly adoption (Befu 1962, 38)[2]—though as the critic Shigeno remonstrates, "To attempt by any such means as adoption to raise up an already extinct house, is like attempting to set in motion the life-pulse which has ceased to beat" (1887, 79).

Further to comprehend free adoption, Hironobu Kitaoji's (1971) argument is instructive. Pointing out the difficulty of grasping the Japanese ie in terms of descent rule or kinship terminology, he proposes "positional succession" as an alternative tool for unraveling the ethnological muddle over patrilineality and bilaterality. Central to positional succession (which to my mind combines the above two features of the ie) is a pair of key positions: househead and housewife. As the incumbents vacate these positions and move into their new roles as retired househead and retired housewife, their successors (the heir and bride) step into the central positions. Represented here, in brief, are three successive generations of paired positions filled by married couples who are also "permanent" members of the house: the retired couple, incumbent couple, and successor couple.

Under the incest prohibition, each generation must recruit a successor-spouse from outside. If the house has a son, his wife must come from another house, a mode of positional recruitment that *happens* to meet the patrilineal ideal. But when the house has a daughter and no son, she stays on and marries a man brought in from outside as an adopted heir and son-in-law (this rule applies also when the house has a son who is not fit as heir). Kitaoji suggests that these two modes are structurally symmetric, reasoning that in both cases one of the paired successors— to the position of housewife or househead—is adopted. Thus in terms of positional succession, each generation is seen to adopt a successor. Adoption of a married couple (*fūfu-yōshi*) then makes sense as a third mode within the same structural framework, in that here successors to the househead and housewife are both adopted.

Kitaoji's proposition is refined and further developed by Jane Bachnik

(1983) from the standpoint of recruitment strategies for succession. In clarifying the order of preference of one strategy over another she suggests that "*all* the strategies" could be viewed "in relation to one another as a gradual widening of the possibilities for accomplishing succession under conditions of increasing difficulty" (1983, 172). Recruiting a male heir from an out-group (son-in-law) and a female successor from the in-group (daughter) is less preferred than the opposite arrangement, that is, recruiting an outsider female successor (daughter-in-law) and an insider male successor (son). But both these options are more desirable than recruiting outsiders for both positions, that is, adopting an already married couple. Nonetheless, all these alternatives adhere to the same rule of positional succession. Even the term *chōnan sōzoku,* succession by the eldest son, a favorite label used by Japanese to characterize their succession rule, should be understood as so polysemic as to cover "the entire positional succession system" (Bachnik 1983, 176), including the least desirable alternative, *fūfu yōshi.*[3]

Let us now return to the kazoku. All the above-cited literature on the ie refers to ordinary Japanese, with a heavy emphasis on rural Japan. Nevertheless, I find the idea of positional succession exceedingly relevant to urban upper-class households as represented by kazoku. Certainly, adoption functioned among kazoku, as among commoners, primarily to ensure positional succession, as the following section will show, but it carried an additional flavor owing to the kazoku's status distinction, which itself was to be transmitted.

Each generation, it should be also noted, is represented by a single incumbent in the position of househead, and thus a genealogy involves, despite the double-headed succession model diagrammed by Kitaoji, a straight line of succession to headship status, with wives being submerged in the chain of male heads. This male bias, a formal expression of general patricentricity, was more pronounced in the elite than among commoners, and may have derived from the structural instability of the status of wife and mother under the historical legacy of polygyny. The 1907 amendment to the 1884 imperial ordinance known as kazokurei (see chapter 2) extended the patrifocal rule of succession, prohibiting female househeadship entirely. Underlying this amendment was a clearer definition of the role of the kazoku in relation to the emperor: a woman could not be a protector of the imperial house; female succession contradicted the imperial model of strict patrilineality (Sakamaki 1987, 333). In actuality, women occasionally did hold a temporary or shadow headship when no man was available, but they were not allowed to assume

Table 7. Frequency of Adoptions over Last
Six Generations

FREQUENCY	NO. HOUSEHOLDS[a]
0	32 (6.6%)
1	89 (18.4%)
2	117 (24.1%)
3	135 (27.8%)
4	84 (17.3%)
5	25 (5.2%)
6	3 (0.6%)
Total	485 (100.0%)

[a]Based on a survey of all the genealogies in *KKT.* Selected
for this table are those households that record ancestry at
least six generations back (including the present househead), making 485 households in total.

the kazoku title. Thus a female head had to submit a special petition to
regain the title when she secured an adopted male successor (son or husband). Gender asymmetry was a major feature of the kazoku structure
and will reappear in the following pages.

The Frequency and Modes of Successional Adoption

Although it is impossible to obtain precise figures for adoption rates over
the generations, *KKT* contains some quantifiable information. (I
restricted my sample to those households that record ancestry to at least
six generations back including the present househead, making 485
households in total.) As table 7 shows, 32 households claim to have had
no adopted son over the last six generations. Such a high number continuing in "natural" father-to-son succession, however, is not supported
by my interview data, making me suspect that adoptions are underre-
ported or underrecorded in *KKT.* In interviews, too, I met one adopted
son whose name appears without an adoption notation in the genealogy
because he had been "adopted as a natural son"![4] Nevertheless, it is
remarkable that out of 485 households, 247, or 50.9 percent, have
adopted three, four, five, or all six successor sons. Over six generations
of 2,910 men, moreover, 1,207 (41 percent) were adopted. Even in view
of the likely underrepresentation of the actual frequency, the figures signify remarkable proportions.

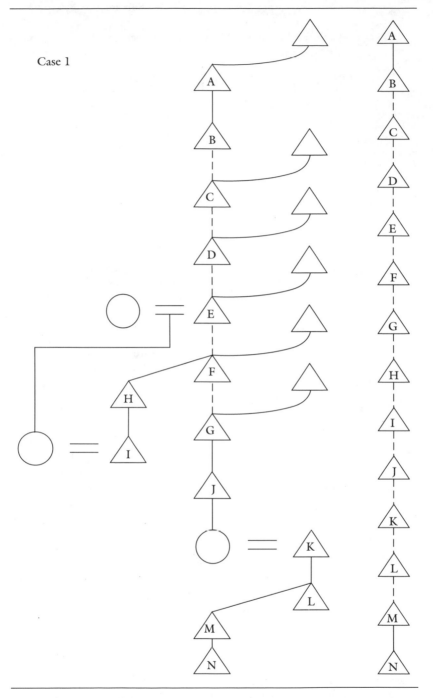

Case 1

Figure 2.   Genealogy and Adoption: Two Examples

Case 2

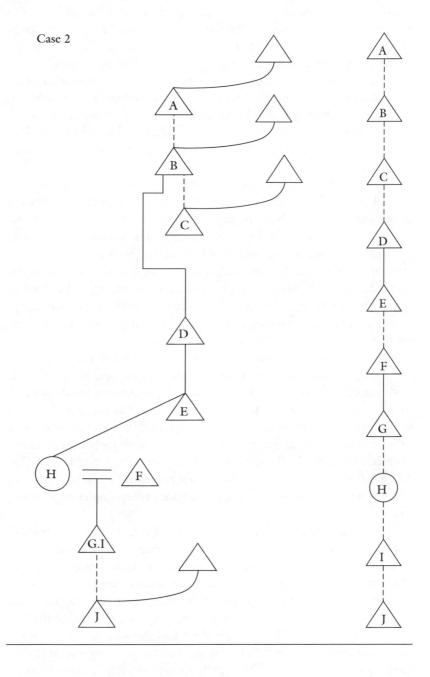

"How often" is one thing, but "who is adopted how" is another important question, one that we will explore in more detail later. For now let me show two striking examples (taken from *KKT*) of genealogy as an introductory illustration (figure 2). Each case is represented by the official straight-line genealogy (right) and by a chart (left) more faithful to natural kinship—my translation of the straight-line version. Dotted lines stand for adoption, solid lines for natural kinship. Curved lines on the left-hand chart indicate the natural link between a man and his son given away for adoption. To show the significance of birth order, siblings are connected by an oblique line. The order of succession is signified by alphabetical letters.

The early history of case 1 is striking for the successive adoptions that took place over five generations in the first half of the nineteenth century. It thus exemplifies a short incumbency for each head (eight years on average) as well as a high frequency of adoption. Further, note that G was succeeded by his adoptive father F's younger brother, H (thus going upward generationally), even though he had his own son, J. J, however, succeeded to the headship two generations later, and was succeeded in turn by his daughter's husband, K (son-in-law adoption); K's son L was then succeeded by his younger brother, M (meaning that the successor brother was adopted as a son).

Case 2 also includes an instance of adoption in which the adopter, B, had a son, D, who only later succeeded the adopted son, C. Further, E was succeeded by his sister H's husband, F (brother-in-law adoption). After F's son, G, held headship for a while, he was succeeded (for an unknown reason) by his mother, H—a rare case of succession by a woman—who after three more years was succeeded by her predecessor, her son, now called I. The same man thus headed the house twice.[5] This peculiar example is indicative of the earlier practice of retirement (inkyo), which was prohibited by the kazoku ordinance except under extenuating circumstances.

These examples confirm the ethnological argument that the Japanese ie defies a notion of descent rule. It may, of course, be assumed that the kazoku had strong reasons or compulsions for successional continuity and therefore adoption. Perhaps, for instance, aristocratic families were less fertile or had higher mortality rates than commoner families. My informants tended to assume that this was the case, attributing the fact to the feeble body produced from close-kin marriage and an overprotected childhood. I suspect this weakness was true to some extent (Lebra 1990); if so, adoption could be regarded as a "cultural" strategy to make up for the deficiency in "natural" birth. But at the same time, the same informants stated that their houses had been continued mostly by children mothered by "side consorts" or "womb ladies" recruited from "healthy" lower-status families. Furthermore, there is ample evidence that sons were adopted even by those houses that had healthy and long-living natural sons. Other explanations are therefore called for.

The Weight of Heritage

The first and obvious reason lies in the weight of heritage to be carried on. Elites and commoners alike need to pass on such things as the family name, the family estate and other assets, and the very authority of the househead (*katoku*).[6] A word is necessary here regarding names. Most kazoku families transmitted not only their family names but personal names as well, at least in part. This latter practice, called *torina*, may be best explained by an example: the successive heads of the Takahashi family may carry a certain character, such as Michi, from generation to generation as part of their personal name—thus, Michitoshi, Michiaki, Michinao, Michiyasu, and so on. Such name succession was only for sons, particularly successor sons. Adopted sons, too, were expected to change not only their family names, but also their personal names, in like manner.

What most distinguished the kazoku from non-kazoku was their hereditary title, the perpetuation of which was mandatory. The privileges and honors formally or informally vested in the title varied from symbolic to substantive, from social to economic to political:

Imperial court ranks of ancient origin accorded automatically at age twenty-one, starting from the minor fifth rank (*jugoi*) and rising theoretically up to the minor first rank (*juichii*);

Hierarchically ordered ceremonial seats in the imperial palace (*kyūchū sekiji*) to be occupied by prominent people, including the kazoku (see chapter 5);

Privileged access to the imperial "benevolence" (oboshimeshi)—ritual, social, or economic (including gifts in cash or kind, and special cases of "commensality" with the emperor);

The right to wear specially styled and decorated court attire (*taireifuku*) indicative of kazoku titles and ranks;

The use of the kazoku group as a legitimate pool of spousal candidates for members of the royal lineage from the emperor down;

The right of each house to install a house law (*kaken*) binding on members of the house;

Automatic or internally elected membership in the House of Peers;

Opportunities for high office in the Kunaishō;

The right to designate certain items of property as "hereditary" so as to keep them immune from seizure during bankruptcy;

The right to send the children to Gakushuin free of tuition;

And so on.[7]

(From Sakamaki 1987, 301–31)

To be added to this list was the general honor of being treated with respect and courtesy by the population at large. Because the kazoku were limited in number, status scarcity was an important factor compelling the title holder to secure a successor, whether a natural or an adopted son. In other words, a kazoku had much to lose by failing to provide a successor. Although the privileges on the above list were taken as obligations, this did not lessen the mission of continuing the line. The compulsion to designate a successor was intensified by a rule laid down in the original kazokurei (which was in part relaxed in a later revision to effect consistency with the civil code) that a successor be designated before the incumbent's death. This rule forced a sonless kazoku to adopt a successor often prematurely and unnecessarily; if the adopter later fathered his own son, a situation of serial adoption was set in motion in which the adopted successor would in turn have to adopt the original adopter's natural son. Such premature adoption offers one explanation why adoption might cause a natural son to be passed over.

If the titleholder died suddenly without having his own or an adopted son, the death was not reported until the family secured an adopted successor. In this crisis, as one informant whose grandfather had died in such circumstances put it, "*Anybody* could have been accepted as long as he was a male." The widow, the informant's grandmother, searched in desperation until she found a third son of a kuge count willing to join the ie as an adopted son-in-law. Offered to choose any one of three daughters as his bride, he picked the informant's mother. It was not until the family completed the adoption procedure that the death of the last incumbent was announced—a modern continuation of a common practice of the Tokugawa period. Both premature adoption and death record falsification amply demonstrate the importance attached to status succession: if one wished to perpetuate only the house, not the kazoku status, these measures could have been avoided.

As far as kazoku status is concerned, the weight of heritage was lifted after the war. Have former kazoku then lost interest in succession and adoption? No, they are still concerned with the continuation of their ie through successors, even though they are less sure of securing heirs than they once were. In the questionnaire I asked, "Do you think your house [ie] should be continued, even by adopting a son if necessary? Please write down your reasons." Of the eighty-eight responses to this question, a large majority (74 percent) were positive (table 8). These responses suggest that the weight of heritage was still felt in connection with the genealogical depth and honor of the house, despite the fact that neither the kazoku nor the ie as a legal entity any longer exists. In my impression, this conservative attitude toward the ie characterizes many Japanese across class lines. Particularly when one faces parental death and becomes a househead, one seems to become sharply aware of the weight of the ie with its transcendent implications. Yet the need to preserve the ie is per-haps more strongly felt in kazoku houses. In the present generation, many households are facing a scarcity of heirs and must allocate them in an optimal way. The daughter of an old daimyo count, age fifty-five, for instance, agreed to give her only son to her natal house—his grandpa-rental house—as an adopted successor. Her commoner husband sup-ported the idea strongly because he thought her natal house, which was old and prestigious, ought to be perpetuated, whereas his own house could be dispensed with.

Underlying this attitude is the cult of ancestors. In questionnaire re-sponses, kazoku informants generally expressed their respectfulness and indebtedness toward their ancestors and emphasized their obligation to keep up the mortuary symbols (most importantly, tombs and tablets) and rituals (daily prayers and death anniversary memorial rites). They would be overcome with guilt toward their ancestors, they said, if the house came to an end during their generation.

Supply of Adoptees

Adopted sons, clearly, were in high demand. But what was the state of the supply side? From the above discussion on the ie structure we know that brothers were dichotomized into two groups: one successor and all other nonsuccessors. Concomitant with kazoku status, which entailed certain privileges of rank, was a greater status distance between successor and nonsuccessors (usually between the eldest son and younger sons, as well as between sons and daughters) than was the case among the non-privileged classes. Only the heir was addressed by positional terms such as "junior lord" (*wakatonosama,* or *wakasama*) and referred to as an "honorable heir" (*o-atotori*), whereas all other children were addressed and referred to by their personal names. Status discrimination within the family (such as the eldest brother being served a meal alone by several

Table 8. Questionnaire Responses, with Example Answers, on the Continuation of a House by Adoption (*N* = 88)

Do you think your house should be continued, even by adopting a son if necessary?

POSITIVE 56 (63.6%)

"As long as Japan exists, it should be continued."

"I don't want to bring to an end in my generation the house status [*iegara*] that my ancestors endeavored so hard to maintain."

"Being a prominent house, it should be continued."

"It is necessary to keep up the tomb for ancestors, and I am proud of my house status."

"We have been living along an unbroken line of descent."

"By all means I want to preserve the family line, which has continued eighty generations."

"I want to continue it forever."

CONDITIONALLY POSITIVE 9 (10.2%)

"It is not necessary to adopt a son, but it would be nice to have someone maintain the ancestral tomb."

"At present I have my son to continue it, but would let nature take its course thereafter."

NEUTRAL 16 (18.2%)

"The future is uncertain."

"It's up to the children."

"I am not thinking about that particularly. I will leave things as they turn out [*nariyuki ni makaseru*]."

CONDITIONALLY NEGATIVE 3 (3.4%)

"There will be no need of adoption in the future."

"Nothing to say."

NEGATIVE 4 (4.5%)

"I don't think so."

"I am only a new kazoku, owing the title to my grandfather's merit. Since it is not a house worth continuing, I have no wish to."

---

servants in a separate room while all younger brothers ate together in the dining room) was recalled vividly and resentfully by nonsuccessor brothers, whereas the successor brother tended to be oblivious to any favoritism. In daimyo houses in particular, younger sons were treated, I was told, as "vassals" (*kerai*) to their eldest brother, as if they were still living in the Tokugawa era. In kuge houses, too, where some "house treasures," including ancestors' writings, had been handed down, it was the eldest son's exclusive right under the rule of *isshi sōden* (one-child succession) to have access to them, keeping all others blind to the house tradition. In other words, nonsuccessor sons were a sort of anomaly. No wonder that I heard scathing criticism, based on egalitarian ideology, of the kazoku institution more from nonsuccessor brothers than from successors—another reminder of the differential awareness of hierarchy and discrimination depending on one's relative status.

Whereas a daughter was expected to marry out, a nonsuccessor son had three alternatives of life course as stated by my informants: (1) to set up his own house independently or, if allowed, a branch of his natal house; (2) to forgo the right to become a household either by staying on in his parental house as a lifelong *heyazumi* (room occupant)—a parasitic and potentially disruptive retainer, unmarried and dependent on his lord brother—or by entering a Buddhist monastery to lead a celibate life; or (3) to be adopted by another kazoku house as its successor. Alternative 2 was hardly an option and I have not seen a single instance of it being practiced; indeed, I suspect informants drew it from historical dramas to capitalize on the deprived status of a younger son. With regard to the priesthood specifically, the Meiji Restoration terminated the rule of priestly celibacy as part of the pro-Shinto policy to suppress Buddhism. Alternative 1 differentiates independence and branching, though the difference between them is not always clear. Among kazoku, the establishment of a branch house entailed the right or obligation to offer a son to (or sometimes to receive a son from) the main house for successional adoption. By and large, the obligatory, subordinate status of a branch house in relation to its main house was a distinct characteristic of the dōzoku relationship in the kazoku, as will be illustrated later. In other words, by branching, a younger brother would have had to prolong his subordination to his elder brother and head of the main house and forgo autonomy for good. Although branching could mean being awarded the title of baron or viscount under "imperial benevolence," thus allowing one to join the kazoku, such cases were exceptional and limited to the highest-ranking or specially favored kazoku such as imperial kin. Independence, in contrast, signified a downright demotion to commoner status.

Compared with these two options, alternative 3 was deemed most attractive by many as the only way for a nonsuccessor son to enjoy an autonomous "lordship." As an adopted household said, "There was nothing you could do as a younger son. You could waste all your life as a heyazumi, or go independent, or enter the priesthood. Nothing else." In other words, adoption was the best deal.

Ray Moore (1970), by presenting contradictory data from samurai families of the Tokugawa period, challenges the widely accepted notion that adoption was a major means by which a poor and bright boy could achieve upward mobility. He demonstrates that adoption took place most frequently within the same class, thus not affecting mobility; in fact, if there was mobility, it was more downward than upward. But as the author admits, this argument is based on the relative ranks (as measured by stipends) of the adopting family and the adoptee's natal family, in disregard of the fact that adoption permitted a nonsuccessor to retain a samurai status instead of losing it entirely. Adoption, in other words, was a means not of status mobility, but of status preservation. The same was true for the kazoku.

Nonsuccessor sons, then, were available on the adoption market and were so understood by would-be adopters. One informant, a second son of a daimyo marquis, received an adoption proposal from a new viscount kazoku. When he turned it down, the proposal automatically went to his younger brother, who accepted it. Consequently, the informant ended up as the only independent commoner in the family, while his brothers all remained kazoku and/or headed a branch house. Another informant, a younger son of a kuge viscount, described how he, as a young man, was inundated with adoption proposals "like rainfall" (a common simile for abundance, usually used for marriage proposals), receiving far more offers of adoption than marriage. Indeed, the adoption market for sons was comparable to the marriage market for daughters, and both marriage and adoption are called *engumi* (tying two partners), the latter marked as *yōshi-engumi*. The above informant declined all the proposals, but even after he was married and became a commoner proposals kept coming, asking him to bring his wife and children with him for collective adoption.

Typically, however, the proposal receiver did not even question whether he should or should not be adopted, nor was he choosy about adopters. When a small child was adopted, of course, the adoptee's compliance did not come into question (see chapter 7). Yet more commonly adoptions involved an older child or adult whose judgment and compliance did count.

For one forty-five-year-old informant, it was when he was a junior high school student that his maternal grandfather, a prince, sounded out his willingness to be adopted. "Grandfather asked me, 'How about coming to my house?' and right away I said, 'Okay, I will.' " His immediate acceptance had childish reasons, such as better food served at the adoptive house than at his poorer natal house (an important consideration in postwar, preaffluence times), greater opportunities to attend sumo tournaments because the grandfather was a strong sumo sponsor, and the like. Not until much later did the informant become aware of the special status of his adoptive house. When he was taken by his adoptive father (natural grandfather) to the great shrine of the deified founding ancestor for a grand memorial rite involving the whole community, he realized what a formidable commitment he had unknowingly made. Eventually he became adjusted to his adopted status ("oriai ga tsuita") and began to find pleasure in following his late predecessor in playing ritual roles for cycles of ancestor rites.

Unquestioning acquiescence with an adoption request was typical of adult adoptees as well. One baronial house of priestly origin, having only daughters, adopted a son, but this engumi ended in *rien* (the severance of adoptive ties; also meaning divorce). Consequently, the eldest daughter, having already married out, was called back together with her husband so that the latter, dean of a medical school, could take over headship. Did he agree? "Me? I decided it would make no difference where I belonged." They changed their name to the wife's natal family name. The wife labeled this adoption fūfu-yōshi, although in fact it was a variety of son-in-law adoption (*muko-yōshi*).

KKT provides some information, though definitely incomplete, on sons adopted out. As a sample, every fifth household on the list was selected—but only if the house included at least one adopted head, and if not, the next on the list was picked up. The 201 households thus selected (a nearly random sample) generated 196 codable households, for which sons of three generations (or less in the case of genealogically shallow or unrecorded cases), going backward from the latest generation born prior to 1945, were counted. Of 553 nonsuccessor sons, 156, or 28.2 percent, were adopted out, mostly as successors to other kazoku houses.

For more precise information, let us focus on the highest-ranking households, the five sekke and the shogunal main house in particular. Table 9 shows the frequency and percentages of adopted sons, both received and given, relative to all successors and all nonsuccessor sons, respectively. The figures show remarkably high proportions of adoptions both into and out of these houses, with the percentages of adopted-out sons being especially striking, in the shogunal house in particular. No wonder that as my informants saw things, *all* sons of the Tokugawa, other than successors, were adopted out. These given-away sons, with few

Table 9. Adopted Sons of Sekke and Shogunal Houses

	SEKKE HOUSES	SHOGUNAL HOUSE
All successors	45	9
Adopted-in successors	16 (35.6%)	5 (55.6%)
All nonsuccessor sons	72	21
Adopted-out sons	34 (47.2%)	16 (76.2%)

Note: Figures derived from *KKT* genealogies, which omit earlier generations.

exceptions, all succeeded to the headship of their adoptive houses. Table 9 may suggest that sons of the top families were more apt to become political pawns to adoption than those of others, but it might also be that adoptions in other families were underrecorded.

We have seen the advantages of being adopted, but calculated interest alone would not seem sufficient to explain such readiness of men to offer themselves for adoption. More important was the fact that adoption, like marriage, was negotiated and arranged not only by the two families involved but often by many others as well who had some say in major family decisions, such as kin on both sides, top-level retainers of both houses, family counsellors, and sometimes the office of *Sōchitsuryō* within the Kunaishō, which supervised the nobility and royalty. For kazoku, adoption as well as marriage was thus a semipublic, semipolitical matter beyond the individual's preference and choice, much more so than for commoners. One reason for this situation was that kazoku were encouraged (though not required) to adopt one another's children in order to maintain the status boundary. Most of my informants were convinced that kazoku were "absolutely" prohibited from marrying or adopting outside the status group.

Individual members were accordingly socialized to be pliable enough to move from one prepared position to another as expected. "Personal preference would have made no difference," said an adopted informant, "because there wasn't much variation in the kazoku career anyway. Everyone would end up as a member of the House of Peers, and the like." He would thus joke with those of his Gakushuin classmates who were also adopted, saying one's adoptive house could well have been another's (*torikawaru*).

The ease of adopting and being adopted may have derived from the positional, structural nature of adoption, implying relative insignificance of personal rapport between parent and child in adoption. In American practice, adoption is primarily between a childless couple and a child whose natural parent(s) are not available, capable, or willing as nurturers; thus it enables both parties to satisfy their personal needs, on the one side parental, on the other filial. Keeping the identity of the child's natural parentage secret seems essential to building an exclusive love and intimacy between the adoptive parties. Adoption in Oceania, though contrastive to the American pattern, is found by some researchers to simulate the relations of natural parent and child, in a way not dissimilar to the American counterpart. Ruth Gallagher Goodenough, for instance, characterizing Trukese adoption, says, "Adoption allows childless adults to validate their adult status by demonstrating their ability to play the role of nurturer, which is highly valued by Trukese" (1970, 337). Writing on Hawaiian adoption, Alan Howard et al. (1970, 48) stress Hawaiian women's strong need for babies and for playing a nurturant maternal role.

In kazoku adoption, such parent-child relations were not entirely lacking, to be sure. Particularly in cases of adoption by close kin, as in the above-cited case of a grandfather adopting a grandson, nurturance and intimacy entered into the relationship. By and large, however, such feelings turned out to be secondary or irrelevant to the mandate of positional succession, and often were completely absent from the adoptive relationship. Adoption was undertaken first and foremost to secure a person to occupy the "situs" of a successor to the ie, a goal that could be realized, for instance, without actual co-residence or even through postmortem adoption. The high frequency of adoption and ready acceptance of adoption proposals among kazoku may indeed have been facilitated by the relative lack of needed investment in interpersonal, exclusive bonding between adoption partners.

THE FREE FLOW OF BLOOD

At this juncture, we must return to the issue of kinship, which so far has been neglected in the name of the ie, defined as independent of kinship. It is important to reconsider kinship in view of the "hereditary" status of kazoku. For my informants, kinship was conceptualized primarily in terms of "blood flow." Sometimes, blood continuity was sharply opposed to adoption, the blood line (*chisuji*) to the ie line (*iesuji*), and so on. Sometimes, however, no such opposition was felt, and adoption and blood continuity were discussed in the same breath with no sense of contradiction.

Whether or not a discrepancy was felt between the ie and blood lines, informants either stressed or took for granted the value of "blood" and some discussed the "legitimate," "true" blood line. A descendant of a sekke house, for example, was stunned when I carelessly asked what he thought of the notion that Japanese easily find substitutes for blood relatives as successors. He strongly disagreed, saying that his house had held a special position in the imperial court for no other reason than heredity. There would have been no justification for his house status, he argued, without the blood continuity from ancestors. He claimed that in his house adoption had occurred only once in the long line of generations, and that the adoptee was an imperial prince and son of a daughter of the house who had married an emperor. The genealogical record does not, however, validate his claim. Obviously, adoption had taken place without disturbing the sense of continuous blood flow. This issue raises the question of how adoptees were related to adoptive parents in terms of kinship.

"Natural" Kinship in Adoption

Table 10 shows that in the 194 codable instances of adoption taken from the 201-household sample of *KKT* (see above; the numbers of codable cases vary depending on the availability of information necessary for the particularly coded items—here, kin relationship), 30.4 percent of adoptees are identifiable kin with relationships including brother to brother, brother's son to father's brother (the relationship most preferred by Chinese), and so on. Although with less frequency, a daughter's or sister's son, too, is acceptable as one's son, as is a patrilateral parallel cousin (one's father's brother's son). "All other kin" includes more collateral adoptions not only in descending generations (BrSoSo, FaBrSoSo), but in ascending generations as well (MoBr, FaFaBrSo). Nonkin adoptions, 69.6 percent of the total, include muko-yōshi (DaHu) and three interesting, and essentially similar, cases of husband adoption (together amounting to 30.4 percent of the total sample). In husband adoption, apparently, a daughter was a temporary househead, and when she married, the headship was taken over by her husband through adoption. Although these adoptees were certainly nonkin, in both son-in-law adoption and husband adoption the blood continued to flow through the daughter/wife. In other words, in 60.8 percent of total adoptions, blood continuity and adoption are compatible.

Is the category of "Other" (39.2 percent of the total) made up completely of outsiders? Although it includes, at best, relationships such as step-kin and remote kin too distant to count as kin, even here blood connections are occasionally discernible, however "thinned" (figure 3). In case 1, A adopts B from outside, but B in turn adopts A's son, C, as would happen in premature adoption or in other circumstances that

Table 10. Adopter-Adoptee Relationship
in Kinship

KINSHIP	NO. CASES
Kin	
Br	31 (16.0%)
BrSo	13 (6.7%)
DaSo	4 (2.1%)
SiSo	3 (1.5%)
FaBrSo	3 (1.5%)
All other kin	5 (2.6%)
Total	59 (30.4%)
Nonkin	
DaHu (*muko-yōshi*)	56 (28.9%)
Hu	3 (1.5%)
Other	76 (39.2%)
Total	135 (69.6%)
Grand Total	194 (100.0%)

Source: *KKT.*

necessitate passing over one's own son temporarily. In such a situation, while the parties to adoption (A and B, B and C) are themselves unrelated, A's blood is restored by his son, C. Similar to case 1 is case 2, where C is A's brother's son rather than his own. Case 3 represents serial adoption, where two blood lines exchange sons in alternate generations. (Also included in "Other" are several cases of dōzoku adoption, to be discussed below.)

Clearly, it is preferable, when possible, to make adoptions compatible with the preservation of blood, even if it is "diluted." In this attempt, the rule of descent often has to be ignored, which leads to the paradoxical conclusion that rulelessness in adoption only demonstrates the importance, not unimportance, of "blood" or natural kinship over and beyond rules. The "natural" blood with all its fluidity cannot be contained in the "cultural" box but leaks in all directions. Looked at thus, the relatively high frequency of brother-brother adoption makes much sense because a brother is the closest available male kin. Similarly, adopting a son-in-law or husband (to keep blood connections through daughters), cousin, uncle, or great-uncle is not as outrageous as it might look to a Confucian.

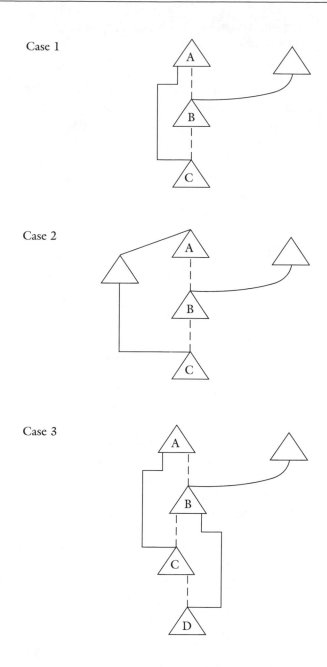

Figure 3. Adoption and Blood Restoration

It is in view of the primacy of consanguinity in this loose sense that Keith Brown's (1966) insistence on the "cognatic" descent as ideology is reappreciated.

The blood flow may be "natural" and ruleless, but the cultural rule of father-to-son succession is rigid. This is why kin adoption was preferred, and why even a brother was considered the "adopted son" to succeed the "adoptive brother-father." If the single-line patrilineal model were not so fixed, there would be less need to "adopt" a kinsman. Because a successor had to be a son, anyone other than a natural son, however close in kinship, would have to be adopted as a son. What appears contradictory is in fact a logical corollary.

The Dōzoku as a Successor Gene Pool

To protect the line from a possible anemic consequence, many houses had branch houses, organized into lineagelike dōzoku, as suppliers of sons in case the main house ran out of its own. The imperial house during the Tokugawa period had four such satellite houses, called shinnōke (houses of imperial-blood sons; see chapter 2). The Tokugawa house, too, had three branches, and later another three secondary branches were added. The dōzoku was characteristically centered on the main house, to which branch houses were subordinated regardless of relative seniority in age of dōzoku members.[8] The main house was entitled to adopt the eldest or even only son of a branch house and, in turn, to "give" its own excess sons to branches as their successors. The blood relationship between the adopter and adoptee might be distant, as when there was no recent transfer of a child, but was translated into kinship by common ancestry, however remote, as well as by the common surname. Within the kazoku, dōzoku formation was undertaken primarily for the preservation of what was regarded as a gene pool, and so its size was kept small. (Large dōzoku, such as those of the Mitsui, Shimazu, and Maeda, were meant to perform other functions as well, particularly political and economic collaboration.)

Not surprisingly, the dōzoku, basically ie-structured, was vulnerable to a split between the ie principle and the blood connection. Disputes flared up over orthodoxy of the line, particularly when the blood was derived from a great ancestor. In one high-ranking kuge house, a nationally eminent ancestor, A, adopted a son, B, from a branch house. Late in his life, however, he found himself the father of his own son by a young concubine. Already committed to the adoption, the house had the blood son branch out. The main ie line, though, soon fell short of blood, whereupon the son of the adopted successor, who himself had no son, prepared to adopt his brother. At this juncture, the blood grandson C of the initial ancestor, A, born in the branch house, emerged to claim his rightful successor status to the main house because he *was* in the "orthodox blood line" (*seitō no chisuji*). According to his relative, this succession dispute landed in court and ended in the blood grandson's victory.

In a more covert way, the orthodoxy of another main-line house was challenged by a branch-house representative. A distinguished ancestor, X, left no son behind, and so this main house headship went to descendants of his brother. Yet some other branch houses still carried the blood of the great ancestor through his daughters. The head of one such branch house and his wife were proud—and somewhat resentful toward the powerful main house—to tell me that theirs and another branch were the only houses in which the "true" blood of X ran.

A member of another dōzoku group, a branch-house head, did not consider his house separate from the main house, because the second-generation head of the main house was an ancestor of his house, and from him the whole line had continued. For the informant, moreover, "It was not adoption. My ancestor actually *returned* to the original house." In so saying, of course, he was repudiating the idea that his house was in any way inferior to the main house.

Historically, dōzoku were indeed ridden with conflicts and fights over succession; I argue that blood played an important role in justifying challenges against the ie structure. Nor is it surprising that, given the potentially disruptive force of dōzoku members, dōzoku size tended to be kept at a minimum and fixed (another point of difference between the dōzoku and the Chinese lineage)—unless a dōzoku group functioned essentially as an economic unit, as it did among commoners.

Integrative efforts were, however, made to bridge the ie and blood lines when they came apart. The best example comes from the Matsudaira, involving a punitive adoption at the transition time. Matsudaira Yoshinaga (1828–90; also known as Shungaku), the lord of Echizen in the late Tokugawa period, was a political activist who opposed the policies of the shogunal government. As a penalty he was not only forced into retirement but also forbidden to have the lordship taken over by one of his two sons. A successor, eight years younger than Yoshinaga, was therefore adopted from a branch house.[9] Later, in the Meiji period, the adopted successor married his son to a daughter of the original Matsudaira so that, in the words of a descendant, "*iesuji* and *chisuji* were converged into one line."

"Naturalization"

Memories are blissfully short-lived. The split that emerges in one generation may be forgotten in the next. The adopted man may have brought his own daimyo culture into the kuge house he succeeded to, but his son, identifying with the culture of his own birth house, not his blood father's, might act as if he were successor to a continuous kuge line. Likewise, the head of a baronial house, after talking about his adopted father, who knew little about the predecessor and the house he succeeded to, responded to my question regarding the continuation of the ie thus: "Yes, I do want our line to be continued forever, because blood cannot be bought with money." Obviously, the "naturalization" of external blood into the "indigenous" blood of the ie had occurred in the informant's mind. The adoptee himself may have resisted changing his personal name, but from his son on the succession of a certain personal-name character (torina) would resume. There is a tendency for a descendant to connect himself to a famous ancestor regardless of blood continuity; Kido Kōichi, according to a biography (Ōdaira 1984), appears to have identified himself strongly with his well-known grandfather, Takayoshi (Kōin), more than with his father, Kōsei, even though he, Kōichi, was unrelated by blood to Takayoshi, his blood father having been Takayoshi's adopted son.

Such aligned naturalization, sometimes involving generation skipping of this sort, was facilitated by the purely cultural representation of blood as a single, rigid patriline of succession, best symbolized by the *bansei ikkei*—a single unbroken line over countless generations—of emperors. Naturalization may occur within the adoptee's lifetime: "Eventually, the adopted son will begin to look as if he were born there," said an adopted head of a kuge house. It seems that Japanese in general have had their own version of "genealogical amnesia" (Geertz and Geertz 1968), aided by the notion of a continuous ie line.

Finally, successional adoptions almost always came from within kazoku ranks. The adopted son could be "anybody," but "of course, he must be a kazoku son." This meant more than the substitutability of status affinity for kinship. Since recruitment of both spouses and adoptees was largely from among fellow members of the aristocracy, there had developed such overlapping kinship networks that everyone was able to find a number of status peers to whom he or she was in fact connected. The mental picture of such groupwide networks was another factor, I think, that contributed to the reconciliation of adoption and heredity. The use of the blood metaphor for genetic continuity also facilitates reconciliation in that it transforms the rigid image of heredity into fluid substance. After all, blood *is* transfusable.

MEMORIALIZING ANCESTORS

Adoption was undertaken for ie succession, which in turn enabled the perpetual memorialization of ancestors through rituals; thus Hozumi (1912) argues in reference to the spirit of the civil code. Our next task, therefore, is to show how successors immortalized ancestors through religious symbols and ritual acts. Although ancestor memorialism was a common feature across classes, some class differences in specific forms of rituals, symbolism, and religious beliefs emerged in my interviews. I will concentrate on these differences.

First of all, in my observation Shinto carried more weight in ancestor rites among kazoku than among commoners. Buddhism, of course, had its place, and the questionnaire responses show that informants were equally divided between Shinto and Buddhism (table 11). Indeed, many kazoku—by far more than the table indicates—were discovered through interviews to be affiliated with both Shinto and Buddhism, like most other Japanese (see below; the validity of the questionnaire result will be taken up later). For kazoku, however, the rites of death and ancestors were connected primarily with Shinto affiliation, while for commoners Buddhism predominated in these areas. To understand this difference, we must look briefly at the turning point in modern religious history called *shinbutsu bunri* (the separation of Shinto and Buddhism), which occurred in the earliest years of Meiji.

Ancestors as Buddhas or Kami

The separation edict (*shinbutsu bunri rei*), issued at the dawn of the Restoration in 1868, was meant above all to sanctify the new government under the slogan of *saisei itchi* (union of rites and government) as embodied by the "divine" emperor. At the same time it exposed, retrospectively, the pre-Meiji fusion of the two religions, the prevalence of which the following quotation makes clear: "In 1868 there were nearly 300 temples at Ise. Recitation of Buddhist sutras before the altars of the *kami* [gods] (on the theory that the *kami* need these Buddhist rites in order to achieve salvation) was a common occurrence, and many Buddhist priests journeyed to Ise as pilgrims and to perform austerities there" (Hardacre 1986, 32).

Since the Nara period, when Buddhism was established virtually as a state religion, the fusion had been theologically rationalized by the idea

Table 11. Questionnaire Responses on Religious
Affiliation, in Percentages ($N = 101$)

Buddhism only	40
Shinto only	39
Both Buddhism and Shinto	14
Christianity	5
No religion	1
No answer	2

of ultimate identity between native kami and Buddhas (*honji suijaku,*
ryōbu shintō, gongen, and so on, terms that entail the notion of manifes-
tation, reflection, or embodiment of Buddha by kami), symbolically expressed by such things as buddha-figured *shintai* (kami body) and mixed
architectural motifs, and institutionally implemented by Buddhist priests
serving Shinto shrines (*shasō*), shrine-temples (*jingūji, honjidō*), and the
like.

The pre-Restoration amalgam was by no means symmetrical but
instead involved an overwhelming dominance of Buddhism over Shinto.
The Tokugawa government's imposition of the *danka* (Buddhist-temple
registration) system on all, including Shinto priests, intensified the traditional supremacy of the Buddhist establishment politically and economically. The Buddhist dominance or license was therefore resented,
attacked, and rejected by many political and intellectual leaders from the
very beginning of the Tokugawa period. These anti-Buddhist sentiments
were ideologically expressed by a variety of Confucian doctrines, Shinto-
Confucian union, pure Shinto, National School nativism, and so forth.
Political suppression of Buddhist temples and promotion of kami and
shrines were carried out in some domains, notably by Ikeda Mitsumasa
(1609–82), the daimyo of Okayama; Hoshina Masayuki (1611–72) of
Aizu; and Tokugawa Mitsukuni (1628–1700) of Mito (Collcutt 1986,
146–47). Toward the end of the Tokugawa era, the anti-Buddhist current was channeled into emperor-focused Shintoism.

In this sense, the separation policy launched by the Meiji government
was not entirely a historical break but rather a formal statewide enunci-
ation of what had long been growing in local quarters. The separation
naturally involved pro-Shinto retaliations against long-privileged Buddhism and was destined to merge with *haibutsu kishaku,* the anti-
Buddhist movement involving removal and destruction of Buddhist symbols from Shinto shrines.

From 1871 through 1872 the government turned from separation to disestablishment of Buddhism. The economic strength of
the Buddhist institution was undercut by the abolition of the old
networks of lay sponsors (*danka*) and by the confiscation of temple lands. Its social position was reduced by the abolition of ranks
and titles for the Buddhist clergy. Far from enforcing the traditional standards of Buddhist clerical life as taught in the *Vinaya,*
the government issued regulations permitting monks and nuns to
grow their hair, to eat meat, to return to lay life, and to marry.
Many temples were closed and some schools of Buddhism were
forced to amalgamate or disband.

(Collcutt 1986, 152)

One informant of daimyo descent stated: "In Meiji, our province destroyed temples completely. Until the twenty-eighth-generation househead, all the deceased were represented by Buddhist tablets placed at
temples, but my grandfather switched to Shinto." Another said, "In the
tenth year of Meiji, [my grandfather] switched from Buddhas to kami.
He sent an announcement to all the family temples, ordering them to
return all the tablets, and thus severed our house from temples once and
for all. In our house we have no *butsudan* [household Buddhist altar],
but only *kamidana* [shelf for the Shinto gods]." In Kumamoto, I witnessed good proof of the radical departure from the Buddhist past: the
Taishōji Temple, owned by the Hosokawa, had been made into a *haiji*
(dead temple), and in its stead a Shinto shrine had been built in the same
compound to enshrine all the Hosokawa ancestors. Before this conversion, the Hosokawa lords were well known, a personal guide indicated,
for their devotion to Zen. The remains of the former temple structure
are now used as a resting place for Shinto-styled ancestor-rite attendants.
    Buddhism in Japan was thus threatened with extinction, but as we
know, the threat was not realized. Shinto, in the end, could not replace
Buddhism, first because, aside from its doctrinal and ritual paucity, which
necessitated a heavy borrowing from Buddhism, its identity was amor-
phous, indefinable, and open to internal debate. The so-called Pantheon
Dispute (*saijin ronsō*), for example, divided "the Shinto world into two
halves, allied with the Ise and Izumo Grand Shrines," respectively, over
whether the latter's central deity, Okuninushi, should be added to the
state pantheon (Hardacre 1986, 51). Second, and at a more pragmatic
level, the problematic nature of the Shinto funeral and ancestor rites
(*shinsōsai*) in terms of death pollution made exclusive adherence to Shinto
difficult, if not impossible. The installation of the Shinto-shrine registration system to replace the Buddhist danka system proved ineffective.

Eventually Shinto was excluded from "religion," partly under pressures to guarantee freedom of faith in the forthcoming constitution: "In 1882 an edict forbade further preaching in the national shrines and the holding of funerals there; in 1884 preaching was forbidden in all other Shinto shrines; and the 1889 Constitution finally granted qualified religious freedom to all Japanese" (Smith 1974, 30). This turn of events is reflected by the rapidity with which the Jingikan, the administrative unit in the Meiji government that oversaw Shinto and shrine affairs, which had been revitalized in 1868 out of its nominal existence under the ritsuryō, and exalted above the daijōkan, was successively reduced to lesser and lesser names and positions.

This administrative demotion did not mean the downfall of Shinto; in fact, the faith came to be promoted above all religions. The proselytizing center for state Shinto was soon moved from the religious to the educational establishment to inculcate the ideology of the emperor-focused, myth-ridden *kokutai* (essence of the state) in schoolchildren (Smith 1974, 30–32). Also notable was the continued influence of activist splinter groups of syncretic sectarian Shinto.

Shintoization of the Imperial House and Kazoku

The large majority of Japanese held a double affiliation with Buddhism and Shinto, leaving matters of death and ancestors with Buddhist priests and temples, and those of life and celebration with Shinto priests and shrines. By and large, however, the populace retained a stronger commitment to the Buddhist institution through a sense of bonding with their ancestors. The kazoku deviated from this pattern in three main ways. First and most obviously, the kazoku as a group were situated closer to the imperial house and its ancestors in an emotional, social, political, occupational, and genealogical sense of bonding. Some kazoku, informants said about their fathers or grandfathers, renounced Buddhism entirely and became staunch Shintoists out of their reverence for the emperor. Reference was also made to a grandfather whose conversion to Shinto was an expression of the nativistic ideology, represented by the National School of the Tokugawa period, which he had embraced. But much more besides was involved in their self-identification with the emperor. Here let us shift our attention to the imperial house, where the shinbutsu bunri led to a great transition as well.

Before the Restoration, the Shinto priest and scholar Sakamoto Ken 'ichi (1983) tells us, the imperial house was inseparably tied with Buddhism: imperial funerals and memorial rites had followed Buddhist formulas for centuries, and the house was connected formally with seven (especially, but in fact many more) temples for *butsuji* (Buddhist matters) as well as seven shrines for *shinji* (kami matters). "The relationship between the imperial house and temples was stronger than one could imagine" (Sakamoto 1983, 471).

For the imperial house, the shinbutsu bunri amounted to a conversion to Shinto exclusively and the renunciation of the strongly Buddhist-biased double or mixed adherence. Shinto conversion was forced on all members of the royalty; royal temple abbots and abbotesses were laicized, and some were later assigned to major national shrines as Shinto priests; the titles of monzeki and *bikuni* (the formal title for female monzeki) were abolished (see chapters 2 and 8 on the monzeki priesthood). Understandably, such compulsory conversion was not always successful, and yet the Shinto mandate was not retracted. Prince Yamashina Akira, for example, himself a former monzeki, apparently remained a devout Buddhist and, before dying in 1898, petitioned in his will that a Buddhist funeral be granted him. The request was turned down (Sakamoto 1983, 509–10). The Buddhist-inspired practice of cremation was halted, and the pre-Buddhist pattern of burial, reminiscent of the protohistoric tombs, was revived, totally separate from temple cemeteries.[10]

The imperial palace itself was "cleaned" up. Prior to the Restoration, imperial ancestors (*kōrei*) were represented by *ihai* (mortuary tablets with Buddhist titles), which were housed in what was called *o-kurodo*, the imperial butsudan, within the palace (then in Kyoto) and served daily by *nyokan* (female palace attendants) in Buddhist style.[11] This state of affairs was terminated by the removal of the o-kurodo from the palace and the enshrinement of the imperial ancestors in a newly built shrine (*shinden*) under Jingikan jurisdiction.[12] Later, when Jingikan was reduced to Jingishō, the shrine was relocated within the palace (now in Tokyo)—a first step toward the final establishment of *kyūchū sanden,* the triple shrine in the palace.

These three shrines stood (and still stand) side by side. On the left was *kōreiden,* the collective shrine for imperial ancestors. The central and most sacred shrine was *kashikodokoro,* containing the mirror, a symbolic representation (*mitamashiro*) of Amaterasu, who is enshrined at Ise. And on the right was shinden, the shrine for the Shinto pantheon.[13] This shrine relocation was meant symbolically to bring the palace into focus as the center of saisei itchi.

The first two being for imperial ancestors, these palace shrines became the primary site of Shinto-fashioned ancestor rites for the imperial house. The ritual calendar was created for the emperor or his ritual surrogate to serve, address, and memorialize particular or all ancestors and gods. Among major rites invented or revived in the Meiji era were the new year's celebration (*genshisai*); the national foundation anniversary (*kigensetsu*), commemorating Emperor Jinmu's accession; the semiannual memorial rites for all imperial ancestors (*kōreisai*) at the equinox; the rite of new rice offering (*ninamesai*); the reigning emperor's birthday (*tenchōsetsu*); and the late emperor's death anniversary. Fifteen years after Meiji's death, the celebration of his birthday (*Meijisetsu*) was added as a major annual rite. (See Irie 1979 for a detailed monthly account of palace rites and ceremonies.) Thus for the imperial house, Shinto and ancestor rites became united.

The kazoku were naturally affected by the Shintoization of the imperial house. Most of my Shinto informants said their families had become converts after the Restoration because "all kazoku were encouraged to switch." One kuge count, personally disinterested in Shinto, admitted that his great-grandfather, as the head of the palace ceremony department, had to go over to Shinto. Some informants were convinced that the kazoku had been "forced" into Shinto by the Kunaishō. "We kazoku had no choice. So we were Shintoist in *tatemae* [outward posture], but remained Buddhist in *honne* [inner feeling]." Forced conversion, however, is an overstatement, for there were kazoku who stayed out of Shinto entirely, as well as those who strongly denied that any such coercion had occurred.

Whether forced or merely encouraged, the kazoku or their transition-period ancestors had good reasons to emulate the imperial house, and their Shinto conversion may be regarded as a small-scale duplication of the imperial conversion. Such emulation was reflected in their version of Shinto, which differed from that of commoners. The kazoku Shinto was an ancestor-oriented family religion, as was the imperial Shinto. It was a private religion, so to speak, catering to the convert's own ancestors and having little to do with the kokutai-inspired state Shinto or communal-shrine Shinto that predominated in the state-engineered commoner version. In other words, as far as modes of ancestor worship were concerned, the kazoku became in essence little imperial houses through Shinto. This leads to the next point.

The second aspect of the different pattern to kazoku Shintoization derives, in my view, from the reorganization of existing shrines and creation of new shrines, theoretically to enhance the spirit of the Restoration and to promote Shinto. The 1871 decree issued by the daijōkan assigned ranks (*shakaku*) to shrines nationwide, dividing them into two classes:

state shrines and local miscellaneous shrines. State shrines were then further classified into *kanpeisha* and *kokuheisha,* depending on sponsoring agencies: kanpeisha, those state shrines that were to receive gift offerings from the imperial house, ranked highest; kokuheisha were to receive the same from the state treasury.[14] Each class of state shrines was ranked according to its physical scale as large (*taisha*), middle (*chūsha*), and small (*shōsha*), a system that in combination yielded six ranks ranging from kanpei-taisha down to kokuhei-shōsha. Above all these state shrines stood the central shrine of the imperial house at Ise, called Ise Jingū. Below state shrines were local shrines, classified as metropolitan (*fusha*), prefectural (*kensha*), municipal (*gōsha*), and village (*sonsha*) shrines and funded by corresponding units of local government. At the very bottom were *mukakusha,* rankless shrines. The shrine reorganization involved the promotion or demotion of gods of existing shrines, and appropriate gods replaced inappropriate ones.[15]

Further, a multitude of new shrines were erected for more gods, emperors, imperial kin, and subjects (see Okada 1966), mainly to display the cause of the Restoration and to validate Shinto tenets. Notable was the construction of the Kashiwara Shrine for Emperor Jinmu to memorialize the founder of the "unbroken line" of dynastic succession, and of branch shrines all over the country to Amaterasu as well as Jinmu as vehicles for the dissemination of state Shinto. Many military, political, and intellectual loyalists from history, predominantly those connected with the Restoration, were enshrined, and some of these shrines were classified as *bekkaku kanpeisha,* a special rank installed in 1873. To glorify the "Middle Restoration" in 1334 of imperial rule, for example, Kusunoki Masashige and other warlords who had sided with Emperor Godaigo were enshrined. This medieval event was obviously recaptured for a double purpose: as a harbinger of the Meiji Restoration, and to quash once and for all the controversy over which of the two coexistent fourteenth-century courts, northern or southern, was of the "legitimate" line—a touchy issue that urged a resolution supportive of the claimed *bansei ikkei.* The enshrinement of the Godaigo camp thus sanctioned the southern court as the sole legitimate line.

These actions had other purposes and rationales not always consistent or based on solid historical grounds. The long tradition of appeasing *onryō* (revengeful spirits) entered the shrine construction project, leading to the enshrinement of exiled or otherwise tragic emperors and those subjects whose lives were ended before fulfilling their loyalist missions. Some of the pre-Tokugawa warlords, including Uesugi Kenshin, Takeda Shingen, Oda Nobunaga, and Toyotomi Hideyoshi, were enshrined because of their "indifference to the shogunal government and loyalist commitment to the court" (Okada 1966, 10).

The shrine construction policy not only necessitated a rewriting of history, but it also stimulated competitive petitions among various sponsors to have their favorite heroes nominated. A movement arose for the former domains to dedicate new shrines to some memorable lords to commemorate their distinguished leadership. The Satsuma, for example, the first such domain, built two shrines, one for Shimazu Yoshihiro, the other for Shimazu Tadahisa (the founding ancestor), as early as in 1869. According to informants, shrines for daimyo ancestors were built at the center of the former castle sites.

In 1873 Tōshōgū, the shrine of Tokugawa Ieyasu, was awarded the title of bekkaku kanpeisha. This gesture of the central government, taken as an exoneration of the former imperial foe (chōteki), triggered those domains that had fought the Restoration war on the Tokugawa side to build their own shrines. Among the first to arise was the Aoba Shrine of Sendai for Date Masamune. These domainal shrines were kensha (prefectural shrines), to be distinguished from the national bekkaku kanpeisha.

Whatever purposes underlay particular cases of shrine construction, it is clear that nonimperial, human "gods" enshrined from the Restoration on, including those of prestigious bekkaku kanpeisha, were overrepresented by the kazoku and their ancestors. Also understandable is the fact that more daimyo ancestors and meritorious kazoku were enshrined than kuge ancestors. Likewise, because the ancestor enshrinement corresponded with Shinto conversion, more Shinto converts were found among the kazoku of daimyo descent and new kazoku than among the kuge.

Shinto adherence for kazoku thus involved the construction of shrine edifices, often vast and awesome (such as the Terukuni Jinja, a bekkaku kanpeisha for Shimazu Nariakira), dedicated to their ancestors and open to public view and worship. Class distinctions thus extended to the transcendental realm: between the enshrined gods and their descendants, on the one hand, and commoners looking up to the shrines, on the other, or between the worshipped and worshippers. In other words, this-worldly ennoblement was accompanied by other-worldly enshrinement. It may be further noted that Shinto-converted kazoku households had collective shrines for all their ancestors, called variously *soreisha, otamaya, oyashiro,* and so on, often built within their residential estates for daily prayer and periodical memorial rites. Here, too, one might find mini-replicas of the post-Restoration imperial palace shrines. Many daimyo kazoku, besides ancestor shrines, had tutelary shrines, predominantly to Inari (a multifaceted god particularly associated with rice and the fox), in their estates, reminding one of the shinden of the palace.

The third way in which the kazoku receptivity to Shinto differed from that of commoners was down-to-earth and even cynical. The pre-Meiji Buddhist establishment had come under attack partly and importantly because it cut into domainal treasuries, not only through the danka system but also through the temples' heavy dependence on daimyo houses for sponsorship and patronage. Typically, daimyo houses, owing in part to the high frequency of domainal transfers as well as to the compulsory double residence in which womenfolk were held as hostages in Edo, felt compelled to support several temples with multiple sectarian affiliations. Speaking about his ancestors, one daimyo count disclosed still another dimension of Buddhist involvement: "It is no easy thing to be affiliated with temples. In the old days, lords belonged to different sects, one to the Jōdo sect, another to the Sōtō sect, and so on. Their wives, too, brought their natal faiths, such as the Nichiren sect, over to the house. Each lord and each lady thus had their own temples built," which their descendants were obligated to maintain.

The Shinto conversion at the Meiji Restoration presented a convenient justification for becoming rid of the Buddhist burden. In a published dialogue, Maeda Toshitatsu, head of the big Maeda house, expressed his frank opinion:

> In Meiji, we became the protective fence [*hanpei*] for the emperor, and supposedly that was the reason for our switch to Shinto, following the imperial example. But even though I have no definite evidence in saying this, I rather think the decision was made by daimyo only to sever themselves from the temples. Still today our house remains tied to a few temples we cannot get rid of. Those bonzes continue, they say, to recite sutras for my ancestors every day. After sutras, the posthumous names [*kaimyō*] are recited, each ending with [a Buddhist marker] *inden* or some such thing, you know. I am the seventeenth generation. From the first ancestor, Toshiie, down to the sixteenth, my father, all the sixteen kaimyō are recited by heart!
>
> (Nanbu and Maeda 1978, 124)

The speaker's language is rough and derogatory, betraying his impatience with the Buddhist obligations that still drag on despite the family's Shinto conversion at Meiji. Several of my informants also explained their Shinto adherence strictly in economic terms: "Only for economic reasons, having nothing to do with the Shinto promotion in Meiji"; "You don't have to worry about Shinto, it costs so little." Here is another reason why Shinto conversion was overrepresented by daimyo houses, the main sponsors of temples. Equally understandable is the fact that most converted households did not relinquish Shinto in the postwar period, when Shinto was openly discredited.

The Shin-Butsu Coupling

The persistence of Buddhism should not be underestimated, however. There were Buddhist devotees among kazoku and even within the imperial family (Empress Teimei, for example), and some households had nothing to do with Shinto. Even a Shinto priest, a kuge kazoku, of a former kanpei-taisha was found to be a devoted Buddhist, faithfully observing the Buddhist rites for his ancestors. The daughter of a daimyo viscount, herself an heiress (that is, she is married to an adopted son-in-law), considers it her responsibility to maintain all five family temples, because "the temples notify us of death anniversaries," and one of the temples has images of generations of ancestor lords and "still keeps intact a room used by one of our ancestors for resting." Financially it is "a heavy burden," but she continues out of her devotion to her ancestors.

More widespread, however, was the double affiliation with both Shinto and Buddhism, thus doubling the funerary rites. Ironically, for the majority of kazoku Shinto conversion meant adding Shinto to Buddhism, rather than lifting the Buddhist burden or simplifying the rites, as some Shinto converts claimed would occur. The two religions, no longer fused, were superimposed one upon the other. Shinto and Buddhism (shin-butsu) are differentiated by various markers: shrines versus temples; shin priests (*kannushi*) versus butsu priests (*sōryo* or *bōsan*) who preside over the rites; symbolic representations of the deified dead by mirrors or other tokens of *mitama* (spirits of the dead) with kami titles versus ihai tablets with *hotoke* titles (*kaimyō*, or posthumous Buddhist names); soreisha or kamidana versus *butsuma* (room for a Buddhist service) or butsudan; *norito* (Shinto prayers) versus *o-kyō* (sutras) for recitation; differences in the modes, places, occasions, and lexicon of rites; and so on. Informants' narratives are full of double-identification experiences, sometimes in confusion:

> Recalled by a sekke daughter: "In our garden there was a shrine containing the mitama of all generations from Fujiwara Kamatari on. One day in fall, as I remember, a kannushi came to give a service there. Oh, no, it was done in butsu? . . . Oh, yes,

there was a butsuma inside the house. The head maid, as her duty, served rice and water there every day. At the Bon (Buddhist All Souls' Day) time, a nun was invited over to recite sutras."

Told by a daimyo countess: "[For ancestor rites] kannushi are invited over on death anniversaries to recite norito, and the equinoctial and Bon rites are performed at Buddhist temples. (How about the *ihai*?) We don't have ihai because ours is Shinto, or rather, the ihai are kept at the temple called Daijōji. And in our butsudan we have Buddha statues. Since my childhood, I have been taught to have faith in Kannon Buddha."

Told by a son of a daimyo count while he was showing me around a large shrine-mausoleum complex: "This [shrine] was constructed a year after [my first ancestor] died. . . . Next year marks the three hundred fiftieth anniversary of his death, and there will be a grand festival for commemoration. . . . In Meiji we switched to Shinto, but when this was built we followed the butsu style. So [in prayer] you must take cautions to fold your palms [in butsu style] *and* to clap your hands [in shin style]."

The successor to another daimyo-count house responded firmly to my ihai question that his house had nothing to do with ihai because of its adherence to Shinto: "We have *mitamashiro* [symbols of the spirits of the dead] only." Then he added in disgust, "But the temples keep making ihai for us without being asked." Yet in his house I saw two equally magnificent gilded altars standing side by side, a kamidana and a butsudan. I was also told that the funeral for his father was in both shin and butsu. "Terribly complicated," exclaimed his wife of commoner origin. After the shin and butsu funerals were conducted separately, the priests of both sides met at a tea house for *naorai* (a dinner party at which one could unwind after the ritual tension, a Shinto idea).

While Shinto and Buddhism were allocated into separate jurisdictions for commoners, the kazoku had to find a way of combining the two faiths' rites of death and ancestors without conflict. Each household seems to have arrived at its own formula, if not always a satisfactory one. The double identity of the dead person may, for instance, be represented at once as a kami (shin) and a hotoke (butsu). A more formal solution is exemplified by a printed list of thirty generations of successive househeads from the first ancestor on, distributed by the current head of a daimyo-prince house at the time of its ancestor rite. Herein each lord down to the twenty-eighth is identified by both a *hōgō* (a butsu title ending with *-den* or *-mon*) and a *shingō* (a kami title ending with *-mikoto*) as well as by his lay name, whereas the two most recent post-Meiji deceased heads hold shingō only. Apparently, the shingō were attached only after Meiji to all the previous hōgō-titled ancestors.

Some households differentiate the two identities in consideration of the individual preferences of the particular ancestors involved. A daughter of a daimyo count said her natal house had practiced Shinto for two generations only and had returned to Nichiren Buddhism in her father's generation. Thus the two Shinto forebears were buried in a cemetery separate from the Nichiren temple cemetery where all the other ancestors had been laid to rest. The informant felt that something would have to be done, but did not know what, to end this unhappy state of separation.

The Tokugawa main house offers Shinto memorial services for its first and third ancestors, Ieyasu and Iemitsu (the former in particular, enshrined as a kami [actually a gongen, a product of shin-butsu fusion] at Tōshōgū), and Buddhist services for other shogunal ancestors, either at Kan'eiji (Tendai sect) or Zōjōji (Jōdo sect), all of whom are buried in one of the three cemeteries. The only anomaly is the last shogun, Yoshinobu, who, because he insisted on Shinto rites, ended up buried at the Yanaka cemetery adjacent to the Kan'eiji. (This anomaly, moreover, reflects his marginal status due to the Restoration government's preclusion of his blood descendants from succession to the shogunal main house.)

Another household takes into account the two stages of a person's postmortem career. The deceased is buried at a Kyoto temple cemetery, given a kaimyō, and memorialized in butsu ritual. On the one hundredth death anniversary, however, the deceased househead, together with his wife, is "promoted" to kami status and placed in the ancestral shrine. "This does not mean they cease to be hotoke," said a daughter of the house, "but we must from then on hold both Shinto and Buddhist rites" at every fiftieth death anniversary (called *kaiki* for butsu and *nensai* for shin). Still another means of differentiating ritual requirements used by another house was gender: from the first daimyo ancestor on, all successive househeads were enshrined as kami, while their wives became hotoke. "But my mother refused to be separated from my father in this way, so she became a kami"—an option that could be exercised only after the war. The most common pattern of differentiation is in terms of public versus private, obligatory or coerced versus spontaneous or voluntary, tatemae versus honne. The first of each pair was represented more by Shinto, the second by Buddhism, but the reverse also occurred.

All this raises questions about the validity of the questionnaire (see table 11). How, in fact, could informants answer whether their households adhered to Shinto or Buddhism? It was a poor question, given that even the stringent Restoration policy of separation did not eradicate but only compounded the centuries-old shin-butsu mixture. Even the imperial house conceded to the demand of Sennyūji Temple to restore some of its previous status as an imperial temple and to allow it to offer Buddhist rites for imperial ancestors, and of the Tendai and Shingon sects to resume their esoteric rituals in the palace (Sakamoto 1983). It might be added, incidentally, that such nonexclusivity in religious identity applies to Christianity as well. A seventy-two-year-old widow said that two funerals had been performed for her late Christian husband, Shinto and Christian, though later memorial rites were Shinto only. (See Reid 1989 on Japanese Christians and ancestor rites.)

POSTWAR VICISSITUDES OF ANCESTOR MANAGEMENT

The end of World War II, followed by the Occupation, brought about an overall degradation—political, economic, and ideological—of religious establishments. The governmental sponsorship and other privileges of Shinto were abolished altogether, leaving the shrines and priesthood abandoned and self-supporting. Neither did the Buddhist establishment remain intact. Postwar land reforms deprived temples of tenanted lands, an important source of revenues. To make matters worse, the impoverished kazoku were pressed to reduce the number, scale, and elaborateness of cemeteries, altars, rites, and other reminders of ancestors. Some kazoku sponsors of certain temples, built and owned by their ancestors, lowered or withdrew their support, which forced the temples to accept other parishioners. In a way, the temples reexperienced the loss that they had suffered at the Restoration.

Nevertheless, ancestral charisma has survived, if on a reduced scale, among kazoku offspring. Some kazoku men have become licensed priests in order to preside over ancestor rites at their semipublic family shrines. Among these is a kuge count who, after a long high school teaching career, became chief priest of the central Fujiwara-uji temple. He considers himself the luckiest man in the world. "Why not? What could be better than making a job out of serving your own ancestors?"

Many informants call themselves *hakamori* (graveyard custodians), as if ancestor services were their main responsibility. For cemetery maintenance, some daimyo houses continue to rely on the services of hereditary hakamori families, who, residing near the cemetery, have been attached to the daimyo houses in that specialized capacity for many generations. But ancestral matters, memorial rites especially, are a personal responsibility of kazoku descendants, more so today than before, when high-ranking servants were in charge of *daisan* or *daihai* (both meaning worship by a surrogate). Nevertheless, ancestor worshippers confess ambivalence. One young princess considers the whole affair wasteful, yet she faithfully accompanies her husband on the annual visit to the major ancestor shrine. The hakamori task may be nothing but an undesirable obligation to many, but they dare not neglect it.

Further, the survival of ancestor worship, I realized, often means that only one member of a family is involved at a time. A househead may pay no attention to ancestral matters because, for example, he adheres to the Christian faith, but then his wife is found to be in charge of the household shrine, temple memorial rites, and so forth. If parents are not interested, a son, daughter-in-law, or grandson may revive ancestor rites. The converse is a more common pattern, however—that is, the parents are involved while their children remain totally indifferent. "I wish my son some day would visit our shrine as my surrogate [*daihai*]," complained a viscount whose well-known grandfather was enshrined for his military leadership in defeating the Tokugawa forces. My prediction is that the son will become involved when he gets older or when he succeeds to the househeadship upon the incumbent's death. In any case, all this suggests how the ancestor cult is inseparable from the ie structure: the cult can live on as long as one representative of the ie, male or female, old or young, is interested; and it may be revived much as a dead ie can be revived.

Meanwhile, as Japan was recovering from the war and working toward unprecedented prosperity, its leaders began to pay greater attention to cultural activities, which resulted in the 1968 establishment of Bunkachō (Agency for Cultural Affairs) in affiliation with the Ministry of Education.[16] Among various projects initiated was the preservation of cultural properties (*bunkazai*), both tangible and intangible (for example, the performing arts). Especially valuable bunkazai were to be designated *jūyō-bunkazai* (important cultural property, abbreviated as *jūbun*), and truly unequaled items among these were to be nominated for *kokuhō* (national treasure) status. Over eleven thousand items, including paintings, sculptures, crafts, and buildings, had been identified as jūbun by 1985, about 10 percent of which were nominated as kokuhō (Bunkachō 1985). The buildings so designated include shrines, temples, castles, tombs, and dwellings; notable historical sites (*shiseki*), such as the ruins of palaces and castles, are also selected for preservation. Such nomination entails financial and technical aid from Bunkachō to assist in repairing and maintaining the property. If the owner is unable to maintain the property, it may be sold or donated to Bunkachō, the local government, or a non-profit organization, to be managed with public funds and thereby to become accessible to the public at large (Bunkachō 1985, 1988).

All these and other preservation policies strongly affect those kazoku who, unable to maintain ancestral legacies, are looking for alternative means of preserving their heritage. Many of their properties and possessions, whether shrines, temples, tombs, castles, gardens, dwellings, paintings, or swords, indeed have been nominated as jūbun or shiseki and today are under public management. Museums and libraries display the archives and treasures that previously had been stored in private homes. One ancestral shrine, for instance, once a bekkaku-kanpeisha, now has come back under public protection as a cultural treasure. The decision in favor of such transfer is not always easy and often involves frustrations over loss of control over the property, but by and large it is accepted as the only alternative to honor ancestors. A recent jūbun nomination suddenly brought into the national limelight the last extant residential kuge estate (of the Reizei), together with its storehouse of "kokuhō-class" treasures—a development that pleases the ancestor-devoted family residing on the estate. Many destroyed shrines and other monuments are being reconstructed to symbolize the resurrection of ancestors. It is ironic that the privatized status identity of former kazoku is being brought back to public attention by state and other publicly sponsored plans aimed at resurrecting these ancestors. But still more is involved in public- and descendant-based cosponsorship of ancestral legacies, as will be touched on in chapters 5 and 8.

FIVE

Life-Style

Markers of Status and Hierarchy

Turning away from the last two chapters' focus on death, the deceased, and ancestors, this chapter looks into the routine life of the latest generations that still "live" in the memories of informants. In contrast to our interest thus far on the time depth of ancestor-successor relations, let us now orient ourselves to the spatial breadth of life conditions. The following pages will, I hope, succeed in translating the previous chapters into a more tangible, this-worldly level of experience with respect to where, how, and with whom our subjects lived. By delineating salient markers of aristocratic life-styles I hope to outline perceptible status boundaries and thereby show the concrete mechanisms that operate behind the hereditary hierarchy.

Life-style is vulnerable to change. "My mother was still wearing *ohiki-zuri* [outer garment with train]," said one informant, "like many other women. But that was stopped overnight by the Russo-Japanese War." In addition to that war, my informants identified two more major turning points affecting life-style: the Kantō earthquake of 1923 and World War II. Numerous fires also added to the list of disasters that disrupted and often irreversibly destroyed the routines to which the victims had been accustomed. These events, however, made most kazoku families crisis-ready. In addition, the insatiable appetite of the nation for things trendy—in which the kazoku shared wholeheartedly—in conjunction with the remarkable pace of Japan's modernization effected enormous change. And yet some aspects of the old life-style are claimed to persist to this day. The use of the past tense in the following account, then, does not always preclude the present condition of life.

147

THE SPATIAL DESIGNS OF STATUS

As Edward Hall (1959, 1969) reminds us, spatial cues form an important silent language whereby social reality is constructed, maintained, or changed. Spatial metaphors for social hierarchy such as "high" and "low," "above" and "below," are of universal use (Schwartz 1981). In this section I will examine how status was expressed spatially in the daily living of upper-class Japanese, as represented by the kazoku. Before delving into more subtle, metaphorical usages of space, however, let us first take a macroview of residential space, an area of cross-culturally recognized criteria for stratification (Warner, Meeker, and Eells 1960).

Residential Geography

As we saw in chapter 2, the Restoration government maneuvered the old aristocracy into settling permanently in Tokyo. Further, for ambitious men who were later to rise into the ranks of the nobility through merit, only the new capital could provide the needed opportunities. There were thus good reasons for the kazoku population to concentrate in Tokyo, with but a few exceptions among kuge who stayed on in Kyoto.

Since this initial resettlement many residential relocations have been made, I learned, either by choice or by necessity. Then too, the war, Tokyo air raids, evacuation, and radical postwar taxation on properties ruined the kazoku's residential distinction, forcing most of them to let their estates go largely or entirely and to live in cramped sections of their former servants' quarters or to disperse into rural areas.

One might therefore think that no more geographical pattern of residence would distinguish the former kazoku. Yet a numerical comparison between the kazoku and the general population reveals that the former are still concentrated disproportionately in the capital. Indeed, in Tokyo Prefecture are located fully 57 percent of all kazoku households whose addresses are known ($N = 916$, according to *KKT*), compared with 11.9 percent for the Japanese population as a whole (Jichishō Gyōseikyoku 1984). In second place, with 16.7 percent of kazoku—versus 6.5 percent of the population generally—is Kanagawa Prefecture, adjacent to Tokyo, where many kazoku owned what once were resort villas along Sagami Bay and later became their permanent homes when their main estates in Tokyo were lost. Thus, 73.7 percent of kazoku live in these two prefectures alone, while the national representation is only 18.4 percent.

Tokyo is divided into the urban area, situated in the east facing Tokyo Bay, and the rest of the prefecture, constituting a large westward-spreading rural area. The former might be delineated as Tokyo City, even though there has been no such administrative unit since 1943. In this urban area of Tokyo are located 74 percent of all prefectural Tokyo households, whereas the corresponding figure for kazoku is 86 percent. More telling is the *pattern* of concentration within Tokyo City, which is divided into twenty-three wards (*ku*). Five wards (Minato, Shibuya, Setagaya, Meguro, and Shinjuku) claim 66.6 percent of kazoku households residing in Tokyo City, compared with only 24.3 percent of general households. Conversely, eight other wards (Katsushika, Sumida, Arakawa, Adachi, Kita, Kōtō, Edogawa, and Itabashi) are home to but 2.6 percent of urban-Tokyo kazoku, but to 35.2 percent of general residents. (See figure 4.)

These figures confirm the impression of a class cleavage in Tokyo residential geography, a cleavage which Japanese are ready to label *shitamachi* (downtown) versus *yamanote* (hillside). The yamanote/shitamachi dichotomy is far from clear or consistent, however. Tokyo City has expanded from its original six-ward district (1869) to the fifteen-ward system (1878; see figure 5), and through the postearthquake urban sprawl to thirty-five wards (1932). The present twenty-three-ward configuration is a product of the 1948 reorganization of the prewar system covering the same area. To add to the difficulty of applying the traditional shitamachi/yamanote designation, ward names have been changed. Yet Japanese still adhere to this usage.

Fujishima Taisuke, a yamanote resident and author, visualizes the yamanote area as "inside the circle of the Yamate railway line" (1987, 13). Others, however, would disagree, since the circle excludes the western wards, such as Setagaya and Suginami, which contemporary Japanese regard as typically yamanote. Generally, the imperial palace ground is taken to divide the two areas, with shitamachi to the east and yamanote to the west. Nevertheless, we find that Chūō-ku, a center of shitamachi, has main shopping streets such as Ginza (created in early Meiji on a Western model) catering to yamanote tastes and business districts that daily absorb white-collar workers commuting from the yamanote. These designations, thus, are more symbolic of class divisions than denotative of geography (Dore 1958, 11–13). Edward Seidensticker, though limiting his analysis to the old city limits, calls the two regions "high city" and "low city," thereby combining physical topography and social class. He takes us back to the historical origin of this division: "When in the seventeenth century the Tokugawa regime set about building a seat for itself, it granted most of the solid hilly regions to the military aristocracy, and filled in the marshy mouths of the Sumida and Tone rivers, to the east of the castle. The flatlands that resulted became the abode of the

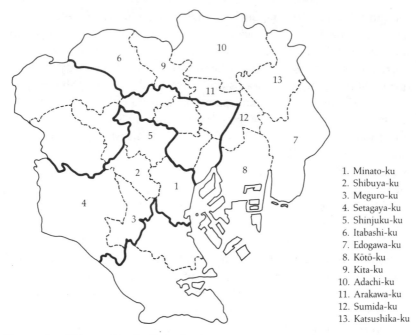

1. Minato-ku
2. Shibuya-ku
3. Meguro-ku
4. Setagaya-ku
5. Shinjuku-ku
6. Itabashi-ku
7. Edogawa-ku
8. Kōtō-ku
9. Kita-ku
10. Adachi-ku
11. Arakawa-ku
12. Sumida-ku
13. Katsushika-ku

Figure 4.   Thirteen Wards (*ku*) of Urban Tokyo, Showing Marked Class Divisions, 1986. Kazoku residence concentrates in the first five ku, in this order of density relative to the general population. In the other eight ku, the proportional difference in density between kazoku and the general residents is reversed, with no kazoku representation in Arakawa, Sumida, and Katsushika. Generally, kazoku concentrate in the southwest of urban Tokyo. Sources: KK 1982–84; Jichishō Gyōseikyoku 1984.

merchants and craftsmen who purveyed to the voracious aristocracy and provided its labor" (1983, 8).

There is reason, then, for the yamanote region to be associated with the "buke *yashiki*" or "daimyo *yashiki*," the mansions of the ruling class. The former kazoku, despite many relocations, continue, if less densely, to cluster in the choice areas of the "high city." That such geographical density must have been much more pronounced in prewar times is inferable from the previous residences revealed in interviews. Most frequently mentioned were two wards of the Meiji-era fifteen-ward Tokyo City, Azabu and Akasaka (presently both part of Minato-ku), which formed the heart of old yamanote. "The Tale of Akasaka," a popular essay by Kōbata Yoshiko (1984), for example, is primarily about the former elite.

Figure 5. The Boundaries of Urban Tokyo, 1878

Confinement

The residential geography of Tokyo is the first clue to the spatial confinement in which the kazoku life was led. Confinement implies one's relative seclusion from the outside world, outside one's household or one's status group. A daughter of a daimyo marquis recalled that, while her "unusually liberal parents" allowed her as a child to visit areas like Asakusa (a popular entertainment district in shitamachi, housing the Yoshiwara quarters of prostitution) on occasions such as local festivals if escorted by "several maids," they themselves would step into such a place "under absolutely no circumstances." To this day, some upper-class yamanote residents are strangers to the heart of shitamachi, though familiar with American and European cities. As an author who only recently discovered the wonder of shitamachi confesses, "Yes, Asakusa was more remote than New York" (Inukai 1989, 37).

In seclusion there was gender asymmetry, with girls and women more strictly bound by the rule of spatial confinement than boys and men. (In fact, boys were allowed and sometimes encouraged to enter the social wilderness of the outside world; see chapter 7.) For older women informants particularly, their girlhood was recalled as confined to the enclosure of the estate. Some were frustrated, but most accepted the stricture as "natural," becoming awakened to the "freedom of mobility" only after their marriage or the war. The old ohikizuri attire epitomizes the woman's indoor life and immobility.

What stands out in kazoku life histories, in sharp contrast to those of average Japanese, is the insignificance or even absence of neighbors—a characteristic of the yamanote in general, and probably more pronounced among the upper class. Beyond perfunctory greetings in accidental encounters in the residential vicinity, there was almost no contact with neighbors until the war, when everyone was forced into a neighborhood association and had to line up for rationed foods. Even children did not find their playmates among neighbors. One woman, the daughter of a count, at age fifty-five recalled being little and temporarily living in an area where she heard the sound of neighbors for the first time in her life. When neighbor children came to invite her to join them in play, she did not know how to respond. She was curious about them and enjoyed watching them, but had no wish to participate in their play. That this lack of neighborly contact may have been due to the Gakushuin subculture was suggested by a baron's daughter: she felt a loss of the freedom she experienced playing with neighbor children when she began to attend Gakushuin.

The only neighbors whose names and homes my informants remembered were fellow kazoku, Gakushuin classmates, high government officials, financial giants, and the like, a fact consistent with the geographical clustering of kazoku residences in selective areas. When there was contact with neighbors, the usual characteristics of neighborliness were missing, such as being always visible and accessible to one another, the unannounced visit, mutual help in an emergency, and so on. "There was no easy way of having *tsukiai* [interaction] with your neighbors. You couldn't just drop in, saying, 'Hi, here I am!' " Even between classmates such behavior was impossible, I was told; parents on both sides had to be informed first, and then visiting was scheduled. An adult visitor was bound not only by such an appointment rule, but also by a dress code and gift-giving obligation. All this class-bound, culturally dictated tsukiai utterly lacked the "natural," informal, spontaneous sociability typical of shitamachi or rural neighborhoods. One of the old institutions essential to shitamachi neighborliness, in fact, is the public bathhouse, where bathers enjoy naked tsukiai. Although yamanote, too, has public bathhouses, and many clubhouses built by ward governments for the elderly have bathing facilities, one ninety-one-year-old woman of kuge origin, married to a wealthy commoner, would shudder, her daughter-in-law said, at the idea of bathing together with neighbors.

Because no household is self-sufficient, seclusion was far from complete, and indeed there was constant interchange between the house and the outside, but only in ways that minimized open exposure of the family to the outer world. Routine domestic labor was supplied internally by a pool of servants, and specialized services such as hairdressing were provided by hired professionals. Necessary goods like food and clothing were delivered by house-calling salesclerks (*goyōkiki*) of certain stores. Not a few informants recalled their curiosity about such salesmen, hairdressers, or gardeners, their only "windows" to the outside.

The limited access of outsiders to the house was symbolized by the rank order of entrance gates or doors. The main front gate, of course, was reserved for important guests and the head of the house. Salesmen were allowed into the house through a back gate; fish vendors and greengrocers used the lowest kitchen backdoor; and sellers of candy and kimono fabric entered through the next higher backdoor ("high" and "low" here being spatial metaphors for social rank).[1] The importance of this gate-rank system to the sense of order can be surmised from the complaint of one woman, as quoted by her niece: "It used to be that the Grand Gate (*ōgenkan*) was walked through only by my father-in-law and husband. But now everything is mixed up and confused." Gate ranks were further distinguished by whether one could ride a car through the gate or not.

Exposure to the outside world was curtailed even when kazoku family members went out. The first thing informants mentioned was means of transportation. To commute to school, go shopping, or pay a visit to some place or person, many walked if the distance was short enough or took public transportation, "like everyone else." If the train had graded cars, they were more likely to take a first-class one. High-ranking and wealthy families considered private transportation mandatory. Historically, vehicles changed from early Meiji on (see Seidensticker 1983), and my informants spoke of the shift from family-owned horse-drawn carriages to *jinrikisha* (rickshaws) to automobiles. Today car ownership is no longer a status symbol, but in prewar Japan it was a special luxury.

Curiously, private transportation was another factor that inhibited access to the outside world. The vehicles were driven by privately employed chauffeurs, who usually lived within the family compound and thus served as guards as well as drivers. (The greatest mischief a girl could perpetrate was to escape the watchful eyes of a servant driver.) Under these conditions, clearly, it was difficult to meet people outside, even one's own kin. The wife of a count, seventy-six years old, recalled that after her marriage she was not free to visit her mother, ironically because she had to be chauffeured everywhere. Apparently, she was bound by the idea that married women belonged exclusively to their husbands and in-laws and therefore could see their natal kin only surreptitiously. It was not until the war, when she lost this private convenience and had to use trains, that she acquired the freedom of mobility and contact.

Whether one walked or took private or public transportation, a chaperon was de rigueur. Servants of the appropriate sex escorted the children—daughters certainly, and sometimes sons as well—from home to school and back home, at least up to about the third or fourth grade but in some cases throughout high school, much to the embarrassment of their charges. Adults, too, were shepherded: in shopping, it was the accompanying servant who discharged all transactions with store clerks, leaving the master aloof from or ignorant about money. As one woman recalled, after an escort servant was lost as a result of the war, "I still kept forgetting to carry a wallet." Even the newlywed couple, some of my informants said with a chuckle, was escorted by an entourage on their honeymoon.

Kazoku women, and to a lesser extent men too, even when they were out of the house, were thus insulated from the outside world, precisely because private transportation and chaperonage kept them from being left alone. Insulation and lack of privacy were two sides of the same coin. Only with the war and postwar demolition of the old hierarchy did the upper classes gain unrestrained freedom for external self-exposure and the enjoyment of privacy. Of course, insulation was a constraint, to be sure, but it also had a protective function, one often called on to conceal improprieties or misfortune. One of my informants had a mentally retarded brother who was being educated and cared for in a school built by the family, thus protecting him from public exposure.

Further inhibiting exposure was the selectivity of destinations for commuting or travel. A large majority of kazoku children attended Gakushuin, and other appropriate schools, which were similarly exclusive to the upper class and narrowly circumscribed classmate contact (see chapter 7). Travel away from Tokyo meant staying at private resort villas or prominent hotels that accepted regular patrons only. Shopping was done at particular stores where the head manager would attend the elite shoppers personally, occasional dining out was restricted to special restaurants or hotels, and entertainment was sought at reputable theaters. Most often mentioned were Mitsukoshi Department Store at Nihonbashi, the Imperial Hotel, Tokyo Clubhouse, the Imperial Theater, Seiyōken (a Western-style hotel in Tsukiji, and later a French restaurant in Ueno)— places that, no longer elitist, used to appeal to yamanote tastes. The Kazoku Clubhouse (Kazoku Kaikan) was another center of recreation for kazoku families. For medical treatment, the imperially sponsored Japan Red Cross and St. Luke's hospitals were most favored. (Both Seiyōken and St. Luke's were in Tsukiji, which was the site of earliest settlement of foreign legations.)

Domestic Space

So far we have considered boundaries between a kazoku person and the external world—external in a double sense to both household and status. Let us now look inward to spatial boundaries within the residential premises.

One can imagine the size of the previous kazoku estates from what has replaced them: school campuses, parks, golf courses, government buildings, foreign embassies, rental office buildings, hospitals, hotels, art galleries, sports arenas, wedding halls, new billionaires' dwellings, condominiums, and so on. The new Prince hotels, constructed by the Seibu Group, a foremost representative of the successful contemporary economic elites, in fact virtually do replace the estates of former royal princes and some kazoku. (For an interesting account of how the Seibu, through their long-range plan, established imperial connections to their business advantage, see Inose 1991.) The prewar main premises of my kazoku informants ranged widely in size from an extreme high of 100,000 tsubo (1 tsubo = 3.3 square meters) to less than 100 tsubo, but most stood between some thousands to several hundreds of tsubo. (One of the largest main estates, commanding 38,000 tsubo, had twenty-two grounds keepers!) Many kazoku also had resort villas on the Shōnan seashore (for example, at Hayama, Zushi, Kamakura, and Ōiso) or in the highlands (Karuizawa, Nasu, and so on) as well as other real estate. The Maeda, the richest of all the old kazoku, owned, in addition to their 50,000-tsubo main residential estate (a large part of which is now Komaba Park in Meguro-ku), secondary estates (*bettei*) in Kamakura, Karuizawa, and Kanazawa, ranches and forests in Hokkaido, and more lands in Kyoto and Korea (Sakai 1982, 120). Some of the new kazoku did very well too, taking over old daimyo estates. Haru Reischauer, for instance, writes that her grandfather Matsukata Masayoshi, who rose from being a modest samurai to count and eventually to prince, owned, in addition to the residential house in Shiba-ku—which once belonged to a famous daimyo, Matsudaira Sadanobu—a twenty-two acre lot (called Matsukata Hill) in Azabu-ku and summer homes in Kamakura, and developed four thousand acres of wasteland in Nasuno into farms, pastures, and forests (1986, 104–5, 117–18). Among the new zaibatsu was Ōkura Kihachirō, ennobled in 1915, whose extravagance in residential estates (Ōkura 1985) can be guessed at from a remaining portion of it, Hotel Ōkura.

In my questionnaire, I asked about prewar and present landownership. Several respondents did not know the prewar ownership, and a greater number, now living in condominiums or rental housing, wrote "None" for the present ownership. By way of a comparison, only those responses that indicated some form of private landownership are tabulated (table 12). High figures in the prewar column indicate several estates put together, including forests, with the average size of the seventy-three prewar holdings being approximately 16,700 tsubo. After the war the reduction was phenomenal: the present eighty ownerships represent roughly 700 tsubo on average, or 4.2 percent of the prewar figure. Indeed, because the sample excludes rental dwellers, the actual percentage is even lower.[2]

The imperial house surpassed (and still does) all in the possession of estates. As of 1937, it controlled roughly 627 million tsubo (about half a million acres), including the central Tokyo palace (637,000 tsubo, or 520 acres), eleven secondary or detached palaces, and many and vast forests, which actually constituted more than 90 percent of the total imperial holding and were the main source of imperial revenue, as noted in chapter 3. (The figures were computed from Kodama 1978, 314–15; quite different numbers are given by Titus 1974, 66.)

A kazoku's main dwelling in Tokyo consisted typically of two architecturally distinct parts—Japanese- and Western-styled—either as two separate houses (*nihonkan* and *yōkan*) or as two sections of a single house. While some had purely Japanese houses, others, including the Maeda, had entirely Western ones. This is one visible indication of how yamanote residents, upper class in particular, in contrast to the conservative, poorer shitamachi people, were influenced by the Meiji slogan of "Civilization and Enlightenment" and lured into the Western way of life, as will be illustrated later in this chapter. It also explains why many kazoku houses were commandeered after the war to serve as lodgings for high officers of the Occupation forces. It might be noted in this connection, too, that the heart of the "high city," where kazoku residences tended to be concentrated, is now densely populated by foreign nationals and embassies.

Table 12. Land Ownership, Prewar and Present

TOTAL AREA (IN TSUBO)[a]	PREWAR OWNERS (BEFORE 1947)	PRESENT OWNERS (1985)
0–100	7	35
101–500	16	32
501–1,000	13	5
1,001–5,000	21	6
5,001–10,000	6	1
10,001–50,000	7	1
50,001–100,000	1	0
100,001–200,000	1	0
200,001–600,000	1	0

[a]10,000 tsubo = 8.16 acres; 1 acre = 1,224 tsubo.

The spatial demarcation of the dwelling was multidimensional, sometimes only in a symbolic or metaphorical way, and sometimes physically, the boundaries being associated with the ranks, functions, or gender of occupants. I detected three partly overlapping dimensions, which, however, do not necessarily appear in the mental map of my informants. The first is the universally recognizable "vertical opposition" of "high" and "low," "above" and "below." Some areas of the premises, conceptualized as low, were marked off from high areas. We have already referred to the imperial palace, where two categories of people were clearly distinguished: denjōbito (literally, "up on the palace floor," namely nobles) and jige ("down on the ground").

The kazoku family occupied the upper domain (*kami*)—the uppermost quarter of which was for the househead and his wife, located at some distance from the nursery which was at the lower end of the domain—and the servants occupied the lower domain (*shimo*). These vertical terms could refer both to the areas and their respective occupants—family (or househead) and servants. (*Kami* can also mean god, and Emperor Shōwa was privately called *okami* by his entourage as well as by the empress.)[3] Servants, and maidservants in particular, who as a whole constituted the shimo domain, were further broken down into kami and shimo: upper maids (*kami-jochū*) attended the master family, while lower maids (*shimo-jochū*) worked around the kitchen or waited on the upper maids. The living areas, bedrooms, and study of the head and his wife thus constituted the uppermost area, and the kitchen area the lowermost. Kami-jochū belonged to two levels: while attending the master family they waited for calls in a room close to the upper quarters; they were therefore designated *otsugi* (lady-in-waiting in the next room).[4] At bedtime they would withdraw (except perhaps one who remained on duty) into the maids' quarters, another low point of the domestic space (see figure 6).

This vertical opposition, universally recognizable, sounds simple. More important, however, and complicating the spatial analysis, is the lateral opposition of *omote* (front) and *oku* (interior), which interlocked with the vertical opposition of kami and shimo in an intricate fashion. Although every informant drew attention to the omote/oku boundary in describing his or her residence, the division turns out to be less sharp and self-evident than it appears in the informant's mental map. It is in this dichotomy, I argue, that an important clue to the Japanese conception of ascribed hierarchy lies.

The front-versus-interior division appeared logical to my informants because in their eyes these spaces were inseparable from the gender of those who occupied them: the omote refers not only to the area in the front of a house but also to male servants; similarly, the oku refers to a house's interior and to the female servants who tend to that space. Further, the omote/oku opposition corresponded to the "public" versus "private" sectors of the house. The omote staff managed the house in dealings with the outside world (thus the space was also called "office"—*jimusho* or *yakusho*); the oku staff, conversely, was in charge of the private life of the kazoku family.

Where did the master family belong in this lateral dimension? And how was the vertical dimension related to the omote/oku dimension? It would make no sense to say that kami is to shimo what omote is to oku, because the kami persons, the lord of the house in particular, belonged to both the oku and the omote. Yet at the same time, there were people who belonged to neither omote nor oku. At this juncture we need to note that the omote/oku opposition entails two subdimensions. The opposite of the "front" is not the interior, but the "rear"; and the opposite of the interior is not the front, but the exterior. The two dimensions are thus restated as front/rear (omote/*ura*) and interior/exterior (*uchi*/*soto*), and can be neatly paralleled with the above/below (kami/shimo) dimension: in sum, we find that rough alignments obtain between above, front, and interior, on the one hand, and below, rear, and exterior, on the other.

Figure 6 implies that the uppermost person (the head of the house) belonged to the innermost and frontmost domains, whereas the lowest

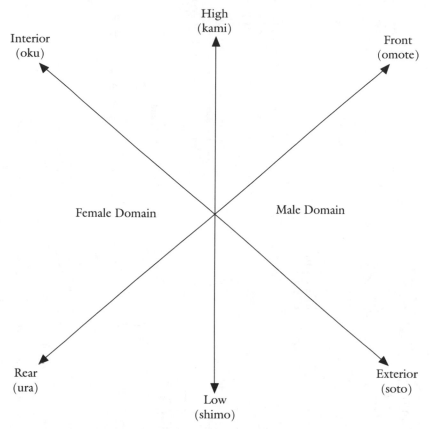

Figure 6. The Tridimensional Domestic Space

persons (janitor and kitchen maid) occupied the outermost and rearmost areas. Other, intermediary residents, whether family or servants, would occupy places in between in variable permutations of the three dimensions. While one might be assigned to a single domain in terms of usual occupancy, varying degrees of freedom or obligation to cross the boundary pertained. An upper maid might be in the interior to attend the master and family (hence she was called *oku-jochū* or otsugi as well as kami-jochū) but would retire at night to the servants' living quarters located closer to the exterior or rear (unless she slept near a child in her charge; see chapter 7). An upper managerial male servant, though usually occupying the exterior, would be privileged to enter the interior to discuss "public" affairs with the master—something other exterior personnel, like jinrikisha men, would never be permitted to do. Figure 7 shows the house plan of a daiymo-kazoku.

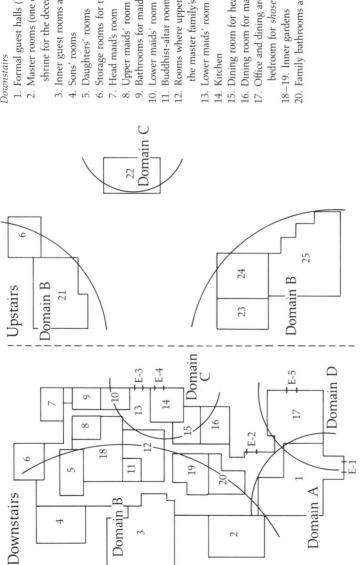

Downstairs

1. Formal guest halls (Western style)
2. Master rooms (one of which later becomes a Shinto shrine for the deceased master)
3. Inner guest rooms and family living room
4. Sons' rooms
5. Daughters' rooms
6. Storage rooms for treasures
7. Head maid's room
8. Upper maids' room
9. Bathrooms for maids
10. Lower maids' room
11. Buddhist-altar room
12. Rooms where upper maids gather, ready to respond to the master family's calls by an intercom bell system
13. Lower maids' room for dining and other purposes
14. Kitchen
15. Dining room for head maid and upper maids
16. Dining room for master family
17. Office and dining area for managerial staff, and bedroom for *shosei*
18–19. Inner gardens
20. Family bathrooms and storage area

Upstairs

21. Children's rooms
22. Mid-ranking young maids' rooms
23. Heir's rooms
24. Bathroom, storage, etc.
25. Inner guest rooms

Domainal division (shown by curved lines)

A. Front
B. Interior
C. Rear
D. Exterior

Entrances

E-1. Front gate for householad and important guests
E-2. Inner gate for other family members and close kin
E-3. Entrance door for maids and salesmen
E-4. Kitchen door
E-5. Office gate for managerial staff and office guests

Figure 7. A House Plan as Recalled by a Family of Daimyo Origin. Shown here is a simplified version to underscore the spatial ranks of residents and visitors and a rough domainal boundary.

While some personnel were thus free on occasion to cross the boundaries, rules of segregation were otherwise imposed. Between the interior and exterior various degrees of sex segregation obtained, more strictly among high-ranking kazoku. And at night, a special door opening from one to the other region was symbolically locked from the interior side. In conservative households, not just daughters, but interior maids as well, were forbidden to step out of the house even for shopping (Yanagiwara 1928, 119).

All boundaries for segregation give rise to marginal statuses or anomalies. The interior/exterior segregation by sex produced an anomalous situation for male members of the family occupying the interior, female domain. The househead, the foremost example of such anomaly, was exempted from the segregation code (indeed, he was *the* innermost person), but sons were not. Some households, especially shogunal and high-ranking daimyo houses, had sons at age seven (the supposedly marginal stage when a child was still totally dependent on his parents and interior maids and yet began to assume sexual identity) removed from the interior to the exterior. Taken away from female servants, they were waited on by young male attendants called *shosei* (student-servant); or they might be removed completely, to all-male dorms away from home (Lebra 1990).

The total removal of a son from the interior was rarely practiced, however. His marginality was well exemplified by a royal prince, whose ordinary day was marked by constant crossings of the boundary both inward and outward: in the morning, the prince would wake up in his exterior bedroom, enter the interior to have breakfast with his family, go to Gakushuin, come home after school, study and play in the exterior, go back to the interior for dinner and stay there until bedtime, then sleep in the exterior.

In conjunction with the interior/exterior sex segregation, there was a rule of vertical segregation within the interior. Lower areas, closer to the rear, were taboo to higher persons, and vice versa. Women informants in particular recalled rooms that they would not go near. Servants' quarters were avoided by the master family, especially the head and his wife. Indeed, the wife, coming from another family, often ended up knowing nothing about the rooms and hallways reserved for the maids, whereas the children, freer to move about, were better informed about the house design. This kind of spatial taboo applied most rigidly to the lowest section of the house, centered around the kitchen. The daughter of a wealthy baron recalled having been told not to walk by the kitchen; when she had to, she ran fast. There was no exchange of words between the lady of the house and lower servants. One sekke daughter, married to a royal prince, said that she did not even know where the kitchen was, and never talked with either the kitchen maids or janitors. One day she accidentally caught sight of a kitchen maid, who, too frightened either to bow or to run away, turned her face aside. Kitchen maids, clearly differentiated from the male professional chef and assistant cooks, were not only in the lowest and hindmost position, but, according to an informant, they "loitered around the kitchen area" with no fixed place to belong.

Another example of marginality in the vertical opposition involves the status of old-time concubines (a subject of chapter 6). When a concubine mothered the heir, her status was raised from that of an attendant, but not all the way up to kami. She resided elsewhere, but when she visited her "master's" house, she had no room to occupy, "neither the otsugi nor okami rooms," and so would be found standing around in the hallway, recalled a daughter of a daimyo-count.

Observance of the spatial taboo was reciprocated by the servants. They stayed away from the rooms occupied by the master, except when they were in attendance. When the head of the house was seated in the uppermost/innermost room, he was spoken to by a servant kneeling outside the room.

The grounds outside the premises were subject to the segregation code as well. Some daughters were not even allowed to step into the garden unless escorted by servants; playing outdoors, most sons and daughters found playmates (*oaite*, humble partner) among the children of the exterior staff, but some were forbidden to have such contact. Boundaries existed within the compound inside which kazoku children were confined, the area of the servants' tenements being especially taboo—for the most daring children, a tempting prohibition indeed.

Interior-Front Double Occupancy

What can be said about the seemingly contradictory nature of the master's double occupancy of the frontmost and innermost regions? Hosting distinguished guests or being invited as such a guest was a regular activity of the head of a kazoku house. Banquets and entertainments were held in the front section of the house—namely, a reception hall built away from the residential interior. In consideration of such guests as foreign dignitaries or Westernized royals, some households would use the Western-style section of the house primarily for such receptions. The master (with or without his wife accompanying him) acted as host or guest chiefly in the frontal section, with personnel of both the exterior and interior mobilized to prepare him (and his lady) for this public role.

At the same time, the lord was a resident of the innermost region of his household, and as such he was hidden and inaccessible. He was "above the clouds"—*kumo no ue*—in the sense not only of height but also of invisibility from earth-bound outsiders. This almost-forgotten term, recently retrieved by a former royal prince in an autobiographical collection of essays entitled *Above and Below the Clouds: Remembrances* (Takeda 1987), refers to the imperial palace, its residents, the nobles who had access to its interior, and people high up in general. A former shosei informant expressed the awe he still felt toward his former master, the lord of Shimazu, by describing him as "above the clouds."[5]

There were good reasons for the double occupancy of the ceremonial front and the hidden interior. For one thing, the status of the *hereditary* elite, imperial and noble alike, was both public and private—public because of their symbolic eminence in the national hierarchy, private because their status was deeply rooted in kinship and ancestry. The public nature of elite status was derived from its private successional prestige, and the latter was in turn sustained by the former. Because of this reciprocity, the public face presented in the front domain was inseparable from the family life led in the innermost domain, however well protected from public view.

In this connection, it is significant that guests were categorized into several groups, an informant of daimyo origin told me, on the basis of this same duality of the hereditary status. Public guests—high officials, kazoku peers, royals, foreign ambassadors and ministers, and so on—were invited into the formal reception hall (front), while private guests—kin of the master family—were privileged to enter the parlor of the interior for intimate contact. Other visitors who were neither public nor private enough, such as former vassals, were met and seen to by the house staff in the guest room attached to the exterior.

The private component of hereditary status, associated with the inner domain of the estate, combined the sacred and profane. The most sacred center of the interior was the in-house shrine for ancestors, tended with daily prayer. The mundane center was the master couple's bedchamber, symbolical of the conjugal reproduction of descendants to ensure the perpetuation of the status. In this context, it makes sense that the lady of the house was called *okugata* (or a more common term, *okusama*).

Separation of the body in the omote and oku was necessary, even unavoidable. To play a ceremonial role on the front stage effectively requires concealment from the audience of what goes on behind the stage. Writing about the British royalty, Ilse Hayden discusses the monarch's "two bodies"—"body natural" and "body politic"—which should be kept apart: "The Queen's body politic is relentlessly on display," while "her body natural is assiduously hidden by 'the impenetrable secrecy' of the Palace" (1987, 11). The "purity rule," by which nature is kept separate from culture, the organic from the social (Douglas 1975, 213), is particularly mandatory for the elite in order to make the staged pageantry effective and to provide backstage relaxation for the actors. It is amusing that Emperor Shōwa, who was known to be so disciplined that he could sustain his body politic (to borrow Hayden's term) for hours, appears in popular biographical accounts as having been in the habit of gargling very noisily as if no one were around, or being childishly untidy in bathing (Togashi 1977; Kojima 1981). Such habits, I think, the emperor considered as rare opportunities to assert his natural self.

Clearly, difficulties are inherent in the double occupancy, since the body is indivisible after all and it is naturally conditioned as well as culturally controlled. A solution seemed to be found in interiorizing the exalted status holder even further. To continue with our imperial examples, Emperor Meiji in 1870, rather than sitting behind the *misu* (bamboo blind) in traditional court dress, was brought for the first time out of the mystical interior into the *front* section of the palace to display himself to the public and foreigners as the "bodily visible" symbol of sovereignty (Taki 1988, 29). Engineered by the backstage builders of the Meiji government, the emperor during his forty-four-year reign made 102 *gyōkō,* imperial progresses outside the capital (Gluck 1985, 74). By mid-Meiji, however, the frequency of these gyōkō was cut down, and eventually Meiji and his successor were increasingly confined above the clouds, invisible and immobile, by Meiji political leaders for a new purpose (Titus 1974): to maximize the flexibility of the political machinery to meet the rapidly changing times by endowing the emperor with *taiken* (omnipotent authority) without burdening him with responsibility.[6] The double occupancy thus resulted in interiorizing, mystifying, and deifying the emperor. This tendency was best symbolized, in my view, by the emperor's seat in the *naijin* of the kashikodokoro, the most sacred innermost sanctuary of the palace shrine.[7] Just like a god confined in the deepest recess of a shrine, the emperor had his mystical potency manipulated not by himself but by the personnel of the exterior.

The imperial example was followed by kazoku on a small scale. Their double occupancy of omote and oku, segregated from the ura-soto regions, necessitated a large retinue to mediate the fourfold regions (see below).

Access to Court and Emperor

The prewar kazoku formed a social layer that served as a bulwark for the imperial family. This did not mean, however, that they enjoyed free contact with the emperor and his kin. Rather, such access was exceptional and held in special honor. In conversation, then, my informants of that generation tended to single out one form or another of privileged intimacy, communication, or copresence with the royalty, whereas otherwise noble status was indicated by distance and segregation from the lower ranks, as discussed earlier. They related themselves or their forebears to the royal family as kin or affines, classmates, dorm mates, fellow members of sports clubs, employees, tutors, advisors, and so on.

The palace was a site for certain kazoku rites of passage, such as an heir receiving the fifth, junior, court rank (*jugoi*) at the age of twenty-one; being awarded a kazoku title to succeed the late predecessor; being promoted; or obtaining new kazoku membership. Further, kazoku, along with high officials and foreign VIPs, were invited into the reception halls of the *kyūden* (the main structure in the palace complex) on major national holidays like New Year's Day and the emperor's birthday. In most cases, the *haietsu* (imperial audience) involved nothing but a momentary glimpse of the emperor and possibly, after having waited their turn, hearing an individually addressed brief imperial message while bowing. At times the highest and most exceptional honor was granted: commensality with the emperor or his family.

One's in-palace status was indicated in spatial terms, with old names of Kyoto palace halls for courtiers' attendance used as status labels signifying proximity to the emperor. The highest rank, which was given to only a few kazoku individuals, was *Jakō-no-ma shikō* (Jakō Hall attendance); *Kinkei-no-ma shikō*, next in line, was granted to many more, including commoners. In 1943 there were five Jakō grantees: Shimazu Tadashige, Tokugawa Kuniyuki, Tokugawa Iemasa, Yamauchi Toyokage, and Yanagiwara Yoshimitsu—four daimyo and one kuge (Kunai Daijin Kanbō 1943, 525). A broader system of in-palace hierarchization was found in the *kyūchū sekiji* (in-palace seat rank), which was defined in the Imperial Ceremony Ordinance (*kyūchū giseirei*). No informant could explain this rank system precisely, though everyone was convinced of the absolute rigidity of the seat hierarchy. One defined it as the order of "standing before the emperor to bow," another as "the table rank for imperial banquets."

The 1926 ordinance stipulated ten ranks, which were broken down into seventy grades. In the allocation of these grades, a variety of criteria were taken into consideration: membership in the royal family, ministerial positions held, other governmental offices held, military ranks earned, the titles of imperial decorations awarded, and so forth. For instance, the prime minister, who stood next only to the royalty, held the second grade, the chairman of the Privy Council the third grade, the presidents of the House of Peers and House of Representatives the twelfth grade, the Jakō Hall attendants the twenty-first, and the Kinkei Hall attendants the twenty-sixth. All kazoku, even without official positions, received one or another palace seat assignment according to either the kazoku title (shaku) or the court rank (i). Princes were given the sixteenth grade, marquises the twenty-second, barons the thirty-sixth, jugoi (the fifth, junior, rank) the forty-fifth, and so on (Kazoku Kaikan 1933, 97–106).

This imperial seat hierarchy was occasionally activated even away from the palace. In the military, when men lined up for national holiday ceremonies, the usual military ranks were superseded by the palace seat ranks. On the emperor's birthday, a baron's heir with jugoi rank who was also an ensign stood before the emperor's picture to bow, next only to the commander—to the great resentment of other officers. If he were higher than the commander in the imperial seat hierarchy, I was told, he would have been sent away that day on some contrived mission to prevent embarrassment. The kyūchū sekiji was theoretically abolished after the war but in fact survives latently (Satō 1987, 15–16), as several of my informants confirmed.

Instead of visiting the palace, to receive royalty at one's own home would be the most extraordinary honor. The Shimazu, for instance, hosted Emperor and Empress Taishō at their Sodegasaki mansion in 1917; the Maeda received the Meiji imperial couple as well as the crown prince and princess at their newly built main mansion in 1910, an event involving extravagant preparation and production as described by a daughter on the basis of her grandmother's recollections (Sakai 1982, 44–51). Also, Haru Reischauer (1986, 101) writes:

> Starting with a visit to Prime Minister Itō's residence in 1885, the emperor and empress began making visits from time to time to the homes of the leading ministers, honoring Matsukata, Yamagata, and Kuroda in this way in 1887. These imperial visits were grand occasions. The emperor would be accompanied by a retinue of imperial princes, chamberlains, and the minister of the imperial household and his higher subordinates. The host would provide elaborate entertainment as well as a sumptuous dinner, and the emperor would give him in return a set of silver sake cups with the imperial crest, a larger gift of an art object, and a thousand yen.

When the emperor traveled far away from Tokyo, he might be offered a locally based aristocratic residence as his lodging. The Mōri, for example, were honored by a series of imperial stays at their residence in Yamaguchi Prefecture. There, the mansion that served as a lodging for

Emperor Meiji in 1911 is still preserved as a "sacred site," constituting part of the Mōri's magnificent garden estate (Usukine 1988).

NOMENCLATURE FOR ADDRESS AND REFERENCE

Just as the spatial design of living, involving boundaries, distance, and proximity, is an important status marker, so is the nomenclature used to address and refer to a person. This is especially true in Japanese culture, which permits the use of personal names for only a limited range of situations and speaker-listener relationships, and which lacks equivalents of "I" and "you" usable independently of a particular self-other relationship. To choose a proper term from a pool of possible forms of address, the Japanese speaker must be sensitive to the relative status of those involved in the communication. The choice varies according to who (speaker) is speaking to whom (listener) about whom (referent), in whose (third person's) presence, and under what circumstance. The speaker chooses one possible term of address for the listener and a similarly appropriate reference term for the referent, all in consideration of the various permutations of relationships involved. In short, it is impossible to exhaust the nomenclature used in the kazoku circle. The following summarizes only the most common patterns, with particular emphasis on class difference. Two terminological sets are employed: status terminology and kin terminology.

Status Terminology

Status terminology implies speech contact between status superior and inferior, kazoku and nonkazoku, master and subordinate. Essential to the kazoku nomenclature was an entourage of servants, important players in the speech community. Table 13 summarizes the status terms used by servants and familiar outsiders in addressing *and* referring to the status holders in the kazoku household.[8]

Not all kazoku family members, however, were status holders to be addressed by status terms. The househead, his wife, the heir, and the heir's wife certainly were central to the positional principle of the ie (see chapter 4). The status of the househead's widow and eldest daughter, however, was not so clear-cut: the head's wife, when widowed, assumed a new status, either higher or lower than her previous status depending largely upon her late husband's influence, among other factors; the eldest daughter in some, but not all, households was given a status term, and definitely received one when she was to be the heiress (that is, to be married to an adopted heir).

The first category of status terms symbolically refers to spatial occu-

Table 13. Status Terminology

ADDRESSEE/REFERENT	TERMS[a]	LITERAL MEANING
Spatial terms		
Househead	Tono-sama (or -san)	Lord Mansion (or Palace)
	O-kami	Lord Above
	Gos(u)san	Lord Palace (gosu = gosho)
	Gozen	Honorable Lord in Front[b]
	Denka	Below the Mansion[b]
Wife	Okugata-sama, Oku-sama	Lady Interior
	Gozen-sama	Honorable Lady in Front[b]
Widow	Go-kōshitsu-sama	Honorable Rear Chamber
Seniority (and spatial references)		
Househead	Ō-tono-sama	Senior Lord Mansion (or Palace)
Wife	Ō-oku-sama	Senior Lady Interior
Heir	Waka-tono-sama	Junior Lord Mansion
	Waka-sama	Junior Lord
Heir's Wife	Waka-oku-sama	Junior Lady Interior
	Waka-gozen-sama	Honorable Junior Lady in Front[b]
Eldest Daughter	O-hī-sama	Little Lady (Princess)
Examples of public titles and ranks		
Househead	Hakushaku-sama	Lord Count
	Ichii-sama	Lord First Rank
Heir (at age 21)	Goi-sama	Lord Fifth Rank

[a]Terms are liberally hyphenated in this table to separate prefixes and suffixes from the stems.
[b]See text for clarification of these four terms.

pancy in the domestic setting (reinforcing the point made in the previous section), which was marked by the lordly mansion or palace. Although the literal translations of *tonosama* and related terms may sound comical, they are given here to underline the spatial symbolism of status. All such expressions for the househead should be translated more naturally as

"Your (His) Excellency." Among my informants, the term *tonosama* was most often mentioned, while *gossan* (derived from *gosho,* the palace, or imperial palace in particular) was evidently for higher-ranking kuge, sekke especially. (The retired Tokugawa shogun, however, was called *ōgosho,* "lord grand palace.") The daughter of a daimyo viscount argued strongly that *tonosama* was a postwar term that, under the influence of popular historical TV drama series, had replaced *okami,* the only proper term. Other informants disagreed.

More intriguing are those terms in table 13 marked with a superscript *b.* The word *gozen* (*gozensama* for the wife, for a reason nobody knew), the sinified version of *omaesama* and a distinctly relational term, implies the speaker in front of whom the addressee is seated. Reflexivity between addresser and addressee is more clearly indicated by *denka* ("below the mansion"), referring to the addresser's humble position, which in turn reflects the addressee's exalted position—in such a logical twist that the term for one becomes that for the other. *Denka* is also used for royal princes and princesses (*hi-denka*). A similar linguistic reflexivity is found in *heika,* an honorific term used exclusively for the emperor, empress, and empress dowager, which is of Chinese origin and literally means "below the stair"—a low position symbolically taken by the imperial retainer in speaking upward to a royal personage seated at the top of the stairlike hierarchy. More generally used is *kakka* ("below the high mansion"), applicable to any dignitary. The spatial terms for wife and widow are self-evident: *okugata (sama)* was more dignified and indicative of "ladyship," while *okusama* is a common term for "missus" shared by the middle class. Because terms listed in the table are only representative ones, variation between families was inevitable. If the mansion had a particular name, its head resident may have been identified by that name, as when the widow of a former daimyo was called "Tokiwa-sama" after Tokiwa mansion, where she resided. Such practices are reminiscent of the origins of kuge family names (see chapter 3). Apparently, *oyashikisan* (*yashiki* meaning a residential estate or mansion) was also used by commoners in reference to an upper family.

Spatial terms were (and are) widely used in both direct address and third-person reference. Consider, for example, the most generic term still used for the royalty, adults and children alike: *miya (sama),* with *miya* referring to a venerable house and also meaning a shrine for gods. A distinctly unflattering label is *heyazumi* (room occupant), referring to— though not used in address, of course—a dependent adult son still living in the parental house. A third example comes from the sixty-nine-year-old daughter of a daimyo count. Speaking about her friends and relatives among the kazoku, she insisted that the family names, let alone personal names, were "never" used. Instead, she said, references to geographic places were mandatory, such as Mita-sama (for a Tokugawa branch family residing in Mita) or Owari-sama (for another Tokugawa branch whose ancestors were daimyo of the Owari domain), instead of Tokugawa-sama. The informant's own family was called Sugamo-sama after the district of its Tokyo residence. All this is quite natural to Japanese, since family names were derived primarily from place names to begin with (see chapter 3).

Spatial identification of a person is generally practiced among Japanese. I may distinguish my uncles by their residences, as, for example, "Uncle of Osaka" or simply "Osaka."[9]-*Dono* (from *tono*) is a common honorific suffix, more formal than -*sama,* attached to the name of any person (including women) in formal address, such as Tanaka Kakuei—dono. *Tono* as an independent term, however, cannot be used for anybody except a person of lordly status. Further, instead of "you," a spatial or directional term may be used such as *anata* or, more politely, *sochira (sama)*—literally meaning "over there" or "the other side." These terms are relative to *kochira* ("over here" or "this side") for "I." A small class difference was observed in the usage of directional terms. My female informants used *konokata* ("this side") for "you," and confessed having had a hard time in changing to *anata* after the war. Also used for "you" were *konatasama* and *sonatasama,* which sound to the ordinary contemporary Japanese like words from a historical novel. (A monzeki nun addressed me as "konatasan.")

The second category of status terms, which were often used as prefixes to spatial terms, refers to age or seniority. Generally, only the junior (successor) generation was marked as *waka* (younger), but sometimes the senior generation (headship) was also prefixed with *ō-* (grand).

The third category refers to the names of kazoku titles or court ranks, which, because of their public nature, were used outside the household, for example by the Kunaishō staff or in public documents and the media. As often happens in Japan, however, the public form of status label was then privately adopted within the house. Thus the househead—the only bona fide kazoku title holder in the family—was addressed by the title, such as "Lord Marquis" (*kōshakusama*), while his wife was referred to but not addressed as "Lady Marquise" (*kōshaku fujin*). The titles were used by doormen, for example, in heralding the arrival of title holders to the hosting personnel and their departure to the servants waiting outside. The announcement went: "X Danshaku Kakka [His Excellency Baron X] is about to leave!" One informant recalled these moments as particularly embarrassing.

Some households preferred the use of tradition-loaded court ranks. Kazoku were awarded five numbered ranks, from fifth to first, each of which was further divided into minor (*ju*) and major (*shō*). One started with "fifth, junior, rank" (*jugoi*) with the expectation to rise to fifth senior, to fourth junior, and so on. In practice, however, only the five numbered ranks were significant. Hence, a jugoi holder was called "Goisama," not Jugoisama. Tokugawa Yoshinobu, according to one of his granddaughters, was called "Ichiisama," Lord First Rank (as well as other names, including Kobinata-sama, derived from the district of his Tokyo residence). Since a kazoku heir was entitled to jugoi rank automatically at age twenty-one, he may have been called such without yet being househead; one informant, for example, recalled how Gakushuin girls had started to address him as "Goisama."

Court ranks were based on seniority. Because one was automatically promoted, a change in terms of address was required from time to time. Speed of promotion, moreover, varied according to one's kazoku title: a prince could rise to the first rank by about sixty-four years of age, but a baron had to wait until age ninety-six and thus had virtually no chance to attain the first rank (Sakamaki 1987, 303). In my male informants' narratives I occasionally encountered remarks like "I would have been third rank by now but for the war."

Status promotion, to be accompanied by a new term of address, could happen unexpectedly. A particular daimyo-viscount family is a case in point. When the head died without a son, the family found in his will that he had nominated his youngest brother as his successor—much to the surprise of the nominee and his family. Immediately, the nominee became "Tonosama," and his eldest daughter, my informant, became "Ohīsama." The case of a forty-seven-year-old informant was more picturesque. Born the third son of a daimyo count, destined to lose kazoku status, he was raised as a "nobody." In his forties, he was suddenly called back to take over the heir's position because of his eldest brother's death, and soon thereafter stepped into the headship upon his father's death. Within a year, he was promoted from "Akisama" (derived from his personal, statusless name, Akitoshi) to "Wakasama" (junior lord, the heir) to "Tonosama" (the lord of the mansion).

The last example suggests a pattern of address for statusless children. Those family members without status, that is, temporary members of the ie, were usually called by their abbreviated personal names plus the honorific suffix *-sama:* a son Yoshitomo might be addressed as Tomosama (with *Yoshi* omitted if it was a common character (torina) shared by other male family members); a daughter Masako would likely be addressed as Masasama (*-ko* being a common indicator of the female gender).

Familial Terminology

Within the family, particularly when the children were involved, kin terms were used. As a general rule, kin terms are used only when speaking to persons senior to oneself; children address their parents and grandparents with kin terms but not the other way around, except when an elder addresses an older child teknonymically or vicariously from a younger child's point of view; similarly, younger siblings address older siblings with kin terms, but not the opposite. To avoid redundancy with common Japanese kin terminology in general, I limit my discussion to those familial terms of address that show some class differences. Table 14 lists terms for parents and grandparents only, sibling terms being less class-distinctive. For comparison, prewar standard (common) terms are listed also.

Let me begin with the prefix *o-* and suffix *-sama*. These are both honorifics, and could be entirely deleted in a child's speech; thus they are bracketed in the table. A small child, for example, might call his father and mother "Toto" and "Tata" instead of "Ototosama" and "Otatasama." Likewise, the childish version of *-sama* is *-chama*, as that of *-san* is *-chan* in common speech. A child was thus likely to be addressed as X-chama. According to one informant, her father-in-law, who had succeeded to the headship when he was five years old, was called by his long-time maid "Tonochama" (Your Little Excellency) into his old age.

Notice in the table that the first-listed term for father, *otōsama,* is identical with the standard *otōsan* except in the suffix, which shows *-sama* versus *-san* (or *-chama* versus *-chan*) to be an important index of class difference. Nonetheless, some kuge informants were emphatic in pointing out that the kuge and royalty alike adhered to *-san* in accordance with the Kyoto palace tradition, whereas "*-sama* was of warrior-class invention." Even the emperor and empress were called "Tennōsan" and "Kōgōsan," royal princes and princes were "miyasan." As far as traditionalist kuge families were concerned, therefore, all *-sama*'s in the table should be replaced with *-san*. Obviously, for them, *-san* had greater elitist appeal.

The table shows another characteristic of kuge terminology. High-ranking kuge, particularly sekke and Seigake (see chapter 3), as well as the royalty, used *omōsan* for father, while lower-ranking kuge used *odei-san;* mother for both was *otāsan*. The sekke terms were identical to

Table 14. Kin Terms for Addressing Parents and
Grandparents

	KAZOKU	STANDARD
Father	Otōsama	Otōsan
	(O)toto(sama)	
	Omōsama	
	Odeisama	
	Papa, Daddy	
Mother	(O)tā(sama)	Okāsan
	(O)tata(sama)	
	(O)kaka(sama)	
	Mama, Mommy	
Grandfather	(O)jiji(sama)	Ojīsan
Grandmother	(O)baba(sama)	Obāsan

those for the imperial family, all collateral royal families, and, as I happened to learn, to those of the two Otani families of the Honganji abbots. The Honganji families, though carrying only the kazoku title of count, were (and are) organized according to the imperial model; but the terminological royalization may be due more to sekke or royal women marrying the abbots. *Toto* and *kaka,* by contrast, were apparently terms of daimyo origin. I found that almost no non-kuge kazoku used male kuge terms (*omō, odei*) but that female kuge terms (*tā, tata*) were widespread across different subcategories, including new kazoku. In other words, whereas use of a standard term for father was relatively common among non-kuge families, the same was not true for terms designating the mother. The latter terms, in my view, were freely borrowed from the kuge, probably through a kuge woman marrying in, while the father term, symbolic of ie continuity, tended to resist such assimilation and change.

English terms—*papa* and *mama,* and exceptionally, *daddy* and *mommy* too—were also used in the families that received exposure to Western influence in some phase of their domestic history. As was already mentioned and will be detailed below, the kazoku life-style was more Westernized than that of commoners; these kin terms only underscore that fact. In many cases, traditional terms such as *omō, toto, tā,* and *tata* were thrown out when Western-educated successors imposed the English model on *their* children. The postwar democratization in nomenclature has resulted in the popularization of *papa* and *mama* at all levels of society, thus divesting these terms of any particular status distinction. Kazoku informants emphasized that now their terminology is no different from anybody else's. The trouble is, the term used in one's childhood cannot be easily altered. If the familiar terms are anachronistic and if one is fearful of sounding snobbish, as many of my informants are, one either has stopped using those terms entirely or else alternates between two sets of terms depending on who is present. A woman told me that she and her son, when alone, continue to speak in the old style, with the son calling his mother "Tata"; in front of her daughter-in-law and grandchildren, however, the two switch to "ordinary" language.

This kind of situational adjustment occurred in the prewar setting as well, though for a different reason. Children would use kin terms for their parents, and the latter would use the same terms as self-references when speaking to the children. Otherwise, status holders were addressed in status terms. We know that status terms were used not only by servants, but also by adult members of the family when situationally appropriate. The wife in particular was a terminological strategist, switching and alternating from one form to another in addressing or referring to her husband. She would use status terms like Lord Count, Lord Fourth Rank, Tonosama, or Gozen if she was talking to a servant or to her husband in the presence of a servant. She might assume a servile position vicariously and temporarily, or go back to a personal name for her husband, like "Michi-sama," when the couple was left alone, and to a kin term like "Papa" in the presence of a child. In many cases, however, the wife used the husband's status name rather consistently, except when talking to her children, regardless of the presence of a servant. Perhaps she simply never became accustomed to using his personal name, as is the case with many old-generation Japanese wives, but instead internalized his status name as his personal identity; it could also be that the couple was rarely left alone by the otsugi servants, who should be always available.

While the wife assumed a terminologically inferior position, the husband did not reciprocate. He might refer to his wife as "Okusama" when speaking to a servant, but more often he called her by her personal name, with or without -*san*. Status asymmetry between husband and wife was thus striking in terms of mutual address such as "Lord Marquis" versus "Yasuko." Some informants did not recall what their fathers called their mothers, whereas the latter's means of addressing the former were clearly remembered. The couple's internal terminology thus shows that the wife was not quite a status holder.

Oshirushi

Another category of names can be cited as well; called *oshirushi,* these were labels or emblems that children received at birth besides their legally registered names. Unlike the formal name, the oshirushi was for private use within a household. Most common were names of flowers and plants (chrysanthemum, lily, plum, wisteria, violet, iris, peach, peony, *hagi* [clover], *nadeshiko* [pink], bamboo, pine, oak, and so on). Also mentioned in my informants' accounts were names of animals (crane, turtle, hawk, sparrow), heavenly bodies or natural elements (moon, star, morning sun, snow), other objects or concepts (jewel, treasure, fortune). Emperor Shō-wa's oshirushi was Wakatake (young bamboo), and the empress's was Momo (peach). There was no clear-cut gender division except that flower names were given more often to daughters and some animal names like hawk were only for sons. That the list of flowers is longest may be because the oshirushi was more important and unforgettable to women than to men. Each name was pronounced and written as, for example, Kikujirushi (emblem of the chrysanthemum) or Umejirushi (emblem of the plum), or pictorially represented unless the name was an abstract concept like fortune.

By attaching one's oshirushi to one's personal belongings, these could be kept distinct from those of other family members. Mentioned as such belongings were chests of drawers, linens, towels, underwear, *furoshiki* (wrapping cloths), trays, dishes, napkin rings, chopstick containers, slipper bags, *hina* dolls (decorative figurines and paraphernalia displayed on Girls' Day), "whatever you brought in as a bride," and so on. The very need for such identification suggests the large numbers of each item in a household. One sekke family, a daughter of the house recalled, had six sets of hina—two brought by the mother from her natal house and four belonging to each of the four daughters, which on Girls' Day, she said, made a splendid show, displayed across three rooms![10]

The question why an extra name instead of one's legal name was used had to do with who handled and maintained these things. It was, namely, servants who put the oshirushi of each member of the family on these possessions and kept them in order. By means of the oshirushi, a servant could maintain a respectful distance vis-à-vis the personal items of the family. The use of a regular name for this purpose, I was told, would have been considered rude. Many informants also explained the oshirushi practice as an expediency "because it is much simpler to write your oshi-rushi than your name." If so, expediency was combined with the servants' refraining from being too personal.

The oshirushi was further employed in reference to a family member when servants talked about him or her among themselves or recorded his or her moves such as going out and coming home. In the house diary, for example, the omote clerk might write, "Lady Chrysanthemum [Kikujirushisama] left for House X at 10:00 A.M."; "Get a car ready at 4 o'clock to go and meet Little Lady Plum [Umejirushisama]." Apparently, for mutual communication among servants depersonalized identification by oshirushi was considered proper. Some informants recalled, too, that oshirushi had been used in direct address in their mothers' generation, though not their own. I also noted that oshirushi could substitute as a convenient euphemism when an individual's personal identity had to be concealed, as in the case of a womb lady.

Whether one had an oshirushi or not marked a rather distinct polarity between the old kazoku and royalty on the one hand and new kazoku on the other. Among the latter, a typical response to my question regarding oshirushi was "Oh, that was only for kuge" or "Only daimyo families had such a custom." Some men did not know what I was talking about. One can only imagine how children without oshirushi felt when their classmates at Gakushuin discussed the subject, as girls often did. One informant thought she should have one and tried to call herself "Wisteria," but then decided the whole matter was silly and gave up. Some women were convinced that an oshirushi was given at the time of marriage, which is understandable in view of the oshirushi attached to the trousseau. Needless to say, the class polarity was not complete, since there is always an opening through which a higher-class life-style flows downward, as with kin terminology. In the case of oshirushi, the culture was carried across classes primarily by kuge or daimyo daughters marrying down. A hypogamous woman thus played a crucial role in aristocratizing the life-style of upstart nobility, especially in the female domain.

Most informants no longer find any use for oshirushi, but a few continue to give such emblematic names to their children and grandchildren for nostalgic reasons. Occasionally one hears an oshirushi still being used for one purpose or another. Classmates of Princess Teru, the late eldest daughter of Shōwa, for example, formed a still-existing club, Kōbaikai, named after her oshirushi, *kōbai* (red peach).

Nomenclature is a pure symbol that can outlast or compensate for what it represents. For an impoverished kuge kazoku, an empty title could be the last remaining source of pride and distinction, however mixed with self-ridicule. Yet the name was not truly empty, but carried social reality, as long as it was used by others around such as servants— which leads to our next topic.

THE RETINUE

Both the spatial and terminological elaboration of a kazoku household implied the presence of servants in constructing an aristocracy. If one were to identify the single most important factor conditioning the aristocratic life-style, it would have to be the omnipresence of a household retinue. Aristocracy would not exist unless there was a commoner class, and in the immediate environment of a kazoku family, servants represented those commoners. The servants sustained and shaped their masters' status. This section details the symbiotic relationship between the master family and the household retinue, and then briefly discusses the provincial bases of vassalage. (More on servants will appear in the following chapters, particularly chapter 7 regarding the part they played in socializing kazoku children.)

The Domestic Symbiosis of Master and Servant

We have seen how the spatial design of an aristocratic residence presupposed that the servants occupied the omote and oku quarters as well as peripheral areas, and how the spatial boundaries between kazoku and outsiders were maintained through the mediating role of the servants. Further, as the above discussion on nomenclature suggests, the lordly status of the household could not be actualized unless he had at least one servant call him "Lord." This symbiotic relationship involved not only a functional but also a symbolic support of the aristocratic status by servants. A "true" tonosama was symbolized by long lines of servants crouching at the main door to the house, having been alerted by a resounding announcement like "His Excellency is about to leave!" or "The lord has returned!" The presence of retainers was so symbolically indispensable that even the poorest kuge household had to have several servants properly dressed and coiffed "for the sake of *taimen* [honor]" of the house.

How were these servants recruited? In a daimyo household, they likely came from the former domain. The upper managerial staff of the exterior were often identified as kerai (vassals), and the uppermost/innermost maids also came from vassal families. Strictly speaking, therefore, these high-ranking servants were of shizoku origin (the stratum below kazoku and above commoners, composed largely of samurai; see chapter 2). Lower servants, including shosei, also were supplied by the province. Their provincial background was associated with local dialects, which they were supposed to shed but which they retained in communicating with one another; these the Tokyo kazoku children overheard and unwittingly learned, to their later benefit. Other households with no provincial base resorted to various networks for recruitment, including professional go-betweens. Generally, the servants tended to become self-recruiting, in that a servant would introduce a relative or friend to replace someone leaving the retinue. Even a poor household could afford several maids because wages were often negligible: service in an upper-class household was undertaken not for the money, but primarily for "etiquette apprenticeship" and to gain credentials (*haku o tsukeru*) for marriage. "Indeed, many such girls showed up, asking to work for us," said the widowed daughter-in-law of a prime minister. Symbiotic reciprocity seems to have been best actualized by the master-shosei relationship, in which the master funded education (usually night school) for the shosei in exchange for the latter's daytime service.

The number of servants varied greatly from house to house. Generally, the retinues of daimyo households were much larger than those of other kazoku households, and ie that ran house enterprises commanded a much larger exterior personnel than those that did not. The largest number of servants I encountered was 136, "if you counted down to yardmen," and the smallest 4. Some informants did not know how many kitchen maids they had had because they had never seen them. Households with small staffs did not even have an omote/oku distinction of personnel, but in large-staff establishments, each domain was hierarchically organized and labeled variously depending on the house tradition.

In a typical daimyo-kazoku household, the core staff was rank ordered into three levels: at the top was the head manager (*karei*, "a new version of karō" [chief administrator-vassal]; also known as *shitsuji* and *sandayū*); he was assisted by deputy managers (*kafu*); and at the bottom were *kajū* (subordinates). (*Ka* is a sinified term for ie, and in some households the staff as a whole was called *kashoku*.) The oku staff, made up of female servants, were also hierarchically ordered, with the head maid (*rōjo, jochū-gashira,* or *jijo-gashira*) supervising other maids and, in some cases, exercising her exclusive privilege to attend the master or to represent him in ancestor rites. In a household with a large retinue, higher maids were served by lower maids. The maid hierarchy was best illustrated by an eighty-year-old woman's description of her natal Tokugawa house. The house had ten oku maids and ten kitchen maids, four of whom—two from each category—were placed together in one servant room as a team, where the kitchen maids waited on the oku maids. At the top of all was the rōjo, "a fussy old lady," who supervised the total oku retinue. "In a twelve-mat room, all the oku maids sat in a row sewing [when they were not attending the family] while the rōjo, seated at the innermost position, watched them with glaring eyes." It was the responsibility of the head maid to train her subordinates in household tasks and etiquette. The larger the retinue, the more clearly the role of each servant was defined so as not to encroach on another's territory. One informant, a daughter of a large daimyo house, had her own chauffeur, who was assisted by another young man whose job it was to "open and close the car door."

Since private life went on around the clock, the oku servants, all of whom were unmarried, lived in the house so that they would be available at any time. The omote servants, in contrast, commuted from their own tenements (*o-nagaya*), provided by the master on the periphery of the estate, where they lived with their families.

Generally, daimyo kazoku had larger, more hierarchically elaborate retinues than other kazoku, but some new successful kazoku also commanded an enormous number of servants. The Mita residence of Matsu-kata Masayoshi, a powerful leader of Meiji Japan, for example, was staffed by "several dozen servants—almost always twenty maids . . . two cooks, one each for Japanese and Western cuisine, and their assistants, three gardeners, two men to cut firewood, rickshaw pullers, coachmen . . . [and] several *shosei*" (Reischauer 1986, 107). Some more examples are shown below in lists of servants, as recalled by informants:

A daimyo-count daughter, age sixty-nine: thirteen-member entourage of closest vassals [*sokkin*], two chauffeurs, one assistant to the chauffeurs, fifteen maids, two cooks, three lowly maids [*hashitame*];

A supposedly "poor" sekke daughter, age fifty-five: upper maids (two attached to parents, two to grandparents, and one to each child), two kitchen maids, three omote men, one shosei, one janitor-yardman;

A new-kazoku daughter, age forty-four: one shitsuji, two shosei, one chauffeur, one Chinese cook, head maid, maids to each child, mother, and father;

A son of a big daimyo family, age thirty-seven: "About one hundred in total, including gardeners, guards, shosei."

Notice that oku maids were often attached to members of the family one to one around the clock. Such maids were called *otsuki* (attached) and had a strong impact on the kazoku life (see chapter 7). While certain households could not afford such personal service, others had two or more otsuki for each child. The heir of a deroyalized branch of the Prince Fushimi house, for instance, said he had been waited on by four otsuki maids.

Status structure is sustained in basic domestic circumstances by demarcating in various ways the separate spheres of kazoku family and servants. Depersonalization was one such cultural design ensuring status segregation—such as the use of oshirushi by servants to refer to family members. Depersonalization took place in the opposite direction as well, however: namely, downward. The family, adults and children alike, addressed the servants in *yobisute*—that is, by their names only (personal names for maids, family names for omote staff), without the minimal honorific *-san*—while they themselves were addressed with status terms or the polite *-sama* suffix. This downward address was mentioned as an explanation for the common practice of changing a servant's name at the master's (or the head maid's) discretion when her name happened to be identical to a family member's name. Thus Yoshiko might become Toshi. In another case, two jinrikisha men were arbitrarily made to adopt the names "Crane" and "Turtle," respectively.[11] These terminological status boundaries were reinforced by the servant's deferential style of speech, manner, and behavior (such as kneeling) and spatial distance (kept, for example, by speaking to the master from outside his room through the closed door).

Such status distance notwithstanding, the family was totally dependent on the servants for almost everything to keep and run the house—for whatever, in other words, the head and his wife would do in an ordinary household. Servants, male and female, upper and lower, in charge of their respective assignments, took care of financial and social or ritual management, domestic chores, child care, chaperonage, and so on. One would become especially dependent on one's otsuki, above all, if she had long been in attendance. One such otsuki (and head maid) wrote in her obituary to her lady: "for these long years, as long as sixty years, from the beginning when I was twenty up until this day when I am over eighty, I have waited on my lady, never leaving her, not even for a moment, accompanying her wherever she went, shopping or whatever" (Shimazu Shuppankai 1978, 191). It is not that kazoku men and women were incapable of managing the house; rather, they simply accepted the status-appropriate role of dependency, with the result that they lost touch. One informant, trained by a professional culinary artist, knew how to prepare French gourmet and other fancy food, but did not know how to cook rice, the main job of a kitchen maid (who was therefore sometimes called *meshitaki onna,* rice-cooking maid).

Some anecdotes reveal an extraordinary degree of dependency. Because actual transactions in shopping were done by an otsuki, the concept of "buying" was not understood by some old kazoku women. One informant's mother, for example, used to say "take" when she should have said "buy," as if there were no exchange involved. Another mother, after the war, never understood why some people could win in a lottery, but not others, including herself. And apparently a certain aristocrat, after he lost his own car and chauffeur, wondered why a streetcar did not stop where he stood. Scandalous rumors of this sort centering on royal princes circulate freely in the kazoku circle. "Believe it or not, Prince So-and-so, when he traveled to England without his closest otsuki, was nonplussed when no food came into his waiting, open mouth." Reportedly, royal (and some kazoku) attendants were all-around caretakers, not only in feeding, but in bathing as well—which produced princes totally lacking in minimal modesty over nudity and private parts! It is said that lack of bodily shame was the very sign of high birth. The "civilizing process" was work done by servants.

Dependency on vassals and servants for house governance had long historical roots. Not surprisingly, then, it was often a chief vassal's decision that determined the post-Restoration rise or fall of a daimyo house. A granddaughter of Toda Ujitaka, the last lord of Ōgaki, in her autobiography gives full credit to the family karō's wisdom in preventing the house from rebelling against the imperial army: the karō saw the tides coming from the west and, in the midst of the civil war, steered the Ōgaki (fudai) domain from its initial pro-Tokugawa commitment to becoming an imperial ally (Tokugawa 1983, 91). Thanks to this sudden reversal, the Toda prospered in Meiji Japan, and Ujitaka married a daughter of Iwakura Tomomi.

In some instances, servants helped a master not so much by their actual work as by their mere presence in the household. One poor kuge count is said to have written a letter in the name of a fictional kafu to a carpenter asking him to repair the kitchen floor; the use of his own name, of course, would have been too self-denigrating (Yanagiwara 1928, 162).

Dependency gave rise to a strong sense of bonding and inseparability. Some of my women informants admitted that they needed their servants to be constantly present, and both women and men stressed that lifelong ties had developed. Dependency, however, also meant that power and authority were conceded to the caretakers. Indeed, budgetary decisions made by the omote managers could not be easily overruled by the lord; major events like weddings were announced in the name of the management. Equally strong was the power of the head maid. In some households, the head maid was the sole person in charge of serving meals to the lord, as well as dressing him. She was also authorized to visit family cemeteries on ancestral anniversaries to perform *go-daihai* (surrogate worship) on the lord's behalf. Decisions on gift giving were also her responsibility. A young bride, a newcomer from outside, was often dominated by a head maid who had been with the master family for decades: "In my days, the rōjo was more frightening than a mother-in-law."

Symbiosis was thus a source of constraint or frustration as well as support. Even when a servant stepped out of bounds, the master, utterly dependent, could not say a word, a situation that only spoiled the servant further. The constant presence of an otsuki or a chauffeur was not necessarily a blessing; it was also a form of imprisonment. Even a servant's diehard loyalty could be a burden. Many an old maid who had devoted her life to the master family without marrying refused to quit even after the war, thus creating the likelihood of role reversal between care giver and care receiver. "Even when you can no longer afford a servant, you cannot discharge someone who has worked for you for years and years."

During the war, kazoku households began to send their servants home for fear of air-raid casualties, and ended up losing them entirely. Asked in my 1985 questionnaire if they had had "helpers" (*otetsudaisan*) and how many, eighty-four of ninety-eight respondents (86 percent) answered "none," four indicated having had one to three live-in helpers, and ten stated that they had had one or two commuters. The older-generation kazoku could hardly adjust to the change; indeed, some of them are suspected to have died prematurely for that reason. But given the general ambivalence regarding servants, many more—women in particular—welcomed the loss as a "true liberation" that brought them autonomy and privacy.

Views of former servants are divergent. Negative views focus on the fact that many kazoku and royal houses were cheated into bankruptcy after the war by omote staff who took advantage of their managerial monopoly. Princess Nashimoto, for instance, writes about the manager of her royal house who, after the war, took charge of selling house treasures on behalf of his master family and kept the money for himself (Nashimoto 1975, 254–55). Positively, warm relationships are still kept up, even between servants and the children of former kazoku families. Househeads are invited to annual reunions of former servants as guests of honor; former servants who now enjoy a middle-class affluence often visit their erstwhile masters, many of whom live in small apartments, bringing generous gifts. Success stories of former shosei (a banker, a government official, a prefectural governor) are discussed proudly by their onetime masters.

Provincial Connections

The Restoration theoretically removed the daimyo houses from their domains, but understandably, severance was not complete. No matter how far the province (kunimoto) was from the Tokyo residence, it continued to affect the life-style of the daimyo kazoku. When the latter-day lord of a large domain visited the provincial capital (the castle town), school-children were mobilized to welcome him, and local residents, I was told, prostrated themselves on the ground (*dogeza*). One kazoku daughter, on a honeymoon trip to the town, was received by local people kneeling in dogeza as well. It may be that geographical distance preserved the charisma of the urban lord in the townsfolk's eyes.

Yet playing a key role in the maintenance of provincial connections were those local men who held samurai identity and served as liaisons between the province and the capital. These vassals—or more correctly, these descendants of vassals (*kyūshin*)—organized themselves into clubs, kept in touch with their lord, gathered in honor of the visiting lord, and "revived" their ancestors, both by taking seats in accord with the rank order determined by the ancestral rice stipend and by speaking deferentially to the lord in a dated, stiff style of speech. In such gatherings, old status terms like *tonosama* were uttered as a matter of course. These vassals' "loyalty" was reciprocated with hospitality when they visited the lord's mansion in Tokyo. Informants of daimyo descent remembered how their parental houses were always entertaining visitors from the provinces. Among the kyūshin were those who had attained the highest positions in the government and military, including prime ministers and generals, who were now settled in Tokyo. On major holidays and in memorial rites, these successful kyūshin, too, paid their respects to the lord. Through such conspicuous affiliations, then, the two sets of elite, old and new, were able to add to one another's prestige.

Lord-vassal reciprocity, needless to say, was built on the shared memory of ancestors. This meant that memorial rites for daimyo ancestors were on local agenda and heavily involved the vassalage. The daimyo descendant felt obligated not only to his ancestors but also to his contemporary kyūshin in the home province, who would remind him of the ritual calendar, pressure him to provide funds for repairing the shrine or cemetery, and prepare for his "return" visit to preside over the rite. Often he had to go along with the local demand against his own desire. One informant, the grandson of a small-domain lord, had to abandon his wish to conduct the ancestor rite in the Shinto style owing to the (extremely courteous) opposition of Buddhist vassals.

Ancestors and successors were thus more than a family matter. Provincial vassals, in fact, were very insistent that their lords keep up ancestor rites and continue their ie lines by securing successors. It was often the kyūshin who demanded that a son be adopted, who searched for a candidate, if necessary, and who requested that the adopted son change his personal name as well. In response to their demands, the lord would take his heir with him to the local mausoleum. All this is understandable in that the vassals' ancestral resources for self-esteem were interlocked with the continuous presence of a lord. As some of my kazoku informants admitted, all these concerns on the part of the vassals involved a search for their own honorable "roots." This situation has not vanished in the meantime: thirty-one respondents to my questionnaire indicated that kyūshin still gather around them.

In one small social gathering of such vassals around their youthful bachelor lord (let us call him Lord A) to which I was invited in 1985, I raised the question of what would happen if the lord had no son. The vassals, who were of the lord's parents' generation, first looked stunned by such an outrageous suggestion, then reassured me that there would definitely be an heir because they would assume the responsibility of finding a healthy, fertile bride for their master. The master, listening passively, assured these "senior vassals" (*jūshin*) with surprising serious-ness that the choice of a bride would indeed be left to them, not to himself.

Today, the search for samurai roots seems widespread, not restricted to provincial enclaves of vassals. In fact, many vassals' clubs, for a long time virtually extinct, have been revived and expanded in the last couple of decades. Major anniversaries of a famous lord, like his three hundredth death day, are promoted by the local government's tourist board and publicized nationally by the media, attracting not only tourists but also self-proclaimed "vassals" from different parts of the country. On one such occasion I witnessed a visitor showing off his genealogy, which indeed impressed the top vassal and organizer of the pageantry. The latter had been in charge of ordering *kamishimo* (the ceremonial outer garment for high-ranking samurai) on behalf of the pageant participants. Each outfit, custom-made and sporting a family crest, together with a helmet, cost 63,000 yen (approximately $400). The procession of some forty kamishimo-styled samurai was the biggest hit of the whole spectacle.

The profusion of claims to special ancestry is double-edged. "True" vassals complain about the intrusion of false claimants who make vassal club membership worthless. In response, several descendants of top re-tainers from four centuries ago formed an inner circle of senior vassals around Lord A, thus proudly setting themselves apart from the three-hundred-strong vassals' club; one of them even claimed descent from the top vassal of those who had committed loyal suicide upon the death of the "first" lord of the domain. Even this cream of vassalage, however, happened to allow in a foot soldier, the lord's protégé, to the express chagrin of the others. (The foot soldier, by the way, was particularly well informed in the history of the domain, which further irritated the high-ranking samurai.) Such antagonism only indicates the extent to which each participant's self-esteem is at stake. I heard about vassals, drunk at a club party, playing one-upmanship over their ancestors' performances, ranks, koku amount of rice stipend, and loyalty. In the case of Lord A's vassals, the anniversary aroused a heated debate over who should take the upper seats, who should precede whom in approaching the altar in the ritual of incense burning, and so on. The inner-circle vassals were strongly opposed to letting contemporary politicians like the mayor and governor outrank them in seating arrangements and the incense-burning ritual. After all, they argued, what counts is descent.

Some lords have resettled in the provinces, as a result of wartime evacuation, in response to local demand for their constant presence, in order to retire from hectic Tokyo life, or to have another career in the country. The heir of the Hosokawa, who moved to Kumamoto where he was elected governor, is a successful example. Lord A, despite his youth, relocated to the castle town, determined to be "buried" there; he hoped to become director of the museum housing his ancestors' legacy, at the same time offering himself as the focus of the vassals' club.

The risk of resettlement is exemplified by Lord B. When he retired from a salaried job to move to his ancestral province, he received many offers of positions in local companies. It did not take long before he realized that these offers were mutually competitive, that his acceptance of one company would alienate another. Further, once he became a local resident, his conduct and whereabouts would immediately become known to fellow residents through networks of gossip. Consider a local election. For whom would he vote? All the competing candidates were likely to be connected with his family—as the grandson of a lord's physician, great-grandson of a vassal magistrate, or whatnot. In other words, Lord B would not be able to be himself, so completely bound would he be to his role as a key symbol. All these possible conflicts were apparently discussed among the local people, and the general conclusion was that he should stay in Tokyo. Particularly those locals who identified intensely with him detested the idea that their tonosama could be bought commercially. "You are expected to be a pure symbol like an emperor then?" I asked this premature retiree. "Yes, but the emperor would have no problem because his livelihood is funded by the state treasury. Look at me, no income! I cannot live just eating mist." When I saw him again in 1989, he said that he had determined to remain in Tokyo.

In the master-retinue network, the kazoku lord stood at the top of the hierarchy, with all the privileges and constraints accruing to the status.

In wider society, however, he found others to look up to. Even within the kazoku "peerage" rank differences obtained, and a new kazoku, descending from vassal status, would have to humble himself in the presence of descendants of his ancestors' lord. Extreme ambivalence was expressed toward such a superior: "natural" and "irresistible" deference on the one hand, and resentment and outright hostility on the other. While the hierarchical orientations among kazoku were thus variable and antagonistic, they converged in veneration of the emperor and the imperial house. Yet there was another apex for the kazoku to look up to, and that was the Western world.

WESTERNIZATION: CIVILIZATION AND ENLIGHTENMENT

Meiji Japan was a zealous convert to the new religion called "Civilization and Enlightenment," for which it sought inspiration in the West, the "faith's" originator. Westernization predated the Restoration, for the Tokugawa and domainal (Satchō in particular) governments had already sponsored Western learning primarily to improve military technology. The post-Restoration oligarchy, committed to sweeping, overall modernization, took a leadership role in effecting the national conversion, as exemplified by the Iwakura mission (1871–73) to Europe and the United States. Iwakura was accompanied by some hundred men, including Ōkubo Toshimichi, Kido Takayoshi, and Itō Hirobumi, the top architects of the Meiji government (Soviak 1971). The urgency of large-scale Westernization was voiced by the political and intellectual elites alike. Some of the proposals were quite radical. Inoue Kaoru urged, "Let us change our Empire into a European-style Empire. Let us change our people into European-style people"; a University of Tokyo professor advocated the Christianization of Japan; Nishi Amane favored the adoption of an alphabet to replace the traditional writing system; and Takahashi Yoshio proposed that the weak Japanese race be improved through intermarriage with Caucasians (Shively 1971, 91–94). (The pro-Westernization fever predominated up until the 1880s, when the nativistic or Confucian counterforces gained momentum, culminating in the 1890 promulgation of the Confucian-inspired Imperial Rescript on Education.)

Conversion

The trend of this time was best reflected in my informants' recollections regarding their grandparents, somewhat less so in those about their parents, and least in their own experiences. While "Civilization and Enlightenment" was a widely accepted slogan, it is unlikely that the commoner class had either the opportunities or the resources to convert it into real life. The urban upper class, in contrast, was well positioned to translate the idea into a life-style, the abstract ideology into a tangible reality. My informants' forebears thus came into direct contact with the Western world. They studied as *ryūgakusei* (students abroad) or cultural apprentices in residence overseas, or under imported foreign tutors. They socialized with foreigners as hosts and guests, and many had diplomatic or military careers requiring years of residence abroad. Through such contact many of these men became fluent in English, French, or German—fluent enough to keep a diary and read newspapers in a foreign language, as some informants claimed about their forebears. One seventy-year-old informant, as a child, had accompanied her father, a military attaché to a royal prince, to England, was schooled there, and as a result feels more comfortable with English than with Japanese, even today. Her talk in interview was interspersed with English words, as if she could not think of Japanese equivalents. Interestingly, Gakushuin students are said to be better at English conversation than grammar, in contrast to students of other schools programmed by the Education Ministry.

Westernization produced many cultural brokers among established and aspiring elites, who had two chief purposes: to fulfill the patriotic mission of contributing to the nation's self-transformation, and to seek advancement through a successful career. Furthermore, being able visibly to display that one was *haikara* ("fashionable," after the high collar of Victorian dress) was taken as an aristocratic status marker. Indeed, "the aristocratic class is itself a sort of Western colony, since its members are almost always expected to be more 'Westernized' than the Japanese middle class" (Miyoshi 1974, 54).

Westernization ended up meaning that one lived a double life, Western and Japanese, trendy and traditional. This (often marked) polarity was expressed by the architectural double of *yōkan* (Western) and *nihonkan* (Japanese) residential space, or better yet by the incongruous combination of the traditional kimono plus *hakama* (long pleated trousers) and Western leather shoes for the Gakushuin female uniform. The daughter of a man who had spent thirteen years in France as a ryūgakusei claimed that she had never in her life eaten *miso* soup and rice for breakfast; rather, breakfast was "purely French," prepared by a French cook who had been brought over by her father from France. Lunch, however, was Japanese, prepared by Japanese cooks, and dinner was a mixture. The daily family life, she further commented, was Western, while major ceremonies, like New Year's observances, were conducted in a strictly traditional manner, attended by kamishimo-styled former vassals.

Many kazoku were enthusiastic converts and went to extremes in emulation, however selectively. As a businessman's daughter recalled, her father, after traveling in Europe and America for less than a year to study industries, returned totally converted. "After that time, he never wore kimono again, his children were always dressed in the Western style, and pajamas were worn at night. No double life." The house was Japanese, but on the tatami mats carpets were spread, chairs placed, and *futon* were replaced by beds. Tokugawa Motoko in her autobiography (1983, 99) describes her grandparents' yōkan as having about fifteen rooms decorated with Louis XVI–style furniture, Persian rugs, and brilliant chandeliers, topped off by a central heating system and water heater. Chandeliers and carpets were mentioned by several informants, daimyo, kuge, and new kazoku alike, as indicating their grandfathers' trendiness. The fashionable grandfather of another informant was the first in the nation to possess such opulent private cars as Rolls Royces, wore only British-made clothing, smoked Egyptian cigars, and had as his family doctor Dr. Baelz, the famous German physician who, at the Japanese government's invitation, came to Japan in 1876, teaching medicine at the University of Tokyo for many years while practicing his profession primarily among the elites. Unequaled in the grandeur of their Western life-style was, again, the Maeda family, who spent years in England socializing with the British aristocracy. Even back home, Lady Marquise "always" ordered dresses following the styles of the English royalty that appeared in an English graphic magazine—that of the duchess of Kent for herself, and that of Princess Elizabeth for her daughter (Sakai 1982, 108).

Westernization in terms of material culture—housing, furniture, food, dress, possessions—is not surprising, but Western emulation had other, more striking aspects. Some Westernized parents, for example, demanded that their children call them "Papa" and "Mama," greet them in English—"Good morning"—or French—"Bon soir"—and even kiss them; the children's room was called the "nursery," in English; and foreign governesses were hired. Some fathers practiced the rule of "ladies first" for their wives and daughters; a man who associated closely with foreign diplomats might entertain them always in the company of his wife, and he was sure to take her with him when invited to embassies; butlers were hired to receive foreign guests; and guests might be entertained at "garden parties" imported from England. According to one informant, once a month the family invited a group of French guests, hiring a whole crew of Seiyōken cooks. A father, while traveling in England, was impressed with the Boy Scouts, took the initiative in organizing Japan's Boy Scouts, and imposed the "Boy Scout spirit" on his own children. Another man, advised by an influential Meiji oligarch well versed in the Western way of life, decided to purchase a ranch because "big Western businessmen have ranches." Sports were a major activity engaged in by many kazoku, men and women alike, because "that is what European aristocrats do all the time."[12]

Rokumeikan

All this links the kazoku to the historical landmark Rokumeikan, a reception hall designed by Josiah Conder, a famous British architect, and completed in 1883 as the first national center to bring foreign and native dignitaries together socially. It was Foreign Minister Inoue Kaoru who decided that Western-style balls, parties, and bazaars held in a Western building would raise Japan's status in the eyes of the civilized Western powers and induce them to agree to proposed revisions of unequal treaties. A number of my informants said that their grandmothers had danced in Rokumeikan. The "Era of Rokumeikan" was short-lived, however, and the building soon became a symbol of notoriety representing superficial Westernism and the extravagant license of the privileged class. Equal treaties did not come about, and Rokumeikan fever subsided under the swelling tide of nationalism. The building was sold to the Fifteenth National Bank (chapter 3), and finally became the Kazoku Clubhouse.

However scandalous the whole affair became, Rokumeikan participants were serious, their descendants recalled. For one person's grandmother, going to the hall was a matter of life and death because "you never knew what was in store for you on your way, where you might fall into an ambush." Far from being jovial and having a good time, she was tense and duty bound to demonstrate the high level of Japanese culture. "Given her strong character, Grandmother must have learned to dance very quickly, because the Rokumeikan's rule forbade a woman to turn down a dance request from a foreign man." When she went out to study English with a foreign tutor, she wore men's clothes for self-protection and was escorted by male servants. She trained herself in horseback riding, too, so as to be able to join foreigners on equestrian outings. The post-Rokumeikan generation, however, began to revert to a more conservative life-style. The daughter of this strong-willed, daring woman led a subdued, domestic life as the wife of a military officer.

Westernization went deeper than the superficial efforts symbolized by Rokumeikan. Many kazoku developed a cosmopolitan outlook; they were unsympathetic to Japan's military expansionism, an attitude that was more or less retained by their World War II–era descendants, who from the very beginning saw the war as doomed to defeat and offended patriots by their irreverent remarks or use of "enemy language." Some, however, went in the opposite direction. After all, military service was compulsory for royal princes and encouraged for kazoku men as well. Critical as he was of the Japanese, and kazoku in particular, being copycats, one informant's father still adored the aristocratic friends he had studied with at Oxford for their *noblesse oblige*. During World War I, his British peers had joined the military as rank-and-file soldiers and were killed one after another in the battlefields. "The British royalty and nobility have a strong sense of duty to dedicate their lives to the state in times of crisis, not like the Japanese kazoku." That is why his son, the informant, became a professional soldier, and his narratives are loaded with serious expressions of status mission.

Westernization for kazoku generally meant emulating the life-style of European aristocracy, and yet the foreign, particularly American, model contained an egalitarian element as well. The "commonerlike" style of a grandfather or father, "atypical of kazoku," was credited to their American education. Further, when fathers or grandfathers, in rejection of their forebears' sexual laxity, remained strictly monogamous, their discipline was often attributed to Western, especially Christian, influence.

In their assimilation of Western people and culture, the kazoku as a whole were at least a few generations ahead of most other Japanese, who began to participate only after World War II. Even the wartime generation of kazoku was not totally rid of the ancestral intercultural heritage; thus Gakushuin, the girls' division in particular, continued to teach "enemy" languages when other public schools dropped them. After the war, the cultural storehouse, handed down over generations, was again tapped to give kazoku descendants a headstart in readjusting to an American-occupied Japan. With fluent English and intercultural savoir faire, many survived the difficult times by filling the role of cultural interpreter or liaison. Some women earned a living in that capacity, sustaining their families and building their careers around it. The same situation produced expectable instances of union between kazoku women and foreign officers.

At present, Japan is faced with the maladjustment problem of returnees from abroad. The same problem was encountered by kazoku returnees before the war. A son of one Meiji leader studied at Eaton, Harrow, Oxford, Cambridge, Harvard—"all these institutions for twenty years"—and became a professor at the Tokyo University of Foreign Languages; yet unable to adjust to his native milieu, he ended up "dissipating all the family property." A kazoku couple, returning from a long residence in Europe, found themselves no longer able to stand the constant presence of a large entourage; they thus moved to a "foreigners' village," taking with them only two maids. Another couple, while living in New York, had enrolled their daughter in a local kindergarten; upon their return, they found her a misfit in the Japanese school system. In such instances, missionary or nonstandard schools like Jiyūgakuen served as halfway stations; Keimei Gakuen, a school built by the Mitsui family that is still in existence, was specifically for the children of diplomats and businessmen returned from abroad.

LEISURE ACTIVITIES

Royal princes, destined to enter the military, were absolutely prohibited from taking up any occupation. Nor were kazoku free in the choice of career (see chapter 8), not so much because their decisions were subject (as they claimed) to approval by the Sōchitsuryō, but because they or their kinsmen constrained their choice for the sake of family honor. Entering the military or taking a seat in the House of Peers was the most legitimate route, but it could hardly be considered a profession. Many kazoku thus opted to spend their time and energy in pursuit of various hobbies. Again, kazoku, thanks to their ascribed leisure—due to both economic freedom from work and occupational restriction—were ahead of today's prosperous Japanese by half a century or more in that their leisure engagement was typically that of postindustrial society, more a primary focus than secondary to work, and more active than passive (Linhart 1988). Leisure activities turned out to be much more than mere pastimes.

Many men and women took to athletic pursuits, mostly of Western origin such as skiing, skating, sailing, swimming, mountaineering, tennis, and horseback riding. Traditional martial arts like archery, *jūdō,* and *kendō* were also practiced. While some athletes were just "play boys" switching from one sport to another, others became devoted to one or another specialty, achieving national or international reputations. One informant's father studied figure skating from imported textbooks first, and then took advantage of his honeymoon tour to Europe by staying there with his bride for two years, visiting "all the skating rinks in Switzerland and Austria," in order to master the technique. "He brought it back home and organized the figure skating association of Japan, which he headed throughout. . . . It was my father who trained Olympic hopefuls." Amazingly, he was a business executive at the same time.

When informants discussed their own athletic involvement, their enthusiasm could lead them to spend the whole interview on the topic. In one two-and-a-half-hour interview, a slim seventy-seven-year-old viscount discussed almost nothing but his athletic career as a runner, in which he attained international recognition. He is proud of having specialized in a sport that is the most "truthful of one's ability, with no room for tricks." His mundane occupation as a company employee was apparently unsatisfactory and not a favorite subject of discussion. He still runs. Another man, a bunke (branch house) head, took to sailing in rebellion against the "feudalistic oppression" of the honke (main house) authority; he has been involved for fifty years in the sport, which brought him an imperial medal.

Traditional martial arts were practiced more for discipline or even for "work" than for sports or leisure. When I asked a certain couple what kind of job the husband had, they said in unison, "*Yabusame* [a ritual performance of archery from a galloping horse] and archery." Before the war, on the fifth of every month, the husband and several of his former vassals performed yabusame before a crowd of commoner spectators, a practice that lasted until all the horses were mobilized for war. The interviewees considered this ritual an obligatory work to preserve the tradition of the ie.

There were other rationales for athletic preoccupations. Athletics built up a "true" aristocratic body and character, tough and disciplined. One informant repeated what his father said in discriminating proper from improper sports: "British noblemen stay away from game sports in avoidance of those sycophants who try to please a master by deliberately losing the game. This is why they undertake one-man sports only, such as sailing, horseback riding, shooting." "The wind would not flatter a sailing king by changing its force, nor would an untamed horse stop being unwieldy when mounted by a king." So the informant sailed and rode from his childhood, and he had his own son do the same, which resulted in a tragedy: the drowning of his only son. In this informant's view, aristocratic sports should be a vehicle for an aristocrat to test his genuine self, to become himself, stripped of status.

A contrary view was expressed as well. Horseback riding was compulsory from time to time in the Gakushuin curriculum for boys, officially as part of martial training (Gakushuin Hyakunenshi Hensan Iinkai [hereafter cited as GHHI] 1981). According to a Gakushuin graduate in his fifties, however, the real purpose was "to train the students to be able to ride with European aristocrats and to handle horses gracefully." I have no evidence to support this claim, but it reminds one of the grandmother quoted above who did ride with Europeans at the peak of the Rokumeikan era. Most likely, a single activity, like horseback riding, served several different purposes: to divest oneself of status dependency or to act out status distinction, to endure solitude or to socialize with status peers.

Sociability seems an important factor in leisure activities, especially when status superiors like royals are involved. Some informants' fathers were tutors for royal princes or princesses in skiing or skating, and informants themselves have participated with royals in sporting events as well. Companionship in athletics, it seems, provided an unprecedented intimacy with the royalty that would otherwise have been taboo. In view of the privileged network thus created through sports participation, the craze in present-day Japan for athletic club membership (in golf and tennis) is not surprising, its epidemic spread across classes only contributing to an escalation in already astronomical admission fees. Associated with this fever, too, may be the exaggerated Cinderella story begun with the tennis match of the then crown prince and princess-to-be (the present emperor and empress).

Kazoku pursued other, less physical hobbies also. One informant's father, a daimyo viscount, while enrolled at Cambridge University took to studying insects, and thereafter tropical fish, then birds, and so on. "According to my mother, his hobbies changed in a five- to ten-year cycle," and each time he became obsessed. At the time of our interview, the father was devoted to photography, with all the paraphernalia for processing and printing—thus following in a long kazoku tradition of being "camera crazed," which even included the last shogun, Tokugawa Yoshinobu. Among other gentlemanly pursuits were ornithology, orchid cultivation, and oil painting, as well as collecting art. Through fieldwork I also found a prewar connection between some kazoku students and Hawaiian music, which has been revived since the war's end.

Traditional arts such as noh drama, utai, waka poetry, calligraphy, and black-ink painting were also practiced, particularly by women; among men, such pursuits were not as popular as things Western. Important to women was the fact that participants were organized into small groups, allowing for periodic reunions of kazoku peers or Gakushuin classmates. One male informant of kuge descent, and an author, however, became so engrossed in Heian literature, *The Tale of Genji* especially, that nothing else interested him. While listening to him, I began to lose a sense of temporal distance between the Genji era and today. He is one of those kazoku who, though deeply influenced by the Westernization fever of their ancestors, connect themselves through their hobbies to the ancient court culture created and expressed by the kuge. Several of these men participate as reciters in the New Year's poetry party (*utakai*) at the imperial palace; one confessed that the event gives him a significant spiritual boost. Some of my informants continue to submit poems to the imperial court (*ken'ei*, dedication of poems to the emperor) monthly as a matter of ritual.

Further, a number of kazoku, male and female, have remained involved in *gagaku*, court music.[13] I observed one instrumental practice session held in a tatami-matted room within the music hall of the palace. Twenty-two players in total were seated in an angular U form, six men and six women on the upswings of the U facing each other, and ten men occupying the bottom line, with an imaginary royal audience sitting on the open-ended side. The seat arrangement, according to one of the players, conformed to the ancient rule, which clearly divided the in-palace nobles (denjōbito) from the ground-bound non-noble retainers (jige): the six men and six women close to the audience were kazoku, whereas the ten bottom-line players were professional court musicians "of jige rank," employed by the Kunaichō.[14] Kazoku lay players, largely but not entirely of kuge origin, were dependent on the professionals—including a drummer, who was an unobtrusive conductor—and yet appeared to make up the main part of the orchestra, playing a whole range of gagaku instruments (winds, strings, and percussion). Toward the end of the one-hour practice, a kazoku leader instructed me, the only nonplayer present, to stand up and the players to remove the floor cushions from underneath themselves, in honor of the late Teimei (Empress Taishō) when her poem was about to be performed. This gagaku club had been formed in response to the empress's personal wish to preserve gagaku. The club, assisted by the jige musicians, would display the fruits of weekly practice for imperial ceremonies on a real stage, replaying their kuge ancestors in full court dress.

In this chapter I have attempted to draw status boundaries within the aristocracy by pointing out salient features of life-style. As we have seen, these status boundaries sustained and allowed the exhibition of the privileges, honor, and prominence of the hereditary elite, but at a great cost. The spatial and social protection of the status holder meant confinement and constraint. The double occupancy of the interior and front regions, without access to the exterior and rear regions—a fact concomitant with the status of hereditary elite as both public and private—ended up further interiorizing the status holder. The emperor, as the most extreme example, was thus enshrined like a god who is hidden and whose supernatural potency can be exercised not by himself but only by magicians outside the shrine.

Spatial segregation and terminological exaltation presupposed the ubiquitous presence of servants, who collaborated in sustaining and enhancing the master's prestige, and even power and economic well-being, but at the same time were in a position to take advantage of the master's dependency on them. That is, inasmuch as dependency entailed power-lessness, the symbiotic relationship between master and retainer could mean the latter's exploitation and domination of the former. Here was a miniversion of the dyarchy of status and power, of symbolic prestige and administrative reality.

If aristocratic status was marked by spatial segregation, it was con-versely enhanced by spatial and social proximity both to the imperial house and to representatives of the Western elite or their culture. The imperial house embodied the roots and justification for the nobility, whereas the West became a model to guide them.

Westernization, too, involved a dimension of duality. On the one hand, as we saw in chapter 3, it provided an opportunity for an ambitious man to shed his humble background and to break into the closed society of the aristocracy. For such a person, Western learning was bread and butter: it promised equality, mobility, achievement, and power. In this chapter we looked at the opposite side of the duality. Westernization not only shaped an aristocratic style of taste but also validated the elite status: thus it played a symbolic, cultural, theatrical role in elaborating and expressing ascribed status and hierarchy. This did not necessarily lead only to superficiality, as exemplified by Rokumeikan; rather, it was pos-sible to go far beyond the instrumental use of Western technology (*yōsai*) while retaining the Japanese spirit (*wakon*), to assimilate the Western way of life culturally and spiritually. Many informants had internalized *yōkon* (Western spirit) as well, both through their own experience and under the influence of their forebears—which in turn, in some instances, had caused profound difficulties in adjusting to Japan's mainstream.

1. The royal wedding of Prince and Princess Kitashirakawa Nagahisa in 1935. The couple is wearing traditional court dress; bride in *jūnihitoe*, groom in *ikan-sokutai*. Princess Sachiko, a daughter of a Tokugawa branch family, is the chief lady-in-waiting upon Empress Dowager Nagako, the widow of Emperor Shōwa. The princess was widowed in 1940. (Photo courtesy of Kitashirakawa Sachiko)

2. Marchioness Hosokawa Kōko, wife of Marquis Hosokawa Morishige, head of a major daimyo family. The marchioness is dressed in *robe décolletée* to visit the Imperial Palace to celebrate Emperor Meiji's birthday. Taken about 1907. (Photo courtesy of Nagaoka Hideko)

3. Viscount Katano Masayuki, born in a daimyo family, the Naito, and adopted into a *kuge* family, is dressed in modern court attire (*tai-reifuku*) to attend the Imperial Palace for commemoration of the late Emperor Meiji's birthday. Taken in 1921, the tenth year of Emperor Taishō's reign. (Photo courtesy of Katano Masahiro)

4.   Members of Count Ōmura's household in front of their newly built residential house in Azabu. Count Ōmura Sumio, an adopted son-in-law coming from a branch of the Shimazu family, is standing on the left side, away from the group. Standing in the front row are the managerial staff; a *shosei* is at the right end. The three women seated in the back row are the countess (an Ōmura daughter); the countess's daughter, who is married to the absent heir and adopted son, Sumihide (an army officer on duty during the Russo-Japanese War); and the uterine mother (*seibo*) of the countess. Among the women standing, who are largely maids, is the count's concubine (*sokushitsu*). The photograph was taken in 1905, with a European camera, and developed and printed by the count himself. (Courtesy of Katsuta Naoko)

5. Katano Masahiro, Viscount Masayuki's son and a Gakushuin student, appears as one of the *osusomochi*, train holders for the empress and princesses during the New Year's reception at the Imperial Palace. In this style, probably after the British court model, the boy has a wide-brimmed, feathered hat and a dirk hanging over his shoulder. The photograph was taken in 1938. (Courtesy of Katano Masahiro)

6. *Kazoku* children with their personal maids (*otsuki*) in 1904. Their grandfather, Fukuoka Takachika, was ennobled to the rank of viscount in 1884 because of his distinguished leadership in the Meiji Restoration and new government. (Photo courtesy of Saneyoshi Momiko)

7. A group of former *kazoku* studying the art of court dressing under the guidance of a representative of a *kuge* house, the Taka-kura, known for its house art (*ieryū*) of dressing. (Photographed by the author in 1982)

8. Samurai-style "vassals" in parade, walking toward the main shrine, in Sendai, of the first ancestor of their domain lords, Date Masamune, to commemorate the 350th anniversary of his death in 1636. The front banner says, "Direct descendants of those loyal vassals who killed themselves to follow their master in death." (Photographed by the author in 1985)

9.   Tokugawa Tsunenari, the eighteenth "shogun," with his wife, a select group of "vassals," and others attending the annual memorial rite for the founder of the Tokugawa shogunate, Ieyasu, at Tōshōgū Shrine, Nikkō, in 1991. Except on such special occasions, the contemporary shogun is a company employee in a business suit. (Photo courtesy of Tokugawa Sachiko)

10. The Shinto-style grave of a royal prince in the imperial mausoleum of Toshi-magaoka, Tokyo. (Photographed by the author in 1982)

11. An estate of a former daimyo house, the Hosokawa, in Kumamoto, with a shrine built in 1878 to deify prominent ancestor lords as Shinto gods. The estate has been converted into a public park called Suizenji. (Photographed by the author in 1985)

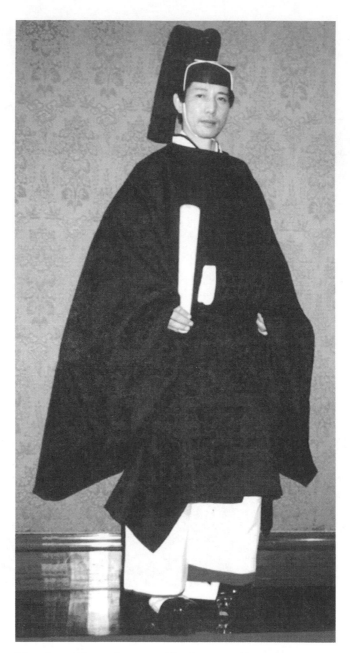

12. Sono Motonobu, one of the former nobles invited to serve as temporary palace ritualists (*shōten*), who assisted the new emperor, Akihito, with the religious and private phase of his enthronement ceremonies (*daijōsai*) in 1990. The Sono is a *kuge* house carrying the *ieryū* art of flower arrangement called Seizan Goryū, and Motonobu is grandmaster (*iemoto*) of the school. (Photo courtesy of Sono Motonobu)

13.   One of the dancing girls, dressed with the help of the two *kazoku* women, to perform the *gosechi* dance to celebrate the 1990 *daijōsai*. The *gosechi* dance, with its long history dating back to the reign of Emperor Tenmu (673–86), was performed in the emperor's presence at various ceremonial court banquets, the most important of which was that of the *daijōsai*. Dancing girls used to be recruited from *kuge* daughters. (Photo courtesy of Yamao Kimiko)

SIX

Marriage

Realignment of Women and Men

In discussing ancestors and successors in chapters 3 and 4, we took individual households as units of analysis, and emphasis was on the lineal continuity of each household. While marriage, too, could be seen in the same light as instrumental to the production of legitimate successors to the house, this chapter examines matrimony more as a realignment between households (or householders), involving cross-generational discontinuity and the reconstitution of the unit house through an outsider's entry as well as the departure of nonsuccessor insiders. Although marriage is the primary topic here, adoption or a combination of adoption and marriage (son-in-law adoption) is also reconsidered in terms of the generational reshuffling of sons, as opposed to the successional continuity of a house. Spouse selectivity is one important measure for the rigidity of hereditary stratification (consider, for example, the caste endogamy of Hindu society). Whether or not a particular kazoku could cross the status boundary in selecting a spouse will be an important point of consideration.

It is safe to assume that among the elite marriage, like adoption, was more heavily "positional"—taking place between social or at least emotional strangers as arranged by a third party—than "personal"—based on the partners' own choice, and possibly motivated by love. The former reflects the interest or discretion of the third party more than that of the principals, and concerns status congruity more than personal compatibility. Nevertheless, the elite tendency to engage in positional marriage notwithstanding, it would be unlikely for the married couple to be aloof from the personal, emotional, and sexual aspects of marriage. In this chapter I examine how the positional nature of marriage was manifested and how the "personal" side of it spilled over and was handled. As might be expected, the positional and personal sides of marriage often diverged, but convergence also occurred. Although personal marriage is more characteristic of today's generation across all classes, it is not in opposition to positional marriage, as we shall see.

The previous chapters have been relatively male-centered, focusing more on male ancestors, successors, and householders, but here we meet more women and enter further into the female realm of experiences. As in other classes and other societies, marriage in aristocratic Japan had a great impact on women's lives, causing a sharp break between two stages of life, pre- and postmarital.[1] Women thus have much to say about it— and had in the past as well, as the stories my informants tell of their mothers and grandmothers make clear. I hope that this chapter will bring to life the cultural notions of gender held by Japanese in general, and the nobility in particular.

FROM POLITICAL ALLIANCE TO STATUS VALIDATION

Positional marriage was first manifested in the form of political alliances in the pre-Meiji period. The ruling class exploited political opportunities in transferring children in marriage (whereas marriage of lower-class children meant simply a gain or loss of laborers for their parents). This practice goes back to the prehistoric or mythological ages: for example, Prince Mimaki, later known as Emperor Sujin, who supposedly emerged as the first ruler of the Yamato region in the early fourth century, allied himself with the chieftains of several distant regions through multiple marriage (Aoki 1974, 23; Philippi 1968, 199).

More familiar to us is the ascendancy of the Fujiwara (see chapter 2), who married their daughters to emperors and crown princes, thus enabling Fujiwara men to control the throne. Their marriage politics began in the Nara period, but the Fujiwara golden age was associated particularly with the line's monopoly of the sesshō and kanpaku (sekkan) offices in the middle Heian period, which were held only by those Fujiwara men whose daughters (or sisters) married emperors and gave birth to imperial heirs. In other words, imperial kin status as either *gaiseki* (affine) or gai-sofu (maternal grandfather, still regarded as "external" to the imperial patriline), achieved through marriage politics, was a necessary credential for sekkan appointments.[2]

The medieval age brought the shogunal-warrior class to the center stage of marriage politics. Daughters and sons were circulated as pawns for alliances between buke and kuge, shogun and sekke, or one warlord and another. According to a Konoe descendant and historian, the five sekke houses alternated throughout the warrior period in establishing nuptial bonds with the shogunal houses. Between warring clans, women were transferred as hostages for peace settlements, as tokens of allegiance, or even as disguised spies. Such ruthless politicization of marriage climaxed during the warfare period leading into the unification phase of Nobunaga, Hideyoshi, and Ieyasu, a span covering one and a half centuries (Kuwata 1972). The Tokugawa shogun, even after their regime was stabilized, continued to offer their daughters not only to loyal or kin-related daimyo, but also to potentially hostile and powerful tozama daimyo houses.

Take the destinations, for example, of the twenty-five children (listed in *KKT*) of Tokugawa Ienari, the eleventh shogun (table 15). Of his thirteen daughters, three were married into Tokugawa branch houses (members of the dōzoku), three into houses of tertiary kinsmen of Tokugawa (shinpan) with the surname of Matsudaira, and seven into other, mostly large tozama daimyo houses such as Nabeshima, Mōri, Maeda, Ikeda, and Asano. Sons were all, with only one exception, adopted into either branch or shinpan houses. These figures show that daughters made better political capital than sons, at least from their giver's point of view. From the receiver's perspective, a shogunal daughter thus marrying down (called *osumaisama,* "lady in residence," referring to the separate mansion built for the bride and her retinue) was usually an unwelcome honor, yet acceptance was politically mandatory. An informant and Tokugawa descendant apologetically expressed her ancestral guilt, saying, "It must have been a vexatious imposition for the receiving house" (as her husband's house had often been). At the same time, the shogunate exercised control over marriages and adoptions among daimyo across domains to forestall seditious alliances, a control that extended to the kuge as well.

It seems that a child, apolitical as long as it remained in its natal house, became politically potent when it moved to another house. The Tokugawa shogunate thus was not concerned about the births of sons at daimyo or kuge houses; it did, however, require a special petition for son adoption (and marriage). Frequently, as a consequence, adoptions (*yōshi*) were falsified as births (*jisshi*).[3]

The most famous political marriage in the last phase of Tokugawa rule was between the fourteenth shogun, Iemochi, and Princess Kazu, a sister of the reigning emperor, Kōmei, and the most coveted pawn in the kōbu-gattai (court-shogunal union) plot. In the post-Restoration era, the brazenly political nature of marriage subsided, but politics continued to play a role. Outsiders, in particular, tended to impute political advancement to the strategic giving and taking of children in marriage or adoption in

Table 15. Allocation of Children of Shogun Tokugawa Ienari
(r. 1787–1837), by Receiving Group

	DŌZOKU	MATSUDAIRA	OTHER DAIMYO	TOTAL
Daughters given as wives	3	3	7	13
Sons given in adoption	6(9)[a]	5	1	12(15)[a]
Total	12	8	8	25(28)[a]

Source: *KKT* 2:140–43.

[a]The actual number of sons was twelve, but three were adopted into two houses serially, all within the dōzoku.

order to build up and use *keibatsu* (cliques based on affinal networks). Yamaguchi Aisen (1932) tells many stories of such *seiryaku kekkon* (political marriages) and of successful careers propelled by keibatsu. The complicated tripartite exchange of sons and daughters involving Itō Hirobumi, Inoue Kaoru, and Katsura Tarō, for example, is seen as an attempt to consolidate the Chōshū faction (Yamaguchi 1932, 60).

My informants, as insiders, did not necessarily project particular political motives, and yet some referred to the "political marriages"—used in multiple senses—of their grandparents, or parents. Political motives were read, for example, into the marriages between the mutually hostile parties to the Restoration war, allegedly engineered to heal wounds or to benefit both parties in the new era. Informants saw political maneuvering in certain marriages between a Tokugawa father and a Chōshū mother, a Tokugawa brother and a Satsuma sister-in-law, a pro-Tokugawa buke and a procourt kuge, and so on. A Tokugawa woman contemplated, "I suppose [my brother's] marriage was a political one, because a Satsuma connection was considered a big plus for the Tokugawa." In some instances the political motive was overread, as when a nuptial arrangement was made between a granddaughter of the last Aizu lord and an heir to a small procourt southwestern daimyo house. The bride, my informant, was flabbergasted to learn that the entourage of her husband's household had been worried about Aizu's retaliation, apprehensive that a big daimyo house like Aizu might be giving away its daughter only as an agent to "wrest the groom's head."

Matrimony between old allies or between a lord and loyal vassal was also regarded as political, particularly if the union was historically unprecedented. When the then crown prince Hirohito became engaged to Princess Nagako, a daughter of Prince Kuniyoshi, the union was interpreted as a maneuver of the Satsuma, the foremost procourt group, because Nagako's mother was a Shimazu woman. In this case, Nagako was considered to belong to her mother's kin group and its domain more than to her royal father, and thus to bring the Satsuma influence with her into the court.

Opposition to certain proposed marriages, whether between former enemies or old allies, whether arranged or love matches, could also have political implications. For instance, it was said that resistance to the above imperial marriage was led by Yamagata Aritomo—who allegedly promoted Chōshū interests against the Satsuma—on the pretext that Princess Nagako carried color-blind genes from her maternal (Satsuma) side. This marriage, which in fact did take place, thus provoked nationwide political turbulence involving pros and cons. For another example, Prince Asaakira, Princess Nagako's brother, was in love with and engaged to Sakai Kikuko; the arrangements, however, were suddenly canceled unilaterally by his family, the Kuni. One explanation, Kikuko's daughter reasoned, was that the Sakai, as a top-ranking fudai daimyo of the Tokugawa, represented a symbolic target of hatred for the courtiers. Furthermore, the Kuni had already been allied with the anti-Tokugawa Shimazu through marriage. The cancellation was thus politically plotted without the knowledge of the young couple (Sakai 1982, 77–82).[4]

Strikingly political were those marriages that resulted from Japan's colonial expansion. Consider, for example, the case of the Korean imperial line. When Emperor Kojong of Korea was forced by Japanese colonialists to abdicate in 1907, he was succeeded by Crown Prince Sunjong. Sunjong was to be the last emperor of the Yi Dynasty, ending his imperial reign in 1910 with Japan's annexation of Korea. His title was then downgraded to "king," and he was made to join the ranks of the Japanese royalty as *ōzoku* (kingly lineage, differentiated from the Japanese kōzoku, or imperial lineage): in other words, he was made formally subordinate to the Japanese emperor. He died in 1926. His younger brother (and crown prince), Yong (Gin in Japanese), had been taken to Japan prior to the annexation, at age eleven, as a ryūgakusei (in the colonial scheme of Japanese rulers, of course, there was to be no more accession; Han 1970, 486). It was for Prince Yong that a matrimonial arrangement was made with a Japanese lady. The Kunaishō sounded out the Nashimoto, a collateral royal house, on their willingness to give their daughter Masako as Prince Yong's bride. It was no easy decision. Yet before she knew what had taken place, Princess Masako was shocked to read in a newspaper the announcement of her engagement, complete with pictures of the prince and herself side by side. Her parents had tried to decline, she writes in her autobiography, but the ministry persuaded them, saying that this marriage was desired by none other than His Majesty as a means of strengthening the Japan-Korea alliance and as an exemplar for people in general. Thinking of her future husband, whom she had in fact not yet met, Masako felt sympathetic and even close to him; after all, they shared the common fate of being victimized by seiryaku kekkon (Ri 1973, 35–38).

Another, later colonial marriage involved Manchukuo, a new state brought into existence in northeastern China by the Japanese Kwantung Army in 1932. The puppet emperor, P'u-yi, who headed this state as a "direct descendant" of the ruling house of the Ch'ing Dynasty, was already married but had not been blessed with an heir. The Kwantung Army selected his younger brother, another ryūgakusei at the Japanese Army Academy, as the most promising nuptial link with Japan. When the initial plan to match him with an imperial daughter proved unworkable because of the Imperial House Law, the army turned to kazoku girls of kuge origin as an alternative. Through a kin network, a picture of Saga Hirō, the daughter of a marquis, reached the searchers; the prince then chose her from among several such candidates-by-picture (Aishinkakura 1984).

Both of these women, although in their autobiographies they express no regrets, since their marriages turned out to be blessed with mutual love, nonetheless admitted that they had served as hostages for Japanese imperialism.

Inseparable from but not quite identical with political alliance as a main motive for marriage was status validation; that is, matrimony was not just politically instrumental, but it also could underscore the status of the spouse giver, receiver, or both. The selection of a spouse was more symbolic than utilitarian. The Tokugawa shogunate, for example, from the third shogun on, looked to Kyoto for wives, particularly among the sekke or royalty, as if to demonstrate its equality with the imperial house.

Table 16 shows the natal houses of the consorts for emperors from Keitai (r. 507–31) to Shōwa (r. 1926–89), and for shogun from the Ashikaga (1338–1573) through Tokugawa (1603–1867). Ninety male emperors in this period were married (including both the southern and northern courts),[5] and their recorded consorts totaled 151 (TDSH). Of these consorts, 64 percent were daughters of Fujiwara men, 23 percent were royal princesses (daughters of emperors or imperial princes), and 13 percent had other origins. Of the shogun from the Ashikaga through the Tokugawa (including Oda Nobunaga, Toyotomi Hideyoshi and the lat-

Table 16. Consorts of Emperors and Shogun

	EMPEROR (N = 90)	SHOGUN (N = 31)	TOTAL
Imperial daughters	34 (22.5%)	7 (18.9%)	41 (21.8%)
Fujiwara daughters	97 (64.2%)	18 (48.6%)	115 (61.2%)
Other women	20 (13.2%)	12 (32.4%)	32 (17.0%)
Total consorts	151 (99.9%)	37 (99.9%)	188 (100.0%)

Source: TDSH 447–62, 471–74.

ter's two successors), thirty-one were married, with thirty-seven recorded consorts in all. These men followed the imperial precedent in favoring Fujiwara women, sekke daughters in particular (49 percent), over other categories of women. Evidently, receiving a sekke consort validated the shogunal status and was politically advantageous as well, while giving daughters to these ruling houses, shogunal and imperial, amounted to a symbolic confirmation of the giver's (Fujiwara's) unparalleled status.

STATUS CONGRUITY

In the post-Restoration period, especially after the installation of the formal kazoku system, marriage, together with adoption, was an important vehicle for building multiple kinship networks that would help create a homogenous "peerage" out of a heterogeneous array of houses. This goal could be achieved only if a status boundary was erected to inhibit matrimonial cross-over between the kazoku and lower strata. While no formal stipulation was erected against unions of kazoku and non-kazoku (indeed, such unions did occur, as will be seen below), nevertheless most of my informants felt strictly bound by the rule of endogamy.

A kazoku had to apply for a marriage license to the Kunaishō, indicating the status of the spouse's family (Kazoku Kaikan 1933, 232–36), to "receive the imperial approval." My informants, in fact, believed that the Sōchitsuryō, the supervisory agency, conducted special investigations in cases of cross-status marriage and exerted its authority formally or informally against any "disgraceful" match that would "spoil the honor of kazoku." Anticipation of such pressures was inflated into statements like "It was *absolutely forbidden* to marry someone outside the kazoku, no matter how rich." In answer to my questionnaire, a number of respondents referred to the severity of kazoku endogamy, to which they either submitted or, with difficulty, succeeded in deviating from. One wrote, "Mine was a *miai* [arranged] marriage. Since [my wife] was a commoner, it was terribly difficult, in those days, to explain the case. But because her family was as prominent as any kazoku, we were able to get approval." The same, or even greater, restrictions were imposed on heir adoption.

Status endogamy sometimes meant more than marriage within the kazoku generally. The daughter of a marquis who married a count grouped the five ranks into two classes—the upper three and the lower two—between which, she said, marriage was rare; the implication here was that viscounts and barons were not genuine nobility. (Recall the ancient promotion barrier between the third and fourth court ranks discussed in chapter 2.) Another woman, who married a commoner after the war, said, "In the prewar period, it was inconceivable for us to marry anyone other than a military officer of daimyo origin"—which is what her father was.

Whether these claims were well grounded is difficult to determine. However, tables 17–19 (based on *KKT* and taking into account only the highest ranks) may shed some light on the question.

Table 17 summarizes the estimated 216 marriages that have occurred since around the Restoration in the fourteen royal houses and the sixty-five kazoku houses with the titles of prince or marquis as spouse takers (and with 1848 arbitrarily set as the earliest birth date of the married individual). What especially interests us here is whether the original house category of the spouse-*taking* house matches that of the spouse-*giving* house. As the table makes clear, that situation holds strongly only for the daimyo (with 57 percent of daimyo houses taking spouses from other daimyo houses) and new kazoku ("Other," at 76 percent). Table 18, in contrast, focuses on correspondence of kazoku titles rather than of house categories. While brides marrying into the royal family come to a significant extent from princely and marquisal houses (41 percent), those destined for kazoku princes and marquises derive fairly evenly from all the three nonroyal categories. Notably, both royal and high-kazoku houses have recruited substantial numbers from among outsiders. The general tendency, indeed, is for spouse takers to marry downward, if not outside the kazoku group.

From these two tables, a variety of conclusions can be drawn. For one thing, it is undeniable that endogamy has been maintained to at least a certain degree. The first kazoku-title awardee may have been already married to a commoner, but his descendants looked to the kazoku group for spouses. Itō Hirobumi, for instance, risen from a humble samurai class and eventually promoted to the rank of prince, was married to a former

Table 17. House Category Correspondence in Marriage

| | | | SPOUSE GIVER | | |
SPOUSE TAKER[a]	Royal[b]	Kuge[c]	Daimyo[d]	Other[c]	Total
Royal[b]	12 (23.1%)	9 (17.3%)	19 (36.5%)	12 (23.1%)	52 (100%)
Kuge[c]	3 (5.1%)	12 (20.3%)	16 (27.1%)	28 (47.5%)	59 (100%)
Daimyo[d]	6 (9.8%)	9 (14.8%)	35 (57.4%)	11 (18.0%)	61 (100%)
Other[e]	1 (2.2%)	3 (6.7%)	7 (15.6%)	34 (75.6%)	45 (100%)
Total	22	33	77	85	217

Source: Based on *KKT* genealogies.

[a]Spouse takers here are restricted to royal houses and those kazoku houses that had top ranks—prince or marquis. "Other" spouse takers were therefore those who originated as shizoku or commoners but later achieved these high ranks. This rank restriction does not apply to spouse givers, who can be of any kazoku rank, with "Other" including commoners as well.

[b]At the top of this category is the imperial house.

[c]At the top of this category are the five sekke houses.

[d]At the top of this category is the shogunal house.

[e]This category comprises those of shizoku and commoner origin. As spouse takers, "Other" is restricted to new kazoku who attained a top kazoku title; as spouse givers, no such restriction applies.

Table 18. Kazoku-Title Correspondence in Marriage

| | | SPOUSE GIVER | | | |
SPOUSE TAKER	Royal	Prince/Marquis	Lower Kazoku	Non-Kazoku	Total
Royal	9 (21.4%)	17 (40.5%)	8 (19.0%)	8 (19.0%)	42[a] (100%)
Prince/marquis	11 (6.4%)	52 (30.0%)	60 (34.7%)	50 (28.9%)	173 (100%)
Total	20	69	68	58	215

[a]The number of royals in this table differs from that in table 17 because here the branch houses of royal origin appear as kazoku, whereas in table 17 they are included in the "royal" category.

geisha, but *KKT* shows that half of his descendants (seven of thirteen) married kazoku.

These tables also make clear that my informants were overstating the "mandatory" nature of endogamy. Difficulty in adhering to strict endogamy is due partly to the limited supply of spousal candidates within a desirable category or rank, a fact more true with higher ranks and with royals and kuge. (The tendency of daimyo to marry among themselves, that is, owes not only to their conservatism but also to the fact that they formed the largest group in the old aristocracy.)

Another aspect of the apparent violation of the endogamous rule, particularly with regard to royals marrying commoners, involves timing—specifically, differences between prewar and postwar generations. Table 19, which includes all the codable kazoku households, reveals a wide gap between the two generations in choice of spouse. Whereas the previous heads married more inside than outside their group, the present heads have reversed this trend sharply. (A similar, though less radical, change has taken place in son adoption.) All this suggests that there has been a definite break in marriage patterns since the war's end, so much so that marriage with commoners is today perfectly acceptable even among former royals and top-ranking kazoku. Indeed, I encountered a number of households in which an informant and all her siblings had been married to kazoku while her children all married commoners. This does not mean, however, that the issue of status congruity has disappeared entirely. One viscount who married a commoner in the early postwar period said that although his generation had married out, younger generations of kazoku are marrying back into their own ranks as their living standard has improved.

A grandson of a well-known daimyo had been reluctant to have his daughter marry the heir of a zaibatsu baronial house; yet he finally gave his consent, and he explained to me why. Having been reared in a daimyo family, he said, he had been trained to be concerned only with affairs of state, and thus to be extremely distrustful of businessmen as selfishly preoccupied with making a profit. Yet the zaibatsu house in question, with its long history, was not like a postwar nouveau-riche enterprise. Furthermore, he said, this mercantile house had, after all, adopted an heir from a distinguished kuge house. Some other informants who were still concerned with status congruity explained their marriages with commoners in terms of their spouses' kinship connections with full-fledged kazoku or, more commonly, Gakushuin background.

Equally informative is what was said by those postwar-generation informants who married within a proper status range about the merits of

Table 19. Marriages and Adoptions of Two Generations of Householders

	PRESENT HOUSEHEAD	PREVIOUS HOUSEHEAD
Marriages		
To kazoku	227 (27.8%)	442 (54.2%)
To outsider	591 (72.2%)	374 (45.8%)
Total	818 (100.0%)	816 (100.0%)
Adoptions		
From kazoku	126 (68.1%)	228 (86.7%)
From outside	59 (31.9%)	35 (13.3%)
Total	185 (100.0%)	263 (100.0%)

Source: *KKT.*

such a marriage. A woman in her thirties stressed the advantage of similarity and familiarity of the two houses in domestic style and speech patterns. Also, her husband's kindred largely overlapped hers, which eliminated affinal readjustment problems. This view, she said, was reinforced by the complaints of her friends about their commoner husbands and in-laws. Another informant at age forty also favorably compared her own inside marriage with conflict-ridden outside marriages:

> *Do you think it is important to select a person of similar background as your spouse?*
>
> Yes, I think it is, and even more so lately. Seeing the marriage of my [male] cousin, I have become more positive that marriage should be between similar houses, of similar level. Otherwise the other party will develop an inferiority complex or, conversely, feel superior [to others] and brag about having a kazoku spouse. That way one provokes animosity from people around. A well-balanced marriage is safest.

That this comment is not an exaggeration is shown by another postwar case of imbalanced marriage. The informant, X, a daughter of an eminent daimyo house, was widowed when her kazoku husband died in the war, and she remarried a commoner, Y, a handsome man with a cosmopolitan outlook who courted her tenaciously. It turned out that throughout their married life Y was pathologically jealous and possessive of her so that she had to forgo her own social life entirely. Far from calming down, though, his jealousy mounted into violence. He raped her numerous times, which resulted in repeated pregnancies. X finally had a nervous breakdown; the couple separated, but Y kept bothering her. An end to this conjugal tragedy came only with Y's death. In X's retrospective interpretation, the root of the matter lay in Y's background. Born the son of a pawnshop keeper, Y, despite his respectable education, was burdened with a tremendous inferiority complex, which he hoped to overcome by marrying a high-ranking kazoku woman. Indeed, he boasted of his marriage and actively used it to circulate and promote himself in high society, both Japanese and American. (An obituary in a weekly magazine, which was brought to my attention by someone else, indeed referred to this marriage as his great accomplishment and evidence of his extraordinary talent.) Then, too, X herself was mobilized to support and validate his claim, showing up at parties as a lively, charming cohost or coguest. Y, however, was not able to transcend his birth inferiority. On the contrary, the more popular she became in his circle of elite friends, the more his resentment grew. Even at home, whenever she talked about her natal house to her children, he took it as a mockery of his own.

While this is a truly poignant case, more benign instances of marital stress attributed to status imbalance can be pointed to. One might fall in love with someone vastly inferior in status precisely because of the difference, marry without parental consent, and, after years of cohabitation, come to the inevitable realization that the marriage was no longer exciting. At this point the status gap would raise its ugly head in one's consciousness as the suspected source of trouble. The daughter of a daimyo kazoku, a divorcée, married a man whom she had met during a stay in the United States and found attractive because he saw her as she was, unlike all the others who were unable to view her apart from her special status. There seems to be no serious problem in this love marriage, except that she feels uncomfortable with his natural style, particularly in the presence of her parents. Whenever she hears her husband talk to her parents, using language so discordant with their status, a dreadful chill runs down her spine. Also disturbing is his manner of eating—a complaint that illuminates the culture-nature opposition. Although the problem may sound trivial, she cannot ignore her gut-level reaction. The very source of the husband's initial attractiveness, that is, his aloofness from status constraint, now upsets her sense of order.

The speech problem was mentioned by many. In this last case, the informant was frustrated because her commoner husband did not bother to rise to her level of speech. Another case, however, concerns just the opposite: the daughter of a baron who must make a special effort to speak in the commoner style of her husband and his kin. "So I feel suddenly relaxed when I talk with my old classmates and their relatives."

Discomfort was shared by a married-up commoner spouse as well. The wife of a daimyo viscount, and daughter of a well-to-do businessman, claimed she had not known about his family background until they married. She was dumbfounded to see her husband in contact with big daimyo X, Y, and Z, and with the royalty, and was embarrassed when his kin asked what kind of family she was from. I detected no sign of marital unhappiness; nevertheless, the wife said, as her husband listened, watching her nervously, that he should have married a woman of equal status. Another woman, discussing cases of mismatched marriage, mentioned an upstart billionaire who had married a daughter of a count: "In such marriage, the noble wife cannot stand her husband's vulgar life-style, such as walking around [in the house] with nothing but underwear on." Conversely, she knew a couple on the verge of divorce because the commoner husband was unable to relax at home. "After all, difference in breeding [sodachi] cannot be erased no matter how hard one tries." The speaker was a commoner married to a count but apparently did not include herself in cases suffering from sodachi difference.

The last remark reminds us that a status match and status-appropriate behavior are often insisted upon by status aspirants who have climbed into the aristocracy through marriage. In her autobiography, Viscountess Torio Tae (1985) discusses frankly how she, the daughter of a wealthy commoner businessman, wanted to marry a kazoku, which she did. She suspects that her mother-in-law was disappointed with this match because she had had the daughter of another viscount in mind and informally had begun to arrange matters. The author reveals that the mother-in-law was from a rural landlord family with no title. Her (Torio's) grandmother-in-law, apparently, was a *maiko* (dancing entertainer) from Gion. Thus three generations of wives were commoners. Still, the author observed, her mother-in-law had become a perfect kazoku lady, with a mastery over special kazoku vocabulary that "sounded like a foreign language" to the bride (Torio 1985, 82). Sodachi, thus, could be erased— or achieved. It may, indeed, be said that the upper status owes the maintenance and renewal of its boundary more to its aspiring marginal members than to core insiders.

Whether status balance is desirable in mate selection even in contemporary Japan may be inferred from the questionnaire responses of present kazoku househeads (table 20). The question was open, and loaded: "From your experience, do you think it better to choose a marriage partner well balanced in status? Or is someone with an entirely different

Table 20. Questionnaire Responses, with Example Answers, on Status Balance in Marriage ($N = 86$)

Is status balance desirable in choosing a marriage partner?

BALANCE DESIRABLE (unconditionally or conditionally)　　51 (59.3%)

"Better to be well balanced. The reason is because you share a similar life environment, customs, speech style, etc."

"Better to be well balanced. You don't have to worry about social intercourse and customs."

"It would be difficult if there is too much difference in the lifestyle, way of thinking and living."

"I chose a house similar to mine, because I thought we could understand each other quickly."

"Imbalance is the root cause of marital failure."

"Better to be well balanced. My wife is from a baronial house."

"Balance is desirable, but not an absolutely necessary condition. My own marriage is well balanced, I think."

NEUTRAL (indifferent to the matter; other things more　　26 (30.2%)
　　important)

"I don't care."

"Status balance does not matter. The personal quality is what counts more."

"I am not concerned about status or balance. More necessary is the mutual agreement of partners themselves."

"In my experience, status did not matter. More important is whether the couple can discuss everything together."

IMBALANCE OR DIFFERENCE MORE DESIRABLE　　3 (3.5%)

"Better to be totally different. A connection with new blood is more important."

"There is no need of balance. A little difference will help you absorb new customs and expand your perspective."

OTHER　　6 (7.0%)

"In my days, balance was important, but it no longer matters now."

"There may be different opinions."

"Being a Japanese is all I care about."

"I don't know."

---

status more desirable? Why do you think so? What was your case?" About 60 percent of respondents—a surprisingly large proportion—indicated the desirability of status congruity, giving reasons largely coincident with those of the above-cited informants. Some 30 percent expressed aloofness from status matters. The responses showed a strain toward cognitive consonance—that is, a general tendency to match one's opinion with one's own marriage. One comment, categorized under "imbalance desirable," said: "It is better to be entirely different. Everything is up to the principals. My wife is from a farming house but is a good homemaker, well liked by everybody, and lives in the present and future. She has left the past behind."

Responses to this questionnaire also indicated that conservatism goes with age (table 21), for older respondents overwhelmingly favored the balanced marriage while younger ones showed a reverse inclination. It follows that older generations of the prewar period were more strictly endogamous and were punished more severely for violating the rule—a rule that, though not necessarily enforced by the Kunaishō authorities, was well internalized by both kazoku and commoners alike. In her fictionalized autobiography, Yanagiwara Akiko, daughter of a kuge count, writes of the upset experienced by the commoner foster family of Sumiko (Akiko's mirror) when they discover Sumiko's engagement to a "lowly, nameless heimin" (Yanagiwara 1928, 399)—even though this heimin was an industrial tycoon. Once married, the bride finds herself unable to adjust to the discrepancy of the two life-styles, kazoku and heimin.

MANAGEMENT OF STATUS INCONGRUITY

Status congruity is an essential element of positional marriage: keeping marriage *within* the kazoku group, or even within a kazoku substratum, was desired, prescribed, expected, enforced, and practiced. Nevertheless, instances of status-incongruous marriage were too numerous to be ignored as exceptions, even before the war (see table 18). Status incongruity, then, must have been managed somehow to make it compatible with the kazoku institution or to minimize potential conflict. How was marrying up or marrying down handled?

Daughter Adoption

When an informant ruled out the prewar possibility of outside marriage, I would say, "But there were so many cases of marriage with commoners!" An immediate response tended to be, "In that case, the bride was adopted by some kazokusan."

Table 21. Opinions on Status Balance in Marriage, by
Respondent's Age ($N = 80$)

	AGE 59 OR YOUNGER	AGE 60 OR OLDER
Balance desirable	11 (13.8%)	40 (50.0%)
Neutral or undesirable	15 (18.8%)	14 (17.5%)

We discussed adoption at length in chapter 4 in connection with succession. Here we encounter another kind of adoption, having nothing to do with succession, and involving women more than men as adoptees. In this case, adoption served to correct discrepancy in the ranks or reputations of the two houses involved in a proposed marriage. The daughter of a low-ranking house might gain status fitness through adoption, allowing her to marry a much higher ranking man. The daughter of a man whose disgraceful conduct (political radicalism or profligacy, for instance) smeared the house reputation to the point of jeopardizing its kazoku status, would be able to dissociate herself from the source of ignominy by becoming a *yōjo* (adopted daughter) of another house, whereupon matrimony could take place. A daughter of Iwakura Tomoharu, grandson of the well-known Restoration leader Tomomi, for example, was thus adopted by Saigō Jūtoku because, according to an informant (the adopter's granddaughter), of Tomoharu's radicalism, which threatened to forfeit the family's kazoku title. The Iwakura daughter thus became the informant's adopted aunt. (Another account of this case is different: Iwakura Tomoharu dissipated the enormous fortune inherited from Tomomi through speculative investments as well as through entanglement with "base" women [Yamaguchi 1932, 36–38].)

That adoption for spousal entitlement was nothing to be kept secret is demonstrated by the fact that such adoptions were often engineered by the office of Sōchitsuryō. According to one informant, her father, during his tenure as the director of the office, was kept quite busy arranging marriages and daughter adoptions: "It was his responsibility to arrange *all* daughter adoptions for the kazoku and royalty."

The best-known recent case of adoption for marital qualification was that of Princess Chichibu, who married Prince Chichibu, Emperor Hirohito's brother. Though a granddaughter of Matsudaira Katamori, the last daimyo of Aizu, Matsudaira Setsuko was nevertheless the daughter of a nonsuccessor son of Katamori—that is, a non-kazoku. When she was chosen and encouraged by Empress Dowager Teimei, the royal mother, to be the bride of the emperor's brother, her family tried to decline the offer by calling attention to its commoner status. This excuse was over-ruled, however, by the suggestion that Setsuko be adopted by her uncle, the head of the Matsudaira main house and a viscount (Ema 1983). Rank discrepancy was thus removed(!), and marriage took place accordingly. Thereafter Princess Chichibu was to appear on kazoku records as a yōjo (or as a niece) of Matsudaira Morio, dissociated from her commoner father.

Historically, the very apex of the national pyramid had long employed such adoption. Some of the principal wives (*kōgō, chūgū*) of emperors were adopted. The Taira daughter Tokuko, for instance, was adopted by retired emperor Goshirakawa so as to qualify as chūgū to Emperor Taka-kura—thus she became the first empress of warrior origin (Ponsonby Fane 1936, 145). Yōjo were also among the wives (*midaidokoro* or *midai*) of Tokugawa shogun. We must now qualify table 16, describing the origins of imperial and shogunal consorts. The eighteen midai of Fujiwara (sekke) origin in fact included nine women adopted by sekke for matrimonial entitlement. Tokugawa Yoshinobu's midai, the daughter of an ordinary kuge, thus first became a yōjo of the Ichijō. The last of the three midai of the thirteenth shogun, Tokugawa Iesada (known as Tenshōin), was born into a small branch house of the Shimazu; though first adopted into the Shimazu main house, when she was nominated as a shogunal wife (or in anticipation of such nomination) she was readopted into the Konoe house.

If nonsuccessional adoption was indeed undertaken for entitlement, it was more likely for high-ranking houses to receive, rather than give, daughters for adoption than lower-ranking ones. And indeed, we find that for the sekke, 8.2 percent of all their daughters (10 of 122) were given away for adoption, while 17.2 percent (21) were received (*KKT*). It is noteworthy that the Konoe, the very top of all the sekke, gave away only 5.9 percent of their own daughters (1 of 17) but received fully 58.8 percent (10), sharply outdoing all the collaterals. The desirability of being a Konoe yōjo for status enhancement is beyond doubt. As for the sho-gunal house, no daughter was adopted out, and only 6.5 percent (two of thirty-one) were adopted in—much lower figures than for the sekke. This suggests either that the sekke continued to be a source of greater prestige than the shogunal house or that the former were more receptive of yōjo than the latter for economic or other benefits.

Daughter adoption for entitlement sounds like empty, or perhaps met-aphorical, adoption, with no *real* change involved but only an "as-if" improvement in nominal status. A yōjo might have lived in the adoptive house for a short time as a rite of transition and subsequently kept ritual contact, or the adoption might have been only a matter of paper work. In the case of Princess Chichibu, according to Ema (1983), Matsudaira Setsuko left her natal home the day before the nuptials and stayed with her uncle's family that night so that the next morning she could proceed directly from the viscount's house to the imperial palace. (Yet according to my informants, the princess's relatives, she moved to the main house months before.)

How could my kazoku informants accept such flexibility in status readjustment while remaining so firm on the issue of endogamy? Obviously, one level of consciousness does not rule out the other: both are stored in the cultural heritage. The same may be said about son adoption for succession. At one level of consciousness, informants believed in genealogical orthodoxy and an unbroken line of succession, while at another level they took the high frequency of successor adoptions for granted. Such double consciousness may be more or less necessary in every society to cope with the inevitable discrepancy between rule and reality, or culture and nature. Discrepancy may result from a natural deficiency (such as inability to produce one's own son) in meeting a cultural standard (father-to-son succession), or from a natural eruption (such as a spontaneous affaire d'amour) in contravention of a cultural rule (the rule of arranged, loveless marriage with a status peer). Indeed, the more rigidly the cultural rules or standards are prescribed, the more necessary it may be to tolerate or encourage such double consciousness. I argue that Japan's hereditary aristocracy, which represented a rigid system, owed its survival to such tolerance.

Be that as it may, adoption was only one strategy available for the management of status-mismatched unions. My informants spoke of many such unions that did not necessarily involve daughter adoption—which raises another historical form of coping.

Wife and Concubine

While some informants described the Sōchitsuryō as a relentless enforcer of status endogamy, others argued that the office was concerned only with cases involving women in the "water trade" such as geisha, bar hostesses, prostitutes—women who would be objectionable for other classes as well. Nonetheless, such women—particularly geisha—figured in a surprising number of kazoku narratives, and often as the narrator's own ancestor. One such informant was quite amused to talk about the "complex" of her father, who was mothered by a former geisha. This informant's grandfather was one of many Restoration leaders whose political life was entangled with women—specifically, the only women available in the sexual market in those days: "water traders." After the death of his wife, then, he had promoted a particular geisha of Gion, Kyoto, from a concubine to his legitimate wife. These women, and Kyoto geisha in particular, took risks too by collaborating with these men of the future. Thus we find unions between geisha and prominent Restoration leaders such as Sakamoto Ryōma, Kido Takayoshi, Itō Hirobumi, Yamagata Aritomo, and Saigō Takamori (Dalby 1983, 62, 316). One is tempted to interpret the kazoku matrimonial regulation against such women as a measure to put an end to this too common practice.

Affairs and marriage with geisha and other "professional women" might be understood as a transitional phenomenon of the Restoration crisis. But one kuge daughter, whose father was also the son of a Gion geisha, referred to the relative recency of the marriage regulation in talking about her grandfather's time. "In those days you were free to live with anybody, because there was no *koseki* [house register] yet." Only after the Restoration, when the koseki law came into effect, did marriage begin to be controlled, she argued. Her grandfather later petitioned to the Kunaishō for permission "to make his concubine, So-and-so, a legitimate wife."

This grandfather had been married to a respectable woman, the daughter of a Restoration leader, upon whose death he raised the geisha concubine to become his second wife. It turned out that the first marriage had been obligatory and that the husband "did not even come near the wife," instead fathering children by his concubine. The informant saw this pattern of dual liaison as having lasted in many upper-class marriages until her grandparents' generation. Her mother was also a concubine's daughter. "The *seishitsu* [main, legitimate consort—or wife] was a mere decoration, and the *sokushitsu* [side consort, concubine] was the real thing." Here is a remarkable juxtaposition of a cultural, symbolic wife and a natural, sexual mate.

This commentary, of course, contradicts the informant's earlier statement about the absence of marriage regulations prior to the koseki law. There was in fact a customary, if not legal, regulation that distinguished a legitimate from a nonlegitimate consort, the one being more open and public, the other clandestine and private. The hierarchical distinction of the two categories of consorts thus ironically helped to perpetuate this semipolygynous practice, offering—from the male point of view— another strategy for managing status-mismatched unions, at the expense of women's integrity. The same strategy is apparently resorted to by high-caste Hindu men, who are otherwise constrained by an endogamy much more rigid than the Japanese counterpart: there "the first marriage," conforming to the rule, "must be distinguished from subsequent freer marriages and, *a fortiori,* from illegitimate unions" (Dumont 1970, 113). For Japanese, either could come first.

Informants spoke frankly about their grandfathers or fathers-in-law because these individuals were too remote to hurt the descendants' self-esteem, but they tended to portray their own fathers as "puritanical" and strongly revulsed by their parents' sexual license. Generally, there has been an increasing commitment to monogamy over the generations, which explains why extramarital affairs have gone underground. The earlier the generation, the more openly conducted was the dual or multiple marriage.

A sixty-three-year-old informant described how his otherwise admirable grandfather, a Meiji leader, had maintained a huge household of about fifty residents, including a couple of concubines and their children as well as a large retinue. In premises some five thousand tsubo in size were five dwellings inhabited by legitimate and nonlegitimate lines all together. The informant, the legitimate-line grandson and heir, had "many" uncles and aunts mothered by the concubines. While this state of affairs disturbed his youthful sense of purity and justice, at the same time he was proud that his ironhanded grandfather had kept this enormous, potentially disruptive household in perfect order, not permitting the concubines to forget their servile status vis-à-vis the ō-okusama.

Another woman declared that she was astonished to witness her royal parents-in-law practically separated while sharing the same shelter. Her father-in-law kept a concubine elsewhere, and when he was about to leave home to pay her a visit, the whole household, from his seishitsu on down to the servants, lined up at the main gate and bowed to see him off. A younger woman told a story of her mother being a concubine in a strangely reversed residential arrangement. As long as she could remember, she said, for some "unknown reason" her mother had lived with her "husband" and his parents always "without any trouble," while the man's "legal" wife resided elsewhere. The children distinguished their two "mothers" by calling their legal mother "otāsama" and their natural mother "mama." The latter was legitimized when the former died. A remarkable aspect of this case is that the informant's father was an adopted son who had married the daughter of the house; apparently, when the marriage was found hopeless his adoptive parents kept him on at the expense of their own daughter and even agreed to his bringing in his concubine. It may be inferred from this case that successional continuity was more important than natural kinship, or that a bright adopted son was more valuable than a blood daughter. I have encountered two other cases of similar marital rearrangement, both involving a termination of the original marriage by divorce.

Again, concubinage as an institution is embedded in a long history. The Tokugawa shogunate developed within its palace ground a large-scale female-only institution or shogunal harem called the ō-oku (literally, "grand interior"), a sort of parallel with the all-male omote bureaucracy of its government. Although constrained to marry royal or sekke women as seishitsu, who would occupy the top quarter of the ō-oku, shogun had access to a wide range of other women as sokushitsu, supplied through the ō-oku agency. Accounts concerning shogunal concubines (Saiki 1946; Takayanagi 1965) stress how numerous such women were, and how lowly (*ikagawashii* or *gesen*) by birth: they included, for example, even bath attendants. At this point I should remind the reader that the numbers and origins of shogunal consorts given in table 16 above are limited to seishitsu. Candidates for sokushitsu were recruited either by the ō-oku female "elders" or picked spontaneously by the shogun himself to join a pool of such women, called *o-chūrō*, some of whom were still "pure" (*okiyo*), while others were already "hands-laid-on" (*otetsuki*) or "polluted" (*yogore*). The number of women thus "polluted" by a shogun is impossible to determine, particularly for childless women. By combining the data contained in Saiki 1946 and Takayanagi 1965 we can derive the following examples of recorded estimates: the third shogun, Iemitsu, had eight concubines; the eighth shogun, Yoshimune, four; and the eleventh shogun, Ienari, sixteen. But this is not all. Iemitsu was also an active homosexual; Yoshimune was a wild womanizer who impregnated at least ten women other than the above-mentioned four, whom he gave to his vassals as gifts (Takayanagi 1965, 232)[6] and Ienari apparently had forty sokushitsu who, altogether, gave birth to fifty-two children (ibid., 257). In other words, even concubines were "ranked"—as either more "legitimate" sokushitsu, who appear on record, or women more hidden or easily discarded.

Turning to the longer history of the imperial consorts we find a looser pattern still. While a shogun had only one principal wife, with a rigid status barrier separating her from concubines, the status of "empress" was not clearly distinguished from that of secondary consorts. The original titles borrowed from China for the ritsuryō system were *kōgō* for empress, and *hi* (or *kisaki*), *hin*, and *bunin* (or *fujin*) for secondary consorts, in that order of status[7]—though the titles did change over time, as will be shown shortly. The emperor was supposed to have only one empress (kōgō) at a time; but from Emperor Ichijō (r. 986–1011) on, another empress was added under the title of chūgū. During and after Kanmu's reign (781–806), new titles for consorts, such as *nyōgo* and *kōi,* were added that eventually replaced *hi, hin,* and *bunin* (Asai 1985, 90).

For twenty-eight imperial reigns of the Heian Period, consorts were distributed as shown in table 22.[8] These data alone indicate the instability or irregularity of the empress status, not only in that an emperor could have more than one empress as kōgō and chūgū, but also in that several emperors had no empress at all while having several nyōgo. (Even in more recent history, Kōmei, Meiji's father, had nyōgo but no empress.) Indeed, nyōgo, theoretically only concubines, came to be held in such high regard as to border the empress's status, and thus they are included in table 16, listing the 151 principal consorts of emperors since Keitai.

What table 22 does *not* show is even more telling of the instability of imperial marriage. Once *nyōgo* came into common usage as a consort title, it became customary for a woman to enter the imperial kōkyū ("rear palace," or imperial harem) as a nyōgo and to be later promoted, with the emperor's favor or in view of court politics, to chūgū or kōgō. Minamoto Kazuko, daughter of the second Tokugawa shogun, Hidetada, was a nyōgo first and later was elevated to chūgū of Gomizuno'o. Even Meiji's wife, an Ichijō daughter later known as Empress Shōken, paid respect to this tradition by entering the palace first as a nyōgo, though she was elevated to kōgō that same day. The subsequent reform of the kōkyū system led to the abolition of nyōgo and synchronization of imperial marriage with the appointment of an empress or crown princess (Kodama 1978, 72).

In the premodern era, still other practices made the status of empress ambiguous. Some unmarried naishinnō (imperial princess of the blood) who had received the title of *junbo* (quasi-mother to the emperor) were promoted to kōgō as an honorary elevation. Also, consorts were occasionally named kōgō posthumously. Making the matter even more confusing is the fact that the title *kōtaigō* (empress dowager) might be conferred—posthumously as well as in life—on the mother of the reigning emperor or even on a nyōgo who had never been an empress. Conversely, there was a time when an empress, even before being widowed, was entitled to the title *kōtaigō* because the two other titles for empress, *kōgō* and *chūgū,* were already appropriated by two other consorts (Ponsonby Fane 1936, 117). It then became customary to confer the titles for three generations of empresses—reigning empress (kōgō), empress dowager (kōtaigō), and grand empress dowager (taikōtaigō)—on women who were not necessarily the emperor's wife, mother, or grandmother (Hashimoto 1976, 139). All this makes it difficult to identify who really were empresses; indeed, the lack of consensus on their total number is hardly surprising (cf., e.g., Asai 1985; TDSH 1966; and Kodama 1978).

Somewhere along the line the imperial consorts tapered off into a group of ladies-in-waiting (nyokan) holding offices in the kōkyū. The multiple meaning of *kōkyū* alone is indicative of the thin boundary between consorts and officials: "the group of buildings . . . behind the sovereign's apartments where the imperial consorts resided"; "the staff of female palace officials . . . assigned to the offices in the service of those consorts"; and the host of consorts below the empress (Miller 1978, 202). The nyokan staffing the central office of the kōkyū, called *naishi-no-tsukasa*, included *naishi-no-kami, naishi-no-suke,* and *naishi-no-jō* (sinified as *shōji, tenji,* and *shōji,* respectively, with different Chinese characters), in this rank order. Kami first began to attend the imperial beds (*jishin*) and thus rise to the level of kōi or nyōgo, but later they were replaced by suke and jō. The jishin attendance by suke (tenji) and jō lasted into the Meiji period, and these women were called *osoba-nyokan* (Kodama 1978, 96; Asai 1985, 91).

Below these were *myōbu, osashi, osue, nyoju,* and so forth. Myōbu, as implied by their other name, *oshimosan* (lady underneath), were also "pollutable," despite their jige origin, for the purpose of bearing princes and princesses. According to Shimohashi Yukiosa, myōbu, while sexually available, were not permitted because of their humble status to speak to the emperor but only to listen; when it was necessary to communicate with him, it was done through upper nyokan like naishi ladies. Osashi, however, though lower than myōbu, were free to speak to the emperor because their job—that of attending him during a call of nature—required intimate communication. "So I hear osashi were most intimate with the emperor" (Shimohashi and Hagura 1979, 20).

This comment sheds interesting light on the court hierarchy: while a rigid hierarchy segregated one rank from another, a low-ranking servant, exemplified by a latrine attendant, was physically much closer to the imperial master than was his higher-ranking consort or empress, who resided in her own section of the palace, surrounded by her own retinue. Anything could happen in such a situation of intimacy between an emperor and a lowly-born woman. It is as if the natural eros flowed upward from shimo while the cultural dignity of status passed downward from kami. Given this paradoxical background, it is understandable why the Tokugawa shogunate ruled that an emperor's children not born of an empress had to be adopted by one of the four shinnō houses (see chapter 2). As long as they stayed on in the palace, these imperial children were

Table 22. Number of Consorts for Emperors from Kanmu Through Goshirakawa

REIGN		KŌGŌ	CHŪGŪ	HI	BUNIN	NYŌGO	KŌI	TOTAL
50th (Kanmu[a])	781–806	1	0	1	4	4	0	10
51st	806–9	0	0	2	0	0	0	2
52nd	809–23	1	0	2	2	2	3	10
53rd	823–33	1	0	2	0	2	1	6
54th	833–50	0	0	0	0	4	1	5
55th	850–58	0	0	0	0	8	1	9
56th	858–76	1	0	0	0	13	5	19
57th	877–84	1	0	0	0	0	0	1
58th	884–87	0	0	0	0	4	1	5
59th	887–97	0	0	0	0	5	1	6
60th	897–930	1	0	1	0	4	13	19
61st	930–46	0	0	0	0	2	0	2
62nd	946–67	1	0	0	0	4	4	9
63rd	967–69	1	0	0	0	4	0	5

64th	969–84	2	0	0	1	0	3
65th	984–86	0	0	0	4	0	4
66th (Ichijō[a])	986–1011	1	1	0	3	0	5
67th	1011–16	1	1	0	2	0	4
68th	1016–36	0	1	0	0	0	1
69th	1036–45	2	1	0	2	0	5
70th	1045–68	2	1	0	0	0	3
71st	1068–72	1	1	0	2	0	4
72nd	1072–86	0	1	0	1	0	2
73rd	1086–1107	0	1	0	1	0	2
74th	1107–23	2	1	0	0	0	3
75th	1123–41	0	1	0	0	0	1
76th	1141–55	1	1	0	0	0	2
77th (Goshirakawa[a])	1155–58	1	1	0	2	0	4

Source: Adapted from Asai 1985, 253–58.

[a]Only three emperors, who are mentioned in the text, are named here.

officially considered as born of unwed mothers and so unentitled to shinnō status (Shimohashi and Hagura 1979, 26–27). In other words, to be designated shinnō, the imperial child had to be adopted twice: first adopted *out* and then adopted *in* (Lebra 1989).

Notably, even concubines, for both shogun and emperors, were supposed to be of respectable origin. Shogunal concubines, for example, had to be at least of the rank of *hatamoto* (shogunal primary vassal), and imperial court ladies were required to come from families of a certain court rank or above. Here again, adoption—father adoption, to be precise—was an acceptable solution to status discrepancy.

I have discussed matrimonial patterns of shogun and emperors at length because they served as models for the aristocracy in general. Yet these models were far from a neat set of rules. The imperial model in particular was strikingly elusive. It is thus small wonder that the kuge daughter thought there had been no marriage regulations in pre-Restoration Japan. Another high-ranking kuge daughter confided that her grandfather had never married, even though he had eight children including her father. A sekke descendant viewed his ancestors as having been initiated in youth into sexual competence through casual liaisons with *ie nyōbō* (in-house female servants) before formal matrimony, dumping the bastards thus born into monzeki temples. Even a descendant of a low-ranking kuge (a viscount), while showing me the plan of his old house, pointed to a room for a servant-concubine. Muramatsu Shōfū, with his strong opposition to the hereditary hierarchy, writes that in the pre-Restoration era royal princes and kuge men, almost without exception, sexually abused their docile housemaids, who were then discharged before their pregnancy was revealed; therefore, "few shinnō and kuge had legitimate wives" (1961, 90–91). Men, in short, had easy pre- and extramarital access to two pools of women in particular: geisha and maids.[9]

For daimyo ancestors, maintenance of a scaled-down version of the shogunal ō-oku was inherent in their status as well as necessary to ensure the birth of an heir. Even a small branch-house daimyo, an informant's maternal grandfather, had three concubines in coresidence, but no legitimate wife. The head of a Tokugawa branch house is said to have had, among many others, four concubines named Spring, Summer, Autumn, and Winter, referred to together as Shun-Ka-Shū-Tō, each syllable standing for a season.

Sometimes it was at the wife's request that the master assembled a number of concubines. One middle-sized daimyo, according to his granddaughter, had five concubines, "not because he wanted them, but because my grandmother, who came over from a kuge house at age fourteen, was a smart woman." She kept giving birth from age fifteen until she fell ill at twenty-five or so. Unable to stand one more birth, she asked her husband to substitute concubines for herself. Another informant discussed her mother-in-law, whose natal family, when she was about to marry a daimyo, proposed that she be accompanied by a good-looking woman of respectable birth as a potential concubine because of the bride's poor health: her family would rather offer a known woman as a safe investment to forestall the groom's involvement with an obscure stranger. The offer was politely turned down, whereupon the family learned that the groom had already been endowed with a concubine.

Under a clear bifurcation among buke between wife and concubines, the latter became increasingly downgraded through the Tokugawa period. Or, if recruited from a pool of housemaids, a concubine remained such without a promotional opportunity. Meiji Japan, ironically, attempted to restore the ritsuryō system of polygyny, upgrading the concubine to spousal status and thus encouraging wife-concubine co-residence. But this ultratraditionalism was later ruled out in the 1898 Civil Code in response to public protest, resulting in the removal of concubines from the husband's house register (Nihon Fūzokushi Gakkai [hereafter cited as NFG] 1979, 631–32). Concubinage remained in practice, becoming a main target of protest, along with institutional prostitution, by women's groups, notably by Christians represented by the Reform Society (Sievers 1983).

Nevertheless, the general trend was toward monogamy, at least in appearance. The registered marriage (*kon'in*) was sharply distinguished from the common-law union (*naien*), the single legitimate wife from concubines, and *chakushi* (legitimate children) from *shoshi* (illegitimate children). In other words, the concept of legitimacy based on an all-or-nothing dichotomy replaced that of gradation from legitimate to nonlegitimate. Articles 3 and 4 of the 1889 Imperial House Law stipulated that in the imperial succession chakushi should precede shoshi, the latter being allowed onto the throne only if there were no chakushi. In my observation, however, what in fact happened among the royalty and kazoku was that concubines were denigrated or simply hidden, while the children, chakushi and shoshi alike, were allowed to share the father's status more or less equally: that is, the patrilineal principle was sharpened.

Prior to this modern change, a concubine, once she became an *oharasan*, or womb lady, and above all if she became the *seibo* (natural mother) of an heir, would have been greatly elevated to a prestigious position, often becoming more powerful than the childless seishitsu and, in some cases, allowed to assume the surname of her shared "husband." In the recallable experiences of my kazoku informants, however, the seibo generally appeared to be kept in a servile status, while her children were integrated into the father's household without stigma, being treated no differently from the legitimate children.

Accustomed to this bifurcation of women in the polygynous practice of the nobility, Yanagiwara Akiko, herself a concubine's daughter, was stunned to discover, after she married a commoner "king" of the mining industry, that her husband did not control his several servant-concubines living in and out of the main estate by the bifurcation rule.[10] Akiko, confronted with a head-maid concubine who would openly overstep the mistress's territory, with the master's acquiescence, and dismayed at the chaotic overall condition of this polygynous household, hired a new maid of her own choice in self-protection, whom she induced to become another concubine. She attributed this disturbing lawlessness to the commoner's way of life, so different from the rule-bound kazoku life-style (Yanagiwara 1928).

In kazoku and royal households, a concubine's children had two mothers: the father's legitimate wife, whom they called "mother" (*otā-sama, otatasama,* and so on), and their uterine mother, who was addressed by her personal name, sometimes in yobisute (without the minimal honorific *-san*). According to some informants whose grandmothers had been womb ladies, these women were at best situated "in between okami [upper domain] and otsugi [rooms for maids in attendance]"; when, after being widowed, they visited their former master houses to pay their respects, they were described as "hanging around in the hallway, neither in okami nor in otsugi." "We children had no idea who these short-haired old ladies were."[11] Some informants, however, did know who they were, and even resided in the same place with them. Nevertheless, none of these informants used a kin term like "grandmother" in addressing these women; all used their personal names instead. "I called my grandmother 'Shige' in yobisute because my mother did so." Such was taken as a matter of course, said these granddaughters. One woman said of the uterine mother of her father-in-law, who occasionally visited them: "All of us were seated in chairs, but this woman sat on the floor and knelt, expressing gratitude. Family members referred to her simply by her maiden name, without *san*."

Ideological justification for concubinage, which has continued into the modern period, derived from the mandate of the patrilineal succession of the ie and ie-attached status. It was coupled with the sperm-centered ethnogenetics in which the male partner is the sole contributor to genetic transmission, the female being no more than a womb-supplier providing the soil for the male seed—a striking example of the cultural distortion of nature. A sperm, the rationale went on, depends for its fertility on the congeniality of the womb, and therefore on its having access to various wombs until its potency is proved. In a peculiar twist of this pseudo-genetics, the child's sex was said to be determined by the borrowed womb, a belief that further rationalized the seed carrier's multiple mating until a male heir was born. The higher the status, the more pressure there was for the status holder to produce a male heir through multiple unions. In this sense, there was no essential difference between wives and other women: they were all "borrowed wombs" (*karibara*). In fact, *hara* (belly, womb) is a trope for women in general, reinforcing the sperm-centered ethnogenetics. Children of the same father and different mothers are identified as *hara-chigai* ("of different wombs"). Women were essentially "natural" as womb carriers, whereas men were more cultural as status-gene carriers.

Nevertheless, the bifurcation rule produced two categories of hara: *honbara* (legitimate, "main" womb) and *wakibara* (concubinal, "side" womb). The former was decorated with cultural trappings and called by a status term such as "okugatasama," while the latter was reduced to the natural womb itself and thus called "oharasan."

Dissociation of male genes from the natural womb was taken to an extreme in the imperial house of Meiji Japan, the ultimate model for all Japanese, and for the nobility in particular. Emperor Meiji, mothered by Nakayama Yoshiko, a kuge daughter and tenji (naishi-no-suke), was nominally adopted by Kujō Asako, a nyōgo to Emperor Kōmei, Meiji's father, who was promoted to empress dowager (kōtaigō) upon being widowed. Meiji himself, formally married to Ichijō Haruko, later known as Empress Shōken, was also attended by five tenji as *otogi* ("talking companions"), and had five princes and ten princesses born to him (Nashimoto 1975, 128–29). Only one prince and four princesses survived, and all of them were dissociated from their natural mothers—Yanagiwara Naruko, who bore the prince, the later Emperor Taishō, and Sono Sachiko, mother of all the princesses—and adopted by their cultural mother, the empress. This dissociation was carried out even more unequivocally than had been the case with Emperor Meiji himself.[12] Correspondingly, Yanagiwara and Sono were more hidden from public view than Nakayama had been.

Meanwhile, the sons of these ladies-in-waiting reigned as sovereigns, and even nonheir children shared their father's imperial status. One informant, aged eighty-three, recalled how she used to know two of Emperor Meiji's daughters through her grandmother, who waited on them as a sort of foster mother. She heard that Empress Shōken, the adoptive mother of the princesses (*naishinnō*), would greet them only after removing her floor cushion from beneath her as a gesture of humility. Embarrassed, the princesses protested that the empress should keep the cushion under her: after all, she was their otatasama. The "wise" empress supposedly replied: "I cannot. I came from a subject family [shinka], but Your Highnesses are His Majesty's children by birth."[13] At the same time, according to my informant, these imperial princesses treated their uterine mother, Sono Sachiko, another former tenji of kuge origin, like a servant and addressed her by her *genjina*, "Kogiku-no-suke," in yobisute.[14]

The mobilization of concubinage to manage status incongruity in marriage certainly worked from a male point of view. It was justified by the mandate of leaving an heir, as a status index, or even in terms of the irrepressible libido of males. Through concubinage, the man's personal whims or emotions could be satisfied. But women in such arrangements were marginalized, and at both ends: both seishitsu and sokushitsu were frustrated; both the childless wife and the uterine mother were unfulfilled, for different reasons. Stories abound of "decorative" seishitsu who wasted their lives waiting in vain for their estranged husbands, almost killing themselves out of agony, or of murderous plots and sorcery undertaken against rival women. The Meiji reforms in some ways only sharpened this gender asymmetry.

Complementary Exchange

Institutional concubinage no longer exists, and Emperors Taishō and Shōwa were both monogamous, the former reluctantly, the latter by personal conviction. Let us now move on to another strategy for compensating status incongruity, one more common in the past and still practiced today in large measure: the exchange of complementary, "heteromorphic" benefits (Gouldner 1960), such as marriage between rank, name, or ancestry on the one hand and brains, wealth, or other tangible desiderata on the other.

As regards certain marriages, some informants tended to see a wide status gap where outsiders might perceive no such discrepancy; these matches they would explain in terms of exchange. The marriage between a daughter of a Tokugawa branch house and the heir to a middle-level daimyo house, for example, though both houses ranked at count status, was seen by one of the latter's relatives as enormously mismatched because one house was shogunal. The Tokugawa daughter was given to a mere daimyo son "because," said the couple's son-in-law, "he was a bright, promising young man."

More common were exchanges involving rank and money, often with poor kuge as a party to the agreement. For example, the head of a wealthy baronial house in business, whose wife was a daimyo daughter, married most of his daughters off to kuge heirs. This was no secret to the daughters: "Our father could spend as much money as he needed," said one of them, "to buy whatever he wanted. But the time came when he wanted what he could not buy with money, that is, status." Marrying into the old aristocracy was the next best step. He did not "buy" status exactly, but ended up reciprocating the gift of status with a generous dowry. Still, such reciprocation was apparently not enough to equalize the original ranks of the couple: when he received his wife's father as a guest, this man would invite his esteemed father-in-law into the uppermost inner room and then kneel—in the adjacent room—to greet him.

A woman from a rich family and married to a high kuge descendant admitted that her father had aided the newlyweds financially, including housing and a supply of servants. When such marriages were treated journalistically (Yamaguchi 1932), however, the conclusion was devastating: a certain kuge marquis, for example, having gone bankrupt as a result of foolish investments and subsequent involvement with loan sharks, allegedly offered his daughter "for sale" at 100,000 yen. A buyer would, he promised, in return for a dowry of that amount, succeed to the rank of marquis as his adopted son-in-law (ibid., 25). By the time of Yamaguchi's investigation, kazoku daughters for sale were too numerous—"like litter"—to raise eyebrows. The bride of another destitute kuge kazoku, Yamaguchi reported, supposedly brought with her a 500,000 yen dowry, which funded their honeymoon trip to Europe and the United States (ibid., 35).

To evaluate the validity of Yamaguchi's claim, I examined the marriages in five zaibatsu families (the main houses of Iwasaki, Kōnoike, Mitsui, Shibusawa, and Sumitomo) involving individuals born after 1848 (based on *KKT*). Of the listed total of thirty-one daughters, twelve (39 percent) are married to kazoku sons (all but one of whom are successors), and nineteen (61 percent) to commoners. As for the sixteen listed sons of the zaibatsu families, ten (63 percent) wed kazoku women, and six (37 percent) wed commoners. Although these findings are inconclusive, zaibatsu men in particular may be said to have married up, given that five out of the ten kazoku wives came from houses carrying the rank of count or higher. In the pre-Restoration family history of the Mitsui, for instance, children married, according to an insider informant, only within the eleven-member dōzoku or the merchant class generally.

Naturally, kazoku informants did not speak crudely using the language of market transaction, and yet some were open about the advantages of cross-status marriage. One kuge daughter who married into a daimyo house was surprisingly frank about such exchange: "No sense of a poor kuge marrying another poor kuge." Her son married a daughter of an "extraordinarily rich man," "one of the richest in the nation," who runs several entertainment businesses. The nobility want money, while nouveaux riches want to raise their status, she said, "and that's why the two are drawn together. It's a matter of supply and demand. We could not have afforded a bride unless her family was wealthy enough to provide all the dresses, for example, that she needed. . . . Both sides are delighted" with the arrangement. "And this is nothing new," the informant added, giving me several prewar examples of such exchange marriages. The only problem, again, has to do with appropriate speech, and so she tries, not always successfully, to use the standard Japanese when her daughter-in-law is around. In my interview sample, most cases of kazoku-commoner marriage involve commoner spouses who are economically better off, often involved in high-technology industries, than their kazoku partners. It is not uncommon for a kazoku groom to be placed in an executive position of a company headed by his father-in-law.

Whether exchange marriage is indeed appreciated mutually or by only one party or otherwise conflict-loaded is another matter. One kuge husband, said his non-kuge wife, talked about "destitute kuge" all the time but never relinquished the *kigurai,* the status-based self-esteem, of his class. Kuge kigurai was blamed by many informants as accounting for their adherence to a life-style far beyond their means, whether in terms of housing, clothing, or the presence of well-groomed servants. This weakness in turn, I was told, necessitated that they seek spouses whom they could depend on economically.

A woman of shizoku origin married a kuge viscount out of what she retrospectively regarded as childishly romantic love, only to realize that there was a fundamental contradiction in the thinking of buke versus kuge. The bride's side had to provide everything: the groom's parents demanded that her family build a house for the young couple, pay for all the wedding expenses, and provide ceremonial clothing for the groom and his sisters as well. Because the husband had no income, the couple was housed in the premises of the wife's natal house and remained parasitic on her family throughout their marriage. This dependency, far from making him or his parents ashamed or worried about burdening her family, was taken as a status privilege: he, as a kuge, deserved such treatment. "His parents in particular felt they were being overgenerous in accepting a commoner woman"; they spoke to or about her family as if they were a bunch of servants. After putting up with such insults and burdens for thirteen years, the informant finally divorced her kuge husband.

Particularly notable among cross-status marriages were those involving royal spouses. Kazoku informants in general were of the opinion that marrying into the royalty was undesirable. I was told over and over again that when a family learned through the grapevine that a nuptial proposal from a royal house to its daughter or son was under consideration, some rationale was immediately invented to refuse without offending the proposing party. The most convincing excuse was that the target person was already engaged—and in fact, the family might lose no time in arranging a marriage with someone else. Such a match was in fact called *miyasama-yoke*, marriage to forestall a royal proposal. Without such an excuse ready, the proposal would descend like a command. So one hears, "My marriage was for miyasama-yoke"—that is, carried out hastily. While such informants' professed feelings should be taken with a grain of salt, clearly a big change has occurred since those days when men of power competed in getting their daughters into the imperial palace—especially in view of the fact that the parents, not necessarily the sought-after daughter or son, are the major objectors to royal marriages.

One reason for such aversion was the extraordinary constraints that the nonroyal spouse and his or her family would be subjected to. Particularly a woman marrying into the main imperial house would be doomed to virtual slavery to palace tradition and continual surveillance by the "nasty" nyokan (female attendants), as well as to the curious eyes of the entire nation. A status barrier between her and her natal family would be created to inhibit their reunion. And so on. This issue was always associated by my informants, who felt partly sympathetic and partly vindicated, with the alleged ordeal of Crown Princess Michiko (the present empress).

Another important reason, one more relevant to the present context, was the economic burden on the bride giver. Royal marriage would require that the bridal family not only pay an enormous dowry and wedding expenses but also constantly present gifts to the whole royal household, from its head down to its lowest servants. In addition, they would have to maintain a life-style appropriate to a royal affine and satisfy social obligations, again including gift giving, within the kin network of royalty and its circle. "No poor kuge family like us can afford to give a daughter to a royal prince."

One should be alert to the likelihood of projective exaggeration on the part of kazoku informants who were around but not inside the royal circle. One insider, however, suggests that the above generalization was not entirely untrue. When it was arranged for this sekke daughter to become a royal princess, the prince's household staff presented a list of items, such as a piano, to be included in her dowry. Among many ex-

pensive things to be custom made were a special court dress called a
jūnihitoe (the common name, wrongly used, for a simplified version of
the multilayered Heian court dress for women), a robe décolletée, and a
tiara studded with diamonds.[15] The princess-to-be had to train in calligraphy, poetry, tea ceremony, flower arranging, koto, and so forth, each
under a prominent tutor and all funded by her own family. After marriage, her mother indeed visited the royal house on such occasions as
Bon, year's end, and the new year, with generous gifts for all from the
daughter's in-laws down to servants in both oku and omote. In the end,
the major provider was not the princess's natal family itself but her mother's wealthy natal family of daimyo origin. "Unless you pleased all of
them, down to chauffeurs, with generous gifts," said another informant,
a peripheral insider, "they would give your daughter a hard time." He
said that it was just such an economic burden that drove Viscount Takagi,
the father-in-law of Prince Mikasa, to commit suicide. All these accounts
suggest that the kazoku "privilege" to marry into the royalty was really
more a liability.

The exchange of rank for wealth has been most common, but other
valuable things were mentioned as justification for marrying children to
commoners. The assimilation of "new genes" was a favorite topic among
a few informants. One nonsuccessor kuge descendant came on strong
with this point: it was his idea to give his daughter to a man of prefecture
X and to take a bride for his son from prefecture Y. To the informant,
the very names of these provincial prefectures indicated that they were
totally alien from the aristocracy. As he put it, such matches had "never
occurred since the age of apes." The meaning of this statement is not
clear, but my guess is that he felt these marriages, so incongruous in terms
of birth rank and so unprecedented, would be like unions between different species. All this scheming, needless to say, was in order to "improve
genes" (*hinshu kairyō*). Although the informant meant to be democratic
and egalitarian, his unconscious prejudice about hereditary status thus
surfaced.

As we saw in chapter 3, the fear of genetic deterioration, considered
inevitable in close-kin marriage, was widely shared. "In this family," said
one informant, "two generations in a row have had a bride from the same
family. There could not be smart children." Similarly, even those who
were not happy about the marriage of the crown prince and princess—
the present emperor and empress—because of the couple's status mis-
match had to admit that "the new blood would do good for the imperial
family." One can detect the profound ambivalence felt by aristocrats
regarding the value of hereditary status.

More subtle currencies surfaced as well involving the exchange of marriage candidates themselves in opposition to their parents and kin. A baron's daughter had gone through arranged introductions (*miai*) to several kazoku men, but turned them all down "because no kazoku men showed enough vigor for living." This was soon after the war, when kazoku men no longer stood tall, buttressed by their noble status and affluence. In the end she married an active, commercially talented entrepreneur, thus overruling the opposition of her kin group.

Another daughter of a wealthy kazoku family practically eloped with the man of her choice, knowing that her parents would not approve of him as their son-in-law. Her lover had been forced by his father's death to quit school and work as the sole supporter of his family. He embodied a type she had never known before, strong, perseverant, full of vitality, solidly rooted "like a weed." Having lived an easy, overprotected life, this daughter of a baron found him irresistible.

In these two cases of downward marriage, if there was any exchange, it was for the tough, vigorous character of a breadwinner. The cultivated gentility of an aristocratic man simply paled beside the natural vigor of a "weedlike" commoner. And in women, too, a tough character was considered desirable. A descendant of a Meiji leader received "many" proposals from kazoku women, from among whom his mother and relatives pressured him to choose. After long thought he decided against them all, because "kazoku women have no spirit, no 'issue-mindedness' [*mondai ishiki*]," and married a commoner with a business background instead. According to the heir of a daimyo viscount who married a commoner woman in the immediate postwar period, almost all his generation married outside kazoku ranks. This was a time when some kazoku men and women saw a great asset in the physical and spiritual vigor of a commoner. "No kazoku woman," said the above count, "would put up with the wretched standard of living" he could offer. "My generation's marriages all worked out very nicely," and "almost no couple has ended in divorce." Once Japan entered its "high-growth" stage and later stability, however, the children of the former kazoku "have gone back to marriage within the same status."

It is interesting that a kazoku mother of commoner origin was no more, if not less, tolerant than an aristocratic mother toward her daughter's choice of a commoner husband, and for the same reason: both objected to such a match "because the two houses are so different in status." The root cause may be that threats to the status boundary are more sharply felt by those on the margin or, conversely, that a marginal kazoku has stronger status strivings.

COMMITMENT

Let us now look into the processual aspect of marriage in terms of how a commitment was effected toward nuptial consummation. In a previous book (Lebra 1984) I detailed "marital transition" as it affects middle- to lower-class provincial women. In the following pages I will focus briefly on the class difference, although a repetition of certain generalizations made in the earlier work is unavoidable.

Arrangement

As might be expected, most kazoku marriages were arranged, formally or informally, by third parties. Even when the principals knew each other and might even have been in love, a formal communication was necessary for a proposal. By identifying how one was matched with whom by whom or through whom, we may gain a clue to the basic networks in which kazoku individuals circulated.

All arranged marriages mobilized kin networks: parents, siblings, collaterals, and affinal kin. These relatives served not only as arrangers or mediators, but as spouses as well. My limited sample of informants includes at least three cases of first-cousin marriage (parallel cousins, both patrilateral and matrilateral), two cases of sibling exchange (a man marrying his sister's husband's sister), two cases of in-dōzoku marriage, and a host of other more distant-kin marriages. Kin marriage was fairly common in Japan, and in fact the upper class followed this pattern as much as, if not more than, the lower class did. Here it should be pointed out that kin marriage and status endogamy reinforced one another. It seems that, partly because of endogamous pressures but mainly because of the spatial confinement and social segregation of kazoku life (see chapter 5), the marriage market was narrowly circumscribed. Kinship was a main network for both mediation and spousal candidacy. "We had no chance to meet any boys other than our brothers and cousins," one informant explained. Heterosexual kin contact was thus made possible by periodic rituals—typically, memorial rites for ancestors. "That's where many, many relatives would get together, arrange, and pick suitable prospects. Isn't it convenient?" said a woman whose marriage to a kinsman had been arranged in this manner. And indeed, it is interesting to see the rituals for the dead pre-empted by a group of debutants and debutantes. Hence, without intentionally choosing to marry a kazoku, "you naturally end up marrying a person with similar background."

The kin network was far from being a closed system, however. It was opened by and linked to the network of friendship involving arrangers or third persons who connected potential spouses. A large number of cases reveals the influence in these matters of the intimate and enduring ties of same-sex friendship built upon sex-segregated co-schooling at Gakushuin. The school bond was in fact an important link giving rise to unions between, for example, a woman and her brother's classmate or a man and his sister's classmate. Two generations could be involved as well, as when two classmates matched their children. Often the word *shin'yū* was used for the closest of such friends. A woman was matched to her father's sister's shin'yū's son through the shin'yū's arrangement. Close classmates, particularly boys, were apparently free to visit one another's homes, where they had ample opportunity to meet the host's sisters. "The father of my future wife," explained a royal prince, "was a few years junior to my father at Gakushuin, and used to come to our house all the time"—a situation that led to this prince's "unplanned" (*nantonaku*) marriage with the daughter of a rich commoner after the war.

Other kinds of friendship, often in combination with Gakushuin alumni ties, played a role in matchmaking as well. One informant was married as an adopted husband to a daughter of his father's friend at the House of Peers, both of whom belonged to the same faction of the peerage. The kinship network was thus somewhat transcended by the same-sex peer bonds molded at Gakushuin, the House of Peers, clubhouses, or through athletic and other associations. The military career formed another such bond as well, producing marital unions between sons and daughters, or between an officer and his superior's daughter. The peer network did not necessarily override the elite boundary, but it evidently facilitated the mixing of the status elite with the class elite. Gakushuin, for example, accepted children of certain non-kazoku families that were often richer, more striving, and more impeccable in many ways than kazoku themselves.

Among other structural arrangers mentioned were Gakushuin teachers, Sōchitsuryō, and the Kazoku Clubhouse. And as in everything else, top-ranking servants and former vassals joined in searching out and evaluating prospects and in negotiating and arranging marriages. Opportunities for arrangement presented themselves also at garden parties, or at resorts like Karuizawa, where upper-class children were freer than back in Tokyo.

For the prewar royalty, there was supposedly no way of rejecting a proposal made by the Sōchitsuryō and presented as imperially authorized. The following is part of a conversation I had with a seventy-five-year-old former princess married to a kuge count:

Was your marriage arranged?
Of course. Ours were all by *chokkyo* [imperial authorization]. Because it was the emperor who made the decision, likes and dislikes were out of the question. . . .
Was it decided by the Sōchitsuryō?
Yes, by the office that looked after the kazoku [and kōzoku].
Were you prepared for that kind of marriage?
Of course I was.

Such a status constraint, which categorically precluded the personal choice, was voiced by many, royals and kazoku alike. And yet, as the above quotation suggests, those who were involved accepted it as natural and did not feel restricted. I recall how many times in one interview a ninety-one-year-old widow of kuge origin disappointed me by giving unexpected answers to my somewhat provocative questions. "Didn't you want to be free?" I asked for instance. "No," she said, "I did not feel constrained at all. I thought such was the way things had to be [*sō yū mon da to omotte*]." It appears that positional training was complete in repressing one's subjectivity. Only in retrospect did this widow and other women realize their "astonishing" or "regrettable" malleability. A sense of patriotic duty was the motive of another young woman in accepting the proposal of a royal prince: since he was a military officer, she thought "the best way of dedicating myself to the state [would be] to marry him so that he could go to the war front without worrying about his personal future." She had no thought about what a husband should be like. This marriage ended in divorce after the war.

Freedom of choice, which some informants enjoyed, was attributed to Western influence on their parents. "Because my father spent years in the West," first as a student and later as an ambassador, "he was able to leave us free to accept or reject his choice of spouses." Even in this case, the selection of prospective spouses was in the father's hands, and a child's freedom to reject was not exercised because the father's choice was "excellent." A daughter whose parents had both lived in Europe for years and were "completely" Westernized in their life-style was nonetheless matched to a branch-house son without her being consulted. In other words, the parents' exposure to the Western way of life did not guarantee the children's freedom in spouse selection. Of course, it is important to recall here that Westernization meant a *selective* Western-aristocratization.

That the individual's subjectivity or choice was irrelevant in mate selection can be inferred from the fact that some of my informants were kept deaf and blind to the ongoing marriage negotiations until they were finalized. Like Princess Masako (daughter of Prince Nashimoto, destined to be wed to the Korean prince above), a daimyo daughter was stunned to read the newspaper announcement of her engagement before she was informed personally. Another daughter of a sekke was told by her mother one day, "You are going, it seems, to marry [royal] Prince K, because his father visited us." Obviously the mother had not been made privy to the arrangements either. It was "as if the whole matter concerned someone else, not me," said the former princess. No wonder that some of my female informants and questionnaire respondents did not know who and how their own marriages came about, a blindness that, to a lesser degree, was shared by men as well.

The irrelevance of the marriage principals' subjective awareness is further illustrated by the fact that proposals were often received when they were in their early teens or even younger. One kuge daughter underwent a miai meeting with her future husband when she was a sixth grader. "I didn't know what the miai meant; I only thought I was gaining a new cousin." Another older kuge informant generalized that kazoku children in those days "had miai at about ten years of age." An extreme was a prenatal engagement. "After my father was born, it was decided that if family So-and-so happened to give birth to a baby girl, he would be engaged to her"—the decision having been made by a large group of high-ranking and powerful vassals. A variety of motives for premature arrangements is conceivable, including political ones. I suspect that the small marriage market was another factor urging some parents to secure suitable mates for their children as soon as possible.

Marriage also took place at a relatively young age, thus interfering with school education. Women in particular, if engaged young, tended to quit school to marry, even when only one more year was needed for graduation from high school or college. I often had the impression that neither they nor their parents cared at all about their school diploma. One of my postwar-generation informants confessed that she agreed to the proposed marriage specifically "in order to drop out" of the Gakushuin Junior College. For men, in contrast, a university diploma was almost mandatory; often, therefore, unions were between a high school dropout and university graduate, making for a sizable age discrepancy between husband and wife. But sometimes marriage preceded the husband's graduation, in which case he became a "married student"—nothing surprising nowadays, but unheard of among ordinary people in prewar days. While a gender gap in education was common across class lines, it was wider, I think, among the elite owing to women's young age at marriage and to the positional requirement of higher education for men.

Of course, not all kazoku women chose marriage over schooling: some completed the highest education level available to women, at a time when the majority of the female population did not or could not obtain more than a grade school education. (For more on education, see chapter 7.)

The miai introduction ranged from formal to informal, and sometimes was dispensed with when the spouses-to-be already knew each other well, as in kin marriage. Kazoku also shared with other classes the practice of staging an "accidental" meeting. Such an encounter was experienced long after the war by the adopted heir to a sekke when he was visiting royal houses to "report" on his adopted status. One of these visits, he later learned, was a staged miai for him and a princess. Marriage did ensue.

Kasumi Kaikan runs a *kekkon sōdanjo* (marriage counseling office), a Japanese euphemism for a matchmaking enterprise. The woman in charge is said to utilize impressive lists of young men and women whose fathers, well known in banking, industry, and government, are connected to the kazoku as members, kin, vassals, Gakushuin friends, and so on.

Ceremonies

The miai itself was in fact a ceremony in that, for older generations, it was more than an introduction; rather, it was a ceremonial confirmation of the acceptance of a proposal. Nevertheless, truly formal rites were conducted for engagements and then for weddings. Generalizations on ceremonial styles and elaboration are difficult to make, given the wide variation even within this small society depending on family affluence, traditionalism or Westernism, status congruity or incongruity of the couple, generational differences within the couple (prewar, wartime, or postwar generations), and the like. Here I shall discuss some features of ceremonies that struck me as status symbolic.

I was told that for the elite, matrimonial ceremonies, whether for engagements or weddings, were quite simple, much more so than among middle-class commoners, particularly if the marriage partners were of similar rank or background. The engagement gifts (*yuinō*) to be exchanged were largely symbolic, typically a hakama (formal pleated skirt-like trousers) for the groom and an obi (a heavy sash for kimono) for the bride. No cash gift was involved, as it was among commoners; only in cases of exchange marriage was any money transferred. Nor was the wedding as extravagant as among rich commoners, a point confirmed by Fujishima (1965, 204–6). Genteel austerity among the old aristocracy was thus stressed in contrast to the theatrical grandiosity displayed by the new rich, especially in regard to matrimonial ceremonies. (This was the reason why one mother was much more nervous when her younger daughter married a commoner than when her elder daughter, my informant, married within high kazoku ranks.)

The main actors in the yuinō ceremony were male servants (of omote): two head servants, one from each house, met halfway and proceeded to his assigned destination for gift delivery. In many cases, the wedding was announced in the name of the top-managerial servant.

The oath-taking ceremony, preceding the reception banquet, was often held at the shrines of family ancestors (see chapter 4). In the Ogasawara-style ceremony, which was practiced by several couples in my interview sample, austerity was such that only the principals, with or without their parents, were present, assisted by a couple of female servants to hand over and fill sake cups to be exchanged.[16]

The reception banquet was another matter, possibly involving a large number of celebrated guests, including royals, noble peers, high officials of government, generals, and the like. When marriage united two daimyo houses, their respective vassal groups would swell the crowd. One such case involved seven hundred people. The austerity principle would thus have to give way to grandeur. The Kazoku Clubhouse, Tokyo Clubhouse, and Imperial Hotel were the most frequently mentioned places used for reception banquets. The Western influence was sometimes expressed in the form of *risshoku* ("standing banquets," instead of the traditional feast at which all guests sat on the tatami floor), which, although today fashionable across all classes, was almost unknown before the war except among the Westernized upper class.

More conspicuously status symbolic were the couple's wedding attire and the bride's coiffure. Asked how kazoku differed from non-kazoku in terms of ceremonies, the son of a viscount promptly replied, speaking of his parents' wedding: "Father wore *ikan-sokutai,* and mother jūnihitoe. I have the picture still. Probably they attended the palace [in those outfits]." The ikan-sokutai—court dress and head gear for male courtiers—originated in the Heian period and paralleled the multilayered female court dress, jūnihitoe. The ancient costume was more popular for a bride than for a groom, complemented by the appropriate hairstyle, called *osuberakashi*. While neither the attire nor the hairdo replicated the Heian court style exactly, they were close enough to stimulate fantasies about the courtly life contemporaneous with the shining prince Genji.[17] This traditionalism in the wedding costume may parallel the "display of symbolic capital or long-standing family court tradition" by Swedish debutantes at court "wearing great-grandmother's train, grandmother's lace, and mama's court sleeves" (Rundquist 1987, 3). A groom, if he already had a title, could opt for a Western-style ceremonial court garment called *taireifuku* or *shakufuku,* as when he presented himself at the imperial palace on official occasions.

MARITAL EXPERIENCES

In many ways conjugal experience among kazoku seems similar to that in other classes, but I noted some subtle differences. Among older generations, husband and wife appeared aloof, as much as or even more so than among common Japanese. Two possible explanations for greater aloofness come to mind: the positional nature of marriage, as discussed above; and the fact that daily chores of domestic life, which might otherwise have brought the couple together—such as the wife looking after her husband's daily needs as in the typical middle-class family—were conducted largely by servants.

Ironically, the kazoku wife answered to her husband more than to other members of the family. "My mother was more a wife to my father than a mother to us children, because my father so insisted." As this remark by the daughter of a viscount suggests, a sort of conjugal bonding resulted partly from the woman's subordination to her husband, the title holder. It appears that the upper-class family in general was more male-centered, with greater authority of the head over the rest of the family than was the case among families of lower classes.[18] This gender asymmetry meant that the wife's conjugal orientation was not necessarily reciprocated by her husband. Wifely subordination was not replaced by the mother-child bonding that would prevail among other classes, because, again, it was servants more than the mother who reared the children (see chapter 7).

Further, the young bride, who in other classes would have been tied more to her in-laws than to her husband, was here relatively free from her obligations as a daughter-in-law, if only because her parents-in-law were waited on by their own servants. In the residential arrangement, too, the two generations could usually afford to live at some distance from each other, in either separate dwellings or entirely separate estates. Interaction between the junior and senior wife was limited to rituals such as daily greetings or weekly visits; at most it extended to sharing meals at the same table. Overall, politeness predominated in in-law interaction. All these circumstances conducive to conjugal pairing were combined with the Western influence, which urged men, especially in contact with Western guests or hosts, to present themselves accompanied by their wives.

The dependence of the wife's status on her husband could be revealed when she was widowed without a successor son, as happened to the wife of a distinguished, affluent daimyo marquis. The widow's daughter recalled that, after enjoying a fully aristocratic childhood in a magnificent mansion staffed by dozens of servants, she and her mother had to move to a much smaller mansion and adjust to a more modest way of life. The main house was taken over by the heir, her late father's brother. I was surprised that the latter's son and present househead did not even recognize the existence of my informant, his cousin, when I asked, as if the sonless widow and her daughter had simply vanished from the family history.

The wife's conjugal tie, while it thus meant her subordination, could also mean her liberation from the overconfined, overprotected life she had been accustomed to in her natal family—if her husband was so inclined to change it. Several women I encountered admitted that they had become "free" of their earlier naiveté and unquestioning compliance, thanks to reeducation by their husbands. One woman said that her Western-educated husband had taken her around to places like cheap bars in shitamachi intentionally to divest her of the old aristocratic inhibitions. Another woman became aware only after marriage of the importance of having and pursuing her own life goal, thanks to her Westernized husband's insistence. Thus "sudden liberation" came for some women with their marriage, before the postwar liberation. Ironically, both occasions of liberation were a sort of double bind, in that freedom was tied to compliance with the liberator's authority.

The ordinary gender hierarchy was maintained, even in the case of an heiress marrying an adopted son-in-law, but patriarchy was somewhat interfered with by the influence of the wife's natal family. The daughter of a zaibatsu family, married to a poor kuge, admitted that she had had her own way (*ibatteta*) with her husband. Even though outranked by his house, which was of old noble stock, her house financially supported the couple almost entirely. But the old status, unless it was extremely imbalanced economically, did count. A daimyo son, married to a royal princess who "descended in marriage" (*go-kōka*), for example, tended to be dwarfed in the eyes of their children. "My mother was the center of the family," said a man in his fifties who, strongly attached to his royal mother, now empathizes with his father's frustrations. A similar status reversal was discussed by a woman regarding her mother-in-law, another royal "descender": "My mother-in-law held the feeling that she was higher than her husband. I thought my father-in-law was great, but inside the house Granny [the mother-in-law] was in absolute charge. My husband also had long believed his mother was superior, and only when [his] father died did he realize his greatness too."

It may be that the bride's status was affected less by the groom's own dominance than by the visible and invisible presence of his parents and other kin. The descending bride, however—definitely in the case of a royal princess—was largely free of the authority of her affines. The daughter of a daimyo count, married to a commoner after the war, admitted that one big advantage of coming from a kazoku family was that "you are treated well by your parents-in-law." From her narrative I detected that her in-laws held her in a kind of awe.[19]

LOVE, ANOMALY, AND LIBERATION

To conclude this chapter, a brief remark is in order on personal emotions that inevitably entered marriage. Thus far, marriage has been viewed from the standpoint of position. Even with regard to the management of status incongruity, the focal point was the relative positions of kazoku spouses. Daughter adoption was practiced to restore positional consistency, concubines were installed to keep the legitimate position intact, and exchange between status and wealth (or robust genes) served to strengthen the hereditary position and avoid its further debilitation.

Personal likes and dislikes, however, were not totally irrelevant, and fortunately in some cases, personal choice and love went together with positional discretion and parental approval. But if personal emotions contradicted the positional judgment, they were overruled. Most of my informants went along with this positional imperative simply because a rejection of the parental proposal had never occurred to them, or because love had nothing to do with marriage.[20] Sons and daughters of the elite appeared more conditioned than commoners to comply with the positional marriage proposal for several reasons: the strength of parental authority; the fact that the ie asset overrode personal inclinations; the highly public, visible nature of their marriage and its control by the Sōchitsuryō; and pressures from vassals and retainers.[21]

Still, there were instances of risk-taking in individual attempts to override the status norm, even before the postwar liberation. Here again we meet gender asymmetry, in that only female rule breakers were stigmatized, whereas men were protected under institutionalized or condoned concubinage. Further, what would have occurred among commoners without drawing public attention was sensationalized if a kazoku woman was involved. An informant's sister, to cite one notable case, fell in love with a *bungaku seinen* (a young man engrossed in literature with no career prospects) and decided to live with him. This affair was eagerly taken up by newspapers, and labeled by the Sōchitsuryō an instance of kazoku disgrace. The informant, who was the head of a count house, submitted to the Sōchitsuryō a voluntary decision to remove his sister from his house register in anticipation of a punitive order that the office would otherwise issue. "Removal" (*joseki*) did not mean actual expulsion, however. Instead it boiled down to a symbolic adoption of the scandalous sister by the informant's commoner acquaintance "to appease the perturbed world." Adoption again! It seems that adoption functioned like a panacea to restore the appearance of normalcy in the face of all sorts of actual anomaly. The sister, by the way, later married another, more respectable man.

Several women mentioned as examples of notoriety were kazoku wives who "eloped" with commoner men. At the time of this research, however, these women were discussed not so much with disapproval as with ambivalent admiration or envy for following their natural feelings. Yanagiwara Akiko, whom we have already met, was a poet and author, better known by her pen name, Byakuren. As a child she was adopted by a Yanagiwara branch house without knowing she had been betrothed to the adoptive father's hidden son, mothered by a concubine. After having been forced into marriage, Akiko ran away, leaving her child behind, an act that led to her incarceration in her natal house. Akiko was then coerced again into an arranged marriage with a widower mining industrialist much older than her who turned out to run a household filled with maid-concubines, as we have seen. This loveless and torturous marriage ended with Akiko's elopement with a young lover, which was sensationalized by her open letter, printed in a newspaper, to her deserted husband demanding divorce (Nagahata 1990). Among less-known scandals was one involving a daughter of a distinguished family who committed herself to lesbian cohabitation with an actor of the Takarazuka, an all-female theater in which the "male" actor is the idolized center of attention.

After the war many kazoku marriages broke down, as if the honor of kazoku status alone had sustained the facade of normal marriage until then. Still, the media continued to go into frenzies over high-ranking kazoku or royal wives who left their esteemed husbands for their lovers. One woman, married to a royal prince, was convinced even after the war that divorce was impossible because of their public visibility and considered suicide by stabbing herself with the dagger given by her family upon her marriage.[22] Finally, her hospitalization for cancer treatment secured her a divorce by consent. Another royally married woman instigated the first court case of divorce; years of struggle ensued until the court finally ruled in favor of divorce—which, of course, was widely publicized by scandal sheets, particularly since she was seen dating another man before the divorce was finalized. Another well-known case involved the wife of a prince who ran away with a masseur. The old term for elopement, *kakeochi,* was used to describe such an "improper" union.

Some kazoku women provided natural links, because of their English fluency and cosmopolitan savoir-faire, between high officers of the Occupation and occupied Japan. In the beginning, they were even mobilized by the Japanese government as communicational lubricant between victors and defeated. Love affairs erupted, exciting the grapevine and magazines. Viscountess Torio, for example, fell in love with an American colonel, presumably second only to General MacArthur in SCAP (Supreme Commander for the Allied Powers) and a man who influenced the earliest policymaking of the Allied Occupation. Both parties already being married, this affair was never consummated by marriage, and it was widely quoted by resentful Japanese as a prime example of kazoku decadence in the postwar era. Nearly four decades later, Torio, then in her seventies, recounted this extraordinary experience in her autobiography (1985).

Some informants both inside and outside the aristocratic circle claim that sexual license among kazoku, kuge in particular, is not new but rather traditional, persisting since ancient times. This claim is associated with classical Heian court tales focused on the uninhibited sexual adventures of nobles and royals. Again we must consider gender difference. It seems that upper-class men, aristocratic or not, have always enjoyed sexual freedom with impunity, while women were under fairly stringent control, even at the Heian court. Women would express their sexual emotions most strongly through jealousy of and protest against rival women or unfaithful male partners, with spirit possession (*mono no ke*) as the ultimate ammunition (Bargen 1988). Lady Nijō, the sensational medieval author of *Towazugatari,* a diary documenting late-thirteenth-century court life with astonishing candidness, had multiple and even simultaneous affairs with retired emperors and nobles, appearing wildly licentious by modern standards. Yet I think that even this extraordinary court lady was more an object of male lust and whims than a subject free to pursue her own passions. From the late medieval through the modern age, rigorous chastity became the norm for upper-class women, deviation from which was severely punished. In this respect, the divergence between men and women of the upper class has been greater than in the lower classes.[23] Postwar scandals, too, I believe, may be understood largely as confirming women's sexual repression. One can only speculate how difficult it must have been for kazoku women to break through the tradition-loaded norm of unilateral fidelity. Most such women, after all, had to make a 180-degree turn away from naive or patient conformism and rigorous chastity.

SEVEN

Socialization

Acquisition and Transmission of Status Culture

The kazoku status, to be hereditary, had to have its culture carried on by successive generations. Chapters 3–6 conveyed *what* that status culture was like; this chapter will consider *how* it was acquired by or transmitted to kazoku members, with a main, but not exclusive, focus on the child. To the extent that "what" cannot be separated from "how," some redundancy, particularly with chapter 5, will be unavoidable, especially in regard to who socialized kazoku children.

The socialization influence flows both vertically—downward from superiors or seniors, or upward from inferiors or juniors (as when a kazoku master was influenced by his servant, or a parent by his or her child)—and horizontally, between peers or age-mates. Kazoku, we find, sometimes felt such multidirectional flows of influence in striking ways. The diversity of socializing agents, indeed, may account for the fact that socialization not only reproduced but also on occasion modified or even created status culture.

THE DOUBLE FUNCTION OF SOCIALIZATION

Socialization performs a double function: to train the child in assuming a series of roles and statuses, on the one hand, and to meet and regulate the child's biological, emotional, and cognitive needs and potentials, on the other. One function involves the social structure and its reproduction, whereas the other focuses on the person and proper growth. Although the two functions, structural and personal, are inextricable, there is likely to be variation from society to society, and class to class, in the primacy of one over the other as well as in the way the two are interlocked. Pertinent to the above generalization is, again, the binary typology of "po-

243

sitional" versus "personal"—as with marriage, but here borrowed from Mary Douglas (1970, 45–48). When one side of the double function is overemphasized, the other, neglected side is likely to erupt in demand of attention.

It is safe to assume that prewar aristocratic socialization was more positional than its commoner counterpart. In the family, a member stepped into a given role rather than made his own role (Bernstein 1971, 185). Individuals interacted more in accordance with the roles and statuses they held in relation to one another than as whole persons with their own needs and emotions. Status distance rather than intimacy, separateness rather than togetherness, predominated in most kazoku families. In this respect, the nobility was surpassed only by the royalty. How the neglected personal side fared and was managed is a point of analysis below.

There were exceptions to this "rule," of course, and some informants (paradoxically, royals in particular) firmly and sometimes resentfully refuted this generalized picture as a stereotype. But such informants tended to add, "My family was different from other kazokusan," or it turned out that distance was so taken for granted that it felt natural. In some instances family intimacy was created deliberately by a parent whose mind was set on reversing what he or she had experienced as a child. Also significant is the fact that "status distance" was not necessarily accompanied by physical distance: even when two persons were in physical contact or copresence, a message of status distance could easily be conveyed. Complicating the matter is the fact that kazoku families on average were much more Westernized than households of other classes in certain aspects of their life-style as a result of overseas education or career and frequent social or official contact with foreign dignitaries (see chapter 5).

Because it would be impossible to exhaust all socialization contexts and agents, the following analysis centers on two main locations or agents: home/family and school/education, with a third, intermediate agent termed "out-of-home."

DISTANCE TRAINING IN THE FAMILY

Family socialization was centered on two pivotal status incumbents: the household and his nominated heir. Since these positions were filled by male members only and primogeniture was the general rule, the children were clearly differentiated and rank-ordered by both gender and birth order. The third son of a count recalled how his eldest brother was trained to be a lord while all the other children were treated indifferently or as subordinates, including not being allowed to have a second bowl of rice

before the heir-brother did. A special status term for address and reference, like "highness" or "junior lord," was reserved only for the heir,
and younger children were disciplined to use honorifics in speaking to
their eldest brother.

Positional distinction of the heir was compounded by sex segregation,
which had much to do with the spatial design of residence (see chapter
5). High-ranking families of daimyo origin, it will be recalled, removed
the heir at age seven from the "interior" family quarters, associated with
women, and put him in the "exterior," male quarters. Some families sent
their sons, even including nonheirs, away from home. One such segregated heir, a former marquis, said that he had had no women around,
except when he was being nursed in sickbed, until his graduation from
university. That he was a sickly boy may suggest a young son's suppressed
desire for female care.

Positional socialization with an emphasis on hierarchy and distance
was further extended to parent-child interaction. Most informants of all
backgrounds characterized their parents as having been distant, remote,
and even "cold." In large high-ranking households, children usually
dined separately from their parents, but when joint dining took place,
conviviality was not to be expected, as a former viscount recalled: "Father
was stern, and there was nothing jovial about the family at the dinner
table. We were forbidden to talk. It was unpleasant. I wanted to talk and
listen freely." Merrymaking was disapproved of as uncalled-for buffoon-
ery (*warufuzake*). On a street one day he witnessed an enviable scene, a
little boy mounted atop his father's shoulders—something absolutely
inconceivable for his father to do with him. The second son of a marquis
repeated the same point: "Today, children and parents joke with and
embrace one another. When I was a child, I had nothing like that." As
a child he felt constrained not to initiate conversation and, when speaking, to use honorifics. "Parents were scary, and we were not able to show
them *amae* [desire for indulgence]." Many informants referred to parent-
child contact as "ritualistic" or "well-mannered, as between strangers"
(*tanin gyōgi*). Said one: "Twice a day we children went to see our parents
for morning and bedtime greetings." The parent-child distance was both
implemented and symbolized by spatial segregation in residential
arrangement. The children's rooms and parental living rooms were quite
separate, often connected only by long hallways.

That the father was a distant figure is not surprising, since as househead he singly embodied the house status, including property, authority,
nobility rank, prerogatives, and prestige, on which the whole family
depended. The positional emphasis in father-child relations was more or

less true with commoners as well, although in a more compromised way, and even now the father's absence, if not his authority, is a common feature of urban middle-class Japanese families. Also shared in a milder form by other classes was positional socialization with regard to gender and birth order. What *did* stand out as a class contrast was the mother's role.

Among commoners, especially middle-class families where there was a sharp division of labor by gender, the mother was characterized by physical closeness and emotional warmth. The aforementioned double function of socialization was performed contrapuntally by mother and father, who thus generated a double image of parenthood as close and distant, warm and stern, supportive and disciplinarian, sympathetic and autocratic—in a word, personal and positional. The mother was autonomous enough to take a role complementary to but counterbalancing that of the father and, when necessary, to shield the child from excessive paternal authoritarianism. The child, legally and positionally, belonged to the father as the househead, but emotionally and personally he or she belonged to the mother. And the mother in turn belonged to the child more than to the father.

This somewhat idealized image of middle-class motherhood was far from reality for the children of aristocrats. The mother appeared in my informants' narratives as conspicuously absent when the child was under bodily care, be it during bathing, dressing, using the toilet, sitting on laps, being held in arms, sleeping, and so on. "All my mother did," claimed the daughter of a marquis, "was give birth, and nothing more [*umi sute*]. She would not have known whether her child was dead or alive unless someone so reported." No doubt this is an exaggeration, but it captures the general feelings of many informants toward their mothers.

Since the war this state of affairs has radically changed, and the middle-class pattern has become predominant. Thus, the prewar-generation mother is now experiencing the "fun" of caring for her grandchildren but at the same time tends to criticize her postwar-generation daughter for being so irrationally attached to and "all over" (*betabeta*) her children. One daughter repudiated such criticism by saying that it was easy for her mother to be so aloof because she did not have to raise her children personally. This is not the whole story, however. Vestiges of old socialization patterns survive, inhibiting some men and women from feeling and acting like ordinary parents. The daughter of a viscount, though determined to be different from her mother, found herself unable to hug her child as she wished to. "After all, you cannot deny your blood," she said. A man who wished to have spontaneous and cheerful conversation with his children over dinner found to his frustration that he was a replica of his stern, silent father. A disproportionate number of postwar mothers in their thirties and forties confessed that they felt cool toward their children and indifferent to the children's high or low performance at school, unlike a typical middle-class "education mama."

To return to prewar times, we have noted that among the kazoku the mother's role was not as differentiated from the father's as among commoners, and that she remained positional like her husband. This fact was explained variously: mother, together with father, was too busy hosting VIP's or accepting invitations from them; father wanted her to remain elegant, aloof from domestic chores; mother belonged to father, not to the children. These explanations suggest, to repeat a point made in chapter 6, that spousal obligations were stronger than mother-child bonding and that the wife joined the husband in maintaining the house status.

The implication is twofold. First, aristocratic families were more patriarchal than families in other classes (as observed of upper-class women in the West as well; see Rundquist 1987; Ostrander 1984), in that, except in extremely hypogamous cases, women readily acknowledged the authority of their husbands. In Japan, this status asymmetry between husband and wife was strengthened by the patricentric rule of succession. Further, while through motherhood and singlehanded home management commoner women would have gained autonomy and even sat on a matriarchal throne (Lebra 1984), the aristocratic wife and mother had no domestic leverage to diminish status asymmetry. And second, aristocrats, as we have seen, were more Westernized than commoners. The primacy of spousal ties over parent-child bonding was thus due partly to the influence of Western culture. In sum, the Western idea of marital companionship seems to have become locked with the patricentricity of Confucian tradition to intensify gender asymmetry.

Another explanation for the distance of the aristocratic mother, readily given by almost all, referred to the ubiquitous presence of servants who performed the maternal role for the children. Questions about mothers often prompted mentions of maidservants who functioned essentially as surrogate mothers: "But we had maids to look after us." Indeed, not only maids, but other types of servants as well were involved in the socialization of kazoku children.

THE ROLES OF SERVANTS

Servants were indispensable to the aristocratic life-style, although the number and kinds of servants and methods of recruitment varied widely from one kazoku household to another, in reflection of estate size, family wealth, and the household's history (see chapter 5).

Servants played multiple roles in socializing the kazoku children, intentionally or unintentionally, directly or indirectly, which resulted in impressing the children with a variety of often mutually inconsistent messages. A particularly decisive role in childhood socialization was played by the maids of the interior (otsuki), who attended the family around the clock. A wealthy family had otsuki on a one-to-one basis, with at least one servant "attached" to each family member, adult and child. According to my informants, these otsuki were high school educated and from "good" families.

In analyzing the socializing roles of nonfamily, I will focus primarily on the otsuki, as the most influential agents, and secondarily bring other commoner personnel, both servants and nonservants, into the discussion when appropriate.

Status Support

The presence and collaboration of servants were indispensable in upholding the aristocracy as part of the social order. Within the household, the lordly status of its head would not be a reality unless he had at least one servant who would call him "Lord"; similarly, the "lady" or "junior lord" would be relying on empty titles if no servant addressed them as such and waited on them with proper deference. Through the servants' respectful speech and manners, kazoku children were socialized to be aware of the hierarchy within the family and at the same time to internalize the status of their family as distinct from that of their servants or commoners in general. The children, like their parents, in turn addressed their servants downward by their personal names in yobisute.

Servants thus bolstered the positional socialization of the kazoku family. No wonder that a kazoku household ceased to be aristocratic not when it was legislated out of existence, but when it lost its last servant during or after the war. The converse was also true: as long as there was at least one servant, the family could retain marks of the aristocratic lifestyle. This difference was clear when I visited homes for interviews, some of which still had one or more "loyal" servants to receive visitors at the entrance and bring tea, while most had none.

Servants also buttressed the kazoku status in the children's minds by mediating between elements—persons, classes, or worlds—that were supposed to be kept apart. The distance between parent and child in the kazoku family necessitated and in turn was maintained by servants mediating between the two. When an informant said, "In my family it was mother who trained us in speech and manners," it often turned out that in fact the mother told the daughter's otsuki what to do.

The children (daughters more than sons) were secluded from the outside world, playing within the fenced premises only with the children of the male servants of the exterior—who, unlike female servants, were married and had families. At school age, the youngsters commuted to school by private carriage, rickshaw, or car, driven by their servant-drivers; this both protected them from direct exposure and mediated them to the street.[1] Such protection was not welcomed by little children, who would rather walk freely in the natural elements. The daughter of a daimyo viscount recalled feeling envy for other children, seen from her rickshaw, walking barefoot and drenched in the rain. Another, the daughter of a rich businessman, protested about not being able to join "all other children" in riding the train.

Many families either could not afford private vehicles or, for disciplinary purposes, ruled out private transportation for the children, and Gakushuin, too, prohibited such luxury during the war, particularly for boys. In those cases, the children were escorted by their otsuki maids, who waited in *tomomachi-beya* (a large schoolroom specially reserved for chaperones) until school was over and then accompanied their charges back home.[2]

Servants acting as drivers or escorts thus mediated kazoku children (and adults too) to the mundane reality of the external world, thereby playing an essential role in the children's distance training. They were in a position to help maintain the status boundary, being located on the margin of the boundary: inside the household physically and functionally, but at the same time outside the *status* of the household. They were "outsider insiders."[3]

The servant was a status prop in still another sense. She represented and bolstered the status of the master family by her very presence, appearance, and demeanor. Not just the number but also the quality of servants affected the reputation of the house. Even children would feel their status pride enhanced before their schoolmates if they were escorted by well-groomed, respectably dressed, and properly speaking servants. Indeed, even the servants, while on duty in the tomomachi-beya, watched one another and gossiped about one another's master households along these lines. Even impoverished kazoku, frugal with food and other basic commodities, had good reason to spend beyond their means on the otsuki servants' dresses and hair. Chaperonage, like private vehicles, not only protected the child but symbolized family status.

I have discussed three ways in which the servant buttressed the aristocratic status of the family and thus instilled an awareness of status distinction in the child: the observable status inferiority of the servant in interaction with family members; her role as a mediator and status protector; and her symbolic representation of the family status and reputation. The servant's support was by no means unilateral, however, but was reciprocated. The parents admonished the child to be kind and considerate to servants and subordinates, to act (or not to act) in a certain way toward or because of them. Several informants, when asked what their parents said to discipline them, could remember only cautions about how to treat the servants. "My parents were strict," said the daughter of an affluent marquis, "in prohibiting us from behaving arrogantly toward the servants [and vassals] 'because they are our treasures.' I was not allowed to say, 'Bring me tea,' but instead 'Will you please . . .' "

There were a variety of house rules, including punctuality, mainly in consideration of the servants. The daughter of a prince recalled, "Looking back, it was like being brought up in a dormitory. There were all kinds of rules, such as what time to take a bath. . . . We were not permitted to wait until bedtime. We were supposed to bathe by three or four o'clock so that the janitor could clean the bathroom before going home for supper." A viscount explained why he became unable to express his feelings in a straightforward manner: his parents admonished the children to be sensitive to the feelings of the servants, not to say, for example, whether the meal was tasty or untasty, because discriminatory appraisals would have caused conflict among the servants, making one cook proud and another miserable.

Socialization focused on the servant seems to reverse what Bateson called the "ternary" mode, exemplified by "parent-nurse-child" and distinguished from "pure hierarchy" and the "triangle": here, "essentially, the function of the middle member is to instruct and discipline the third member in the forms of behavior which he should adopt in his contacts with the first. The nurse teaches the child how to behave toward its parents, just as the N.C.O. teaches and disciplines the private in how he should behave toward officers" (Bateson 1972, 96). The typical ternary mode, which likely derived from the European example of the upper class, did occur among Japanese aristocratic families (see below), but my informants more vividly recalled the reversed ternary, where they were taught by their parents how to behave toward and on behalf of their servants. In the reversed ternary, one might also expect the parents to train their daughter to be polished in manners so that the servants watching her might emulate her as their model. This point was made by a student of high society in Victorian England, Leonore Davidoff (1973), and in Japan, too, such behavior would have been consistent with the conventional status name for a servant: "etiquette apprentice."[4] Yet in only two cases of my sample (a baron's and a viscount's families) was this kind of instruction actually given, while all other informants (including these two) stressed considerateness and empathy for servants. In fact, the exemplary role and modeling role were more often reversed, as will be seen below.

Surrogate Parenthood

More important in the informants' memories than the servants' role of status support was their direct and personal responsibility for rearing and looking after the children. While bolstering positional socialization, servants also looked after what was thereby omitted—that is, personal socialization, the gratification and regulation of the child's biopsychological needs and development. In a word, a servant was a surrogate parent, filling the role left vacant by the real parent.

In the first place, the mother's role in mother-child bonding was transferred to the otsuki in terms of intimacy and interdependence. Surrogacy began at birth. Some families hired wet nurses for various reasons: because the mother had no lactation; because the mother's milk had been artificially stopped; because the mother was supposed to stay young, beautiful, and free; and so on. Even when the mother breastfed her baby, it was done more or less as a matter of necessity, with the rest of caretaking left to a servant. It was the otsuki hired either after or simultaneously with a wet nurse, who was generally recalled with the fondest memories: "I cannot remember myself ever left alone. Ume was always with me. She was there waiting when I woke up, she was there when I went to sleep." In some households, each child ate alone, waited on by his or her otsuki. It was the otsuki's job to bathe the child, and the otsuki slept near the child.

The recollection of a prince's daughter depicted a striking intimacy:

I have never sat on mother's lap. [But] I had an otsuki who, luckily, stayed with me from my birth until my marriage. She was a truly devoted servant. I played with her nipples and pretended to nurse—only pretended, because she was not a wet nurse. I feel that her daughter and I are real sisters. Now it is her grandchildren's generation, and as if we were kin, we keep in touch. . . . Yes, she slept at the edge of my bed. [Every morning] it took her an hour to fix her hair [in a Japanese style], which I could not stand, because that kept me away from her. We were together wherever we went.

It was this maid, instead of her mother, who kept a "developmental diary" for her, recording her weight, vocabulary, and the like. In the living room of her present tiny apartment, this woman displays a picture of her late surrogate mother. As indicated in the above quote, such bonding was a product of long otsuki service for the same child. In most cases the maid quit to marry, but in some she remained single and dedicated her entire life to her charge, accompanying her mistress when the latter married.

The warmth and indulgence of the otsuki was typically contrasted to the aloofness or formality of the real mother, attachment to one contrasted to indifference to the other, one's leniency to the other's authority:

> We were most scared of mother, but never cried for her when she went out. It was when the servants went home on holidays that we cried and screamed.
> If I had had to choose [between mother and otsuki] I would have sided with my otsuki.
> When my mother died I did not cry, but when my otsuki passed away I did.
> In my house I was free to go and see my mother whenever I wanted, and my mother also could come into my room. But the otsuki was closer to me. I could sit on the lap of my mother or grandmother, but only in strangerlike etiquette [tanin-gyōgi]. Toward them we had to behave deferentially. With the otsuki, I was free to say whatever I wanted, free to fight. Parents were absolute.

This type of contrast, granted that it could be an overstatement, is nonetheless significant. The son and heir of a marquis, while his parents were always accessible, had a maid from his birth on, who defended him when he was scolded by his father, and even talked back to the father when she thought he was being unreasonable. This sounds like a scene from an ordinary family where the mother protects a child from a harsh father. Another male informant recalled how unruly and rebellious he was as a child and how parental punishments were revenged by mischief. It turned out that his disobedience was expressed not against his father, the very source of authority and discipline, but against the maids. Here we can see a displacement of aggression from the real target, the father, to a weaker object, the mother, as embodied by the maid.

As much as the ordinary mother-child bond can intensify to an unhealthy exclusivity and generate psychological conflict, intimacy between child and maid could produce similar stress. Some otsuki, though not many, as their former "surrogate children" recalled, came to identify themselves with the children so much that they lost their own identity. One result was sibling rivalry created and, in a sense, taken over by the maids. An eighty-eight-year-old woman, the daughter of a count, recalled otsuki servants, each in support of her favorite child, fighting one another over which child should or should not receive an apple or "some such silly thing." The heir's otsuki, not surprisingly, was arrogant and aggressive, as if she were privileged to be—which the others challenged. In one instance, two maids did not speak to each other for nearly a year, their rivalry had grown so heated.

Often the children were onlookers, embarrassed or disgusted. But in one case a child was actually abused by a jealous otsuki in charge of the victim's sister. The informant, the youngest of three daughters but stronger than her immediately older sister, always bested the latter in games, school athletic contests, school reports, and whatnot. She was also her grandmother's favorite. All these circumstances upset the otsuki of the middle sister, and so she punished the younger sister by verbal and physical abuse. Did the victim's own otsuki not protect her from the assailant? The jealous maid was in fact so mean to the informant's otsuki as well that no woman would stay as her otsuki long enough to be protective, and this fact was picked up by the punitive otsuki as proof of the victim's allegedly perverted character. The eldest sister, co-interviewed, turned out to be the victim of her own otsuki, a former schoolteacher who acted like a contemporary "education mama": "I was constantly pressed to study, study, study every day. When I got a poor score in a Chinese-character writing test or something, she was mortified and vented her anger by scratching me. At times I bled. I did not know why I was abused so." It never occurred to either sister to report to their parents what was going on. While certainly the parent-child distance in space and status contributed to this information blockage, the victims also feared the inevitable retaliation of the maids—"It's like you can't take a grievance about your immediate boss, the section chief, directly to the company president." This deplorable situation, the younger sister explained, was caused by the "hysterical" outburst of an unmarried woman trapped in a small, isolated world.

Overall, servants may be said to have provided the child with personal warmth, nurturance, and a feeling of kinship (though sometimes going to a pathological extreme of identification), in compensation for the relative distance and aloofness of family members, whether parents or siblings. It is ironic that there was a deeper intimacy between an aristocratic child and his or her commoner maid than between the members of a same-status family. While a commoner servant reinforced the distinctiveness of the aristocracy positionally, more "equality" resulted from personal intimacy across different statuses than within the same status. One might wonder whether this is true as well across societies in the culture of the elite. Yet a Maeda daughter, who spent her childhood in London, wrote in her autobiography (Sakai 1982, 8) and stated in interview that British servants and their upper-class masters never developed such intimacy, even after three years of live-in service, as did the Japanese counterparts.[5]

Servants could hamper children and turn them into weaklings through their overprotectiveness and indulgence. A daughter of Konoe Fumimaro, a prince and prime minister and head of *the* top-ranking sekke, recalled what her father had said: he was constantly waited on by his servants, and when he washed his face it was a servant's job to wipe it. He had no chance to walk by himself; indeed, he had to practice doing so before his entry into Gakushuin (Shūkan Yomiuri Henshūbu 1987, 268–69). A former viscount told me he was so used to his in-house playmates, children of the omote servants who looked up to him as their lord, that he had a hard time at Gakushuin, where students were equal. He had "what people today call 'school phobia.' "

Along with such pampering, kazoku children were subjected to discipline as well. Here parents played a greater role than in nurturant mothering, as implied in informants' remarks that their parents were "scary," "frightening," "absolutely compelling," "always giving us orders." But in discipline, too, servants played surrogate parent to some extent by conveying the parents' instructions. Again, it was not uncommon that informants associated their home training more with their "strict" or even "frightening" servants than with their parents—and the higher the family rank, or the older the generation, the more so. The daughter of a viscount repeated what her mother used to say about her head maid: "She [the maid] would say, 'It's not me, but I am telling you as a surrogate of your mother [*otāsama ni kawatte mōshiagerun desu*].' " In her mother's days, parental authority had been "totally delegated" (*zenken*) to the head servant, and the children had no recourse to their parents except through these delegates. "Mother used to say, 'If you sat with your feet sticking out, your otsuki would step on them. If you screamed she would say it was your fault.' " A sekke daughter stressed the severity of family discipline: she was not allowed, for instance, to use a floor cushion for herself or to wear a coat in the presence of her parents or grandmother until they gave her permission. Such injunctions came, however, from the head servant. Here is a good example of Bateson's ternary mode, where a child was trained by a servant to behave deferentially toward his or her parents.

Yet the locus of ultimate authority was not always the parents. A woman marrying into a large household, for instance, could be taken in hand by the domineering head servant who had waited on her parents-in-law and husband and was now in a position to teach the bride about the family's life-style (*kafū*). The daughter of a prominent daimyo house suffered under such a servant when she married into an equally prominent kuge house: "She was criticized," said her sister sympathetically, "as having a 'warrior style' in everything she did." In this case, the stereotypically shrewish image of the mother-in-law was embodied by none other than the head maid. This raises questions of how a servant could impose her authority so thoroughly on her master. Informants said that servants used polite language such as *asobase* to give orders; evidently, the "order" was a higher message contextualizing the solicitous polite expression and could be a respectful but stern command. Apparently too, double communication of this sort was subtly employed.

These examples suggest that discipline was focused on manners and demeanor, particularly for daughters. To mention a few more examples: ladylike movement in the house ("Don't run in the hallways"), courtesy in receiving guests, Ogasawara-style table manners ("Don't start with the pickles"), selection of appropriate dresses, keeping the room tidy ("Don't leave your kimono lying around, but fold and put it away immediately after use"). Such instructions were delivered more often by servants than by mothers.

Important above all was a proper style of speech, particularly in the use of keigo (honorifics). It was here that the servant's role was particularly crucial because, I was told, parents could not tell their child to speak to them with honorifics, nor could they use keigo in speaking to their child. Thus the otsuki or head servant scolded the child for using the "bad" speech he or she picked up outside the home, especially from Gakushuin classmates (see below). Children also learned keigo more "naturally" and unconsciously through hearing their servants use it with them, their parents and siblings, and guests. One such learning chance might come when a maid spoke on the phone in a high-pitched formal style to a representative (though also a servant) of another noble or royal household. It is therefore ironic that although servants, especially maid-servants, supposedly entered upper-class households to learn etiquette and other aspects of high culture as apprentices, they were the ones who taught the master's child, not only by instructing and "scolding," but also by being an exemplary model. The roles of trainer and trainee were thus reversed. The new apprentice-maid learned etiquette primarily from senior servants.

For school-age children, especially sons, discipline also involved character development—austerity, self-reliance, and perseverance—which of course required the efforts of male servants. The staff of the exterior were quite authoritarian and even punitive, as a woman recalled regarding her father, a collateral royal prince. When her father was a Gakushuin student, she said, many families were switching from carriages or jinrikisha to automobiles. Discontented with the old-fashioned carriage kept by his family, he, on behalf of himself and his siblings, demanded that the manager replace it with a car. Instead of seeing his demand met, he was ordered to sit in formal style and listen for half an hour to the manager's lecture on the virtue of frugality. Such authority of the managerial staff, I was told, stemmed from their exclusive power over budgetary decisions.

OUT-OF-HOME DISCIPLINE

The home setting was generally considered inadequate for socializing sons fully, however tough their fathers or servants happened to be. Boys were thus moved away from home to "training centers" both near and far from the home base. There were two directions of discipline regarding status: one was to reinforce status distinction or conformity; the other was to offset status.

Provincial Vassals and Townspeople in Status Reinforcement

The emphasis at home on speech style, manners, and demeanor was intended primarily for children to learn what was expected of them as aristocrats. There, not just status insiders, but status outsiders such as servants and commoners generally instilled and reinforced status identity in the children. The commoner apprentice-maid expected her master (at least at one level of consciousness, because I do not preclude status resentment at another level) to appear and conduct himself like a lord for the sake of her own self-esteem. Indeed, former apprentices respect truly upper-class-like families but look down on those who are basically no different from themselves in life-style (Lebra 1984).

This sort of cross-class collusion in bringing about status distinction may be the case elsewhere as well. One of my informants said that while living in England to learn the life-style of the British aristocracy he and his family had to dress formally for dinner every evening because otherwise their British butler would have refused to serve them. In my fieldwork, the loudest evidence for such expectations came from self-styled "vassals," for the good reason that their vassal identity depended on the presence of a lord.

I met one latter-day "vassal" from the castle town of the former domain who would wait on his "lord" every time the latter came from Tokyo to reenact the role of his lordly ancestors on ritual occasions. This lord, a third son who had been a commoner for a long time, had been suddenly called back to assume the heir's position and soon thereafter the headship. He thus had to train himself to fill the role of a "junior lord" and then "lord" within a year. In this resocialization, a large part was played by the self-appointed local vassal, through correspondence and telephone conversations conducted in an old-fashioned samurai style. In his direct contacts with the lord in the town, the vassal bowed and spoke to him in a stiff style as if he were acting in a samurai drama, much to the lord's embarrassment. To me it was clear that the old vassal was dramatizing his status in order to give this upstart an intensive course on how to be a lord. The vassal confided to me that he could not stand the man's Gakushuin classmates hanging around and freely touching him, with no respect. He wanted his master to remain distant and aloof. And indeed, when I saw the lord for the second time, he did appear more aristocratic, more distant, more silent, and less spontaneous than on our first encounter.

Some daimyo families made sure that their heirs maintained regular contact with their respective provinces, which meant that the provincial vassals socialized the "junior lords." One informant spent every summer of his childhood at his ancestral home, so as to be in touch with "ancient" vassals who remembered his grandfather, the last lord. One of the oldest vassals told the visiting junior lord that after the Restoration he had been taken in his childhood by his father to the lord's mansion for an audience. To his astonishment, he said, his vassal father, kneeling, bowed "as flat as a flounder" toward the lord seated in the remote distance. He, the boy witnessing this, wondered why his father, so dignified in his own home, would humble himself to such an extent here, and concluded that this old lord must be an extraordinary man. "Then, turning to me," said my informant, "[the old vassal] said, 'You are none other than this great lord's grandson. As such, you must do your best.'" The ancestor's image, when described by such local vassals, left an unforgettable impression on the heir's young mind.

Status expectations of this type were not limited to servants and vassals, who after all partook of the master's prestige. Commoners outside the household also imposed status constraints on members of the nobility and royalty, in some circumstances more so than insiders did, by virtue of their stereotypic expectations. I was told over and over how Gakushuin children were made conscious of their status when as a group they encountered townspeople on school excursions, and how kazoku children had become a center of attention during the war when they were evacuated to the countryside (especially those who were thrown individually into village schools rather than staying together in Gakushuin groups). One woman remembered a classmate who had been a tomboy at Gakushuin but returned from the rural site of evacuation totally transformed into an elegant lady. Village children had straightened her out.

Commoners, both inside and outside the aristocratic household, thus socialized kazoku children (and even adults) in the ways of status conformity, often against the latter's natural inclinations. It is in fact no wonder that few of my informants deplored the abolition of the aristocracy; instead, most felt "liberated" from all the constraints attached to kazoku status. Women in particular would never trade the freedom, privacy, physical mobility, and anonymity thus gained for the status prominence, economic security, leisure, or convenience of elite perquisites.

Socialization in Status Neutralization

Besides engendering status conformity, discipline for kazoku children was intended to neutralize or compensate for a status environment conducive to dependency, hampering, or ineptitude. For daughters, some families provided this counteractive socialization in the home. After the Kantō earthquake, for instance, one informant's father decided that the children should learn to do everything by themselves, to become totally self-reliant. The informant and her sister thus took turns doing all the housework from cooking to toilet cleaning, even though the family had many servants ready to do everything for them. In another case, a grandmother kept the daughters at home to instruct them personally in all domestic chores: "She was afraid that we children would be spoiled [by outsiders] if left free to go outside the home."

For sons, self-reliance took a more severe form in out-of-home training. Some kazoku fathers were particularly concerned that their sons, being confined within a small elite society, would grow up unable to adjust to the wider society; these boys were thus pushed out of the home to be raised by outsiders. Motives behind this practice varied, however, ranging from tough- to tender-minded (for the son to be "buffeted about in the rough storm of the outside world," or to become sensitized to the hard life of commoners); from elitist to antielitist (to build character and competency for leadership, or to prepare the boy to live like everybody else); from socially restrictive to unrestricted (a situation of complete sex segregation, or contact with people in all walks of life). Some fathers feared an imminent revolution that would destroy the whole status system and so were trying to prepare their children for a dire future.

Boarding Houses

At the intermediate level of education, boarding schools kept some kazoku sons away from home except on weekends and vacations. For periods of time Gakushuin was a boarding school for boys, as were some other private schools like Gyōsei, attended by upper-class sons. Yet there were other facilities as well. Top-ranking daimyo families in particular maintained the tradition of having their sons trained with their age-mates by distinguished teachers in all-male private boarding houses (generally called *juku*) specially built by the families for that purpose, even while the sons were also attending Gakushuin as regular students. One inform-ant talked about his family's juku, established to discipline his father, an adopted son, and make of him a fully qualified heir under a great tutor; he was joined by several bright boys, all brought from the home province. They were taught, among other things, swordsmanship and Chinese clas-sics like the *Analects* of Confucius. The informant was put into the same juku when he was a third-grader at Gakushuin, to be trained similarly. A daughter of the shogunal house felt sorry that her late brother, in accor-dance with family tradition, was removed from home at age seven to live in the family's boarding house (called *gakuryō*), just as his father had been. He was waited on by co-resident shosei and taught by a tutor, though he also commuted to Gakushuin for regular school. While he was allowed to visit home on the weekend, he had to return to the gakuryō for the night. His sister interpreted this family tradition, which by his time had become anachronistic, as a way of having the heir achieve man-hood away from the feminine influence of home.[6] These and other similar cases of boarding-house training were distinctly elitist, the purpose being character development for a future lord and the very model coming from the imperial palace school (*gogakumonjo*) for the crown prince. The pro-tective environment, the fact that servants were in attendance, and the location of the boarding houses near or on the main estate meant that, although the goal was to develop strong character away from home, training was nonetheless status-centered.

There were semipublic juku as well that accepted sons from kazoku families other than the founding house and its former domains. One such house, called Jishūsha, trained a host of distinguished men, according to a son of its first superintendent, including Kitashirakawa princes, a Saionji, a Matsudaira, and businessmen like Mitsui, Kōnoike, and Ōkura. "They were toughened, for example, by taking cold baths." Another such juku, called Shūitsukan, was built by Konoe Atsumaro, a prince and president of Gakushuin, with the intent personally to drill twelve accepted kazoku sons (Kanazawa, Kawakita, and Yuasa 1968, 224). Although semipublic, these boarding houses still confined enrollees to aristocratic circles.

Some totally unprotected exposure to the world of commoners did occur, however. The sons of one marquis of daimyo origin, for example, were sent not to Gakushuin, which their father considered too soft, but to a national school famous for its rigor. At the same time, each was put under the custodial care of an individual schoolteacher, "probably to make us feel close to common people," one of them recalled. From the teacher's house he would go to a neighborhood public bathhouse (it was not until the informant got married and had his own house that he tasted the wonderful convenience of a private bath), and meals were so poor that even *nattō* (fermented soybeans) was considered a luxury and served only occasionally. My informant, at seventy-eight, still resented such overdiscipline, and confessed he felt no warmth toward his parents.

As a future lord and leader, a kazoku heir could have high public visibility, which in turn could foster in him a precocious awareness of status identity. Some kazoku men stressed that they had had no genuine childhood, that from the very beginning of their lives they had been treated like adults. Their status visibility prevented them, I think, from indulging themselves with childish amae toward mother figures, whether real mothers or otsuki maids. A gradeschool-age boy would accompany his father as junior lord on visits to the home province. On occasion, the son went alone as a temporary lord, substituting for his father (*myōdai*), and presided over ancestor rites, surrounded by vassals and townspeople. He might in fact step into the permanent lordly position as a mere boy if his father died prematurely. Thus heirs, in particular, had reasons to skip "natural" childhood and enter straight into more "cultural" adulthood. Even a publicly visible girl would experience the same fate. A royal princess told me a similar tale about the precocity forced upon her as a small child, as well as the impeccable performance expected of her. Some informants expressed regrets, but by and large such training in adult ways was appreciated for instilling confidence: "I don't have any timidity. No matter how great the person is, I don't feel frightened."

FOSTERAGE

Boarding-house training tapers into fosterage (*satokko* or *satogo*), a practice with no uniform pattern (thus its inclusion here as a separate section). Fosterage was something "natural," I was told, even automatic, for every birth, from the royal family on down. This is an exaggeration, of course, but it is common knowledge that the late Emperor Shōwa and his brother, Prince Chichibu, were raised by foster parents, the Kawamura. Some royal daughters too, such as Emperor Meiji's daughters, were foster children. And the last shogun, Tokugawa Yoshinobu, had his children, all born of concubines, reared by a number of commoner foster parents.

The child's health was a major concern in the decision to seek foster care. It is said that the strikingly high mortality rate of royal children motivated Emperor Meiji to send his surviving children, and later his grandsons, to foster homes so that they would grow up strong and healthy away from the palace. In fact, the high mortality of princes and princesses in the history of the imperial household is attributed in part to the unhealthy and dangerous conditions of palace life, specifically: jealousy among attendants, involving even possible murders; the nannies' lead-heavy cosmetics, which a child might lick; sleeping drugs for putting children to sleep quickly; and so on (Kawahara 1983, 12). Among non-royal kazoku families, too, the child's health was an important consideration: many foster families were selected because the "mother-to-be" was a healthy woman who had just given birth and so afforded a large quantity of "natural milk." Thus she combined the roles of foster mother and wet nurse.

Health was not the only reason for sending children into foster care, however. One informant, the youngest of sixteen children ("from one single womb!") of a baron, was immediately taken away to a peasant family to be nursed by a new mother. But he stayed on with the foster family. Why? Was it because his parents wanted to bring him up strong so that he, a nonheir, could live in the wilderness of the outside world? "That reasoning would be only a face-saving excuse," he interjected to deny my guess. He claimed instead that he had been unwanted and "abandoned." His foster parents used to tell him that his parents, having so many children, never bothered to come see him and only dispatched a steward to deliver a small fosterage fee (*satobuchi*) once a year. "So they said, 'This child is not wanted at all. But we farmers need as many boys as possible [as farm hands]' and they were about to take me as a *sato-nagare* [unretrieved foster child, much like *shichinagare*, a forfeited pawn]." But he was retrieved unexpectedly by adoptive parents—as it turned out, his own uncle and aunt—when he was three years old. When his aunt came by rickshaw to meet him, she could not tell him from the farmer's children, in his straw sandals and sucking bamboo-shoot skin. Overnight, however, he became a junior lord of a kazoku house that commanded six servants.

This incredible story was not unique. The recycling of *satonagare* into the commoner class may, historically, have been a not totally unlikely fate for upper-class nonheir children, since keeping such children would not only dissipate a family's resources but might cause family conflict. All that parents could hope for such children would be to marry them off or adopt them out. Apparently economic complementarity was at work as well, in that working-class foster parents wanted the children as laborers. A woman of kuge origin read in an ancestor's diary that all his children except the heir had been placed into fosterage upon birth, for reasons unknown. She suspected that the family had been too poor to feed excess children and that fosterage had been resorted to for "mouth reduction" (*kuchi-berashi*). The daughters, the diary reported, were later retrieved at about the age of ten but were at once sent away again, this time to live with the families of their future husbands. And the sons? Born of different women away from the home residence and strangers to their father, the boys were placed immediately into foster homes; much later some of them returned and were formally recognized as his children. With this weak or nonexistent tie between father and nonheir sons, satonagare recycling likely occurred.

Discipline, the central topic of much of this chapter, did not enter into these cases of fosterage. But an extreme instance of alleged discipline is found in the story of a great-grandson of a nationally eminent Restoration leader and heir to a count. What he called his foster family, indeed, sounded like a bunch of bullies.

> When I was eight, I was put into the custody of Satō Sensei, a teacher in Chinese studies, together with two other boys [one the son of another kazoku, the other of a wealthy businessman]. I was there from age eight through age eighteen.
>
> *Was that your father's idea?*
>
> Generally all the boys of our clan were sent out for fosterage. My father, born the youngest [of a big daimyo family, later to be adopted out], was fostered by a rice trader; one of my father's older brothers, who was also adopted [into a kazoku house], was fostered by a stone mason; and another brother and heir was fostered by a pawnshop keeper.
>
> [In the foster house,] as if we were shop apprentices, each of us was given a box in which you kept your rice bowl, chopsticks, and other utensils. You used the box as your table as well. The box with each person's name on it was placed on a shelf, to be brought out only at mealtime. Utensils you washed yourself after the meal, then put them away in the box and back on the shelf.
>
> *How was such a foster house selected?*
>
> Every kazoku house had several counselors who looked over the candidates and reached a consensus.
>
> *What was the purpose of such fosterage?*
>
> To learn etiquette, and not to become eccentric. Training was extremely Spartan. We were disciplined more severely than ordinary boys—to keep our rooms clean and orderly, to scrub the hallways, to clean the toilets and yard.
>
> *Together with the children of the foster family?*
>
> Oh, no, they were warming themselves in *kotatsu* [a quilt-covered footwarmer]. We were there for training, but among us trainees there was discrimination. My father never bothered to visit the sensei but only sent his messengers; the parents of oth-

ers, however, did come to pay respect. In winter, they [the family and fellow boarders] were all sitting around the kotatsu, eating a rice cracker, but when I entered the room they hid the cracker. Very mean. But all that was for my discipline.

Do you think it was a good experience?

Yes, to some extent. The character [of the foster parents] should have been better investigated. But thanks to that experience, I can endure any kind of hardship, and also understand how people in lower positions feel.

Did you come to feel that the foster parents were like your real parents?

That would be impossible. But when I was in the army, the hardship I had as a foster child did help me a lot. . . . [As a foster child, however,] I was crying all the time. In winter, my hands were frostbitten and hurt as if pricked with needles.

Even on Sundays we were told to study and study. In the morning, after study, we cleaned the toilets and yard, with nothing else to do in the afternoon. So I would go out for a walk, and [one time] I deliberately tore off the straps of my wooden footgear [to create a good excuse for returning late] and went to a movie.

Under such circumstances, might you have developed hostility toward the people around you rather than kindness?

Yes, there was such feeling. When I did something wrong, the sensei's wife ordered me to sit in the wooden hallway in formal style for two or three hours. Yet I never apologized. She and I vied in the contest of stubbornness. When there was a fire in the neighborhood, I wished to go out to look but would not volunteer to apologize [to be released from the sitting punishment].

Did you, then, feel warm toward your own parents?

I hesitate to say this, but toward father I had no warmth at all. Heaven might punish me for saying this, but even when he died I did not touch his finger. When asked to help cleanse his body with alcohol, I refused. No feeling of kinship at all.

Who have you shared the closest intimacy with in your life?

There has been nobody. Spartan education seems to make your life miserable. I have no confidant.

It is hard to believe that this account was that of the seventy-year-old great-grandson of a national leader, who as a child was addressed as "Junior Lord" by as many as twelve family maids. This unusual account, indeed, makes us wonder whether such "discipline" was really intended to develop character. My informant entered a business career after postwar repatriation but, he admitted, has been a failure in whatever project he undertook. As his narrative shows, some status outsiders—in this case, foster parents—certainly did socialize kazoku children to break through their status identity, but not always in a positive direction and possibly with the result that character development was curtailed. This narrator, according to one of his kinsmen, is so devious, cheating money out of many fellow kazoku, that nobody trusts him now.

I assume the above case was anomalous. Fosterage, like adoption, served many purposes and generated various kinds of relationships. In general, the commoner parents and aristocratic foster child likely developed warm, unbreakable ties. Satonagare could have occurred not only because the child was unwanted by the natural parents, but also because he or she was too strongly wanted by the foster parents. If the latter continued to resist the natural parents' recall, it could become too late for the child to be retrained for the aristocracy, thus resulting in its abandonment (Yanagiwara 1928). Two autobiographical authors (Yanagiwara 1928; Ōkura 1985), both of whom were mothered by concubines, write about the warmth and love they had for their foster parents and vice versa, and about attempts to subvert the recalls from their natal households.[7]

SCHOOL EXPERIENCE: GAKUSHUIN

As we have seen, kazoku children were socialized both in and out of the home by parents, servants, vassals, boarding-house teachers and fellow boarders, and foster parents. But probably even more important was the role of regular schools, particularly Gakushuin, in instilling in kazoku children a sense of peerage, or at least in homogenizing children of heterogeneous family backgrounds.

Not all kazoku children were sent to Gakushuin; some parents chose other schools for various, often contradictory reasons. Some parents considered Gakushuin as not rigorous enough for boys, academically or morally, whereas liberal or cosmopolitan parents saw the school as too regimental. Gakushuin was too elitist for some, but not elitist enough for others. This diversity of views on Gakushuin is indicated by the range of other schools selected—from academically distinguished and competitive schools like Tokyo Metropolitan middle schools (the so-called number schools, like the "First" and "Fourth" middle schools) and the lab school of the Higher National Teachers' College (Kōshi Fuzoku) of Tokyo, to missionary or other private schools such as Gyōsei, Keiō, and Seikei. Girls went to, among others, the lab school of the Women's Higher National Teachers' College (Jokōshi Fuzoku), Seishin (Sacred Heart), Futaba, Jogakkan, Morimura, and Jiyūgakuen. Further, in reflection of the military career encouraged for kazoku men, the navy and army academies were also opted for. As for foreign education, we have already seen ryūgakusei referred to in connection with the Western life-style in chapter 5. To be added in this context were foreign schools established within Japan, which some parents favored over native schools. Haru Reischauer (1986, 3), for example, attended the American School in Japan before going to Principia College in rural Illinois, at the insistence of her American-born mother, a Christian Scientist.

A majority of my informants and their parents, however, attended Gakushuin either for their entire educational career or at least for the lower level of education before transferring elsewhere. (Sixty-three out of the eighty-nine male questionnaire respondents, or 71 percent, fall into this category; and women would have yielded an even higher percentage.) Most of my interviewees took Gakushuin enrollment as a matter of course, even as mandatory ("You would have had to get approval from the Sōchitsuryō if you had chosen another school"). Further, Gakushuin experience left an indelible impact on the graduates—which leads me to Gakushuin socialization.

Institutional History

Thus far I have referred to Gakushuin as if there was a clearly bounded, constant, single entity so called, but in fact its identity is elusive in reflection of its historical fluctuation in several dimensions. The origins of Gakushuin can be traced in the official Gakushuin history (Gakushuin 1978; GHHI 1981–87) to a lecture hall installed for court nobles in 1847 within the Kyoto palace grounds at Emperor Ninkō's (r. 1817–46) initiative. (Staunch Meiji Restorationists would have linked it further back to the ancient Daigakuryō [see chapter 2] under the ritsuryō system.) This Kyoto prototype of Gakushuin underwent further reorganizations and renamings until it was more formally established in Tokyo in 1876 as Kazoku Gakkō (Kazoku School) on imperially granted land under the sponsorship of the Kazoku Kaikan, built two years earlier. The next year, at the time of the opening ceremony—which was honored by the presence of Emperor and Empress Meiji—the school was renamed finally as Gakushuin (meaning "Hall of Learning") by imperial decree. In 1884, when the modern (Meiji) kazoku was institutionalized, Gakushuin was made a state school (*kanritsu*), though under the jurisdiction of the Kunaishō instead of the Ministry of Education, which oversaw all other schools in Japan. Gakushuin enrollment was required of kazoku children as a rule, and at the same time was opened to selected commoner children.

The name of Gakushuin remained fluid to accommodate the placement of girls in the institution. In 1885, a separate campus was founded specifically for girls, with the name of Kazoku Jogakkō (Kazoku Girls'

School). This gender segregation was symbolized by the presence of the empress but not the emperor at the institution's opening ceremony (which, by the way, set the precedent for subsequent school ceremonies to be honored by female royalty alone). The girls' school, thus separated from the male-centered Gakushuin in name as well as geography, was renamed Gakushuin Jogakubu (Girls' Department of Gakushuin) in 1906 to mark its reintegration into the Gakushuin system. But later still, in 1918, separation was reinstated under another new name, Joshi Gakushuin (Girls' Gakushuin), which this time had its own (male) president. This last version, which was to last until the end of the war, implied that the name Gakushuin referred to the male campus(es) only, while this campus was marked by the presence of *joshi* (girls). Informants were explicit on this difference.

Not only the name, but also the system of academic years and levels was revised almost constantly as if no long-term plan existed. This was made all the more complicated by the difference between the male and female units in terms of grade sequencing (table 23). Because of the school's deviation from the standards set by the Ministry of Education, the Gakushuin administration was concerned with level equivalencies between Gakushuin and other schools. According to the grade system shown in table 23, completion of *kōtōka* (the higher grade) in the girls' Gakushuin was determined to be equivalent to completion of a standard girls' high school program, whereas kōtōka graduation from (the boys') Gakushuin was deemed to correspond to completion of a standard higher school (*kōtō gakkō*) course of study or the preparatory grade of university (*daigaku yoka*). This consideration was important given that Gakushuin graduates would likely wish to (or be encouraged to) continue their education. Gakushuin made several attempts to instate its own university from 1893, but abandoned this goal in favor of another alternative: to clear the way for its male kōtōka graduates to enter existing imperial universities without necessarily taking examinations. Finally, in 1922, the latter option became formally sanctioned. Just among my informants I found many graduates from imperial universities (table 24; the entry "Gakushuin" there refers to Gakushuin University, created after the war [see below]). Indeed, it is remarkable that fully 42 percent of the respondents to this question graduated from either Tokyo or Kyoto (Imperial) University—a good indication of the privilege of Gakushuin kōtōka graduates and their equivalence to graduates of elite "number higher schools."

The Gakushuin identity was made further elusive by frequent relocations, necessitated by fires, earthquakes, campus separation by gender and

Table 23. The Gakushuin Grade Systems

The Joshi (female) Gakushuin System, installed 1921
  Honka (basic grade)
    Zenki (initiatory period):   4 years
    Chūki (middle period):   4 years
    Kōki (last period):   3 years
  Kōtōka (higher grade)   2 years
The (male) Gakushuin System in 1922
  Shotōka (elementary grade)   6 years
  Chūtōka (middle grade)   5 years
  Kōtōka (higher grade)   3 years

Source: GHHI.

Table 24. Questionnaire Responses on University
Education (*N*=94)

Gakushuin University graduate	8 (8.5%)
Tokyo or Kyoto University graduate	39 (41.9%)
Graduate of other national or public university	10 (10.6%)
Graduate of private university	27 (28.7%)
Other[a]	5 (5.3%)
No university education	5 (5.3%)

[a]Includes Army University and foreign universities.

grades, the need for expansion, and so on (table 25). These relocations and place-names were vividly remembered by old informants in connection with specific modes of transportation and commuting. During the war, too, younger Gakushuin students were evacuated in school units to Shiobara, Nikkō, and Shuzenji, and middle- and higher-grade students, like all other school students, were mobilized as a labor force away from home. In the meantime, most of the Tokyo campuses were destroyed by the 1945 air raids.

In 1908 the middle- and higher-grade boys moved to the new Mejiro campus, and Gakushuin became a boarding school for them. This earliest stage of dormitory history is closely associated with the retired general Nogi Maresuke, who, as Gakushuin president from 1907 to 1912, lived in a house adjacent to the six-ward dormitory monitoring the students

Table 25. Relocations of Gakushuin Campuses

	MALE OR FEMALE GAKUSHUIN (MG OR FG)	DISTRICT
1876	Unsegregated	Kanda Nishikichō
1885	FG	Yotsuya-Nakamachi (Owarichō)
1888	MG	Sannenchō, Kōjimachi-ku (Toranomon)
1889	FG	Nagatachō, Kōjimachi-ku
1890	MG	Owarichō, Yotsuya-ku
1908	MG (middle/higher grades)	Mejiro
1918	FG	Aoyama

Source: Adapted from chronological table, GHHI, 984–1017.

around the clock as a stern *and* warm father figure. The boarding-school system, like many other features, was later discontinued, only to be revived from time to time on a compulsory or optional basis.

As was mentioned before, Gakushuin admitted a limited number of nonkazoku children, who in time were to outnumber kazoku enrollees. But status inequality was retained by the fact that nonkazoku students had not only to pass examinations but also to pay tuition, while kazoku children attended Gakushuin tuition-free. Further, nonkazoku were admitted only to the elementary and middle schools, being barred from the higher school. These inequities were abolished in 1924, however, which meant that kazoku children were also charged tuition, at first in an amount less than that paid by nonkazoku, but eventually with no difference in amount. One last barrier to nonkazoku was the kindergarten, *yōchien,* which, unsegregated and attached to the girls' campus, was reserved exclusively for kazoku until the postwar collapse of the entire hereditary hierarchy. This meant that kazoku children could form an inner circle before they went on to elementary school, where they met new faces. Whether one attended Gakushuin's prewar kindergarten was, therefore, a crucial point of status demarcation.

Postwar democratization affected Gakushuin immeasurably, probably more than any other school. Gakushuin almost died, divested of all the privileges it had enjoyed as the only kanritsu school supported by and under the jurisdiction of the Kunaishō. Nevertheless, it was reborn as a totally transformed "private school" (*shiritsu*), open to all, with new goals consistent with Japan's new constitution, and subject to the authority of the Ministry of Education like all other schools. Owing to the school's sudden impoverishment, the Gakushuin administration had to work hard raising funds from the private sector, and this resulted in consolidating parent as well as alumni associations, something new in Gakushuin history (Gakushuin 1978, 116).

The dual system of Gakushuin for boys and Joshi Gakushuin for girls was eventually replaced by a more unified system under a single president, even though gender segregation was retained for the middle and high school levels. With the 1949 creation of a coeducational university (which later added a graduate school) and, the following year, of a women's junior college (upgraded from the division that had long existed above the girls' higher-school department), Gakushuin became a self-sufficient, "complete" educational institution encompassing all levels from kindergarten to graduate. It has thus become one of those "escalator" schools that do away with the intense competition for entrance at intermediate levels. After several more relocations to temporary shelters in war-ravaged Tokyo, Gakushuin is now located in three campus zones: Toyama for girls from middle school through junior college, Yotsuya for coeducational elementary, and Mejiro for all the rest.

The popularity of postwar Gakushuin may be measured by the tough competition for admission to its kindergarten and elementary school, an inevitable feature of an escalator system. It is said that entrance examinations are absolutely fair, utterly ignoring family background. When former kazoku lodged bitter complaints about postwar Gakushuin having "lost its true quality," it often turned out that their children had not passed the entrance examinations and thus, to their embarrassment, were forced to attend other, inferior private schools or examination-free public schools. Indeed, special kindergartens exist to prepare children for entrance to the Gakushuin elementary school, and mothers whose minds are set on Gakushuin for their children are now typical "*kyōiku* [education] mamas."

Has Gakushuin really lost all its prewar character? This question draws our attention to the education of the children of the emperor, whose "hereditary" status, although reduced to a ceremonial office, survived the postwar reform. Crown Prince Akihito, if the war had not intervened, would have moved to the palace school (gogakumonjo), as his father had done, after Gakushuin elementary. Instead he stayed on at Gakushuin, as did his brother and sisters, and his children too are affiliated with Gakushuin. In this sense, the imperial house remains strongly associated with Gakushuin, perhaps even more so than before. True, it has no authority over Gakushuin, nor do the imperial children stand out on campus as much as they used to, according to a contemporary adminis-trator: for example, "Princess Nori looks and behaves like anybody else at school," said the Gakushuin president about the present imperial cou-ple's daughter. "You really don't notice her presence." Yet in the eyes of many Japanese, Gakushuin still draws its prestige from the imperial connection. Indeed, special ceremonies at Gakushuin, such as the hun-dredth anniversary of its foundation (1977), have been highlighted by the presence of the Shōwa imperial couple and other royals. Emperor and Empress Heisei (Akihito and Michiko) occasionally appear on cam-pus, not as office holders, but as the parents of students and, in the emperor's case, as an alumnus as well.

Instructional Features

Like the institution itself, instructional emphases also changed largely in reflection of political tides and partly of the school president's ideology. From former students' recollections I discerned three instructional cre-dos of prewar Gakushuin. One concerned the imperially centered elitism by which kazoku were supposed to play the role of hanpei (bulwark) for the imperial house. The underlying reasoning was that kazoku and Gaku-shuin owed their existence to the imperial benevolence: "We were taught all the time not to forget our *on* [moral indebtedness] to the imperial house." Interlocked with this sense of being a special beneficiary was the self-image of a Gakushuin student as a future leader of the nation: "You are going, teachers used to say, to stand above people [*hito no ue ni tatsu*] and therefore must study that much harder"; "We were told again and again to become an exemplar [*kagami*] for Japanese women." Elitism thus instilled turned out to produce a sense of reverse discrimination in that "excellence in performance was taken for granted [*dekite atarimae*] but any slightest wrongdoing or mistake would immediately attract attention."

A second preponderant credo in instruction, one mentioned especially by male graduates, was the "Spartan" discipline modeled after military training. Like General Nogi, many of the school's presidents were navy or army officers and assimilated martial arts and military drill into Gaku-shuin's compulsory curriculum as *buka* (the martial program). Dormi-tory life was punctuated from morning to bedtime by trumpet calls, "ex-actly like the army," and there were daily roll calls (*tenko*) and midwinter drills (*kangeiko*). The stern discipline was equated with Gakushuin's slo-ganlike idiom *shitsujitsu-gōken*—referring vaguely to a moral principle combining toughness, simplicity, sincerity, and austerity—which one in-formant after another commented was the "best" feature of Gakushuin experience.[8] The emphasis on bodily strength involved the importance of physical education and sports in general, which merged with martial training.

This military austerity was best symbolized by the Gakushuin uniforms. Gakushuin was the first school in the nation to adopt a uniform for boys styled after a navy officer's. For girls, despite some fluctuation between the traditional kimono and Western-style dress, the uniform was eventually fixed to the "sailor" style. Older informants, however, wore a kimono-hakama ensemble with leather shoes; only in school ceremonies could the regular kimono of modest quality be replaced by one of better-quality silk with the family crest. Adoption of uniforms was explained as a way of restraining kazoku children from displaying wealth, luxury, and extravagance. Yet discipline extended to academic performance as well. Teachers of the boys' units, for example, presumably did not hesitate to display lists of students in order of performance, and to make the grades of the entire class available in print for sale to parents. "Gakushuin teachers," it is said, "flunked students right and left," unlike instructors at other Japanese schools.

Third, Gakushuin stressed Western learning, offering Western-language courses even to elementary school children. This orientation may seem inconsistent with the school's military and nationalistic propensities, and indeed, the Western-language instruction for elementary children was suspended at times. But cosmopolitanism (or more correctly, Westernism) and the emperor-centered martial spirit went together without contradiction partly because Emperor Meiji encouraged kazoku at once to pursue a military career and to study abroad. President Konoe Atsumaro (1895–1904), for his part, revived the Western-language courses for the elementary level in 1898 in an effort to encourage Gakushuin students to enter the foreign service. This last feature was reinforced by home education with foreign tutors or governesses, as well as by post-Gakushuin overseas study (see chapter 5).

Commoner Teachers and Aristocratic Pupils

There was general consensus as to the high academic quality of Gakushuin teachers. It was pointed out that higher-level units had faculty as good as any university's, many of them in fact borrowed from Tokyo Imperial University. Writes a former student:

"It was in 1918 that I moved to the Mejiro campus as a *chūtōka* [middle school] student. Bright classmates went to Itchū [First Middle], Yonchū [Fourth Middle], or Fuzoku [the lab middle school of Tokyo Higher National Teachers' College], while we

Mejiro campus students felt somewhat embarrassed about being left behind. However, the teachers were of extraordinarily high caliber, considerably above those of metropolitan middle schools at that time."

(Gakushuin 1978, 72)

The author went on to the Gakushuin kōtōka to be further inspired by first-rate instructors, so that "when I later entered Tokyo University, nothing surprised me." Kōtōka students, both male and female, were blessed with a roster of nationally prominent scholars, some with doctoral degrees, and well-known artists, and "it was up to us students to take advantage of this academic luxury."

Still, some social barriers stood in the way of average students becoming unquestioning admirers and fans of the faculty. Hereditary status, for example, set teachers and pupils on different levels. Although a few instructors came from kazoku ranks, most were commoners and at best shizoku. The daughter of a viscount, when asked, could not name a single teacher as an inspiring mentor. In retrospect, she realized why that was so: "In that school we students were perfectly aware of ourselves ranking above the teachers"; some teachers "were [descendants of] retainers of our house." Many informants discussed how Gakushuin teachers used honorifics in speaking to their students. A teacher would say, for example, "May I ask you not to do that," instead of "Don't do that"; "Will you say it," not just "Say it." Even an instructor in military drill would give orders in polite form. It was because of this status contradiction that Gakushuin education was considered too soft by some fathers, who enrolled their sons in public schools instead. How could a commoner teacher really be stern with a prince's daughter or a marquis's son? How could the Gakushuin discipline truly be as "Spartan" as it was proclaimed?

Teachers, for their part, displayed by their behavior an awareness of each student's family status. For example, a child named Kujō would be addressed with a polite -*sama* as "Kujōsama," a former student mimicked, while the same teacher did not hesitate to address a commoner student in yobisute. Students observed such weakness on the part of teachers with either amusement or contempt. "Sugimoto Sensei asked Prince K, 'Would you please graciously answer this question?' We students all burst into laughter. And Prince K was unable to answer the question." Rumor had it that some teachers carried class rosters with the students marked according to their specific kazoku titles. Such stories circulated quickly among students and parents to denigrate a teacher's respectability. According to one informant, the student directory indicated three basic categories: kazoku, shizoku, and heimin.

Yet narratives tell even more. A teacher's status or reputation, particularly on the girls' campus, was apparently determined by the family status of her students. The daughter of a marquis who had descended to kazoku status by branching out from a collateral royal house (miyake) gave an illustration:

> According to my mother, to be assigned to a class having the emperor's daughter [naishinnōsama] was the greatest honor for the teacher. The next highest honor was to have any other princess (miyasama). Our class had neither. Yamamoto Sensei, who was in charge of our class, had been teaching at Gakushuin since the time my mother was a student. She knew my mother well. Apparently, Yamamoto Sensei told her that even though her class had no royal princess she did not mind because of my presence [and that of another royally related girl].

Indeed, at Joshi Gakushuin, Princess Teru, Emperor Shōwa's eldest daughter, held a uniquely distinguished status, the highest of all royal princesses. Hence, both students and teachers, when they happened to meet Princess Teru, were supposed to stop and bow. In ceremonies, royal princes and princesses were seated conspicuously in a front row to impress and reaffirm their position at the very top of the school hierarchy. Royal students were addressed by teachers and fellow students alike with status terms such as "Denka" and "Miyasama." In interviews, royal names often appeared as reference points for the interviewee's Gakushuin class: "I was in Prince Hitachi's class"; "My class was one year below that of the empress."

Paralleled with this image of a royally centered hierarchy was the sense of injustice felt by students whose class lacked a royal princess. Much discrimination was recalled, particularly in association with school events off campus and in contact with townsfolk. "My class was discriminated against because we had no princess. The classes above and below us were privileged because of Princesses Kuni and Fushimi. On excursions, these classes were given souvenirs." And a member of a "royal class" at the elementary school recalled:

> When we had a school excursion, we were put into a brand new train, for instance. What surprised me was that the train conductor, when we were about to get off the train, came out and covered the exit steps with newspapers. We were shocked into silence. None of us welcomed that kind of treatment. . . . [Also during school excursions] local schoolchildren were lined up to meet us; the princesses headed our group, and we followed the princesses. We detested this [Iyadana!]. Smart princesses [particularly] loathed this intensely.

Another informant connected the presence of princesses with behavioral constraint: "On school excursions, we were met by mayors and governors. So we were specially trained to behave properly during outings." (Recall here the role of outside commoners in socializing kazoku children.)

Schoolmates: Hierarchy or Equality?

Royal princes and princesses, especially the reigning emperor's sons and daughters, were thus singled out as special. But what kind of relationship bound the rest of Gakushuin students to one another? As was briefly discussed in chapter 3, there were two polar views on this subject. One stressed the overt and covert hierarchy and discrimination. In this view, the status boundary was clearly drawn between kazoku and nonkazoku students. Indeed, the latter were sometimes labeled "new students" because they joined Gakushuin at the elementary or middle grade level, not in kindergarten. An heir to a count house, whose mother was a "descender" from a royal house, said in his late fifties that he and his friends still called former classmates who were middle school entrants "new enrollees" (*shinnyūsei*).

Torio Tae (1985) was one of two commoners admitted in 1919 to the forty-member class of the Joshi Gakushuin elementary school. She recalls how she was humiliated by kazoku classmates throughout her eleven years of attendance. One day, when she was on her way to deliver the monthly tuition to the office, a classmate noticed it and said, "What is it? Oh, tuition! We don't have to pay." The same girl asked Tae what kind of dress she was going to wear for the annual cherry blossom viewing party at the imperial Shinjuku Gyoen (Garden), to be hosted by the emperor personally—knowing full well that only kazoku families were invited. Despite such mortifying experiences, Tae responded with delight when the same little lady suggested that they go together to see movies at the Kazoku Kaikan (in those days the clubhouse showed new, quality films to kazoku children a few times a month, occasions that, according to the author, also provided a "girl-hunt" field for boys). Although admission was a kazoku privilege, the friend assured Tae she could go as her guest, and in excitement Tae got a special dress and shoes ready. The day before the movie day, however, her host told her, "It didn't work out for tomorrow's event. It is only for kazoku, after all, they say. Not for commoners." Such humiliations drove Tae to decide, rather than rebel against the unfair status system, to break into the kazoku circle through marriage, an ambition she would realize.

Discrimination was experienced not only by commoner students, but by kazoku students as well for one alleged reason or another. The daugh-

ter of a new kazoku with the title of baron repeated discriminatory remarks made in routine conversation by her classmates: "You are a tozama, aren't you?";[9] "She is from our vassal's house." Children of
"upstart kazoku," who overshadowed poor kuge daughters with such
conspicuous marks of wealth as posh foreign cars that brought them to
campus each morning and picked them up each day after school, provoked "blatantly derogatory remarks." "Money was something despicable to begin with. In school, it didn't matter how rich you were; even
someone like the Iwasaki [of Mitsubishi] was looked down upon as being
beneath the penniless, sunken kuge."

The kazoku ranks were made visible by the decorative ribbons and
laces attached to the formal hat and garment (taireifuku or shakufuku)
worn by kazoku men for court ceremonies and, on cars, by color-differ-
entiated flags, the five ranks being symbolized, in descending order, by
purple, red, pink, greenish blue (*asagi*), and bluish yellow (*moegi*) (Sakamaki 1987, 306). (A baron's daughter remembered a classmate making
fun of her family, referring to them as "purple"—even though baronage
was indicated by bluish yellow, not purple.) Yet none of my informants
remembered the whole spectrum of colors completely and correctly, and
even their own color had often been forgotten, particularly by lower-
ranking kazoku. Details did not matter. What mattered was that there
was the color classification which was displayed on occasion.

These allegations about humiliating discriminations of one student
against another were refuted by louder voices, however. Many more
informants stressed the prevalence of the unwritten law of "amazing" or
"absolute" equality: "Teachers may have been aware of our differences,
but among us students there was absolutely no mention of who was a
sekke, who a commoner, and so on." Even for a new entrant, the Gakushuin class was "shockingly" equalitarian. In fact, nonkazoku students
were "highly regarded" because everybody knew they had passed the
examination with their brains. "After all what counted most was one's
school performance, even at Gakushuin," and it was usually a nonkazoku
student who won the top seat in the performance hierarchy. "No one
made fun of a bright student." Even a princess, said the daughter of a
baron, remained obscure unless she showed character or smartness. Interestingly, some informants named among their closest friends atypical
kazoku representatives, individuals who had rebelled against or deviated
from the aristocratic code of conduct—be it a romantic eloper, an active
socialist, or a feminist—as if they wanted to prove their egalitarianism.

Does this mean that the first viewpoint reflected a false consciousness
or, as is often maintained, a preconception carried over from outside?
There may have been an element of self-fulfilling prophecy, to be sure. I

think, however, that both sides of the argument carry weight. I suggest the following three viewpoints in an attempt to reconcile the oppositional arguments regarding equality and inequality at Gakushuin.

First, many pointed out that at Gakushuin one remained virtually anonymous; after all, there were too many students from distinguished families for any particular individual to be singled out. A boy who had been the "junior lord" to his vassal playmates was thus suddenly reduced to a "nobody" in a Gakushuin class. One girl from a daimyo house first attended another school, where she stood out as a princess and was adored and fussed over by both teachers and classmates; when she switched to Gakushuin she felt thrown off balance, for nobody paid attention to her, and she later came to detest the way the first school had spoiled her. Yet I would argue that anonymity at Gakushuin indicates not so much the students' indifference to as their active awareness of one another's family status, with so many prominent families so concentrated in one school. If so, anonymity would be unlikely to do away with classroom-centered family-rank difference completely.

Second, despite the anonymity of students generally, the royalty, and particularly a smart naishinnō like Princess Teru, did stand out at the very center of a class or a whole school. Sakai Miiko, a classmate of Teruno-miya, writes how ferociously, even violently, the girls competed to come near the princess, to touch her, to hold her hand; how they invented and played a game to "kidnap" the princess; how they imitated the princess by possessing the same things as the princess had (hat, pencil case, handkerchief), so much so that the teacher finally stepped in to prohibit such behavior (Sakai 1982, 95–96). This phenomenon may explain why another transfer student found herself, to her annoyance, a center of attention at Gakushuin much more than at her previous school: she was a royal princess.

A woman from a nonkazoku family related this royalism to Gakushuin's equality principle. There were only two classes at Gakushuin, she asserted: royals (miyasama) and subjects (shinka). No distinction was made between kazoku and nonkazoku, or between marquises and barons: they were all subjects. This dichotomous picture of royal versus nonroyal, however, does not in my view preclude graded hierarchy, but rather entails it. The royal group itself was hierarchically graded by descent, closeness to the reigning emperor, and rank order in succession rights to the throne. "Subjects" were likewise graded according to closeness or access to the imperial house or collateral royals through marriage and kinship: the emperor and his family were held in intimacy by some kazoku, while for others they were up "above the clouds."

A third reason for emphasizing equality at Gakushuin was that family background was a taboo topic. "We refrained from talking about one another's families because you might turn out to be a cousin of the gossip target." Avoidance of talking about family background was thus one result of the general awareness of a thick kinship network binding kazoku families, which generated a feeling of "We are in the same boat, good or bad." Given this sense of kinship, the students were inclined to protect one another's family secrets (such as a mother being a concubine) by desisting from gossiping. More positively—not just defensively—many informants described Gakushuin as a group of kindred, a sense reinforced by the fact that often two successive generations of a family, both parents and children, had been enrolled at Gakushuin from kindergarten on. Thus classmate bonding was intensified by the combination of the horizontal and vertical axes. Here again, though, the kinship network or the feeling of belonging to a single kin group was not shared by all members of a class; more likely, this element served as an implicit barrier between Gakushuin insiders and outsiders.

All these accounts validate the egalitarian argument while entailing some indication of hierarchical order. Equality thus seems to encompass hierarchy, or vice versa. It is not surprising, then, that Viscountess Torio (1985), when as a nonkazoku student she encountered the vexing humiliation inflicted by a classmate, did not rebel against the hierarchy but rather resolved to upgrade herself into the kazoku ranks. In other words, a victim of the hierarchy became a strongly motivated supporter of it. Or, to put it yet another way, hierarchy and equality likely stimulated each other to produce something more or less homogeneous—what might be called Gakushuin culture—that transcended the family-based heterogeneity.

Homogeneity was best expressed linguistically. There was a Gakushuin vocabulary (not entirely unique to Gakushuin, of course), which the whole student body assimilated. One simple example is the use of one word, *gokigen'yō,* to cover all greetings that most Japanese would use during the day, such as *ohayō* (good morning), *konnichiwa* (good day), and *konbanwa* (good evening). The extremely common *arigatō* (thank you) was, for Gakushuin speakers, *osoreirimasu.* It took some time, I learned, before the gokigen'yō group managed to switch to the ohayō vocabulary as part of their postwar linguistic readjustment.

Linguistic homogeneity did not override the gender boundary, however. In fact, there was a clear distinction, possibly sharper than among commoners, between the male and female languages. While girls were generally committed to the correct use of respectful or polite expressions, like the -*asobase* verb ending, male speech deliberately violated rules of deference, particularly in conversation within an intimate group of peers. When I asked a man if he had ever used words like *konokata* (this person) for "you" while a Gakushuin student, he was emotionally provoked, as if I had seen something feminine in him. "For heaven's sake, *no!*" he shouted: he had never used anything but the rude *kisama* for "you."

Underlying such juvenile male speech may have been a combination of three attitudinal propensities held by upper-class children: to create equality and intimacy among close friends, to act out a small rebellion against the family-based hierarchy and gentility, and to enjoy a reverse snobbery in opposition to the conventional snobbery exhibited by pseudo-aristocrats. In a word, this may be understood as a linguistic "liminality." Once outside the peer group, a little boy would adjust his speech style to accommodate both the person he was speaking to and the person he was speaking about. Thus, Gakushuin boys (and girls too, though to a lesser extent) alternated linguistically between liminal equality and structural hierarchy. Both men and women characterized Gakushuin speech mainly in terms of an extensive repertoire that allowed the speaker to switch from one style to another freely and naturally in accord with given speech communities or occasions. This mastery of linguistic versatility and command of the inner language of Gakushuin circles together must have contributed to the creation of a more or less homogeneous status culture.

Courtly Companionship and Attendance

I have already referred to the kazoku privilege to mingle with royalty in various contexts, be it in palace ceremonies or in Gakushuin classes. I also mentioned that emperors and empresses made royal visits to Gakushuin to play an honored role in its ceremonies. Let us now focus on more specific forms of contact privilege (or obligation?), enjoyed by some or all Gakushuin students. The students who shared a class with the emperor's son or daughter were designated, formally and informally, *gogakuyū* (honorable classmates), and a number of them (or the whole class) were invited in rotation to the palace to be *oaite* ("humble partners"; here, more accurately "honorable company") with the prince or princess in study and play. After school, recalled a former classmate of Princess Yori (Emperor Shōwa's third daughter), the five students assigned to royal companionship changed into clean uniforms and were taken with a teacher to the palace, specifically to Kuretakeryō, where the naishinnō and her attending staff lived. Together they did homework and then played outdoors. At three they were treated to tea and cake, after which the students were driven home with a take-home gift. In this case, all the princess's classmates, including commoners, were invited in turn. "Gakushuin was very sensitive this way, I think. They never discriminated against anybody."

But some gogakuyū appear to have been more equal than others, in that a select few, and not necessarily only kazoku, were invited regularly. One of my oldest informants, a Tokugawa daughter, was a regular companion for Emperor Meiji's daughters, who lived and studied within the palace. As soon as Gakushuin classes were over, she and two other girls— a Shimazu and a Matsukata—hurried to the palace. Joined by two Kitashirakawa princesses, they played the oaite role for Meiji's four naishinnō in studying the tea ceremony, poetry, social dance, and so forth. Through this exposure my informant learned the palace language, which retained Kyoto palace usage. Another younger gogakuyū informant was so privileged as to be invited alone to palace events like duck hunting, something she was told not to mention to fellow students.

In the case of Prince Hirohito, later to be Emperor Shōwa, five kazoku boys were selected as preschool playmates for him and his brother, and twelve gogakuyū were put into his special class at Gakushuin elementary when Nogi was president. After the death of his grandfather, Meiji, he moved to the Tōgū Gosho (Crown Prince Palace) of Takanawa and, after his graduation from Gakushuin Elementary School, studied at the newly created Palace School for the Crown Prince (Tōgū Gogakumonjo), with Admiral Tōgō Heihachirō as its first superintendent. Teachers of high caliber and staff were appointed, and five new gogakuyū were selected— a fact that the children of these five, when interviewed, did not neglect to mention. When the gogakumonjo was abolished after the war, Emperor Shōwa's son, Prince Akihito, attended Gakushuin throughout, surrounded by *his* gogakuyū. The gogakuyū or oaite system, which is still in practice, though more informally, was designed primarily to socialize imperial princes and princesses, but at the same time it functioned to socialize Gakushuin peers. The parents were pleased and proud.

Male students attended the court in still another capacity. In the New Year's palace receptions, at which royal consorts (princesses by marriage) were present, Gakushuin boys were mobilized to hold their robe décolletée trains. Again, according to some informants this role, called *osusomochi* (train holder), was assigned only to kazoku sons, while others said it went to all Gakushuin boys rotationally. In one informant's recollection, only kazoku heirs were appointed to be osusomochi, and then only on reaching thirteen years of age—as he and his father, a viscount, had been. At age fifty-six, he remembered his osusomochi debut vividly:

You wore a British style: purple velvet garb, with white pompoms attached, a black tie, white stockings, enameled shoes, carrying a dirk slung over the shoulder; knickerbocker-like pants, and a large cap with a feather, not for your head but hung on your back. Formerly, each uniform was privately ordered, but later the Kunaishō stored and lent them out, and you would go there for outfitting. In December there were rehearsals for the New Year's three-day receptions: the first day for members of the royalty and kazoku, the second for diplomats, and the third for government officials and bureaucrats. The empress was attended by four osusomochi, and princesses each by two. . . . At the center stood the emperor and empress, with a line of princes on the emperor's side, princesses on the empress's side. A couple of us stood behind each princess. . . . Guests would enter the hall one after another at the name announcement by the Kunaishō staff, proceed toward the emperor, bow, and leave by the opposite door. Facing them, we watched all this. What impressed me most was the lively appearance of ambassadors and other representatives of foreign states, all dressed in taireifuku. Their wives, in their best, curtseyed. How marvelous!

This event was the last opportunity for this recaller to be in the palace. He was very nervous throughout the ceremony, after which these pagelike boys were offered lunch and wine, as well as gift watches. He recalled how everyone, including his own father, the Gakushuin president, and his class teacher, stepped forward to make *saikeirei* (the deepest bow). It is regrettable, he deplored, while looking at a picture of himself in a brilliant osusomochi outfit, that all that beautiful tradition has to come to an end. Whether or not other participants share such nostalgia, attendance at court as honorable companions or train holders may have reminded those Gakushuin students so privileged of the pre-Restoration courtier's life.

Enduring Classmate Ties

As with other Japanese schools, Gakushuin attendance meant an involvement in enduring friendships. Former classmates in their fifties, sixties, or older still get together once a month, for example, in small groups of about five to ten. In answer to my question regarding friendship, my Gakushuin-educated informants almost invariably mentioned their classmates: "The twelve years of togetherness in the same classrooms could not help but unite us emotionally." This tendency was reinforced by the overlapping of two networks: classmate and kin. Not only fellow students, but also their siblings, parents, and children, often formed the bases of such enduring bonds. A Tokugawa daughter, who was not free to choose her friends, "luckily" found among her classmates a Shimazu and a Konoe, both her close relatives whom she was allowed to associate with. Another woman from a new kazoku house became intimately acquainted with the Tokugawa main family through one of their daughters, a classmate; was well liked and indulged by the Tokugawa father, the seventeenth-generation "shogun"; and now has a grandson who attended school with the present (eighteenth) "shogun." Royalty, too, is involved in her classmate network through similar chains. One can understand why she, now in her seventies, is still active in reunions. Even for those kazoku who attended another school, chances are they would be drawn through kinship into the Gakushuin networks; as one such person put it, "All my relatives are Gakushuin graduates."

Although women's ties are stronger, men, too, have kept up school bonds, thanks to Gakushuin's escalator system. One of my male interviewees in his fifties said, "Your kindergarten classmates are the dearest to you, closer even than your wife."

What do they do when they get together? Some groups have specific engagements like studying or appreciating poetry or noh drama, cooking, dressmaking, doing embroidery, playing golf or tennis, horseback riding, traveling, and other leisure activities. Whatever they do, their main purpose of reunion is to enjoy friendly, relaxed conversation over tea or dinner. Informants all emphasized that Gakushuin classmates are especially open to one another, with nothing to hide, no need of defense, pretense, or circumspection. Again, language is an important tool for creating such spontaneity and removing distance. The rude language used by boys in their school days, for example, is reproduced. For women, a mixture of speech levels serves the same purpose: on the one hand, they revive the Gakushuin vocabulary, which is more polite or deferential than their routine speech and which comes back naturally to them; on the other, they intersperse this with deliberately discourteous expressions. Both extremes belong to the liminal sphere, exemplified here by the reunion of former schoolgirls. Relaxed into the common language of an intimate circle, even Empress Nagako (the empress dowager) was said to chat continuously. It appears that such intimacy of classmates may compensate for the positional distance maintained or internalized in family socialization and other social interaction. Unlike intimacy with one's otsuki, here is intimacy based on peer equality.

All this does not deny that animosity did exist among classmates, which was attributed to status differences. Nevertheless, in retrospect Gakushuin graduates recall and write about their student days with idyllic nostalgia (see, e.g., Ishimoto 1990), precisely because the prewar Gaku-shuin is irretrievably gone (recall Lasch's [1989] definition of nostalgia).

There is variation in the persistence and cohesiveness of classmate associations. Again, it is the royal family that provides an attractive focus around which friends gather. Thus, classes with princes or princesses prove more durable, active, cohesive, and better organized than those without. A female group called Sumirekai (Violet Club) centers on Princess Chichibu, another group on Princess Takeda, a younger group focuses on former Princess Yori (Mrs. Ikeda), and so on. I already mentioned the group called Kōbaikai, named after the oshirushi (chapter 5) of its central figure, the late Princess Teru (Princess Higashikuni). Among male groups is Shō'ōkai, named after the first character, *aki* (read as *shō*), of the name of Prince Higashikuni Akitsune (later Marquis Awata), and formed of the prince's kindergarten and elementary classmates. Prince Hitachi is the focal point of another group, meetings of which are scheduled at the prince's convenience. And around Prince Akihito a tennis club was organized called Ikuyokukai that consisted of several of his classmates. Before the war, Empress Nagako was absolutely inaccessible to her classmates, but after the war the taboo was lifted, and since then class reunions have been held several times at the Kunaichō (Imperial Household Agency, downgraded from the prewar Kunaishō, a ministry) and elsewhere. "Nagasama" even gave her friends a guided tour around the new palace building (*shin kyūden*) constructed in 1968 on the site of the ruined "Meiji" palace.

Royalty as the focal point of group solidarity, incidentally, holds true for kin grouping as well. Members of a kindred tend to be more willing participants in reunions if a royal member is at the center of the group, such as a kinswoman married to a prince. "Those of us who carry the blood of Tokugawa Keiki [Yoshinobu] are a group of about eighty, and we get together around Princess Takamatsu [Keiki's granddaughter]." Given the strictly patrilineal principle that binds royalty together, a royal connection was made through a woman marrying up into princesshood or a royal daughter marrying down into kazoku ranks. Kin associations centered on the imperial house often bear names containing the word *kiku* (chrysanthemum—the imperial symbol), such as Kikueikai, Kikuyūkai.

Gakushuin's umbrella alumni clubs are called, for men, Ōyūkai (The Cherry Blossom Friends' Club) and, for women, Tokiwakai (The Everlasting Club). These groups engage in their own activities, in which relatively little interest was shown by my informants. Tokiwakai, however, seems to attract more active members than does Ōyūkai. Recently, too, this women's club gained notoriety for its conservatism in allegedly opposing the crown prince's marriage to Shōda Michiko—a Sacred Heart graduate, not a Joshi Gakushuin alumna and Tokiwakai member as every other royal consort until then had been. It would be difficult to determine the truthfulness of this "rumor," which every Tokiwakai member I met strongly denied. Still, one can imagine how this royal marriage, involving as it did an outsider, might have hurt leading members of Tokiwakai.[10] In this respect, the crown princess's commoner status may have mattered less than her non-Gakushuin background.

SOCIALIZATION AND STATUS BOUNDARIES

Socialization, whether at home, away from home, or at school, mediated kazoku children to the outside world in various ways, with status outsiders or those on the margins of the status boundary playing a crucial role. The result of this mediation, however, was twofold. On the one hand, it contributed to raising status walls, promoting an elitist self-awareness, and cultivating a more or less homogeneous culture of peerage centered on the royal lineage, all involving the complicity of insiders and outsiders in consolidating and reproducing the hierarchical structure. On the other hand, mediation opened up the small circle of kazoku so that insiders and outsiders interpenetrated. Kazoku children expanded their horizons, for example, through intimate contact with commoner servants, and Gakushuin brought students of various backgrounds together into the same classrooms, forming a stimulating environment for all concerned. Later, the Gakushuin affiliation was to provide an important network— one that crossed the status boundary—for spousal candidacy, mediation, and all manner of opportunities for oneself and one's siblings, children, and friends. A Gakushuin diploma became a passport for a commoner woman to cross the status boundary through marriage. As one kazoku husband hastily pointed out after telling me of his wife's commoner status, "Of course, she is a Joshi Gakushuin graduate." In other words, the Gakushuin identity worked for commoner women much like adoption in rectifying family status, but in a much more substantial way than symbolic adoption in that such women in fact participated in or contributed to Gakushuin culture. Looked at from the opposite side, kazoku men, through such marriages, gained entry into the upper crust of the bourgeois class, which these women represented.

Gakushuin connections benefited one not only in marriage but in political and occupational careers as well. My informants concurred that kazoku in general were aloof from one another, even from kin, and would offer no help when their peers were in trouble. In that case, Gakushuin circles may have formed the very core of whatever solidarity existed among kazoku. Kazoku Kaikan (now renamed Kasumi Kaikan) and its subdivisions, which served as the bases for the House of Peers, would not have been so successful in attracting members without the help of Gakushuin alliances—a point to be taken up in the next chapter.

EIGHT

Status Careers

Privilege and Liability

We have examined how kazoku children were reared and trained in the home, boarding houses, and schools; let us now take up their adult careers. In so doing, we will be more in touch with the public realm, which so far has been treated largely as the ground for private, domestic life. By placing kazoku in the public arena, and by paying attention to institutional as well as individual biographies, we will gain a better idea of how the upper layer of Japan's social structure as a whole was shaped.

The main question here is whether kazoku status in any way affected one's career: whether it provided career opportunities and propelled advancement or, conversely, whether it limited a career repertoire and put a ceiling on how far one could go. In other words, we want to know whether and how ascription and achievement agglutinated or repelled each other. Did personal aspirations match career choice? The main actors in this chapter are men, with women playing a role only exceptionally, particularly before the war; for this reason, the generalized "person" will be genderized as "he."

CAREERS AND GENERATIONS

I begin by presenting a tabulation of careers based on the questionnaire (table 26). My focus here was intergenerational change, involving three generations: the respondent, his predecessor (*sendai,* or previous house-head—namely, the father or adoptive father), and the respondent's successor (*kōkeisha,* the son or adopted son). The table is confusing mainly because individuals often had multiple or shifting careers owing to personal or family circumstances or, more importantly, to the wartime and postwar crisis, which forced a radical career change on either the respondent himself or his predecessor. Obviously, then, the main (numbered)

285

Table 26. Career Patterns of Three Generations ($N = 101$, all from G-II)

	GENERATION I (PREDECESSOR)[a]	GENERATION II (SELF)	GENERATION III (SUCCESSOR)
Career Status			
With career	67	96	54
Without career	9	0	0
Ambiguous	25	0	0
Inapplicable	0	0	18
No answer	0	5	29
Career Tracks			
1. Government or Politics			
a. House of Peers	26 (28%)[b]	3 (3%)	0 (0%)
b. Kunaishō (-chō)	11 (12%)	4 (4%)	0 (0%)
c. Other	9 (1.0%)	14 (15%)	0 (0%)
2. Military			
a. Career officer	23 (25%)	2 (2%)	0 (0%)
b. Technical officer	0 (0%)	8 (8%)	0 (0%)
c. Draftee	0 (0%)	5 (5%)	0 (0%)
d. Postwar Self-Defense Forces	0	1	0

	G-I	G-II	G-III
3. Priesthood			
a. Shinto	4	4	1
b. Buddhist	2	2	1
c. Other	1	0	0
4. Professional			
a. Academic/educational	9 (10%)	15 (16%)	4 (7%)
b. Engineer/technical	5 (5%)	10 (10%)	9 (17%)
c. Iemoto master	2	2	0
5. Business			
a. Financial (employed)	7 (8%)	17 (18%)	5 (9%)
b. Other (employed)	23 (25%)	49 (51%)	34 (63%)
c. Independent	3 (3%)	10 (10%)	4 (7%)
d. Real estate	3 (3%)	5 (5%)	2 (4%)
6. Mass media	0	3	3
7. Administration	8 (9%)	10 (10%)	6 (11%)
8. Nonprofit organization	1	4	0
9. Honorary office	10 (11%)	12 (13%)	0 (0%)

[a]Three generations refer to a successive line of householdship seen from the point of view of the questionnaire respondent as the present head and second generation, who identifies his natural or adoptive father as his predecessor (first generation) and his natural or adopted son as his successor (third generation).

[b]The (rounded) percentages given in this table are all in reference to the total number of those individuals "with careers" and with "ambiguous" careers combined: 92 for G-I, 96 for G-II, and 54 for G-III. The percentages do not add up to 100 because of multiple self-assignment to categories.

categories of career tracks are not always mutually exclusive, nor are subcategories within a category. Only "Career Status" presents a straightforward picture. A response such as "a member of the House of Peers; master of ceremonies at Kunaishō," for example, was entered as "With career," 1a and 1b. Even though respondents with multiple careers were asked to mention only the two most important jobs, some gave more than two, which I decided not to waste. One man, for instance, began his career in the Ministry of Agriculture and Forestry, then was drafted into the Imperial Guard cavalry, remaining on military duty until the end of the war, after which he launched a new career as an owner-rancher in Hokkaido, where he was continuously reelected to the Hokkaido legislature. In this case the entries were "With career," 1c, 2c, 5c, and 5d. Two more examples of multiple careers: an employee at F. Electric Engineering Co. and then Mitsui Bank, a consultant at a metallurgy company, manager of golf courses, and so on; and a bank employee, store manager, and iemoto master.

"Full careers"—a single, consistent occupation continuously held for twenty or more years—are also found in the questionnaire sample. Here, consistency may lie in the specialized job itself, while the jobholder moves from one employer to another. Among such cases in generation (G) II are a researcher at the marine research institute in the Ministry of Agriculture, Forestry, and Marine Industry, for thirty-seven years; an assistant professor, then professor, at Tokyo University of Technology and professor at Tokyo University of Physics; an electrical engineer throughout, but moving from the (prewar) Ministry of Communication to the Telegraph and Telephone Public Corporation to the Postal Ministry to the Matsushita electric research headquarters. Career consistency may also be attributed to a single employer, while jobs and positions change—a familiar employment pattern in Japan—such as an employee at Mitsubishi Trading Company (MTC) for thirty years who ended as a board member of one of MTC's subsidiaries ("child companies"), or an employee of Japan Air Lines who moved from steward to purser to assistant pilot to captain.

Whether an individual had a single or multiple career is not always obvious, however, because many respondents listed temporary jobs held before their career was launched and postretirement jobs without differentiating them from the primary "single"-career tracks. Then too, the table omits certain entries that would likely have been added had the respondents seen the whole range of categories given in this table.[1] These problems notwithstanding, the table does show striking differences among the three generations in career pattern.

First, "Career Status" points up the disappearance of careerless men over generations: whereas thirty-four men in G-I (34 percent of the total) had no career or an ambiguous career, no one in G-II or G-III is so classified. Even if silence ("no answer") could mean careerlessness, only five men in G-II fall in that group. This difference may stem in part from generational variability in the definition of a career: what was a career for the older generation may not be so defined by the younger generation (as will be illustrated below when we come to subjective narratives). Nonetheless, it is certain that the career identity has become sharpened and mandatory for G-II. G-III includes eighteen "inapplicable" cases, where the successor was too young to have a career or where no successor had been nominated; and most of the twenty-nine silent responses may be also inapplicable cases. In any event, in no applicable case is the career absent or ambiguous.

Generational fluctuations are observable in career tracks as well. (In this part of the table, percentages are provided only where the numbers of actual cases alone do not elucidate intergenerational trends. The "totals" for percentages refer to the numbers of "With career" and "Ambiguous" [for Career Status] combined: 92 for G-I, 96 for G-II, and 54 for G-III. The subcategorical or categorical percentages cannot be added for the above-stated reason that they are not necessarily mutually exclusive.) As expected, the oldest generation is sharply overrepresented in careers in the Kunaishō and Kizokuin (House of Peers). In "other" governmental or political careers, where G-II exceeds G-I, the latter tended to occupy high-level positions including that of cabinet minister. None of the successor generation figures in this category. As for the military career, the twenty-three G-I representatives were all professional career officers of relatively high rank, including a general and a vice admiral, while G-II has only two military professionals but several technical officers (e.g., navy engineer) and draftees. No successor has entered the military career, not even in the postwar Self-Defense Forces. These linear changes are in fact predictable. Careers in government were adversely affected when the Kizokuin was abolished and the Kunaishō lost its prewar prestige and power, being diminished to the Kunaifu (1947–49) and then further to a mere agency called the Kunaichō. The military, of course, was wiped out by the pacifist constitution, and its partial revival in the Self-Defense Forces is being questioned as to constitutional legitimacy.

This transgenerational change does not apply to category 4, the priesthood, and for a good reason. The priestly career was included here on the assumption that it would indicate possible links between kazoku status and occupations, since a number of prominent "priestly houses" are of noble status (see chapter 2 for this history; note also other categories, like "Real estate" [5d] and "Honorary office" [9], delineated for the same purpose). The total number of priestly careers shown in the table is small, but significant is the relative stability of that number, suggesting that the priesthood is in fact an ie-attached occupation. The best-known example in Shinto is the Izumo Shrine chief priest, the Buddhist counterpart being the head of Honganji, the main temple of the Jōdo-Shin sect.[2] In my sample, it turned out, one Shinto house and two Buddhist houses had transmitted the chief priesthood from G-I to G-II.

From category 4 on, we find a relative preponderance of the younger generations. Outstanding in professional careers are educators, largely university professors (whose specialties, when indicated, are in natural science, medicine, law, foreign languages and literature, and art), but including some high school teachers as well. G-II has produced as many as fifteen academics and schoolteachers. This generation in fact doubles the predecessor generation (10.4 percent versus 5.4 percent) in engineering and technical fields, including architecture and medicine. This trend of technicalization rises to 16.7 percent for G-III. As for iemoto masters (4c), the two men of G-II each succeeded to the headship of a school of arts inseparable from their houses.

The intergenerational change we have seen in professional careers is duplicated in business careers, where G-II more than doubles G-I percentage-wise, a trend closely followed by G-III. The only exception is the real estate category, which, it should be noted, includes all businesses relating to land and property. In three cases, family-owned lands are the basis for businesses such as farm and ranch management and "high-class" rental housing for foreigners. In other cases, ownership per se is not clear, as in "land enterprise." And in still others, employment in real estate is meant, such as "section chief in Mitsui Realtors." Except for the cases of family-owned estates, inclusion in this subcategory may have nothing to do with kazoku status. Two households involve two generations (II and III) in the real estate industry.

Category 5, mass media, is indeed a new career, with no representatives in G-I. However, six men of younger generations have followed this path, in newspapers, radio broadcasting, and television, some of whom in fact work as producers. In interview, one man who is a media producer and executive explained his occupation in terms of his kuge background rooted in court culture: he had always had a strong taste for rituals as theatrical performance, best represented by court ceremonies.

Category 8, administration, refers to any position in a bureaucratic structure involving managerial or supervisory responsibilities (commonly indicated by the rank suffix -*chō* or -*yaku*), but exclusive of presidency of one's own company (to avoid redundancy with 5c). Here the percentage distribution shows a slight edge of the younger over the older generations, probably in reflection of generational differences in the number of "employees" (potential administrators). More significant differences emerge within specific ranks. In G-I, all administrators but one rose to the very top or executive level of the total organization (president, vice president, director, chairman), whereas G-II includes lower ranks like departmental chiefs (*buchō*), and half of all G-III administrators are still section chiefs (*kachō*). Obviously, this difference reflects seniority as a key to rising to the top; but I suspect there is another reason as well.

The older the generation, the more likely it is that one might have been offered a high position without first having to "rise" from the lower ranks of the bureaucracy. When the kazoku title carried with it a distinct reputation, a titled man may have been invited to cap the organization, thus lending it prestige and credibility. In such cases, an executive position may well have been more like an honorary office, merging with category 9. For younger generations, particularly G-III, no such "outsider" track exists; one must rise through the inside ladder by competing with peers. (Note that this interpretation is not based on solid evidence, but drawn only from what some of my informants said about their fathers or grandfathers.)

"Nonprofit organization" (category 8) refers to positions in a foundation, association, or institute formed for the purpose of charity, research, or other public benefits. Under "honorary office" (*meiyoshoku;* category 9) fall such ill-defined titles as advisor or consultant (*komon, sōdanyaku, san'yo*) and officer (*yakuin*). What was true regarding generational differences in administrative ranks seems even more relevant to this last category: seniority and the titular status of kazoku together may have favored older generations in being offered such offices by companies and other organizations, while no G-III representative holds an honorary office.

From this survey of generational change in career patterns, we might conclude that the oldest generation followed more status-relevant careers, the youngest predominates more in status-neutral careers, and the middle generation—the respondents' generation—involves a mixture of the two career types. In this sense, ascribed status may be said to have affected one's career one way or another (for the older generation) or not at all (prevalence of status-irrelevant careers for the younger generation). This generalization conveys nothing surprising, but provides a background for more personal data to be presented below. While occasionally referring back to the questionnaire, we now turn to what interviewed informants said about careers and look at their subjective views and experiences.

At this point I should be prepared for the problem of keeping my informants anonymous. Given the small size of the kazoku group and its dense network of informational circulation, plus the fact that individuals may pursue a career over a long period of time, a person's identity is likely to become disclosed at least within the group, even under a pseudonym. To protect anonymity, then, I avoid giving a continuous account of any particular individual's entire career but instead offer general, admittedly simplified patterns of careers or segments of careers. However, salient subject-informants will be identified by initials assigned by order of appearance: Mr. A, Mr. B, and so on; and, for women, Ms. Z, Ms. X, and so on.

POSITIONAL CAREERS

Kazoku and royals were supervised by the Kunaishō's Sōchitsuryō, which ensured the maintenance of honor worthy of their title, whether in the matter of choosing a spouse, adoptee, or school, or of upholding a proper life-style and decorum generally. Deviants, in short, jeopardized their kazoku status. Career choice, of course, was expected to conform equally to status honor; this meant that the job market for kazoku was as limited as the marriage market. Royal princes were destined to enter the army or navy, with no freedom to pursue a nonmilitary profession. As for kazoku, while a military career was not mandatory, it was strongly encouraged, and taken by many. In this sense, all kazoku men and their heirs were largely bound at some phase of life to a positional career (as represented in table 26 by status-relevant careers held predominantly by the oldest generation). In what follows I shall discuss a number of salient career patterns of positional type, though the reader should be aware that this list is by no means exhaustive, nor are the individual positions mutually exclusive.

Career Ambiguity

The positional constraint dampened career motivations among some kazoku heirs, unless the military profession happened to meet their desires. This predictable situation was reinforced by economic security based on regular proceeds from real estate, stocks and bonds, and other properties. Even "poor kuge" received dividends—enough for subsistence—from deposited imperial gift funds. In combination, these conditions sometimes produced men with careers that can only be called ambiguous, in that they were transient, temporary, part-time, titular, nameless, or simply nonexistent. This pattern, not surprisingly, prevailed more in older generations than in my informants' generation (G-II), more among older than younger informants, and more in the prewar than the postwar stage of a career.

By labeling this career type negatively as ambiguous or unidentifiable I display my bias for associating a career with an occupation. But many kazoku children shared my bias and, indeed, employed an even more stringent definition of career in discussing their fathers' noncareer careers:

> Kuge count, age forty-three: "All my predecessor [the previous house-head and the informant's adoptive father] had to do was occupy the headship."

> Daughter of a daimyo marquis, forty: "My grandfather had no particular occupation. . . . [He ran] a research institute but only as a hobby. . . . I don't know what father has done, which means he was not working. He had something to do with the Japanese Red Cross."

> Daughter of a daimyo viscount, sixty-five: "Father stayed around the house, engaging in gardening and other hobbies."

> Daughter of a daimyo count, forty-three: "Father knew nothing but horses. Horses, horses, all the time."

> Daughter of new kazoku, and granddaughter of a big daimyo, thirty-five: "None of my relatives had a job. That's why I still don't know the rank order of salaried men. I don't know which is higher, departmental chief [buchō] or subsection chief [kakarichō]. [Her husband is a section chief in a large company.]

The last remark reveals that children tended to equate a "job" with salaried employment in a bureaucratic organization. The daughter of a marquis of royal origin recalled her brother mercilessly interrogating his father about his occupation because he, the boy, had to write an essay on "My father" as a school assignment. He refused to accept the father's membership in the House of Peers or a long list of "titular" positions, insisting that "you have no occupation unless you commute to the workplace every day." She gathered her brother was embarrassed in front of his classmates, whose fathers were company men and whose work sustained their families. Her father later told her that in the prewar days the lump-sum allowance he had received from the emperor when he descended to kazoku ranks, amounting to one million yen, made him wealthy "enough to buy land, build houses, marry, employ staff, and live

an entire life without working." Another woman denigrated her antiquated father thus: "We say he is bound for a museum, hopelessly
unemployable."

In these cases, a positional career was opposed to or incompatible with
the modern occupational career, one being a career of "being," the other
a career of "doing." The former went along with the pursuit of leisurely
activities (see chapter 5). It was not that these men were inept; in fact,
all of them were highly educated, a large number having graduated from
Tokyo or Kyoto Imperial University, and some from Princeton and other
prominent foreign universities. But higher education often proved irrelevant to one's career choice or opportunities. This is exemplified by a
kuge marquis who majored in applied chemistry at Kyoto University but,
after a period of joblessness, entered the Board of the Ceremonies (Shikibushiki) in the Kunaishō. Among his assignments was an on-site study
of the system of ladies-in-waiting at the British court. "He did not utilize
his speciality," said his ninety-one-year-old widow. "In those days, people were not worried about livelihood at all, never doubting that everything would take care of itself. In my day, all kazoku were like that, so
unconcerned."

In this widow's retrospective view, the careerlessness of some kazoku
men was attributable to their lack of motivation. Yet this interpretation
does not apply to all careerless men, nor were all so malleable to the fate
that status dealt them. A number of men had a clear notion of educational
specialization and related career goal but were forestalled. One man, for
instance, wished to specialize in agriculture with the view to managing
farms and ranches and developing the family-owned land, but he was
overruled by his family and omote servants because of the prevailing,
leftist-instigated agrarian unrest. He majored instead in history at Tokyo
University and ended up careerless.

Endowed with money, leisure, and energy, some kazoku pioneered or
excelled in certain specialties, without, however, making career professions out of them. However highly regarded they became as "scholar,"
"scientist," "author," "artist," "photographer," "skier," "equestrian,"
or "alpinist," their activities often fell short of a career simply because
they were not applied within the commercial labor market. Emperor Shōwa's marine biology is a prime example of a professional "hobby," even
though his massive publications are said to be of professional quality. The
emperor himself reportedly said that his study was only a by-product of
his outdoor exercise and did not quite come up to a scholarly standard
("Tennō Hirohito" 1988, 273).

These men must have felt quite frustrated under such positional restraints. After all, pursuit of a hobby without professional commitment can be a constraint as much as a privilege. In some cases, extraordinary preoccupation with one hobby or another may be seen as the very expression of frustration or rebelliousness. Prohibited from following any acceptable occupational career, the heir of a viscount involved himself deeply in music and sailing. Now at age seventy-six, he explained his interests "as an outlet" and a signal of "rebellion," because he knew even these activities were not approved. He still resents the "feudalistic" oppression that led to his careerless life—the oppressor in this case being the main house of which his was a branch.

In the questionnaire I asked whether the respondent's occupation matched well with his desires or whether kazoku status had in any way affected his career choice. Contrary to my expectations, 50 of the 101 respondents indicated a good fit between their career and personal desires, and 51 (including many of the above 50) denied that kazoku status had influenced career choice. These responses differ markedly from what informants told me in interview. One possible explanation for this gap is that some people may not have thought a given career to be a matter of choice but simply took it for granted. If so, the question itself was inappropriate. Another explanation may be that open admission of status constraint would sound too overbearing. As if to offer a tacit confirmation of these two possibilities, about one-third of the total respondents gave no answer. During interviews, however, I had strong impressions of positional constraint on career choice, exercised both by informants and by their families.

The House of Peers

Membership in the Kizokuin was an exceedingly prominent positional career and indeed was mentioned by many informants as the career (or noncareer career) of their fathers, fathers-in-law, or grandfathers. What these forebears had done as peers, however, was unknown or of little interest to my informants—an attitude that may reflect their retrospective view of the House of Peers as only decorative, being so overshadowed by the *Shūgiin* (House of Representatives), the real center of politics, as well as their reluctance to recognize their predecessors' political role in prewar Japan.

Some older informants were peers themselves at the tail end of the Kizokuin's fifty-seven-year history, when Japan was already entrenched in the imperialist escalation in China heading toward the fateful Pearl Harbor attack. Mr. A, whose late father had been a leading peer, was himself elected in 1939 and remained a peer, without standing another election, until the May 1947 abolition of the Kizokuin. He was one of the few informants who was eager to discuss the role of the Kizokuin, but more as an inside historian than from his personal experience. By then, of course, the military dominated politics so thoroughly that no debatable issue seemed to surface. In any case, Mr. A and his contemporaries were too young to have their voices heard in the Kizokuin. (Another former peer, who sounded as if he had had some clout, was described by his daughter as "a mere *jingasa* [backbencher] seated there only to applaud other speakers.")[3]

The Kizokuin, together with the Shūgiin, was set up to form the Imperial Parliament in 1890, the memorable year of its first session, as stipulated by the 1889 Imperial Constitution and *kizokuinrei* (ordinance of the House of Peers). Because the 1884 kazoku reorganization was politically aimed at the bicameral parliament then projected by governmental architects, it was no surprise that the kazoku formed the major constituency of the Kizokuin. The Kizokuin included three other groups as well, however: royal princes, imperial appointees (*chokusen*), and "highest taxpayers" (*takaku nōzeisha*). Later, representatives of the Imperial Academy (Gakushiin) were added. Recruitment processes also varied internally. For royal princes and kazoku of the two highest ranks (princes and marquises), membership was hereditarily automatic or obligatory, while all other kazoku members were to be elected through "mutual election" (*gosen*) within their respective ranks. Because of this difference, kazoku peers were identified according to their titled rank— "baron-peer," "viscount-peer," and so on. Imperial appointees were selected from among those who distinguished themselves through meritorious accomplishments for the state or through learned expertise. As for the high taxpayers, initially one member was elected from each prefecture out of the fifteen top national-taxpayers in that prefecture. Being male was of course mandatory for all categories, and the minimum age was set at twenty for the royalty, twenty-five for kazoku, and thirty for the rest. When Academy seats were added, the mutual-election principle was adopted. Elected members in all categories served a seven-year term; all other appointments were for life.

Table 27 presents seat distribution (in actual occupancy) in House sessions from 1890 to 1925. Owing to changes in allocated seats through amendments of the original ordinance (KK 1985, 296–301) as well as new ennoblements and promotions, during these thirty-five years change is especially noticeable. For example, the number of baron-peers more than tripled between 1890 and 1925, to fill in the initial gap between them and viscounts. This change reflects a sharp increase of new barons,

Table 27. Distribution of Peers by Qualification Category, 1890–1925

	1890	1904	1911	1918	1925
Royal	10	13	14	14	18
Prince (kazoku)	10	10	16	13	15
Marquis	21	30	31	37	31
Count	14	17	17	19	18
Viscount	70	70	70	73	66
Baron	20	56	63	72	65
Subtotal	145	196	211	228	213
Appointee	61	125	124	123	120
High taxpayer	45	44	45	47	66
Academy	—	—	—	—	4
Subtotal	106	169	169	170	190
Total	251	365	380	398	403

Source: Adapted from Kizokuin Jimukyoku 1947.

ennoblements made largely among the highest-ranking military officers. Further, imperial appointees increased almost every year until by 1904 their original total had more than doubled. The Kizokuin, then, had room to absorb new elites, thus allowing a better balance between kazoku and nonkazoku, but not without a ceiling.

In 1925, the hereditary elite (royal princes and kazoku) numbered 213 (53 percent of the Kizokuin membership), while nonhereditary peers totaled 190 (47 percent). The preponderance of kazoku peers in the Kizokuin is perhaps best symbolized by the fact that the seven House speakers were all kazoku of kuge or daimyo origin except the first speaker, Itō Hirobumi, the foremost architect of the Meiji government. The fourth speaker, Tokugawa Iesato, held the position for thirty years, as if he were above political dispute as the emperor was. I suspect that, his highly credited personal merit aside, in the eyes of peers he continued to stand out as none less than the sixteenth head of the shogunal house, second in prestige only to the imperial house.

How competitive was "mutual election" for kazoku candidates? The ordinance stipulated that the number of seats allocated to each rank not exceed one-fifth the number of title holders of that rank. Table 28, which shows the results of the first election, would seem to indicate that 1 in 4.4 title holders gained a seat; in fact, however, competition was even

Table 28. Title Holders and Kizokuin Seats for Kazoku from the First Election of the Imperial Parliament (1890)

KAZOKU TITLE	NO. TITLE HOLDERS	SEATS ALLOCATED
Count	74	15
Viscount	297	70
Baron	95	20
Total	466	105

Source: Adapted from SK (1982a, 28).
Note: Imperial Parliament elections were primarily for the House of Representatives (Shū-giin); the House of Peers (Kizokuin) was only partially open to elections and only among privileged circles, including kazoku.

less tough because not all title holders stood for election. Some were precluded on the basis of insufficient age or jobs incompatible with politics; for example, it was ruled that holders of major court offices (KK 1985, 301) and military positions, if still active, be ineligible for Kizokuin membership. Further, many eligible kazoku preferred to stay away from politics. The kazoku candidacy for Kizokuin election, then, involved only mild competition, if any. "The number of counts was so small," said the heir of a count-peer, "that virtually every candidate was elected." In fact, the system of "mutual election" practically did away with election itself in the strict sense of the word, even in a large rank group like that of viscounts.

According to Mr. A, each rank group formed a nominating committee: "In the case of viscounts, [the committee] was called Shōyūkai. Speaking from my own experience [as a candidate], if you wanted to run, you would ask Shōyūkai leaders to recommend you. Then the leaders would discuss whether you should wait a little or should be recommended right away as an important candidate, and so on. If recommended, you would be on a list of sixty nominees." A nomination amounted virtually to election, since "voters" went along with the committee's recommendation: "Each voter wrote down the names of the sixty nominees." The whole process was "very clean indeed," commented Mr. A nostalgically.

The mildness or absence of competition, as well as "election" through internal negotiation, was in Mr. A's opinion symbolic of the unique significance and strength of the Kizokuin. Under these circumstances, the Kizokuin could play a politically neutral role, checking the overpoliticized, short-sighted moves of the popular election–dependent Shūgiin and thereby stabilizing the whole national polity. Another informant, a former baron-peer, seconded this view, saying that the rationale for the Kizokuin's very existence lay in its immunity from party politics.

Given the composition of Kizokuin membership, it is not surprising that the Kizokuin played a more conservative role than the Shūgiin, but whether it was a politically neutral force is a matter of opinion. The Kizokuin in fact acted against Shūgiin decisions on many occasions—opposing a land-tax increase passed by the Shūgiin in 1899, for example, overriding the Shūgiin's decision to revise the Peace Preservation Police Law and permit women's participation in political assemblies (1907), and stalling a Shūgiin bill to eliminate the tax requirement for the right to vote (1924–25). The Kizokuin's conservative outlook reflected its members' special sense of mission: its task, as it saw things, was to protect the emperor's political immunity or sovereignty. Mr. A recalled how Prime Minister Tanaka Giichi (1927–29) was "hazed" by the Kizokuin because Tanaka explained his failure to dismiss a minister from his cabinet under the pretense of following the emperor's venerable wish (*yūjō*): "That was a lie. Men like Prince Konoe and Marquis Hosokawa whipped Tanaka with strong words for being so impudent to the emperor."

A more zealously nativistic loyalism entered into the Kizokuin's role in the 1935 dispute over the *kokutai* (the "body politic," connoting the mystic essence of the state merging with the emperor)—an event that ominously foreshadowed a coup d'état by young officers the following year known as the February 26th Incident. The kokutai dispute arose in association with a constitutional interpretation by Minobe Tatsukichi, an imperially appointed peer, of the emperor as an "organ" of the state. When a fellow peer, Kikuchi Takeo, who was a baron and an ex–major general, rebuked Minobe in a Kizokuin session, the rightist argument quickly escalated and spread, invoking proclamations from both houses, the government, and the military against the "organ theory." Minobe was spared prosecution, but he resigned from the Kizokuin. "It was a difficult issue," Mr. A said. "The 'organ theory' was valid in a legal sense, but if you had any respect for the emperor you could not have stated it in such terms. I agree[d] with [Minobe's] scholarly view, but it was wrong to use this word [*organ*] in the session. It lacks reverence."

The wartime nationalism was apparently fully shared by the Kizokuin (SK 1982a), although my kazoku informants tended to stress the cosmopolitan and antimilitary atmosphere of their own homes. The chronological table (SK 1982a), for example, lists the Kizokuin's unanimous decisions to present "a statement of gratitude to the army and navy" and expand military budgets, as well as its dispatch of supportive messengers to the war fronts. Such actions, though perhaps meant only as lip service to the military, were taken after the Manchurian Incident, and they became increasingly frequent as Japan's war involvement deepened and broadened—an understandable development in view of the large number of peers with military background.

In brief, the Kizokuin was far from being a mere accessory to the Shūgiin or standing above mundane politics. It was, in fact, deeply involved in the political process of modern Japan. Nevertheless, the Kizokuin's accomplishments as a policymaker do not loom large in its chronological table, probably because its primary function was reactive rather than proactive. More striking are the vicissitudes of its internal organization, with constant fissions and fusions, formations and dissolutions of subgroups or factions, joinings and defections, group renamings, and so on. Indeed, the bulk of the Shōyū Kurabu publications concerns organizational matters (SK 1980, 1982a, 1982b, 1984). Factions were formed either along or across ranks or categories of membership; one source (SK 1984, app. 2), in a complicated genealogy of the Kizokuin's organizational fissions and realignments, identifies twenty-seven main "political associations" and twenty-nine other affiliate groups. Though immune from "party politics," the Kizokuin was clearly not immune from factional politics. Indeed, the lack of parties and the fact of noncompetitive election through internal negotiations probably fostered organizational instability.

The most powerful faction of all was the Kenkyūkai (Study Group), consisting predominantly of viscount-peers, the "tyranny" of which came under attack from baron-peers. According to one of the latter, following the Sino-Japanese and Russo-Japanese wars there was a sharp increase in ex-military kazoku, and hence in baron-peers. They therefore decided that it was "ridiculous for us to be pushed around by the pompous kuge and daimyo of the Kenkyūkai," and so new group called Kōseikai (Justice Group) was formed. For this baron-peer, the Kōseikai-Kenkyūkai struggle was the most memorable event of his Kizokuin tenure.

The relative organizational power or commitment of these two peer groups—viscounts and barons—compared with that of peers of higher ranks may be inferred from the fact that the two groups survive symbolically to this day. Their respective clubhouses have been newly rebuilt with funds derived from collectively owned real estate, in collaboration with giant corporations like Mitsui Realtors, Inc. Located across from the central clubhouse, Kasumi Kaikan, are Shōyū Kaikan, representing the former viscount-peers and their descendants, and Shōwa Kaikan, for baron-peers and their descendants (though actually, membership is extended to all viscounts and barons). Eligibility for membership is less stringent than for Kasumi Kaikan (Shōwa Kaikan, for example, accepts nonsuccessor sons and adopted-out sons), but the gender requirement is maintained across the board (I was admitted into guest quarters, but not into the bar and billiards area). Both clubs occupy the top floors of super-modern high-rise office buildings, remaining solvent through office-space rentals on other floors. As nonprofit corporations, both clubs, along with the central club, Kasumi Kaikan, engage in charity activities. According to a Shōwa Kaikan representative, part of the club's income (some 500 million yen per year) is donated to social welfare agencies—to aid the mentally retarded, for example—and used to support foreign students.

The mention of money calls attention back to the Kizokuin and the peers' salaries. In 1920, Diet members received a pay raise: from ¥5,000 to ¥7,500 for the speaker; from ¥3,000 to ¥4,500 for the vice speaker; and from ¥2,000 to ¥3,000 for members (SK 1982a, 109). This did not apply to automatic and obligatory peers, however: prince- and marquis-peers were paid "not a single yen." No wonder Kizokuin membership was not considered a career by the children of high-ranking peers. Conversely, elected peers apparently took their office quite seriously; 3,000 yen, after all, was "more than enough" to keep a family alive. "That is why poor kuge were particularly eager to seek a seat," said a former baron-peer prejudiced against old nobles. "They were so covetous of the 3,000 yen annual pay. Some were despicable indeed: they as a group would support a candidate in order to share the pay. They were really pitiful, those parasitic kuge." This probably exaggerated statement is nevertheless a revelation to those who dismiss Kizokuin membership as a mere medal of honor. Service in the Kizokuin was raised to a full-fledged career when the honor was backed up by pecuniary reward. In this regard, kazoku status was a strong asset on which to build one's career.

Careers at Court

Notable among positional careers were appointments in the Kunaishō, or more correctly, in the imperial court. Indeed, according to my informants the court, like the military, was a major employer of kazoku men (and to a lesser degree women). Even though the kuge had been abolished, its legacy was thus partly renewed in the modern court. Some followed a courtly career as the only alternative to a military one, while others found their "postmilitary" life in the court. In many instances, court jobs were taken as the last stage of a career, thus attracting postretirement job seekers. Yet as we shall see, the relationship of kazoku status to a court career was not as simple as it might at first appear.

Four court offices were especially important in influencing, shaping, shielding, and executing the imperial will, in keeping the imperial position above politics and government, in supervising imperial behavior, and in controlling outsiders' access to the emperor: these were the offices of the lord privy seal (*naidaijin*), Kunaishō minister (*kunaidaijin*), grand chamberlain (*jijūchō*), and chief aide-de-camp (*jijūbukanchō*), referred to categorically as *sokkin* (entourage to His Majesty). The first three theoretically belonged to the Kunaishō, and yet the naidaijin was semi-autonomous as the head of the naifu (the court's internal bureau). The autonomy of the jijūbukanchō derived from the *tōsuifu* (the supreme commander bureau), which attached the military directly to the emperor as the supreme commander, separate from the rest of government. Table 29, indicating the number of kazoku (by rank) who held these four offices from their inception to termination, demonstrates a strong—and in the case of naidaijin, perfect—correlation between these top court offices and kazoku status. In addition, the chair of the privy council (*sūmitsuin*) was 100 percent kazoku-held until 1945. This might give the impression that the pre-Restoration kuge institution had not really vanished. To dispel this impression, let us look at other key positions of the government as a whole. The offices of prime minister, home affairs, foreign affairs, and finance were occupied by 254 men in total between 1885 and 1945 (Takayanagi and Takeuchi 1974, 1257–66). Of these, 161 (63 percent) were kazoku. It was not because of their kazoku status that these men reached the apex of the government hierarchy; rather, it was through their outstanding performance that they earned not only these top positions *but also* kazoku titles. Members of the *hereditary* elite who figured large in key positions were very few, notably Sanjō Sanetomi and Saionji Kinmochi, and even for these men their kuge status alone would have helped their careers but little; particularly Saionji's three terms as premier would have been inconceivable without his extraordinary brains and performance.

The same was more or less true of the four court offices as well. The chief aide-de-camp is a case in point. He was always recruited from among generals (as exemplified by Honjō Shigeru, who held this office in 1933–36 after having been commander-in-chief of the Kwantung Army) to represent the army in dealings with the court (for Honjō's role in court, see Hane 1982). None of the holders of this office were hereditary kazoku; indeed, the five kazoku among them were newly ennobled. As for kunaidaijin, only two (Iwakura [1909–10] and Matsudaira [1946–47])

Table 29. Kazoku Status and Top Court Offices

RANK	NAIDAIJIN (LORD SEAL)	KUNAIDAIJIN (MINISTER)	JIJŪCHŌ[a] (CHAMBERLAIN)	JIJŪBUKANCHŌ (AIDE-DE-CAMP)
Royal	1	0	0	0
Kazoku prince	5	2	4	0
Marquis	1	0	0	0
Count	2	4	4	0
Viscount	1	2	2	1
Baron	1	3	2	4
Nonkazoku	0	2	4	3
Total	11	13	16	8
Percentage kazoku/royal	100	85	75	63

Sources: Kodama 1978; *KKT*.

[a]This office has survived the postwar constitutional change, but because of changed functions and capacities, only those appointed under the prewar constitution are counted.

were hereditary kazoku. Even grand chamberlains and lord keepers of the privy seal were largely nonhereditary kazoku, or even nonkazoku, though among them a good number of hereditary title holders are found as well (seven grand chamberlains: Tokudaiji counted twice, Kawase, Higashikuze, Takatsukasa, Ōgimachi, and Tokugawa; and four seal keepers: Sanjō, Tokudaiji, Prince Fushimi, and Kido). The majority of these newly ennobled kazoku were awarded their titles in recognition of excellent performances prior to appointment to these offices.

All this reflects the unwritten rule in favor of appointing "outsiders" to the higher offices of the imperial court, a policy that meant the appointment of "bureaucrats" from external ministries as the personal consensus–based oligarchy of the early Meiji was replaced by a ripened government bureaucracy, with all its sectional competition (Titus 1974). Even Kido Kōichi, a marquis, had had extensive bureaucratic experience before becoming the "last" naidaijin: after the typical educational course from Gakushuin to Kyoto University, Kido entered the Ministry of Agriculture and Commerce, then held the office of secretary general to the naidaijin, that of Sōchitsuryō director, and three ministerial positions.

The outsider recruitment policy was confirmed and explained with regard to the present Kunaichō by an informant, a retired chief steward to the crown prince (*tōgū daibu*): "The Kunaichō as a whole is a 'household,' and the business there is basically domestic"; this is why, he said, the higher echelon of the Kunaichō hierarchy is staffed by outsiders nearing retirement after long careers in other ministries—as had been his experience. "If you started your career in the Kunaichō and stayed on there throughout, you would have no opportunity to develop administrative leadership and judgment on statewide affairs." Curiously, this bureaucrat's explanation for outsider recruitment centers on the career development of individual officials—an indicator of the Kunaichō's downgraded function. In the prewar Kunaishō, however, a more important reason was at work: highly experienced and successful outsiders would keep the Kunaishō viable, whereas outmoded insiders with no broader knowledge of the world beyond the court would be deadly to its function.

Yet was kazoku status really irrelevant to the four offices, particularly to those of naidaijin and jijūchō? Clearly not. Take Prince Kido, for example. Kido was recommended to the office of secretary general to the naidaijin by Prince Konoe and Viscount Okabe, who were intimate with Kido as fellow kazoku, as fellow students at Gakushuin and Kyoto University, and as co-members of a Gakushuin golf club and a literary club. Further, during his tenure as secretary general Kido circulated largely among fellow kazoku, particularly hereditary kazoku sharing club membership (Titus 1974, 196–99; Odaira 1984). This initial, private networking, even though it later gave way to more official outsider contacts, must have contributed greatly to his career advancement. To be sure, kazoku status, coupled with the Gakushuin background, was neither a necessary nor a sufficient condition for attainment of a top court office, but it did give one a headstart.

To be noted in connection with Kido's rise and with the relevance of the old aristocratic status to modern court politics was the role of Prince Saionji, who, as the last surviving genrō (former Meiji statesman), was behind virtually all major decisions on appointments (and thus was called a "cabinet maker"). Emperor Hirohito's most trusted advisor, Saionji practically became a surrogate emperor—reminiscent of a regent in the Fujiwara heyday—whose opinion or sanction was sought out by the imperial entourage. As secretary general to the naidaijin, for example, Kido often had cause to contact Saionji on behalf of his superior, Naidaijin Makino, either directly or through Saionji's ubiquitous secretary, Baron Harada Kumao. The advocacy by the imperial entourage (except the chief aide-de-camp) of a pro-Western, liberal constitutional monarchy is also credited to the influence of Saionji, who spent many years of his youth in Paris, was educated at the Sorbonne, and, after his return, expressed his ideology of "liberty and people's right" in his own newspaper. The question might, of course, be raised whether Saionji's influence as a surrogate emperor would have been as indisputable had he not been a prominent kuge who could sit with the emperor almost as an equal.

When Saionji withdrew from the genrō position because of age, his role as imperial surrogate was taken over by Naidaijin Kido Kōichi. The result was a double-headed entourage represented by the naidaijin, backed up by two other civilian officeholders, on the one hand, and by the chief aide-de-camp on the other, both of whom competed in influencing the imperial will (Titus 1974). To digress a little here, it should be noted that in these palace politics, Emperor Hirohito was far from a passive listener to these sokkin; rather, he influenced them by his *gokamon* (imperial questioning), which was often understood as a challenge, or by his pronouncementlike remarks, which were later conveyed by the sokkin to the source of the imperial irritation or pleasure. It was through such subtle utterances on the part of the emperor that even the jijūbukan was kept in line (Titus 1974; Kojima 1981). And yet the emperor, confined to the interior of the palace and surrounded by the sokkin and thousands of retainers (the "ninefold fences"), had no chance to talk directly to the people. Hence the structure of "dyarchy" was maintained intact.[4]

The least politically involved of the sokkin, the jijūchō headed the office that attended to the emperor's personal, domestic matters; he was thus most intimate with the master. If the genrō or naidaijin was a surrogate emperor, the chamberlain was the emperor's shadow that accompanied the master wherever he was. It would be only natural, then, to find more court insiders, and hence hereditary kazoku, on the board of chamberlains. And indeed, except for the last period from 1929 to 1946, when the jijūchō were all retired navy officers (to counterbalance the army's domination of the office of chief aide-de-camp), grand chamberlains largely were court insiders—including Tokudaiji Sanenori, a kuge prince and the elder brother of the adopted-out Saionji, who held the office for twenty-eight years. This office alone survived the constitutional change because of the primarily private nature of its function.

The major court jobs that my informants or their fathers held were those of grand or rank-and-file chamberlainship, similarly of personal nature, in attendance to emperors, empresses, empresses dowager, crown princes, and other members of the royalty. Generally tongue-tied on personal matters of the imperial household ("My father said not a word about what happened at the palace"), some interviewees divulged interesting and even surprising bits of information:

> The daughter of a kuge marquis, age ninety-one: My family waited on the imperial house generation after generation. My father was a chamberlain [to Emperor Meiji], commuted to the Kunaishō on horseback or by a horse-drawn carriage [which was sent from the office every day]. . . . My brother was *kōgōgū daibu* [chief steward to the empress[5]—in this case, the present empress dowager] after retiring from the Ministry of Communication. Actual caretaking was done by the *nyokanchō* [chief lady-in-waiting], but on formal occasions [*omotemuki*] it was my brother's duty. . . . When the crown prince [Akihito] was born, my brother carried the baby prince in his arms to the kashikodokoro [to be introduced to Amaterasu]. Clad in the heavy court dress [ikan-sokutai] and with the special court footgear on, he was frightened of dropping the prince.
>
> The daughter of a daimyo count, eighty-eight, to the question "What did a chamberlain do?": A servant's job. Today, it is not too bad, but it used to be a tough job. Ordinary chamberlains did everything, but my father [as grand chamberlain] accompanied Emperor Taishō when he went out. In those days, it was chamberlains who combed the emperor's hair, helped him bathe, and everything else. Because Emperor Taishō was such that while a chamberlain was shaving him he would not sit still, my father,

watching it, was scared to death that the emperor might "sweat" any second [*sweat* being the palace word for "bleed"].

Both quotations focus on the attendant's responsibility for the safety of his charge. The second informant could not resist telling more about Taishō: the emperor indulged himself with cigars and wine so much that the empress tried to stop him. But the emperor had something more on his mind: when Yamagata Aritomo chaired the Privy Council, he would visit with Taishō, who communicated his carnal desire and asked Yamagata to find a woman for him. "Yamagata told him off firmly, 'No, Your Majesty, that cannot be done.' So nothing happened and he died from meningitis, poor thing."

Mr. B was an active chamberlain when I interviewed him in a room of the shabby Kunaichō building. Determined to pursue a scholarly career, he had been reluctant to accept the court job offer, but was persuaded by a chamberlain whom he regarded highly just to "try" it. Since he came from a kuge family and his father had been an attendant to Empress Taishō, this course was considered sensible by his father and strongly endorsed by his mother. Once at court, Mr. B found the emperor such a pleasant person that he appreciated his presence every day for the next four decades. "No regrets." He described Emperor Hirohito as full of "humanity," "tolerance," "humor," and "the world's best employer." In his view, the emperor's extraordinary quality was recognized more by foreigners than by Japanese. Mr. B had many anecdotes to tell. For example, when he accompanied his master to the United States, "Americans were expecting, according to my American friends, to meet a Hitler stepping off the plane. At the Williamsburg airport, they stood ready only to glare at him, when an old, feeble-looking [*shoboku-reta*] man descended. Immediately, they decided that this man was unable to do anything evil."

Mr. B, speaking while Hirohito was still alive, did not think court life changed after the war. "Even under the old constitution, His Majesty lived in the same spirit as under the new constitution; he has never been status conscious. He was believed to be a god only by outside people, not by himself. He is the same as ever. . . . The only difference is that he has no military duty any more." There was no change in his consumption style either, because he was always personally frugal even when the imperial house had a huge property amounting to 1.6 billion yen. "Even then he asked us to buy a three-and-a-half-yen book only if it was within budgetary limits."

A chamberlain's work is like that of a housewife—not that he has to do domestic chores like cooking and cleaning (such tasks are carried out by specialized staff), but his job is not well defined; it is multifaceted, diffuse, and generalized like housewifery. When he has nothing to do, he must still be present in the "waiting room": chamberlains (six in total now, in addition to the grand and deputy grand chamberlains) take turns, in two-member teams, keeping duty all night in the palace. When the emperor is receiving guests or visiting various places as the guest of honor, the chamberlains' work and concerns become intensified and their ability and perseverance are tested. Here the analogy with housewifery ceases to apply. A chamberlain's responsibility may be diffuse like the housewife's, but it is also much more extensive, heavier, and tougher, as the following episodes illustrate.

Irie Sukemasa (1989), the late grand chamberlain to Emperor Shōwa, describes, among hundreds of other things, problems of imperial lodging. In the prewar days, unless on a visit to Hayama or Nasu, where there were imperial villas, the emperor and his retinue had to take lodgings at a local public building such as a school, prefectural government office, or municipal auditorium. Regular hotels were ruled out for fear that hotel owners would try to capitalize on His Majesty's selection to promote their business or would completely refurbish the structure to impress the distinguished guests. Yet it was difficult to sleep in a temporarily rearranged office "bedroom." In 1947, when the emperor stayed at a regular hotel (*ryokan*) for the first time, he discovered the surprising convenience and comfort such lodgings could afford (Irie 1989, 55–60).

Imperial travel must be well planned in advance to minimize unexpected troubles. The chamberlain's responsibility includes locating the lavatory at the travel destination and checking its quality, so that he can guide the emperor there if nature calls. Irie himself once made a special advance trip for the sole purpose of locating the lavatory. But something unexpected always seemed to happen. Once, when the emperor was about to be welcomed by schoolchildren on a schoolground, he wanted to use the toilet. But the ground was so tightly enclosed by red-and-white curtains hung to celebrate the occasion that no one could pass through. Irie and two others tried desperately to tear a corner open for the imperial passage to the lavatory located in advance, but in vain. The emperor ended up at one of the tiny latrines used by gradeschoolers (Irie 1989, 170–71).

This kind of work, however hard, remains hidden from public view, and chamberlains and similar court attendants seem to consider it their duty to remain as unobtrusive as possible (another housewifely, and shadowlike feature). What really frustrates these men, judging from their writing and remarks in interview, is that the public not only does not appreciate their invisible efforts but even accuses them of standing between the emperor and the people—accusations that I heard, too, and not just from total outsiders ignorant of court affairs but from some kazoku themselves.

Often, the Kunaichō and palace guard receive severe criticism for blocking free contact between the emperor and the people. But the court retainer reveals another side of the barrier. Irie repeats how strongly he wished to see the emperor meet ordinary people freely and spontaneously in natural conditions. The trouble is that the emperor, once he steps out of the palace, would not be allowed any private, anonymous moments. Ubiquitous reporters and photographers would lose no chance to catch even a momentary glimpse of the emperor, and crowds would form immediately, overwhelming the scene. While struggling with the human waves, attendants would have to forestall delay of the planned event, lest the emperor be late for the specially chartered imperial train. And so forth. Further, there is a gap between local interest and statewide concerns. During the 1954 imperial visit, a mayor in Hokkaido wanted to play a conspicuous role as the emperor's guide to the exhibited local products. But circumstances, including the emperor's fatigue, prevented this mayor's dream from coming true. Having missed this opportunity for glory, the mayor went into a rage and berated the Kunaichō official in charge for "thwarting the reverential petition [*jōsō*] to the emperor," which became inflated into a huge headline. Irie comments regarding this incident that if such a request were accepted in one town, under the golden rule of fairness every similar request would then have to be accepted as well (Irie 1989, 68–69). Despite the seeming consensus that the emperor and people should have freer, more natural contact, then, a wide gap exists as to just who and what stands between them.

Court attendance, as represented by chamberlainship, demotes the otherwise lordly kazoku to the position of a servant. Why would anyone from an aristocratic family want to be a servant? In cases of poor kuge, some court offices involving no real work were granted out of "imperial benevolence" to provide income. But most career courtiers were (and are) promising men who, educated at Gakushuin and Tokyo University, could have pursued other careers. Being offered a court job, thus, was apparently a high honor difficult to turn down. Further, judging from essays written by active chamberlains (Irie 1980), to share the imperial private life so intimately, as no one else does, and thus to be part of the imperial charisma may be taken as an unparalleled privilege, one that more than compensates for the sacrifice involved.

Chamberlains also play ritual roles as imperial surrogates. Every morning a Shinto ceremony is conducted at the palace shrine, and, except for major annual rites or anniversaries that require the emperor's personal participation, it is one of the chamberlains on duty from the previous night who becomes the presiding ritualist on behalf of the emperor. The surrogate ritualist purifies himself by bathing, appears in full court-priestly attire, and receives all the courtesy due the emperor himself.

There are other court attendants who specialize in rituals and ceremonies as well, serving in positions less demanding than the chamberlainship. The palace ritualists or priests, called *shōten,* are no longer public appointees but, under the constitutional separation of religion and state, private employees of the imperial house. Among these, as among chamberlains, we find a concentration of former kazoku. The five shōten, under the chief and deputy chief shōten, take turns in assisting the emperor or his surrogate (a chamberlain) with Shinto rituals at the palace shrine.

Mr. C was a new shōten at age fifty-six. A member of a kuge family, he quit Gakushuin to enter the Yōnen Gakkō (preparatory army academy) to become a career officer like his father, but the war ended before he reached this goal. After the war, when the Self-Defense Forces were created, he joined the ground force, where he stayed for more than twenty years; then, upon retirement, he was invited to be a shōten "because my grandfather was a shōten." Like any convert, Mr. C took this new position seriously, strongly identified himself with his master, and explained the detail of rituals to me with missionary zeal. Convinced that the court is the center of Japan's ritual culture (*saishi bunka*), Mr. C insisted that its tradition, which is "one thousand and several hundred years old," should be carried on intact. In fact, the ancient ritual code is being followed in every detail, he claimed: "For example, Their Majesties appear in the traditional court dress and hairstyle in annual rites." He emphasized how sacred the kashikodokoro is, how no one but the emperor can enter its inner chamber. Mr. C sounded as if, after long years of military life, he was rediscovering his own kuge roots in the most sacred site of the court, where his ancestors had waited on emperors for centuries. He neglected to mention that the palace practice of Shinto rites, together with the construction of the palace shrine, had been a post-Meiji creation (see chapter 4), though he did admit that even the kashikodokoro, an otherwise off-limits sanctuary, had been exposed on television at the time of the 1959 wedding of the crown prince (Akihito) and princess. Mainly, he seemed to adhere to the idea of the "timelessness" of imperial tradition, which was in turn closely connected with his own identity. (Incidentally, it is the shōten who, during the one-year mourning period after an emperor's demise, assume the role of the new emperor in conducting rituals at the palace shrine. The successor, being in mourning, is unable to be in contact with Shinto gods, for whom death is a taboo.)

There are also five female shōten, called *naishōten*, about whom very little is known. According to two insider informants interviewed separately, these unmarried women, who serve the daily food offering (*o-nikku*) to the kashikodokoro and kōreiden (the shōten are in charge of same for the shinden), seldom leave the palace, sleeping in a dorm on the palace ground, waited on by their respective maids. They dress in kimono and hakama, and wear "a strange hairdo." The naishōten "say all sorts of things to the kami, like 'It has become cold now,' as if they were speaking to people. Such communication with kami is better done by women, I suppose." According to this informant, the naishōten office is a modern successor to the ritsuryō nyokan office called the naishi-no-tsukasa, which had been in custody of the sacred regalia (see chapter 6). Although the office used to be staffed only by kuge daughters, now commoner graduates from schools specializing in Shinto and daughters of local shrine priests predominate. In the kashikodokoro, it is the naishōten who, as personal servants to Amaterasu, enter the inner-inner chamber (*nainaijin*), the absolutely taboo area for everyone else including the emperor, and respond to the emperor's prayer by ringing bells. One of my Kunaichō informants believed that the naishōten office was the last repository of court tradition.

More secular than the role of shōten is that of *shikibukan,* ceremonial officials—that is, members of the Shikibushiki (Board of Ceremonies) who oversee the progress of imperial ceremonies and events of all sorts, from authentication of top-level state appointments to the New Year's imperial reception of VIPs, to the court poetry party, to semiannual ceremonies for the granting of imperial awards, to garden parties and banquets hosted by the emperor, and so forth and so on. Here, too, many kazoku found temporary, postretirement, or sometimes career employment, being drawn into the job because they were supposedly accustomed to courtly protocol and etiquette and to conducting themselves with lordly dignity in front of exalted guests. Above all, their "cosmopolitan" experience was regarded as a valuable resource, since ceremonies often involved foreign dignitaries, including heads of state and monarchs, as imperial guests and it was believed they knew how to manage international hospitality at such a high level. Thus, most kazoku who were on the ceremonial board had been abroad. One informant, a daimyo viscount who had been trained in the livestock industry at Tokyo University, ended up as a career shikibukan only because he had spent years in Europe. With or without foreign experience, it was also believed that "there is something universal about lordly comportment" which communicates itself across national borders. We are told how, during the Occupation, shikibukan with kuge or daimyo background were mobilized to disarm the top-level American officers invited from the General Headquarters with their charming courtly repertoire, which included duck netting and cormorant fishing (Takahashi and Suzuki 1989, 53–58).

The Military

We have already referred to kazoku involvement in the military career, and table 26 has confirmed its preeminence, particularly among the older generation. Japan's modernization went hand in hand with the buildup of strong armed forces, and the emperor himself was supreme commander-in-chief, with the title of *daigensui* for both the army and the navy (super–field marshal and super–admiral of the fleet). Reviewing the troops in parade and maneuvers was the major duty of the uniformed Emperor Shōwa. As a young prince he had been well trained in military science by the best possible instructors at the gogakumonjo (Kojima 1981, 1:92–96). Theoretically, all royal princes were to become army or navy officers, and kazoku sons were indoctrinated at Gakushuin, if not at home, to follow the royal example as a matter of status destiny. For some daimyo descendants, the martial career was accepted as consistent with their ancestors' way of life, but even kuge sons did not resist this career. And of course, many generals and admirals of the modern military, like samurai warriors who had fought the Restoration war, were new kazoku.

Mr. D expressed the status mission underlying his naval career most clearly. Born the heir of a daimyo viscount, Mr. D was under the strong influence of his father, who had been educated at Oxford and had witnessed the patriotic sacrifices made by British aristocrats. The father, combining two traditions—that of a daimyo family and that of the Western upper class—disciplined his two sons to go into the navy. Once in the navy, Mr. D became disillusioned with his fellow officers, who were not dedicated in heart and soul as he was but were concerned only with their self-promotion. After the war, Mr. D decided to continue his military career with the Self-Defense Forces, because he thought it his vocation to protect the country, having been so well trained for a naval career at such a great cost to the state. His narrative, however, revealed that his postwar reentry had been motivated by something more specific: he was alarmed by the ominous signs of revolution discernible at that time, which in his eyes threatened to dismantle the imperial house. He therefore joined the ground force, rather than the marine force, so that he could stay in Tokyo, ready to rush to the emperor's rescue in case of true emergency. So seriously committed was he to his cause, he said, that he found many faults with his colleagues here again and, unable to get along, fell ill and retired.

Being a kazoku sometimes exerts pressure on one to be morally self-defensive. In this regard I should mention another case, for in the war the kazoku status was actually considered a social handicap as well: in such dire times, namely, there should be no such privilege. To overcome this handicap (or guilt?) and to "let people know what a kazoku could do," an informant's husband, a daimyo count, volunteered for a suicidal-attack (*tokkō*) unit. Fortunately, the war ended before he had a chance to make a fatal attack on an enemy ship.

These were not typical cases. Unlike the former officer corps characterized by Theodore Cook (1983) as fully devoted to the cause of the imperial army, many kazoku officers apparently had no strong ideological commitment to a military career:[6] they joined the military because no other career was conceivable, because one's father was an officer too, because no other source of income was available, and so on. Some took the military course only reluctantly, suppressing what they really wanted to do. Many were technical officers with no combat duties. Baptized in Western liberalism, some set themselves clearly apart from the zealous chauvinism generally associated with General Tōjō. The military inspiration for Mr. D, for example, came from the British aristocracy. In the interwar period, too, some kazoku men were military attachés to embassies or to royal princes stationed abroad, and their life-style was much like that of an exalted diplomat circulating among the foreign elite. The daughter of Marquis Maeda Toshinari, a brilliant graduate from the Army College and an army attaché in London, for instance, describes the incredible splendor of the life she and her family enjoyed in the British capital during that period. These men, of course, were not immune from criticism. According to one former officer, royal military officers played a largely decorative role, and their presence hurt more than helped the efficacy of military leadership. The same was said to be more or less true of hereditary-kazoku officers as well.

Whether committed to the cause of the war or not, those who were already well advanced in a military career through the war, if they outlived Japan's defeat, lost everything, too late to start a second life. Kazoku officers as well as government leaders, too, were among those imprisoned for war crimes, and many more in various fields were purged from public office. In encountering this "cataclysm" and demoralization, my kazoku sample was no different from Cook's (1983), and probably was even worse off relative to their prewar condition. My kazoku ex-officers seemed less successful than Cook's ex-officers in finding their way to "rebirth." Only engineering or other technical officers could take up their old careers, and only young men whose military careers were not yet ripe at the war's end could start a new life in business, the media, academia, and so on. Others, their children said, died prematurely in spirit, if not in body. Ironically, if they were born again, it was often through a retrieval of their kazoku background in one way or another, as will be shown.

The Priesthood

Another positional career was the priesthood. From the Meiji period on, Ise Shrine, the central symbol of Shinto, has been headed theoretically by emperors, but practically by imperial surrogates recruited from among royal princes and princesses: Prince Kuni, Prince Nashimoto, Princess Kitashirakawa, Princess Kazu, and Princess Yori (the last two being daughters of Emperor Shōwa and both married to kazoku). The appearance of princesses on this list reveals the Restoration attempt to revive the ancient tradition of sending a maiden imperial daughter to the shrine as a new *saigū* or *itsuki no miya* at every turnover of the imperial reign, a tradition that had a legendary beginning in the reign of Emperor Suinin (29 B.C.–A.D. 70) and lasted until Emperor Godaigo's reign (1318–39). Called *saishu* (master of rites), this office was activated only when there were major rituals at the shrine.

Among regular priests we find some kazoku descendants, of kuge origin particularly. Mr. E, after retirement from a long career as an electronics engineer and researcher, was invited to head Ise Shrine as *daigūji*, grand chief priest. When I met him in his shrine office, he called himself a "first-grader" in this second job. Despite his totally unrelated career background and the fact that he and his family adhered to Tendai Buddhism, he felt it was not inappropriate to assume this position; after all, his family, one of the sekke, had been "so close to the imperial house" for many centuries. After having contributed his technical expertise to Japan's industrialization, Mr. E was now ready to serve the kami, and especially the imperial ancestors, for the rest of his life.

Ise Shrine, though now separate from the state, "remains strongly tied to imperial private affairs." While the staff priests under Mr. E were professionally trained at Kōgakkan or Kokugakuin University and are promoted internally through the institutional hierarchy, he alone was picked from outside. From Mr. E's remarks it was apparent that the shrine, despite its lack of public status, is inseparable from countless support groups of "private citizens." The biggest event is the *sengū*, shrine transfer, occurring every twenty years and involving the construction of an exact replica of the entire shrine complex (including many subshrines and all their contents) on plots adjacent to the existing structures. Preparation for the sengū goes on continuously in the immense shrine compound. It is indeed a remarkable symbol of "periodically renewed timelessness," but involves an enormous economic cost and arduous human labor. The main channel of monetary support is through sale of the shrine's charms (*ofuda*) distributed to homes by local shrine agents. (About eight million such charms were in circulation at the interview time.) Rev. E was a little apprehensive about the success of the next sengū, scheduled for 1993.

Other Shinto shrines where former kazoku work either as career or postcareer priests include Meiji Shrine and Yasukuni Shrine of Tokyo, Heian Jingū of Kyoto, and Kasuga Taisha of Nara. These are all *choku-saisha*—imperially sponsored shrines that receive the chokushi (emperor's envoys), who deliver imperial offerings (*heihaku*) for major rituals. The chief priest of the controversial Yasukuni Shrine, a retired military officer, told me of two categories of shrine rites: one is to "console the spirits of the war dead" (who are enshrined there), and the other to "pray for these spirits to protect the state and imperial house" on such national occasions as the new year, *kigensetsu* (the prewar name for the national foundation day), the emperor's birthday, and the like.

What about the Buddhist priesthood? We have seen that royal priests of Buddhist temples were laicized after the Restoration in line with the separation of Shinto and Buddhism at the expense of the latter. But the old monzeki temples, concentrated in Kyoto and Nara, never entirely relinquished their old prestige. In 1945, Mr. F, a former royal prince and later a kazoku, renounced his academic job (he was already a well-known religious-art historian, according to one kazoku informant) to accept the head priesthood of a major monzeki temple, a position his grandfather had held before laicization. Unlike the Shinto shrine figurehead, a Buddhist priest required a period of special training. Mr. F endured some tough discipline, including repeated prostrations, cold-water bathing before dawn, sutra recitation, and secret finger movements unique to esoteric Buddhism as a way of attaining the "unity of body, mouth, and mind" and thereby "becoming one with the Buddha." Only after this indoctrination was he considered fully qualified and awarded a priestly name (*hōmyō*). Rev. F is married to a woman from a daimyo kazoku and has adult children.

Less known and more intriguing is the life of a monzeki nun, or *bikuni*. One of "eleven" monzeki nunneries in Kyoto was headed by Ms. Z, seventy-two years old.[7] With her mother's death and the remarriage of her father, a kuge marquis, she was selected at a very young age as a suitable candidate to be a monzeki successor at the temple.[8] One day, the then monzeki came over "to see me for a miai and told me to stand up, which I did immediately." Impressed with her nonresistant character (*sunao*), the incumbent accepted Ms. Z then and there. "So I passed the examination." This incumbent nun was also a kuge daughter, as the one before her had been, but before that, I was told, the temple had always been headed by a daughter of the reigning emperor (naishinnō). (This special status was a major source of pride: this nunnery, according to Ms. Z, was one of only four in the whole country that had been headed consistently by naishinnōsan.) The kuge successors were thus considered surrogate imperial princesses.

Ms. Z moved in at age five. Such a young age was desirable because a small child would still be uncontaminated by the mundane life of the outside world. The predecessor monzeki was a "beautiful and kind lady" who loved this successor, took baths with her, and combed her hair. Indeed, the unmarried nun practically adopted the child nun-to-be as a daughter and lavished maternal love on her. (Though Ms. Z called the predecessor "Big Sister," she also used to say she had "come out of Big Sister's belly.") The "adoptive" mother was also a teacher who taught the child both manners and sutras. At school age, Ms. Z entered a local school, but after the schoolday studied, in addition to sutras, the Chinese language (*kanbun*) and read Confucian classics. At thirteen, after graduation from grade school, she went through the ceremony conducted by the topmost priest of the Rinzai sect to enter the priesthood. Dressed in black, she had her head shaved and received a Buddhist name. She was now totally severed from her natal family. (Upon becoming a nun, Buddha's follower, "you are not supposed to bow to your parents, not even to an emperor.") Overwhelmed, Ms. Z cried.

Nevertheless, the life-style here was more like that of the court than an ascetic nunnery, as the temple's main function was to preserve its royal tradition as well as to conduct memorial rites for imperial ancestors. The temple structure was a tiny imitation of the Kyoto palace, and the living quarters of naishinnō nuns were preserved as a *goten*, or palace. In the prewar days, when the temple was more generously funded by the Kunaishō, it had a courtly "retinue." (When I spoke with her, however, Abbess Z had only one subordinate nun, of samurai descent, who, although older than her, had been nominated as her successor.) As a young girl, Ms. Z enjoyed reliving the ancient court life by reading with her teacher-mother *The Tale of Genji*, *The Tale of Ise*, *Kokinshū*, and the like, and participating in the monthly poetry party (utakai) held at the temple.

Among the tokens of the glorious past were many dolls—ranging in size from one to three feet tall—given to generations of monzeki nuns. Showing a picture of each doll, Abbess Z and her assistant identified who or what it was. Some were models of real persons ("This is Emperor Taishō in his childhood, this is Emperor Kōmei . . ."), and all the dolls had names ("This is Chiyoko-san, that is Harunaga-san. This is a gift doll from Empress Dowager Shōken, which was a gift to her from Emperor Meiji"). The important point was that all these dolls had been possessed and played with by monzeki predecessors and handed down to successors. It was strange indeed to see two elderly women talking excitedly about dolls as if they were living persons. These dolls are displayed in the goten on special occasions—as I saw them when I visited the temple again three years later, though the rewards of my visit turned out to be more than just sentimental.

On my second visit I saw a crowd of people, mostly middle-aged women, strolling through the magnificently kept garden and looking around the temple structures. Many temple treasures were on display— painted folding screens, scrolls, and, above all, the dolls. These women, it turned out, were students in various classes—tea ceremony, handicrafts, dyeing, and so on—sponsored by the temple as a last economic resort for temple maintenance. I was surprised that the "palace" was so casually opened to outsiders, remembering how tightly it had been closed on my previous visit. From a young apprentice nun I learned that this open house was being given at the request of a leader of the temple-support association. Obviously, it was a reluctant concession by the monzeki. Still, said the young nun, "To make this place a tourist attraction would be unthinkable to Her Highness [gozen], with her pride." These unwelcome "intruders" were gazing at the dolls admiringly, listening to old male teachers explain what they were and thus vicariously sharing the remnants of the temple palace's glorious history. It suddenly occurred to me that the dolls have served for generations as concrete, humanlike links between the past and present, between lower-ranking kuge daughters and imperial princesses, between commoner onlookers and elevated monzeki nuns.

In a reception room, the outsiders, allowed into the temple for the first time, were bowing and looking up to Abbess Z with awe. The latter, who had had a stroke, was sitting in a wheelchair, and she acknowledged the bows with only a slight eye movement. Clad in a flowing purple priestly robe, seated upright with dignity despite her paralysis, she looked like a true princess, outranking her former kuge self. With the people seated around her waiting eagerly to hear her "royal" voice, the monzeki kept her mouth shut, looking aloof. I was about to suspect the onset of senility, when suddenly she recognized me in the crowd and broke the silence—"You are from Hawaii? Come over here"—and, to my embarrassment, spoke to me exclusively, disregarding her fans utterly. Through her paralyzed mouth she tried to tell me what she had omitted in her last interview. There was no trace of the successor nominee. Was she dead? I had no chance to ask. Later, though, I did find out that the young novice I had talked with was Abbess Z's successor now, which I took as a signal of the monzeki era being over.

NONPOSITIONAL CAREERS

As shown in table 28, kazoku are substantially represented in nonpositional, ordinary occupations as well, such as business, professions, and the mass media. As an index of the success of kazoku in nonpositional careers and in joining the viable elite of today, it may be pointed out that a reputable *Who's Who of Japan* includes 207 former kazoku—representing probably one-quarter of existing kazoku households—on its list of 110,000 select individuals (Jinji Kōshinjo 1985); of these, 106 persons were active in business and 33 were in various professions.

The question remains, however, whether this positional/nonpositional bifurcation really makes sense. The above *Who's Who*, for example, while mentioning nonpositional accomplishments of the kazoku listees, also identifies them by their ancestry and genealogy in 185 cases (89 percent). In this section, I focus on nonpositional careers, but at the same time look into where the nonpositional career shades into the positional one. Informants tend to declare that the kazoku background is meaningless or useless, if not disadvantageous, to the postwar generation, but interview data do not necessarily support this claim. The outdated status can and does translate into often unacknowledged, updated "capital," even for young men and women launching and succeeding in "nonpositional" careers.

One postwar nonpositional career was generated by the Occupation itself. After studying English intensively, Mr. G found a job at the United States Information Service (USIS) in the SCAP, then at the American Embassy, which led to his permanent career in the Japanese branch of an American-based multinational pharmaceutical company. Mr. G often travels to New York on business. He claimed that his career was absolutely self-made, having nothing to do with his family background. Still, I wonder if his cosmopolitan home environment did not have some influence: his father was a versatile athlete who, after mastering skating techniques while living in Europe with his wife for two years, became Japan's pioneer in this Western sport.

This speculation on my part was stimulated by some women who worked outside the home, in some cases as the primary breadwinner.[9] A typical job for older kazoku women was in cross-cultural communication, whether as an interpreter, translator, or language teacher for foreigners. These women were able to mobilize foreign experiences of all sorts, having lived abroad with a father or husband, studied under a foreign tutor, or hosted foreign guests as a function of their father's or husband's job. What made them different from most other Japanese was the cultural— not just linguistic—ease with which they handled and communicated with foreigners. This was during the postwar era, when expertise in international communication was scarce and in high demand. By the time I began my research, Japan had risen to the status of a world power, attracting many foreign students, and I found several of my female informants working with them as tutors in the Japanese language.

Kazoku background appealed to many Japanese as well. A kazoku woman could, by recapturing her impeccable training in manners and speech, teach such comportment to those fellow countrymen who were now ready economically and mentally to learn the upper-class style of behavior. One kuge woman who had been tutored since her childhood in the tea ceremony and flower arrangement, for example, emerged as an iemoto master. Journalism, for its part, was an open market for anyone with a knack for writing and willing to disclose his or her personal life as a kazoku or royal. Starting out as best-selling autobiographers, a few even established themselves as writers or journalists. A prominent name or birth made a person, if endowed with an attractive personality, irresistible as a media star or a public relations representative in business. Proud kazoku, of course, shunned such publicity, but there were those who succumbed to the seduction of fame and money.

Mr. H was a prewar career journalist, an exceptional case among kazoku in those days: in his word, his career was "heretical." After Gakushuin grade school he attended Tokyo's elite metropolitan middle and higher schools and then Waseda University, each time passing a tough examination. Immersed in the "liberal" tradition of these institutions, he first worked for a major magazine known for its liberalistic stand, until it was discontinued under "fascist censorship." He then switched to a national newspaper, thus becoming the first reporter with a kazoku title. He gathered the newest information quickly, partly thanks to his access to political leaders like Prince Konoe, who leaked information from his

Karuizawa villa. He was, for example, one of the first to know about the Potsdam declaration, Hitler's suicide, Roosevelt's death, and so on. It was also he who scooped Konoe's prearrest suicide, an event he had known would happen a few months beforehand, for Konoe, dead drunk, had confessed his intention during a social tête-à-tête at Karuizawa. Mr. H prepared an article in advance that was printed at the same time as Konoe's suicide. His journalistic career may have been heretical, but his kazoku status, inherited from his famous grandfather who had been a leader of the Meiji government, likely helped establish a special rapport with top Shōwa leaders like Konoe—a crucial advantage for a political journalist.

Many men went into business, especially in the banking industry, where staff reputation—to which a kazoku name certainly must have contributed—is invaluable capital. Marriage was another inducement to a business career. Some entered a firm as the son-in-law of the company president and as the likely successor. Most important of all resources in starting one's own business or in excelling in an employed career was the kazoku social network. Our journalist Mr. H, though a self-proclaimed maverick ideologically unable to accept his own kazoku status, found a postretirement job after the war at Japan Air Lines as a PR man. His success, as he admitted, was directly due to the extensive elite network, which he strategically utilized (and which would have worked even more to his advantage had he been a full Gakushuin graduate).

Ms. Y, from a wealthy business family, was another rebel. As a child she questioned why she was not allowed to play with neighbor children, and as a Gakushuin student she was repulsed by the existence of classes even on the campus. She wanted to discard her well-known family name and was happy, after the war, to replace it with a commoner name when she married without the blessing of her family. After being employed in various businesses, Ms. Y started her own Japanese language school and soon rose to become one of the most brilliant leaders in this field of education. As a nonprofit corporation, the school had to rely on donations and grants. While circulating in the business community in search of supporters, she was stunned to learn that many business leaders had been heavily in debt (*on ni naru*) to her grandfather, claimed to owe their present status to his support, and so on. Thus Ms. Y came to realize that her grandfather was still breathing in the lives of many businessmen, who were more than willing to make donations as tokens of repayment to him. The former rebel could not resist visiting the grave of her grandfather to say thanks.

Many facets of these careers are combined in Mr. I, who succeeded in making a postwar rebirth. Born as the heir to a daimyo prince and now the seventieth househead, his ancestry going back to a god, Mr. I was brought up as "junior lord" at the Tokyo estate, with the occasional duty of substituting for his father to highlight special events in the home province in western Japan. He never questioned his future lordship over the vestiges of the enormous domain possessed by his ancestors. As a student leader at Gakushuin Elementary School he led the morning exercise on the schoolground, with Crown Prince Akihito among those exercising at his command. Mr. I then switched to another school to prepare for Yōnen Gakkō (the army school that trained middle-school-level boys toward the next level: the army academy), determined to follow his father's steps into a military career. (His father, a military attaché in Germany, was a good friend of Hitler's!) There and in Yōnen Gakkō, the future officer was well trained, particularly in war strategies and decision making. His "dream" was to become a torpedo-plane pilot.

Before his graduation from Yōnen Gakkō, however, the war ended. Mr. I's family was thrown into the postwar turmoil, selling the bulk of their property, including the Tokyo estate ("In our old estate grounds stands S. Hotel now"), to pay taxes and moving to the hometown of the domain. For the first time in his life, Mr. I began to question the importance of his family background and to resist parental authority. At the local middle school he joined fellow students in farming, carrying buckets of nightsoil, harvesting rice, and so on, but he was unable to get along with these country boys. It was indeed "a culture shock, and I thought I was going to die." The school principal's attempts to dramatize the presence of the "domain lord" on campus by having him lead school ceremonies only irritated the boy. For him, this was a period of extremely low morale and alienation—a truly antipositional interlude.

But it did not take too long before he bounced back. He returned to Tokyo for higher education at Seikei, a private higher school (later promoted to a university), which, sponsored by the Mitsubishi zaibatsu, catered to boys from "elite families" in business and the professions. Mr. I studied economics, getting straight A's, and at the same time internalized the "Seikei spirit" of pragmatism, "not like the theory-obsessed Tokyo University and Hitotsubashi University." After graduation he was hired by a lending bank involved in international business and, through the system of employee transfer and *shukkō* (experience gained by working in other companies),[10] accumulated experience and expertise in a variety of business fields—domestic and international, private and governmental—and took a leadership role in all kinds of company projects. The strategic training he had received at the military schools proved extremely useful in this business career after all. In the meantime, his networks expanded to such an extent that "nobody, not even a top government official," could frighten him. Energetic and confident with his English fluency cultivated in youthful days, he talks with foreigners on international calls as a matter of routine.

Has Mr. I left his kazoku background entirely behind? At fifty-five, he retired to make his "descent from heaven" (*amakudari*) and head a "child company" (a peripheral member of the business "lineage") of his original employer. He had risen to an executive position at the parent company but not to its presidency. Although he had once been regarded as a promising candidate for that role and thus was transferred to so many different places to gain a whole spectrum of experience, at the same time the company executives tacitly understood that he would have to assume the lordly responsibility of running his provincial estate, which would keep him from full-time devotion to the firm.

As the amakudari president of the child company he is busy five days a week, and travels to his hometown for the weekend to supervise the foundation that, named after his family, runs a museum and the daimyo estate as a prefecturally maintained "cultural property." His, moreover, is the main house of a large dōzoku, commanding three dozen branch houses. After the war, almost all the member houses went bankrupt, resulting in the virtual disappearance of the dōzoku organization, but recently its holding of reunions has been revived. The dōzoku ties have proved beneficial to members as another base of networking, not only expediting one another's business interests but also allowing them to share the honor of imperial kinship. When a branch house member became engaged to a royal prince, the dōzoku club meeting had its biggest turnout ever. Vassals or quasi-vassals residing in Tokyo, too, have resumed the meetings of their own association. Among the members are many successful businessmen, including company presidents and board chairmen who are in a good position to help members and are generous donors to the I-family foundation. Mr. I has thus made a full career circle back to his ancestral identity.

Before closing this section, I should mention those cases that might be called "antipositional." Some kazoku sons and daughters chose careers where nothing but personal talent is revealed or counts—such as musician (Konoe Hidemaro and Dan Ikuma, for example), painter, or film actress. A famous actress, Kuga Yoshiko, the daughter of a Seigake (the kuge lineage next to the sekke, awarded the title of marquis; see chapter 3), was disowned by her grandfather, an act that, practically speaking, amounted to her nominal adoption by an uncle (adoption again!). By prewar standards, the acting career was absolutely incompatible with being a high-kuge daughter. She persevered, however, and was reintegrated into her natal family after the kazoku title became obsolete. Her mother was credited as having influenced her unorthodox career choice.

ANCESTOR-RESURRECTING CAREERS

The careers of my contemporary informants by and large display relative freedom from ancestors, but ancestry has not entirely disappeared, as we have seen, even from the lives of nonpositional career men. The ancestor's identity, of course, is inevitably fused with one's own. People may find themselves involved with their ancestors either after retirement or as a part-time job on the side of a primary secular occupation. In some cases, a midlife conversion may take place, leading from an ordinary to an ancestral career. To conclude this chapter, let us look at "ancestor careers" and the ways in which ancestors are resurrected, thereby harking back to chapters 3, 4, and 5 from a career perspective.

Reorganizing the Dead

One ancestor-career pattern involves reorganizing the symbols of the dead. Old kazoku houses typically have many cemeteries, particularly, in the case of daimyo, as a result of domain transfers, the mandatory double residence under the Tokugawa regime, or personal temple choices by lords or ladies. Descendants often become obsessed with imposing some order on this chaotic situation of the dead, dedicating their free time or postretirement life to centralizing them, possibly in a single cemetery. Given the number of ancestors involved, the size of each cemetery, and the weight of the gravestones, as well as the temples' frequent objection to such removal projects, a full-time effort is certainly required. In the course of reorganizing the cemeteries, tombstones are often collectivized as "House X's tomb for generations of ancestors," at least for the most recent generations, so that "all descendants from now on will enter under this same stone."

Other symbols are involved as well. Mr. J, a baron and businessman, became keenly aware of his responsibility as househead upon the death of his widowed mother, who had been the main caretaker of ancestors, and began to study his "true ancestors." At the interview time, he was, at age sixty-four, preoccupied with ousting false ancestors (mostly matrilateral kin) from the *kakochō* (the recorded roster of the dead) and sending them back to where they really belonged. Each name removal requires the ritual intervention of a priest. Apparently, Mr. J's occupation as a company president has become secondary to this newly assumed ancestor career. Among various factors necessitating such reorganization of the dead I discern an internal urge on the part of the reorganizer to straighten and purify his own identity by locating himself on a single patriline.

Investigating and Documenting the Ancestor History

A number of informants are amateur "historians" whose area of specialization is their ancestors—they do not just watch popular dramas but actively collect and read whatever is published on their ancestors or the history of the Japanese elite. In interview, I was often given the titles, and sometimes gift copies, of such publications. Academic historians solicit these people's help for access to their family records, and archeologists excavate their ancestral mausolea in coordination with the descendants' own reorganization efforts. Such academic stimuli in turn motivate individual kazoku to study their ancestors in reciprocal collaboration with the scholars, whose help is particularly needed in deciphering the old-styled handwriting of ancestors.

One purpose of historical study is to discover or verify the extraordinary character, performance, or caliber of this or that ancestor. Ms. X, a history major while at university and daughter of a kuge count, has delved into the house archives and examined the diary kept by an ancestor of hers from Restoration times. She admires this particular forebear because he stayed on in Kyoto during the mass exodus of kuge to follow Emperor Meiji to Tokyo. This man's refusal to go along with the changing times seems to mirror Ms. X's own determination to stay in her natal Kyoto house and perpetuate its tradition.

Historical study is also tied up with genealogical inquiries, the family tree being one of the most important records for the hereditary elite. If a genealogy is not quite credible, descendants will often go to considerable effort to dig up archives to substantiate it. For Mr. K, a naval and later civilian engineer, now retired, the whole archival endeavor seems geared to validate the claimed genealogy of his house, which is one of the seven kokusō embedded in mythological time (see chapter 3): he has traced his ancestry to a god who accompanied Ninigi in the descent from heaven to earth, followed Emperor Jinmu on his eastward military expedition, and was assigned to rule a province. The survival of prehistoric ancestral shrines in that province is his best evidence; yet, this contemporary descendant admits, verifying the godly origin of his family is difficult—"as difficult as [verifying] the origin of the imperial house." Even as he commented with skepticism on the mythological tale, he nevertheless produced one document after another that purported to substantiate his claim. In a second interview he showed me a neatly printed genealogy, this time going back to Ame-no-minakanushi, "preceding the origin of the imperial line."

The mythological tale of Mr. K's family origin, closely linked to the national myth, suggests that what matters in a historical investigation is not genealogical depth alone but the place of ancestors in the national hierarchy of lineages (uji). Genealogical study is in fact heavily oriented toward the most prestigious lines—topped by the imperial and followed by the Fujiwara and Genji—in terms of descent or at least of alliance or vassalage. The prestige of Mr. K's kokusō house derives not only from its long duration but also, and more importantly, from its primeval ancestors, who belonged to the group of heavenly gods (*amatsukami*) that, allied with the imperial ancestors, came down from heaven to conquer the natives. Implied in this narrative is an invidious comparison between Mr. K's own and the Izumo Shrine's kokusō house. "They were natives; they were defeated. . . . We were with Emperor Jinmu and came down as occupation troops. . . . They were *kunitsukami* [earthly gods]." (But see chapter 3 for Izumo's claim to its own unparalleled superiority.)

For Mr. K it did not suffice to establish an ancestor's alliance with the imperial line in the mythological age; his ancestors, he declared, were repeatedly connected with the imperial family at later times through marriage or descent. For example, Emperor Sujin married a daughter of Mr. K's kokusō ancestor who then gave birth to Princess Toyosuki, the first chief priestess (saigū) of Ise Shrine (predating the other "first" saigū known as Princess Yamatohime); and Emperor Kōgen's grandson fell in love with a daughter of Mr. K's kokusō ancestor, which resulted in the birth of Takenouchi-no-sukune, the legendary figure of the early Yamato court. Mr. K took the trouble to verify every such statement by pointing to a particular document—impressing me, certainly, with the intensity of his "research."

Preserving and Displaying the Heritage

The treasures that have been handed down in a family are a major vehicle to connect ancestors and descendants. If a kazoku household was lucky enough to escape air raids and is still in possession of valuable treasures such as archival materials and notable art objects created or collected by ancestors, it must carry the heavy and costly job of maintaining them. Many such items, along with historical buildings or other sites associated with kazoku ancestors, have been designated "important cultural properties" or "historic sites" and are cosponsored by the national or local government and various foundations (see chapters 3 and 4). Even then, the original owners have not relinquished their custodial responsibility entirely. Portions of their estates may be used as museums or libraries, of which the househead may be appointed director.

In the case of daimyo houses, their cultural properties are attached to the provincial castle towns as landmarks of local history. Under such circumstances, the original owners, like Mr. I, must maintain two residences if they are still pursuing their primary career. Mr. D, for example, is a museum director who commutes between two places constantly, and although he feels overburdened, he is devoted to this mission as the descendant of a distinguished lord he particularly admires.

Clearly, the lordly duty to visit the castle town at the request of the local office that manages the domainal cultural properties interferes with a regular career. The employer may tolerate the periodic absenteeism of the lord-employee if the name he brings to the firm enhances the company's reputation. Yet such a situation may well block the employee from getting promoted to an executive position, let alone presidency, of a company just as easily.

A retired dean of a medical school, Mr. L has turned a room of his home into an archival library, writes and lectures on his ancestral history to groups of fellow descendants of the Fujiwara clan, and repairs the family's tattered scrolls for exhibition. Given the time, labor, and money he pours into these activities, his, too, is a full-time commitment, his private clinical practice being only secondary. Interestingly, he is the son-in-law, not the son, of a priestly baronial house of sekke-monzeki origin, yet he is more committed to these ancestral matters than is his wife, the natural descendant of the house.

In some cases, a residential house that is still in use is designated a cultural property. A recent example is an old kuge house in Kyoto, whose resident family, now with no control over their own home, cannot help feeling ambivalent about the situation—about being tied to an inconvenient old-style house instead of being free to replace it with a modern concrete building. Still, the Reizei accept that this arrangement is the only alternative if they are to preserve the ancestral legacy—and that, after all, supersedes all other considerations. The widowed mother of the family was actually delighted that the designation of her house as an "important cultural property," an event well publicized in the media, had attracted royal attention, resulting in princes and princesses coming to visit.

In another such house (of small-daimyo origin), an old couple appeared completely tied down and as immobile as the hina dolls that were on display in the house-treasure museum. Our interview revealed that their whole life has been taken up with replicating the ancestral way of life, performing the house rituals and arts such as noh drama, the tea ceremony, and martial arts. Perhaps partly because of their age (the husband was eighty-six, the wife eighty-one), they looked like living ancestors themselves.

Preservation of the ancestral heritage, then, amounts to its public display. Some kazoku shy away from the display role and are critical of those who seem overeager to "show off." Yet many more are aware that their ancestral heritage could not be preserved for posterity without such public access. To this end, particularly enterprising lords have updated their museums with audiovisual mechanization.

The effort of reorganizing cemeteries and other ancestor symbols is likely to go hand in hand with redesigning them for public display. A baron, the head of a "top-ranking branch" of the Maeda and now retired from a long career as an engineer, devotes all his time to his ancestors, deciphering archives and writing a family history. His ancestral mausoleum, which occupies part of a vast hill preserved solely for the burial of the entire Maeda lineage, has been cleaned up, and signs have been erected—clearly for the benefit of curious tourists—with a map and brief biography of each ancestor buried there.

Among the kuge are houses that have handed down the art of court dressing. As interest in the ancient court life-style spreads and intensifies, such arts are not only studied and taught but also displayed, in the form of actual garments worn or received as imperial gifts by ancestors of the house. At one such exhibit in a busy shopping area of Tokyo, I joined a crowd of enchanted women who stood gazing at sets of multilayered colorful court dresses, headgear, footgear, belts, and other accessories set up on brilliant display. The court rank of the wearer was indicated, my guide, an expert in court dress, told me, by the color, material, form, and accourtrement of the dress. The guide punctuated almost every statement with, "This was worn by the third rank or above only." A dress show like this is probably one of the most effective ways of resurrecting noble ancestors in the minds of viewers.

Reenacting the Ancestors

Ancestors are reorganized, studied, documented, preserved, and displayed. They can also be replicated in live form. Affluent and reflective, Japanese today are massive consumers of "historical tourism" (V. L. Smith 1989) in response to enticing programs organized by the travel industry in collaboration with local governments and business promoting the reconstructed historical monuments of the provinces. Grand festivals (glossed as *ibento*, events) are organized as major tourist attractions, featuring rulers of the feudal age, daimyo, and samurai vassals. Among the most popular are the *sennin gyōretsu* (thousand people on parade) in Nikkō, commemorating the transfer of the remains of Tokugawa Ieyasu from the Kunōzan to the Tōshōgū mausoleum, and the *hyakumangoku matsuri* (million koku festival) in Kanazawa, reenacting Maeda Toshiie's accession to lordship of the province. Daimyo descendants, invited as guests of honor, may come to watch their ancestors being resurrected in carnivalesque shows.

In some provinces, where remnants of the former domains still provide a focus for provincial solidarity, contemporary "lords" are mobilized into a more active role. Mr. M, for example, is from a province that local residents say is "strongly unified around the *tonosama* [lord]." Its castle town is also very active in converting its history into a tourist attraction. A huge budget was allocated to reconstruct the castle, with accommodations for group tours; the restored samurai mansion attracts a million visitors a year; the Restoration war and the collective suicide of young soldiers are major themes of museum displays. The mayor's idea of a parade featuring the civil war has developed into a main annual event, with local high school students impersonating the suicidal soldiers. Politicians compete to be selected as top-ranking samurai to parade on horseback, but no one is so audacious as to volunteer to be lord for fear of town gossip: "The lord must be the lord himself, they insist," says Mr. M, "and so I am pushed into it." Yet, this retired salaryman confesses, it is not easy to reenact his grandfather, a true lord and the last one—after once falling from the procession's horse, he has been frightened of horseback riding ever since.

Another example comes from scenes I actually observed and centers on Mr. N. The event began with a solemn memorial service at the shrine located on the castle site. Seated on one side of the main hall were about twenty priests, and on the opposite side were some thirty lay participants, including Mr. N, his wife, and representatives of the "vassal"-run foundation as well as various associations such as the shrine support group and the neighborhood organization (*chōnaikai*). A usual Shinto ritual was under way, involving the norito recitation; the elaborate offering by the priests of food to the gods, followed by all the lay attendants taking turns each to prostrate themselves and offer a sprig of sacred tree at the altar; and ending with the equally elaborate withdrawing of the food. Court music was played by three lay musicians. The sleepy monotony was broken twice by a loud "Wo-o-o!" uttered by one of the musicians to signal the appearance of gods—once when the interior door of the altar was opened, and again when the kami body (*goshintai*) was transferred into the *mikoshi* (portable shrine). The gods were four ancestors of Mr. N.

After the ritual, the stage was moved to a banquet room located behind the main shrine hall. The lord, still dressed in a black priestly robe, was seated on a stool at the upper center of the room so as to look down on everyone else, including his wife, sitting on the floor. One after another senior man in a dark suit entered and bowed deeply to the lord, who acknowledged the obeisance with a nod. These men, ten in total, selected from among the ritual participants, were invited to share in the take-out lunch with the lord. There was not much conversation, and no one spoke to the lord, the old temporary "vassals" apparently inhibited from talking to him in such a formal setting—which made me think that not only inferior but even superior persons are treated as if they do not exist.

The lord left for a costume change, this time to be dressed, with the help of a loyal "retainer" about his father's age, in a bright-colored combat outfit suitable for horseback riding. Starting from the shrine ground, a long procession of some two hundred people moved along the city's main streets, with children dressed up like pages, young men in samurai style, and several older men on horseback impersonating high-ranking vassals and imperial envoys. A group of white-robed young men were carrying the mikoshi. At the midpoint of the procession was the lord, mounted with dignity. Behind each horse men shoveled up the dung and dumped it into a wagon. Although it was drizzling and the expensive costumes were getting spoiled, the parade was conducted in high spirits, presenting an exciting pageant for local residents and tourists standing along the streets. When the procession returned to the shrine after the three-hour show, the city fire brigade stood at attention at the entrance and bowed to two objects: the mikoshi carrying the ancestor gods, and the live lord. Later, Mr. N told me that he saw the shopkeepers and pedestrians watching the parade bow to him as if in prayer.

Various agents with their own purposes and interests are involved in such projects: the tourism industry, the locality proper, representatives of national or local government committed to cultural preservation, and the kazoku themselves. To some extent these entities complement one another, but frictions are inevitable. Some of my informants were upset with the excessive commercialization of the "memorial rite," which "desecrates my ancestors." The selling of "silly" things like candy on the mausoleum premises infuriated one youthful lord who was seriously devoted to the shodai warrior ancestor buried there. The staged self-presentation as a lord on parade aroused ambivalent feelings in these instant "actors" as well. Although a sense of elevation at being the focus of attention or even reverence of the huge crowed was a pleasurable element, Mr. N acknowledged, at the same time a feeling of humiliation at the "clowning" inevitably crept in. The whole affair was, of course, a serious matter involving a man's obligation and dedication to his ancestors; still, he could not help but see a collusive play going on. By and large, older, experienced lords took the negative side (humiliation and play) for granted, while younger, fresh lords had positive expectations (elevation and seriousness) and thus resisted the strong touristic element.

The center of another ancestor-reenacting drama was Mr. O, around whom stood an inner circle of four senior vassals (jūshin) to assist, advise, and "discipline" this young lord as their ancestors had, without being bothered by the rank-and-file vassals, contemporary city politicians, businessmen, or tourist industry. At my request, Mr. O "summoned" the jūshin, who rushed right over, abandoning whatever obligations they had that day. Seated around a restaurant table, they introduced themselves to me in turn: Vassal A, age sixty-three, a descendant of the retainer who was uppermost among those who had killed themselves following the death of the first lord (in the early seventeenth century); Vassal B, age fifty-one, descendant of another suicide following the second-generation lord's death; Vassal C, age sixty-four, descendant of "the right-hand man" of the first lord, credited as responsible for the latter's success; and Vassal D, age fifty-two, descendant of a front-line fighter killed in the Restoration war.

These latter-day vassals and lord were co-actors in a drama to replicate and revitalize the esteemed status of their ancestors, and in so doing they supported one another in enhancing their own identities. The surrogate ancestor role was played not only as a serious matter involving the player's identity and ancestor worship, but also as a jovial pastime. Later that evening the same group, this time joined by the head of a branch house of Mr. O's dōzoku, gathered again in a tatami-floored booth of an old-fashioned Japanese bar-restaurant for a drinking-dining party. Relaxation and conviviality, as sake cups were exchanged and emptied, threw the participants into a playful mood for acting out their ancestral roles. The vassals addressed Mr. O as "Your Highness," called one another by the ranks and personal names of their ancestors, and spoke in the old samurai style. Everyone looked happy, and declarations that the lord be helped to "reestablish the house" (*o-ie saikō*) were heard often in the speechmaking. Infectious euphoria prevailed. The lord, apparently feeling good and encouraged, remained dignifiedly reticent, but smiling. Such mobilization of ancestors back to life, it occurred to me, produces a most effective therapeutic psychodrama.

Thus far I have concentrated on daimyo kazoku, but kuge, too, often replay ancestral roles. The court-centered festivals that originated in the Heian period, for example, involve kuge descendants in prominent parts. One informant, for instance, the son of a kuge count and president of a media production company, occasionally plays an imperial envoy (choku-shi) at the annual Aoi festival in Kyoto, consisting of a long parade of Heian courtiers. The New Year's poetry party (utakai) at the imperial palace gives another annual opportunity for a group of kuge descendants to replay their courtier ancestors: they recite a selection of poems submitted in competition by people from all walks of life; also, a dozen kazoku participate in a court-music (gagaku) club (see chapter 5).

More relevant to a career are the courtly arts that have been handed down in some kuge houses, such as incense art, tea ceremony, flower arranging, poetry, calligraphy, and court music. According to my informants, supposedly "each" kuge house developed and passed on its own style of art as a matter of course.[11] This subject, having been touched on in chapter 3 in connection with iemoto, needs only brief elaboration here from a career point of view. Although no fixed name like *iemoto* applies to kuge house art, for the sake of convenience let us call it *ieryū*, as some of my kuge informants did.

The ieryū as an ie-embedded style was far from a profession; indeed, it was not even necessarily practiced by the househead but was often relegated to retainers.[12] Said one contemporary practicing ieryū master about his predecessor: "All he had to do [to be called the master] was hold the headship." It is said that the ieryū art used to be transmitted to only one heir in each generation (the rule of isshi sōden) or at least kept strictly within the house never to be released outside (a prohibition known as *otomeryū*).

Many ryū became totally extinct after the post-Restoration abolition of the kuge status. But some kuge houses, either after the Restoration or, more commonly, after World War II, began to revive their ieryū legacies and make professions out of them. These houses now do what their ancestors never did: hold classes to teach the arts, exhibit the results of training for publicity, and issue certificates for graduates; moreover, they recruit disciples and audiences from the former commoner class, which is now affluent in money and leisure time and receptive to the culture of the bygone elite. "In the seven-hundred-year history of this house," said Mr. P, "I, the twenty-eighth-generation headmaster, am the first to make

a living from this art." (Though a pupil once asked him, to his amusement, what his occupation was—as if teaching art were his hobby!) The
ieryū is thus evolving into something like an iemoto, a social organization
developed among the warrior and commoner classes and in which the
original creator and master of the particular art still plays a prominent
role as the ultimate authority for orthodoxy (as implied by *moto,* meaning
"origin" or "stem"). For a kuge family's ieryū, however, because there
was no attempt to "teach" it or build it into a "school," the identity of
the original master is not always certain. According to Mr. P, ieryū styles
evolved naturally. Nevertheless, as part of the overall metamorphosis, the
term *iemoto* has been adopted by these kuge houses as well.

After assuming the iemoto-master position, Mr. P studied and wrote
in the iemoto-school magazine about the life of the house shodai (first
ancestor), who served a thirteenth-century retired emperor. As the first
career professional in the ieryū, Mr. P felt "as though I had returned to
the shodai," and he assumed the same professional title (gō) as his ancestor. According to his narrative, which was loaded with philosophical con-
templations, he is living in a world beyond here and now, in a timeless
universe inhabited by successive ancestors and descendants.

The best known of the presently active kuge iemoto are the Sanjōnishi
in the art of incense, the Sono in the flower art, and the Reizei in poetry.
Professionalized as they are, these art schools still retain features of their
nonprofessional predecessors. The headmasters, for example, were proud
to say that they did not build up iemoto-like networks for commercial
gain. Mr. P, for instance, had contemplated the meaning of iemoto and
come to the conclusion that his responsibility was to transmit the art style
to at least one person of the next generation (who could be his own son).
For him, neither money making nor network building was relevant to
his role; rather, he said, "my duty is to teach what I believe in." In
teaching style, too, these kuge iemoto masters tend to present themselves
as coparticipants instead of imposing their authority on their pupils. Further, the kuge arts are intended to be enjoyed as recreation rather than
to be studied for spiritual, moralistic discipline, as the Zen-inspired buke
(warrior-class) arts are said to be.

It might be suspected that such nostalgia toward ancestors is parochial,
destined to die out in the course of Japan's internationalization. Yet in
fact I found two men, both of the postwar generation, who became truly
committed to the role of iemoto master only after traveling abroad. As a
young man one of them, Mr. P—who was not even born into the ie but
had been adopted from a branch house—had had doubts as to whether
the iemoto position was worthy of his entire life, and so he left Japan in

search of a resolution to this inner conflict. During an eight-month journey through Europe and exposure to different countries he became convinced of the unique value of Japanese traditional culture, and especially of his ieryū art. He returned a true believer.

The other man, Mr. Q, had been long unsure of what he desired for his life, except he knew he wanted to "absorb" anything new. He thus accepted an invitation from an American friend and went to live in the United States at the time when campus unrest was at its peak, making friends with Berkeley students. His travel extended to South Asia, the Middle East, and Europe, during which time he supported himself with a variety of odd jobs. India particularly intrigued him with its life-style that had "endured for millennia"; indeed, in the end it "liberated" him to accept the fact that he, despite all his learning experiences, could not change basically but had to return to his homeland. Back in Japan, when his mother fell ill Mr. Q was ready to take over her role of iemoto master in the tea ceremony, and he set about to retrieve what he had learned in this art as a child. He did not like to dramatize his foreign experience as a turning point in his career, but admitted that his American friend-host was surprised by his transformation. At the same time, the friend also astonished Mr. Q by his total metamorphosis from a long-haired rebel into a respectable lawyer. In one another the two men saw themselves.

As these instances suggest, internationalization does not necessarily subvert atavism but rather can trigger its reactivation. More generally, in a postindustrial society like that of Japan, where people are subject and sensitized to new information that is continuously produced and instantaneously circulated on a massive scale, perhaps a nostalgia for the order and stability attributed to centuries of ancestors is all the more likely. It does not matter that resurrection is itself an invention, and in fact no "tradition" may be revivable without an inventive alteration. What matters is the participant's *faith* in preserving and reproducing his ancestors and their symbols in their pristine forms. And in this playback of "tradition," it seems, kazoku descendants perform a particularly key role.

I have shown how kazoku status has affected careers in a variety of ways. In some instances or periods of life, the status was a liability that bound one to a positional career at the expense of personal aspirations or chances of achievement, while in other cases the status placed its holder in a privileged career course. Even for those who pursued nonpositional careers, the shadows of ancestors could not be wiped away. Willingly or unwillingly, all kazoku assume a double career—ancestral and this-worldly.

NINE

Conclusion

To conclude this ethnographic journey, I will attempt to pull together salient features of the hereditary status and hierarchy that have appeared and reappeared across the preceding chapters. In the introduction we encountered a series of oppositional concepts presented for interpretational purposes; here these oppositions will be useful again for drawing some generalizations. The second half of this chapter sums up the relationship between emperors and aristocrats—for, as we have seen, the emperor is an important focal point for the aristocracy. Here I reconsider the idea that the kazoku served as a sort of hanpei (bulwark) for the imperial house.

OPPOSITIONS IN INTERACTION

The oppositions in question may be understood as manifestations of a duality inherent in stratification in general and the Japanese hereditary hierarchy in particular. Among the salient oppositions are: status vs. power/wealth/class, ascription vs. achievement, genealogy vs. performance, hierarchy vs. equality, structure vs. practice, rigidity vs. mobility, culture vs. nature, cultural capital vs. economic capital, symbolic vs. real, formal vs. informal, public vs. private, positional vs. personal, decorative vs. substantive, and so on. To this list may be added more specific oppositions such as gentility vs. vitality, patrilineality vs. blood flow, cultural blood vs. natural blood, monogamy vs. polygyny, distance vs. intimacy, interior vs. exterior, and front vs. rear.

These pairs overlap or correlate to a large extent, as exemplified by the parallels of status vs. power, ascription vs. achievement, and genealogy vs. performance. But correlations are not perfect. Public vs. private does seem to correlate with formal vs. informal, positional vs. personal, decorative vs. actual, structure vs. practice, culture vs. nature, symbolic vs. real, and front vs. rear, but not with interior vs. exterior. Culture vs. nature, far from overlapping with ascription vs. achievement, seems rather to cut across it. One opposition may thus either reinforce or interfere with another.

The opposite concepts of each pair may be represented by two persons (e.g., wife vs. concubine); two sets of people or classes (master family vs. retinue, old aristocracy vs. nouveaux riches, elites vs. commoners); two institutions (emperorship vs. regency, two houses of the Meiji parliament); two objects of possession (prestige vs. wealth); two modes of orientation (rigid vs. flexible). The opposites link up somewhere between two extremes—agglutination and distantiation, mutual attraction and repulsion, or alliance and collision—with exchange, conversion, negotiation, reconciliation, collusion, complicity, double standards, double consciousness, ambivalence, dissonance, or repression being the result. These terms reveal multiple dimensions of the relationship: social (alliance, realignment, networking); psychological (the individual's feeling and awareness); and rhetorical (metaphor, legitimation, conflation).

To illustrate dynamic interaction between opposites, I focus on three main features of hereditary hierarchy that have emerged in the preceding chapters: status negotiability, vertical symbiosis, and asymmetric dyarchy. As will become clear, these features should be taken more as variables than as fixed characteristics.

Status Negotiability

As a hereditary status group, the aristocracy, by definition, is set apart from the lower strata by the ascriptive criterion of birth, without which there would be no aristocracy. We have identified the status boundary of the kazoku in various contexts, a boundary not easily crossed over. It should be recalled how elitism was locked with the idea of genealogical orthodoxy; thus, economically poor court nobles of ancient origin were in the top layer of hierarchy, while wealthy nobles with a shallow genealogy were at the bottom, as if status and wealth stood in perfectly inverse relation. At the same time, we saw repeatedly that kazoku status was negotiable to a surprising degree. This negotiability, as juxtaposed with the highly structured principle of heredity, is apparent from kazoku history, in which "new" nobles acquired aristocratic titles based on performance, either their own or that of their recent ancestors. But negotiability is a complex notion; after all, the achievability of kazoku status was rigorously limited.

Heredity was made negotiable primarily through adoption: nonsuccessor sons, destined to become commoners, were redistributed among kazoku households lacking their own sons, thus becoming "hereditary" nobles (see chapter 4). We have observed how the ie carried, transmitted, and perpetuated its hereditary status through a series of adopted successors, a practice that in turn allowed the ie line (iesuji) to diverge from the blood line (chisuji). This does not mean that "blood" connections were unimportant. On the contrary, they were essential; the rule of descent was in fact ignored so that, in search for adoption candidates, blood connections could be traced in all possible directions.[1] This fluid, multilineal, multilateral, ruleless consanguinity was then elevated to a blood "line." Natural disorder was thus converted into cultural order, the practice of adoption into the patrilineal structure, informal into formal.

What is remarkable is that such negotiability of heredity did not subvert the structural principle of patrilineal succession, along either a single continuous line from father to son or even a more unambiguous line of successive "eldest" sons. Patrilineality was not disrupted by divergence between the ie line and blood line, or by the common practice of brother-to-brother succession, father-in-law–to–son-in-law succession, or even by age (or generation) reversal between successor and heir. In a couple of generations, or even within one generation, the "blood transfusion" would be absorbed, muted under the model genealogy of the "direct blood line" carrying the hereditary status, and sublimated to a continuous line of eldest sons. In fact, the patrilineal model, otherwise so rigid, was kept alive by the very negotiability of heredity. Similarly, negotiation was necessitated by the model, in that any successor other than a son had to be "adopted as a son," even in the case of a brother, to conform to the model. The opposition was thus to endure.

Successor adoption remained largely, but not entirely, within the kazoku group. Nevertheless, my kazoku informants insisted that adoption from outside the kazoku class was "absolutely" forbidden. Here again, we find the claimed nonnegotiability of the status barrier for adoption juxtaposed with what was in fact a practical negotiability, however limited. In this case, status negotiability is likely to have been facilitated by another kind of adoption—symbolic adoption—that would enable one to cross the status barrier to become entitled to a position (office or successional adoption) over and beyond one's original status.

Empty adoption of the latter type as a device for genealogical reconstruction took place more often for women than men, and generally as a prelude to marriage (chapter 6). A commoner woman, even of "base" origin, could thus cross the marriage barrier by becoming an adopted daughter of a high-ranking nobleman before marrying upward, or she might gain a courtly office or the exalted seat of a royal nun (monzeki), for which she would otherwise be unqualified. (Strictly speaking, then, this practice should be called "father adoption" rather than daughter adoption.) The same symbolic contrivance could dissociate a woman from her father who had scandalized the family by his political radicalism, dissipation, or otherwise improper style of life. Conversely, a child who deviated radically from the aristocratic norm could just as easily be adopted out to keep the family honor intact. In other words, adoption was a cultural panacea for status negotiation—for constructing, revising, or removing a "hereditary" status.

With such recourse to adoption available for genealogical reconstruction, ascribed status was made so malleable as to be interchangeable with achieved status, elite status with nonelite status, rigid hierarchy with mobility. And yet malleability was not limitless, not enough to wipe out the status boundary. Instead, status malleability served as a key to supplying the hereditary aristocracy with new vital blood. The aristocratization of the peasant Hideyoshi is a historical example (chapter 2) in making a mockery of the entire system of hereditary hierarchy, but at the same time dramatizing and reproducing it.

In terms of the patrilineal principle of heredity, women were more adoptable for genealogical reconstruction when they participated only as "womb loaners," rather than gene contributors. Such ethnogenetics made marriage more flexible than successional adoption as far as crossing the boundary is concerned. In fact, status negotiability in marriage was so extensive that the premarital symbolic adoption of a bride-to-be was often dispensed with. Marriage involving an exchange of status for wealth, name for money (and vice versa), was, while subject to gossip, so prevalent that commoner blood and money both flowed into the hereditary elite. In this case, status negotiability amounted to convertibility or complicity of status and wealth, that is, of symbolic and economic assets. Yet here again, the conversion of hard currency into symbolic currency did not lead to the devaluation of either.

Further, laxity in marriage practices with regard to monogamy—common particularly among upper-class men even under the Meiji civil code—allowed sexual union between an aristocratic man and shizoku or commoner woman (chapter 6). Such a union, particularly if the woman was a "water trader," such as a geisha, was unlikely to be consummated by legitimate marriage (except during the transition time of the Restoration), but sometimes a concubine was raised to the wifely status as successor to the late legitimate wife. As we have seen, however, commoner or shizoku concubines were more likely than high-born wives to bear aristocratic offspring, including heirs. Many of my informants had two paternal grandmothers (and in some cases two maternal grandmothers as well): the respectable obabasama and a subservient concubine who, though called by her personal name, was the biological grandmother. The formal/informal opposition of wife and concubine thus corresponded to that of cultural mother and natural mother. A concubine's son, even if he was heir to his noble father, may have felt stigmatized for a while (though my informants claimed there was "absolute" equality among children, legitimate and illegitimate), but the stigma would have vanished by the next generation. This is why informants talked about their concubine grandmothers more frankly than about their concubine mothers or polygynous fathers.

If concubinage was a surreptitious route for status conversion, the Gakushuin diploma was a more open alternative, a valid passport for a commoner woman to be admitted to the aristocratic marriage market (chapter 7). In fact, a commoner graduate from the prewar Gakushuin was considered a more qualified bride than a kazoku graduate because she had to pass the school's highly competitive entrance examinations and rigorous inspections of family background, from which her kazoku classmates were exempt. The Gakushuin education, moreover, contributed to creating and instilling a homogeneous culture of "peers" and "peeresses" across all classes, kazoku and non-kazoku alike, which later contributed to the formation of durable networks for adult careers. Crown Princess Michiko, had she been a Gakushuin alumna, would have been more readily accepted by traditionalists as *kōhai* (junior graduate), *dōhai* (same cohort), and *senpai* (senior graduate), thanks to support from members of the Gakushuin alumni clubs.

Status negotiability, or even fluidity, whether through adoption or marriage involving the conversion of status and other commodities, clandestine unions, or membership in the Gakushuin "family," was not unlimited, however. The Sōchitsuryō kept such negotiability under control by accepting or rejecting applications, or even taking an active role in matchmaking, for marriage and adoption. Many of my informants were adamant in saying that they had had "absolutely" no choice but to marry other kazoku.

Apparently the status structure was operating at two levels—structural nonnegotiability and practical negotiability, or public and private, formal and informal. Patrilineal succession (bansei ikkei) involving a single, continuous blood line, genealogical orthodoxy, status endogamy, and in-adoption were all constitutive of the structural formula. If these were often violated in practice, such practical negotiability was juxtaposed with or fed back to the rigidity of the structural formula; no undermining of the status structure was condoned. Negotiability in succession and marriage was conflated or sublimated to the fixed discourses of patrilineal descent and of status endogamy. This relationship is well illustrated by the upwardly mobile person, whether within or across classes, who proves more likely than a core insider to become an alert sentinel at the status gate. The two levels may be understood as psychologically compensatory, in that the rigid structural principle was more unequivocally enunciated when its fluidity at the practical level was in play.

Vertical Symbiosis

Hierarchy, while open to status negotiation, involved a vertical symbiosis between superior and inferior. The aristocracy, in short, was bolstered by the presence of commoners; and commoners, as represented by servants, supported, reinforced, and protected the positional distinction of the aristocratic house by their omnipresence, their respectful speech and behavior, their use of status terms for address, their performance of mundane chores for their masters, their role of mediating interior and exterior, front and rear, the house and the world outside (chapter 5). The indispensability of servants to the aristocratic status was made abundantly clear when the house lost its last servant during or after the war. Truly lordly status was best displayed by lines of servants kneeling at the main gate, to see the master off and to meet him on his return home.

The status dependency of a superior on an inferior is a matter of universally recognized social logic. There may be differences, however, in the degree of cultural association between aristocracy, on the one hand, and independence, idiosyncracy, and freedom, on the other. I would conjecture that in Japan the latter qualities were not regarded as inherent to aristocratic status, as they were in England. For the Japanese superior, rather, reliance on inferiors was a necessary price to pay, not for independence, but for status-bound respectability. This situation probably reflects historical differences in the relationship between the aristocracy and the monarchy, a point to be touched on below.

Servants played a crucial role in socializing their kazoku masters. Children learned their positional identity primarily through their contact with or observation of the servants. They learned etiquette and speech proper to their aristocratic status from these "etiquette apprentices," who served as both instructors and exemplary models. The twist involved in this interaction may be best illustrated by the double message implicit in the polite, respectful language used by a servant in firmly ordering the obedience of her master-child (chapter 7).

Vertical symbiosis also meant a total dependency of the kazoku masters, adults and children alike, on servants for their all-around caretaking. Intimacy evolved, and enduring attachments were forged through personal service, so much so that masters lost not only their autonomy, but also their privacy. Emotional dependency on otsuki maids was particularly striking among kazoku daughters. In many ways, commoner servants played the parental role both in disciplining and in indulging the children. Even in retrospect they were recalled as closer, warmer, more available, and more missed than the parents.

For daimyo kazoku, vertical symbiosis involved vassals either residing in the provincial castle towns or forming "prefectural associations" of Tokyo settlers. The contemporary lord was the central focus of such organizations, and memorial rites for his ancestors were signal occasions for reunions. Again, the mere presence of vassals was a compelling reminder of the lord's special status as well as of his obligation to his eminent ancestors. The lord-vassal tie still survives, or has been revived in new forms for new purposes, including tourist attractions in which daimyo ancestors and their vassals are resurrected in pageantries.

While verticality implies asymmetry, symbiosis amounts to mutualism. Just as the elite depended on the rank-and-file, so did the latter rely on the former, however asymmetrically. Servants expected their masters to appear and behave "lordlike" according to their status; noncompliance would result in disappointment or scorn. What "lordlike demeanor" was varied, but it seemed to tie in with praise of someone as awe-inspiring. A servant's expectation of status-appropriate bearing or "status-personality," moreover, apparently stemmed from his or her own self-esteem interlocked with the master's estimableness. Being trusted and needed by the esteemed master was also gratifying and self-elevating.

For a young maid, *oyashiki bōkō* (service in a mansion), even with very low wages, was a way of earning credentials for bridal qualifications (Lebra 1984). A former otsuki maid for a baronial household said in interview—in impeccable speech—that being a maternal caretaker for a daughter was the best training she could have had. For a young male servant (shosei, or student-servant), reciprocity was more tangible. Shosei had various tasks, depending on seniority, ranging from serving tea to visitors at the omote office and running errands to escorting a son or the master. In exchange they were allowed to attend night school, with tuition, in addition to room and board, paid by the master. Daimyo households typically recruited shosei and maids from their home provinces. For promising boys from poor families, a shosei position used to be virtually the only route to a career. One former shosei, who had studied at a higher school of commerce, some fifty years later still felt grateful to and even awed by the sight of the contemporary lord, whom he had served and whose father he had served.

Psychological, if not economic, symbiosis was especially noticeable in the lord-vassal relationship. Just as the lordly status depended on the existence of a vassalage, so a vassal needed a lord to establish his samurai identity. Thus, although the feudal system has been nonexistent for several generations, vassal descendants retain some sense of attachment to the progeny of their ancestors' lord as a matter of personal self-esteem, and those with unclear ties might construct a genealogy specifically to link their ancestors as vassals to a daimyo house. Despite the fact that some vassals made their way to the very top of the political, economic, or military hierarchy of modern Japan, still they or their descendants continued to pay respect to their contemporary lord. The result was a symbiosis of an old and a modern elite lending and borrowing prestige from each other.

If the master's child was emotionally dependent on his or her otsuki maid, so was the latter on the former. The otsuki's dependency could even extend to overidentification with her charge, resulting in a sort of sibling rivalry with fellow otsuki over their respective charges.

The thesis of vertical symbiosis could be further extended to the general public. Not only servants or vassals but also commoners in public socialized those persons "above the clouds" by acting as a watchful audience down below. In this way they contributed to sharpening, rather than diffusing, positional awareness in members of the aristocracy or royalty.[2] Recall how Gakushuin students were reminded of their special status during school excursions and pressured to conduct themselves accordingly in front of townsfolk (chapter 7). Recall, too, the tomboy who surprised her classmates with her transformation when she returned to Gakushuin following the war: her schoolmates at the interim village school had straightened her out into an aristocratic lady (again underscoring the fact that people marginal to the kazoku status were often found to be a reservoir of status culture).

In present-day Japan, people still want to borrow honor from the old elite. They wish to see a noble or royal descendant head a Buddhist temple, for example, thus following the monzeki tradition, or cap the priesthood of a major Shinto shrine. It is the rank-and-file parishioners, I was told, who are trying thus to maintain the temple's monzeki status or the shrine's imperial prestige. It was also said that support groups, prone to be recalcitrant, could be kept under control only by the noble or royal prestige of the chief priests or priestesses.

Rehabilitation of the vanishing aristocracy as central actors on the tourist stage, such as in daimyo parades, is another nostalgic sign of vertical symbiosis in a broad sense. So is the popularity of the estates and museums housing treasures of former rulers, or the choice of a kuge-headed iemoto school for learning a court art. In the meantime, the pool of aristocrats and royals who might fill such newly created roles is dwindling, which only raises their value. The feverish excitement at the latest royal marriage (of Prince Aya and Kawashima Kiko) may be a compensatory overreaction. In my opinion, much more than "cultural hegemony" is at stake in this extreme vertical connectivity.

All this appears to confirm the "vertical society" thesis, but by no means does it preclude equality. The point is, equality was conditioned, compromised, or framed *under the vertical umbrella*. Internally, kazoku were a group of "peers" who supposedly transcended the prior inequality. Furthermore, the early-Meiji Westernization, particularly American and Christian influences, had some egalitarian impact on the urban upper class, as informants proudly mentioned in reference to their parents and grandparents. Yet equals were not necessarily partners likely to form an intimate symbiosis.

We found that members of a single kazoku family tended to be more distant from one another than from their otsuki servants or, in many cases, from their foster parents. As personal caretakers, servants were copresent or even in bodily contact (as bathing assistants, for example) with their masters more frequently than family members, who lacked such a caretaking role. It is not surprising that a househead could have easier access to his maids than to his status-bound wife, who was waited on by *her* maids. Indeed, the status gap could foster, not inhibit, intimacy, if the two were giver and receiver of personal care. As for the mutual distance within a family, some informants interpreted it as indicating the "individualism" and "independence" characteristic of kazoku, while many others thought the kazoku family was simply "cold." In any event, the intrafamilial "individualism" or distance was certainly afforded or even produced by symbiotic interdependence and intimacy with servants.

Stepping outside the family, we see a similar distance predominating between kinsmen or among unrelated kazoku families. "Kazokusan are cold with one another," I was told over and again. In contrast to status unequals, status peers were inhibited from building intimate solidarity.

It may be that verticality can be manifested in two contrastive forms: in asymmetry and status distance; and in interdependence, mutuality, or even intimacy. The latter set of attributes, in the Western preconception, goes with horizontal, equal relationships. To understand the kazoku world, however, it is necessary to reconsider this Western association and to see mutuality in hierarchy, intimacy in verticality.[3]

As we have observed, intimacy between equals was not entirely lacking. A small subgroup of Gakushuin classmates, for example, might form an extraordinarily intimate and enduring bond, one lasting from kindergarten well into adult careers. The children's classmate bonding was often doubled by the parents' peer bonding. Although student solidarity is widespread across all classes, Gakushuin classmates seemed bonded particularly strongly, probably for two good reasons. On the one hand, kazoku children needed to feel and act out intimacy with their peers to compensate for the status-bound distance prevailing among equals inside and outside the home. On the other hand, they needed to enjoy equality-based intimacy all the more because intimacy available at home, such as with servants, was locked into verticality. Thus, the Gakushuin peer interaction within such a small group tended to release both unusual intimacy and wild equality, in total disregard of the ordinary decorum that accompanied distance or verticality. It was in this context that kazoku children became adamant in their denunciation of snobbery. Gakushuin-based solidarity, far from representing a mere liminal phase, was structurally significant, for such peer subgroups were interconnected into extensive networks that in turn determined opportunities for marriage and careers (chapter 8). But again, this equality-based intimacy was enjoyed only within an inner circle exclusive of outsiders, within a status boundary that in the end only reinforced overall status barriers and hierarchy. To borrow Joy Hendry's (1990) terms, "unwrapping" inside the group— that is, dropping status defense—was nothing but a "wrapping" of the group against outsiders.

Vertical symbiosis was far from an endorsement of status-conscious elitism or snobbism. A "true lord" was said to transcend status difference and to present himself "like a commoner." This distinction, too, derived from the vertical structure, in that his commonerlike behavior was especially appreciated *because of* his lordly status. It was for this reason that Emperor Shōwa's obliviousness to his unparalleled status was a favorite subject among my informants.

Of course, vertical symbiosis is not immune from conflict, nor is intimacy or interdependence free from ambivalence. The omnipresence of servants could become synonymous with constraint, with dependency on their service obligatory rather than desirable. Conversely, in some instances commoner servants harbored class resentment. Even during the prewar period class antagonisms in a broader sense were not absent: kazoku elites were ridiculed in the media, and, as we have seen, an imminent "revolution" was seriously anticipated by some kazoku men, which prompted them to train their sons in shedding the aristocratic status identity and developing extraordinary fortitude.

In the long run, however, cross-class conflicts were more or less repressed or misdirected. As far as my informants' recollections show—and I do not deny that these are biased like any other recollections—conflicts were experienced for the most part only within their own small world. In a family, for example, a younger brother, resentful of his elder brother, the heir, might be more susceptible than others to an egalitarian ideology condemning the kazoku system. Such "revolutionaries" within kazoku ranks often took it upon themselves to scandalize their families or the kazoku as a whole. On the Gakushuin campus, similarly, a commoner student might be humiliated by a kazoku classmate, a baron's daughter discriminated against in turn by a daughter of an old kuge house. Likewise, a concubine's son, feeling unequal to his half-brother born of the legal mother, might rebel against the shared father. Yet these sound more like tempests in a teapot than like "class conflict," as my informants admitted.

Further, the kazoku class was ridiculed inside as well as outside, not necessarily for egalitarian reasons, but, on the contrary, from a conservative, elitist point of view: the Meiji kazoku was not a "true," "genuine" nobility but included a bunch of crude, self-promoting "upstarts." Here one finds animosity within the elite stratum, between the old and new, though often such a regressive stance did find conversion into a progressive, egalitarian ideology.

By and large, hierarchy contextualized equality, as Susan Pharr (1990) shows when she separates egalitarian grievances from other kinds of protest. In an attempt to demonstrate how Japan has maintained governability despite being perennially fraught with conflict and protest, she argues that in Japan, because it is a basically hierarchical society, authorities are resistant to status protests and egalitarian demands (such as for gender or age equality) whereas they tolerate and even respond to other kinds of grievance (such as environmental protests). In such conflict management, moreover, the leadership characteristically resorts to the model of benevolent paternalism, which further reproduces the hierarchical structure.

Asymmetric Dyarchy

The negotiability of hereditary-elite status was not without a psychological as well as a structural ceiling, for in the end charisma accrued to the "hereditary" source of status. Negotiability therefore varied by rank: the higher the rank, the greater the need to justify it in terms of heredity, thus allowing less negotiability. In other words, with increased rank, the more bound the title holder was to the enunciated structural principle, to the positional—at the expense of the personal—life-style, marriage, and career. This situation has held unequivocally for the modern emperors as embodiments of the highest hereditary status and supreme state authority. (Recall the explicit injunction on royal adoption in the 1889 Imperial House Law.)

The hereditarily based status charisma was not to be diffused but protected, not to be compromised but kept pure. As a result, its carrier tended to be deprived of active engagement in practical matters, thus minimizing the risk of exposure. This meant not simply the separation of the "body politic" and the "body natural." In chapter 5 we discussed the double occupancy of the residential space by the househead to keep one body separate from the other, his private, natural self being confined to the innermost area so that it would not interfere with his public, cultural image presented on the front stage. From another angle, double occupancy could be seen as providing the occupant with "time out" to restore his natural self. In either case, the boundary was to be maintained without compromise.

Even though it must be spatially split, the body is nevertheless indivisible. Further, as we have seen, the front/public status of the hereditary elite was deeply embedded in the interior/private domain of birth, kinship, ancestry, and reproduction. The two bodies had to merge into one; separation could not be complete, either socially or biologically. It was in this indivisible body that the hereditary charisma resided. The general tendency would then be to isolate the charismatic body by pushing it further into the interior. Such spatial confinement made the status holder all the more dependent on his subordinates and retainers, whose inferior status permitted them to be mobile across spatial boundaries; thus, he became all the more entrenched in vertical symbiosis.

Limited status negotiability and vertical symbiosis together, then, would give rise to asymmetric dyarchy, with a split between symbolic representation of hereditary status and "real" exercise of the status potency. The decision-making responsibilities vested in the status holder, the head of an aristocratic household, would ultimately have to be left to his subordinates. We have seen how not just mundane but even ritual roles were taken over by high-ranking subordinates or servants as delegates of the master. Indeed, I argue that the hereditary hierarchy is bound to require not merely assistance, but full-fledged surrogacy of a superior by an inferior.

Given such routinized surrogacy, dyarchy, involving a jurisdictional separation of the original-status incumbency and its enactment, is inevitable. Spatially, if one was confined to the interior and front, the other dominated the exterior and rear as well as the boundaries. One embodied the status, the other implemented it; one authenticated the decisions made and executed by the other. This dyarchical arrangement accounted for skillful management of financial and other domestic matters, inasmuch as a company can run well with competent and loyal employees under a figurehead president. Many informants acknowledged the post-Restoration prosperity and success of their houses as owing to the foresight and loyalty of the managerial staff. When the former lord took over house management after the war, his gullibility often led the house to disaster and bankruptcy.

Often, however, I was told of the kazoku's plight under the domestic dyarchy, in which a sort of reverse hierarchy arose, with top servants taking advantage of their master's naiveté, appropriating his authority for their own benefit, and looting the house assets. The postwar bankruptcy that plagued many kazoku households was attributed not only to taxation and status loss, but also to such swindles by staff. Even when the house servants were loyal and well-meaning, they could be overbearing in their control of the house, leaving family members frustrated and helpless, unable to say a word in protest. A woman from a prominent princely house who married the heir of another princely house became enslaved not by her mother-in-law but by the head maid. In this case, the house retinue was more a source of constraint and unhappiness than a provider of security and comfort.

The kazoku version of domestic dyarchy epitomizes the familiar story of the Japanese polity in general, characterized by various multilevel dyarchies as we saw in chapter 2. Although the Restoration was meant to terminate this state of dyarchy, instead it sharpened it with the emperor as the symbol of taiken (sovereign authority) and new men of power defining and exercising the taiken.

Analogous is a Shinto god whose presence, forever invisible, is symbolized by a shrine building, as if the shrine itself were the god. Even when the god is brought out in a festival to make his annual tour around the community, he is transferred in a mystic rite from his residential shrine into a temporary portable shrine (mikoshi) with no moment of exposure. This spatial confinement of the god likely has magical implications, for, as T. M. Luhrmann (1989) argues, invisibility generates supernatural potency. (As if to ensure invisibility and thereby maximize magical efficacy, mystic Shinto rites are often conducted in the dark, between midnight and predawn.)

The emperor, then, was not only a ritual worshipper possessing privileged intimacy, including commensality, with his hidden ancestor-gods (who are central Shinto gods), but he himself embodied godlike potency, which was preserved and enhanced by his invisibility. Like a god confined in the hidden interior of a shrine, he was in no position to use his potency; instead he could only make it available to a magician outside the shrine, to "the carrier of the mikoshi," who invoked the name of the august one inside, hidden, invisible. Guarding the shrine of the emperor-god was the enormous bureaucracy of the Imperial Household Ministry.

The two parties of a dyarchy were interdependent and complementary, and thus came into vertical symbiosis, in either alliance or collusion. But the duplex also opened the way to a reversal of the hierarchical order, to the point of virtual usurpation. Nevertheless, the formal structure of duplexity was not destroyed; neither party supplanted the other to claim a "mono-archy." Indeed, the imperial authority was expropriated but not destroyed precisely *because* the dyarchy was asymmetric, and thus basically complementary, not symmetric and competitive. Although the Tokugawa ruler could and did exercise shogunal hegemony over the imperial court, even at the peak of Tokugawa power he needed to wrest shōgun senge, the imperial authentication of shogunal investiture, from the royal entourage. The military rulers, despite their control of the politico-economic currency, cherished the symbolic status of honor conferred by the powerless court in the form of empty court offices and ranks, and preferred to be known by these. The assassination of an emperor did not mean that the assassin wanted to put an end to the sun dynasty. Emperor Hirohito is said to have been targeted by ultramilitarists, but he would have been replaced, in the assassins' plot, by Prince Chichibu, his brother. The mikoshi carrier was not free to replace the god in the mikoshi by himself or a man of his choice.

Dyarchy has been reproduced extensively in nonpolitical organizations as well, particularly where hereditary status is involved. A clear example is the institution of the iemoto school, which was in the past (and in some cases still is) capped by a nonpracticing noble househead as authenticator of the highest professional degree of the art, but actually taught and led by the practicing iemoto master. Dyarchy, in my view, is a paradigm of Japanese social organization.

THE ARISTOCRACY AS IMPERIAL HANPEI

The official raison d'être of the kazoku, which appeared repeatedly in the personal recollections of my informants, was its mission as hanpei (shield or bulwark) for the imperial house. This mission has been cited as a foremost reason why kazoku entitlement was limited to the male househead

(Sakamaki 1987, 333), even though the women I spoke with were no less emphatic about their hanpei role. What the idea of hanpei signified is not clear or simple. I detected the following three meanings, and found that the last one weighed the most.

Unicephalous Centralization of the Elite

First, the hanpei, in support and defense of the imperial throne, was to be incorporated into a single, unicephalous pyramid of the state, with the emperor at its apex as the sole carrier of the nation's highest legitimate authority. This meant a radical centralization of the elite under the throne, putting an end both to the dyarchy of the imperial court and the shogunal government and to the feudal polyarchy. The kazoku class, functioning as a single, homogeneous hanpei, was to supersede the previous divisions that had existed between the civil and military elites, daimyo and kuge, old and new, as well as between regions. Centralization took various forms. The daimyo were forced by the 1870 ordinance to move to Tokyo for permanent settlement, and most kuge eventually moved to Tokyo as well (see chapter 2). The result was a heavy concentration of the elite in the new capital, where a new imperial palace (later known as the Meiji Palace) was built on the moat-surrounded ground of the fire-ruined shogunal castle. To this day kazoku, despite many relocations and dispersals into rural areas through and after World War II, cluster in the yamanote region of Tokyo (see chapter 5).

Besides residential centralization, many other sites, facilities, or institutions brought kazoku of varied backgrounds together either socially or symbolically. Among these were the Kazoku Kaikan founded in 1874; Gakushuin, founded in 1876 under the sponsorship of the Kazoku Kaikan; the House of Peers, installed in 1889; and above all, the imperial palace, where kazoku were invited to attend imperial ceremonies.

Further diluting the "unique" tradition of each household was the fact that marriage occurred largely within the kazoku group, with few mates coming from outside. The prevalent, though not mandatory, practice of status endogamy necessitated that kazoku disregard the history of households offering suitable marriage partners. Thus we find many instances of marriage between kuge and daimyo, old and new kazoku, tozama and fudai, northerners and southerners, Aizu and Satsuma, shogunal and imperial children. Such "incredible" matches occurred not only because of the limited marriage market, but also as a matter of politically engineered realliances or reconciliations. Adoption to secure successors was also generally carried out within the group. The result was a diffusion of status culture from one household to another as well as the development of a kin network that encompassed the entire kazoku group.

This does not mean that kazoku became a harmonious group: a sense of kinship does not necessarily equate with harmony or solidarity in Japan. Animosity, disdain, resentment, and estrangement were constant features of kazoku relationships. Nor did the Meiji restructuring of the national hierarchy erase the historical residues of domainal identity. Particularly the 1868 Restoration war (see chapter 3) was a sore point of recollection loaded with enmity and indignation. Descendants of the shogunal house and of northern-provincial daimyo who had sided with the Tokugawa camp repeated, as if it had happened in their own lifetime, what their parents and grandparents had told them about the foul play and horrendous abuse perpetrated by the "imperial army."

No hostility was targeted at the emperor or imperial house, however; instead, unequivocal loyalty was confirmed and reconfirmed. Descendants of civil-war losers called their enemy the "western army," not the "imperial," and their own camp the "eastern army," not the "rebel." Yet Aizu became stigmatized with the dishonorable label *chōteki* (enemy of the imperial court), a fact that agonized Aizuites more than their defeat. When a granddaughter of the Aizu lord was selected as bride to the imperial brother, Chichibu, the jubilant Aizu seized on this event as an opportunity to be purged of the chōteki stigma.

In short, centralization of the elite as hanpei for the imperial house was decidedly focused on the emperor. If the imperial throne depended on the peerage for its strength, so did the latter require the emperor as a unifying symbol. The unicephalous pyramid, then, involved a distinct and dynamic process of interdependence between royalty and nobility.

Binary Assets: Performance and Genealogy

Centralization notwithstanding, kazoku drew their reputation and prestige from various assets. Particularly important were two sources of prestige: first, personal performance, such as administrative, political, military, professional, scholarly, or industrial leadership, expertise, or valor; and second, genealogical distinction to justify the "hereditary" status of kazoku. These roughly corresponded with the two categories of kazoku: meritorious or new kazoku, and old kazoku ennobled by virtue of their pre-Meiji ancestor status. Performance and genealogy together qualified kazoku as imperial hanpei, which reflected the dual role of the emperor himself.

The modern emperor was expected to come out of the inner sanctuary of the palace, to represent the new Japan's promise, talent, prestige, power, and strength—in short, its performance—both internationally and domestically. The hanpei's mission was to put this new performance role embodied by the modern emperor into practice, and in this endeavor

Western learning played a key part. In his instructions to the kazoku given in 1871, Emperor Meiji urged them to serve as a model for the nation by studying abroad in order to make Japan competitive with foreign powers in wealth and strength. Many kazoku did go overseas to study or live as cultural apprentices, or they were trained by hired foreign tutors. Some took ambassadorial and other foreign service careers, and many were converted to Western life-styles. More important, Western knowledge became a major asset allowing commoners to rise to kazoku status. Westernization was taken to great lengths—recall Rokumeikan, a caricature staged and played by new kazoku (chapter 5), probably in part to shed their humble origins.

Another primary area of performance was the military. Japan's modernization went hand in hand with the construction of strong armed forces, the emperor himself was transformed into the supreme commander-in-chief, and all royal princes were supposed to assume military duty. Kazoku were thus strongly urged to follow a military career as true imperial hanpei, and many did. Even kuge kazoku, whose ancestors, unlike daimyo ancestors, had had nothing to do with things martial, became professional officers, and the Gakushuin curriculum had military training, side by side with foreign languages, as a compulsory course. Like expertise in Western studies, military achievements also resulted in top-ranking officers of commoner origin being ennobled. These two important areas of performance related clearly to Japan's position in the world: in one, Japan presented itself as a humble, open-minded learner from the West, and in the other as an aggressive and defensive force against the outside world.

The performance aspect of the hanpei mission was complemented by genealogical distinction, a quality attributed to the old nobles. The emperor himself, of course, was unsurpassed in genealogy as successor to an unbroken line from time immemorial (bansei ikkei) stemming from mythical ancestors, which legitimized the imperial authority and made it immune from accountability. The emperor, while representing the new, vital Japan in competition with Western powers, also embodied prehistoric, archaic Japan. As Fujitani (1986) points out, imperial rituals of the Meiji period alternated those of the past with those of the present, the former symbolizing continuity and tradition, the latter change and power; often, too, a spatial swing between Kyoto and Tokyo occurred in the staging of these rituals, with similar significance.

Likewise, the hanpei role of the kazoku was split between performance, to promote Japan's new position in the world, and genealogical orthodoxy, to legitimize their hereditary kazoku status. Implicit in the importance of genealogy was the folklore of *kisen* or *sonpi,* or the distinction between noble and lowly. Hence, despite the attempted centralization of kazoku, they were divided and graded by their genealogical status. The old kazoku thus stood above the new; and within the old aristocracy, kuge ranked above daimyo, with all kuge in turn topped by the Fujiwara main line, which goes back to a god contemporary with Amaterasu and co-residing in the heavenly plain.

Performance and genealogy placed kazoku in contrastive roles within the modern dyarchy. Performance represented the operational side of the dyarchy to implement, define, or even appropriate the imperial authority, while genealogy in essence made lesser emperors out of them. One embraced the instrumental role complementary to the symbolic authority of the emperor, the other the symbolic role by which the ancestral mystique of the imperial throne was duplicated and validated. It was the genealogical distinction, I argue, that made the kazoku a unique hanpei at a time when the entire nation was mobilized into one huge hanpei. Even the performance of an original title awardee was destined to be counted as a genealogical asset when his heir took over. In some instances, particularly in the Meiji period, a kazoku title was given to the successor of a deceased individual whose performance warranted the title. The entire generation of my informants can be regarded as genealogical, ascribed, hereditary kazoku in this sense, regardless of the status of the initial awardees. Which leads to the next point.

Privatization

Conceiving of the kazoku as a genealogical hanpei is problematic, in that their status could not be considered a public commodity, despite the prominence of the kazoku in the national hierarchy. That is, ascribed status, owing to ancestry, descent, kinship, and birth, belongs to the family and thus becomes privatized, whereas achieved status, owing to the individual's performance, can be fully public. Indeed, kazoku status as a public or private entity became a subject of debate in the early Meiji years, even though it was linked to such distinctly public institutions as the House of Peers. Questions were raised, for instance, about whether the rules stipulated in the 1884 kazokurei and its subsequent amendments should supersede state laws such as the house register law and civil code when contradictions arose (Sakamaki 1987). No conclusive answers to these questions were found, and covert concessions were made to deviate from the stipulated rules, such as male primogeniture, exclusion of women from succession, and prohibition of inkyo (retirement from house headship), which were supposedly "mandatory" for kazoku but not so for the general citizenry subject to the civil code. At best, kazoku status may be regarded as something *between* public and private, or as a fusion of the two spheres. The imperial status, it might be noted, was and is an extreme case of such fusion.

The kazoku were placed under the jurisdiction and supervision of the Kunaishō (Imperial Household Ministry) through a special board called the Sōchitsuryō, successor to the Kazoku Department (Kazoku Kyoku). Nevertheless, it was understood that kazoku entitlement and rank promotion would result from the emperor's personal benevolence (oboshi-meshi). Even descendants of the former ruling house, the Tokugawa, attributed their kazoku status to the imperial favor. Imperial favoritism extended to financial aid, particularly for the pauperized kuge kazoku, who came to depend on this imperial money gift (gokashikin) for living. The kazoku-emperor relationship thus tended to be privatized as much as hereditary status, both royal and noble, was, and imperial favor was reciprocated by kazoku loyalty.

It follows that the most gratifying privilege enjoyed by kazoku was personal access to the royal family, the emperor in particular. Symbolic of this privilege was the kyūchū sekiji (seat rank in the imperial palace), assigned to every kazoku as well as governmental leaders and VIPs, and enacted in palace ceremonies and banquets (chapter 5). Further, the kazoku provided a pool of spousal candidates for the royals (though this was an unwelcome obligation more than a privilege for many kazoku, as implied in the practice of miyasama-yoke, a hasty marriage to forestall or decline a royal proposal; see chapter 6). Most important in the narratives of my informants was intimacy with the royalty, a scarce and exclusive privilege indeed. Such intimacy was derived, in some cases, from kinship connections through marriage or branching, but in most cases from childhood associations rooted in Gakushuin (chapter 7). Invitations to the palace to play and study with royal classmates, or to participate in royal sports circles as players or instructors, entailed the special privilege of being physically intimate with princes or princesses.

Further, the court was a major employer of kazoku (see chapter 8), primarily in positions involving personal attendance to or role surrogacy for the royalty. Also, kazoku staffed the Board of Ceremonies (Shikibu) and served as palace-shrine ritualists (shōten), providing personal assistance to the emperor in ceremonial and religious rites. On the whole, kazoku were active not so much in visible, public leadership as in invisible and intimate roles, behaving much like a shadow that followed wherever the royal master was.

The third aspect of the hanpei mission, then, lay in the intimate, private realm of the imperial life space. Kazoku provided a shield or buffer to protect the privacy of the royalty by virtue of intimacy built up through shared Gakushuin experiences and court employment. In my view, this privatized role took precedence over the other aspects of the hanpei mission.

Vestiges of Hanpei Connections

Do former kazoku have any role in democratic Japan today in relation to the emperor? It goes without saying that the kazoku no longer constitute a centralized force supporting the throne. Although a large majority still reside in the capital, and the clubhouse in the heart of Tokyo, now called Kasumi Kaikan, provides a central focus for survivors, by and large former kazoku are today more scattered than centralized. Nor do they exhibit the prestige associated with the kazoku status, but rather maintain a low, cryptic profile and joke about their having become *shin-heimin* ("new commoners," a post-Meiji name for former outcaste). What, then, survives? To answer this question, we must first look at the emperor's postwar role.

The postwar emperorship is humanized and secularized to a degree unimaginable by prewar standards. In the television age, the emperor appears to viewers relaxing in their living rooms foremost as a happy husband and father, a man totally devoid of the mystique surrounding the prewar throne. Yet despite this public, media-oriented visibility, he plays quite another role as well, one more continuous with the prewar imperial persona; namely, it is his duty to satisfy a highly staged ritual role, a key assignment of monarchs everywhere.

The postwar emperor plays a symbolic role in authenticating or highlighting state power and authority, as when he reads his imperial statement (*okotoba*) at the opening of the Diet session. But the emperor's association with power is largely suppressed in consistency with his depoliticized status, and instead a more social and cultural aspect of imperial ritual is promoted, as when he hosts foreign and domestic dignitaries in the palace banquet hall, the splendor of which event the mass media play up for mass consumption.

If these rituals represent the present, new Japan, another set of ceremonial dramas conveys the ancient origins of imperial status and culture, which transcend the constitutional change. These rituals, held in the triple palace shrine (kyūchū sanden), are loaded with mystical symbols of Shinto and of the Heian, Nara, or prehistoric court life. They are conducted in many different cycles, ranging from daily to annual, centered on the death anniversaries of emperors, life transitions of the imperial family (birth, initiation, marriage, accession, death), and so forth. On special occasions, these rituals also penetrate the living rooms of citizens via television screens, thus breaking the prewar taboo that prohibited such public exposure of "secret" rituals. Interestingly, urban TV viewers are likely to find these rituals so extraordinarily archaic as to border on the "exotic."

Today the two sets of imperial rituals, contemporary and ancient, are held in alternation, just as they were in the Empire of Japan—a contrast dramatized in the recent (1990) enthronement ceremonies for Emperor Heisei. It is in such rituals of the imperial house that former kazoku reclaim their imperial connection. Chamberlains (jijū), ceremonial officials (*shikibukan*), and palace-shrine ritualists (shōten) are recruited from among former kazoku to serve the emperor side by side with the staff mobilized from the Kunaichō, the Imperial Household Agency. As in prewar times, they assist the emperor in the execution of rituals: witness the jijū's rotational role in praying at the palace shrine every morning as a surrogate of the emperor, in full court dress and assisted by shōten, as the emperor would be.

The two realms of the imperial household, public and private, though once fused, are now more sharply divided, in conjunction with the privatization of Shinto following the constitutional separation of state and religion. Shōten are now private employees of the imperial house, and jijū and shikibukan, while they are on the public payroll, play a similarly privatized buffer role for the emperor. In other words, today the kazoku maintain their connection with the imperial house in large part by replaying their privatized hanpei role as personal attendants and protective servants.

From the previous chapters it should be clear that the emperor, or royalty as a whole, was not *primus inter pares,* but stood above the aristocracy. Kazoku, waited on by their subordinates and respected by status inferiors, in turn looked up to the royalty as their masters and models. Verticality worked upward as well as downward. Even a kazoku or, for that matter, a member of the royalty had no autonomy in the face of the emperor's wish. Once an imperial proposal was expressed, it had to be complied with. By and large autonomy, like equality and privacy, was a scarce commodity for aristocrats, who were vertically tied both to inferiors and to their imperial superiors. No more autonomous was the emperor himself. The imperial will, though absolute, was hardly expressed by the emperor in person, but only through his surrogates, who guided, reformulated, or implemented it.[4]

In England, too, the aristocracy is seen as centering around the monarchy, and the two are considered closely interdependent: "Without a sovereign, the Fount of Honor from which the peerage springs, a titled aristocracy would be pointless. . . . For better or worse, the Queen would probably be a less mystical figurehead without [her] supporting lords" (Perrott 1968, 94). Yet we are also reminded that the British aristocracy carries the historical memory of "revolt" and "opposition to royal tyranny" (Bush 1984, 112). It is this heritage that may well explain the apparently greater autonomy and individuality of both the British aristocracy and royalty than are enjoyed by the Japanese emperor and his hanpei.[5]

Epilogue

The End of Shōwa

Emperor Shōwa's terminal illness and eventual demise on January 7, 1989, threw Japan into a state of shock, as judged from the media coverage of the widespread *jishuku* (voluntary abstinence from festivity and entertainment) and prayer and mourning. Thereafter, open debates about the emperor and the imperial institution as a whole ensued, and publications began to fill the bookstores. The loudest voices came from two extremes: from the strongly pro-emperor advocates on the right, and the anti-emperor critics on the left. One camp demanded a constitutional amendment to redeify the emperor, while the other took Shōwa's death as an opportunity to demolish the reactionary, wasteful institution of emperorship. The debate is still going on. Arguments over the emperor's role in the war, a topic that predominates in the foreign media, are likewise dichotomized: for one group, the emperor was a staunch pacifist whose voice was indispensable in terminating the disastrous war and thus saving the country; for the other, he was the worst war criminal of them all. Neither position is embraced by the silent majority, however. According to a late-1989 public opinion poll, 81 percent of nearly two thousand respondents age twenty or older prefer to keep the status quo of the imperial institution as constitutionally defined.[1]

The debate extends to the issue of the constitutional separation of religion and the state, involving the controversial role of Shintoism in the imperial transition, marked first by the funeral rites for Emperor Hirohito and then by the succession rites for the new emperor, Akihito. For the funeral, an awkward compromise that alienated everyone, left and right, was made, in which a double, sequentially staged ceremony was mandated, the first part being Shinto-loaded and thus "private," the latter more secular and public. It was a clumsy but characteristically Japanese solution to the dilemma. More problematic were the succession ceremonies of November 1990, particularly the heavily Shinto *daijōsai* (the grand rice-offering ceremony).

Although the above poll found that most people support public funding of the succession rites—79 percent being for and 5 percent against the accession ceremony (*sokui no rei*), and 63 percent for and 13 percent against the daijōsai—still the constitutional problem of religion-state separation was at issue. The government's rhetoric was again ingenuous. The accession ceremony would be a straightforward state affair (*kokuji*). The daijōsai, however, with its strong religious component, could not be a state event, nor should it be reduced to a totally private one. It was therefore designated a "public affair of the imperial house" (*kōteki kō-shitsu gyōji*), to be funded from the court treasury.

The double ceremony of succession symbolizes the emperor's double occupancy of the omote and oku space—the sokui no rei as an exoteric front-stage ritual, the daijōsai as an esoteric interior ritual. It is in the latter exercise, to my mind, that the union of the imperial public position and private connection with ancestors is enacted by the indivisible body of the new emperor. The government's naming of the daijōsai as a public affair of the imperial house, thus, is a barely disguised attempt to link the two "bodies" of the emperor, public and private.

For kazoku, Emperor Shōwa's death seemed to matter more than Emperor Heisei's accession. Shōwa's demise signaled for many informants the final death of the kazoku as a status group, if not as a cultural legacy. According to a daimyo viscount:

> There were some dissatisfactions about the imperial funeral [among kazoku]. Formerly, all kazoku were privileged to attend the wake and funeral. This time we had absolutely no such privilege. So there were complaints asking, "Why are we, so close to the imperial house, not allowed to attend?" Only the officers of the Kasumi Kaikan were invited. [In fact,] for the *hinkyū shikō*, that is, the wake in ordinary language, volunteers from the Kasumi Kaikan had been invited by the Kunaichō.[2] But then too many, over three hundred, volunteered, too many to be handled.

Some surviving kazoku were mobilized to conduct mortuary rites. Of eighteen lay ritualists, called *saikan,* and eighteen assistant saikan, half were kazoku, as was the saikan chief and one of two deputy chiefs; the rest were retired Kunaichō staff members. (The shōten, or palace-shrine ritualists, could not perform this task because they were to be kept "pure" from death, pure enough to wait on the shrine gods.) These saikan took turns attending the sealed imperial coffin around the clock during the wake (hinkyū shikō), which lasted thirty-three days, and receiving and assisting mourners. After that they participated in the "private" half of the funeral, and then engaged in the cycles of postfuneral Shinto rites, including daily food offering, on rotational duty, at two locations: the burial site in Hachiōji, where the coffin awaited formal interment upon completion of a new mausoleum; and the temporary shrine (*gonden*) within the palace (kyūden), where the symbol of the deceased was tended during the year-long mourning period (*ryōan*), after which time it was incorporated into the kōreiden, the section of the three-fold palace shrine for imperial ancestors.

The saikan's job was no easy one. When on duty, the saikan had to stay overnight. In attendance, he had to control and regulate his comportment, indeed every motion, according to detailed rules specified in a manual that he had learned and rehearsed together with fellow saikan. The physical constraint was increased by the court dress: a greenish-black robe specially designed for imperial mourning, together with court-style headgear, footgear, and other paraphernalia.

Some of the kazoku nominees had to decline nomination because their age or ill health made them unable to stand this tough duty. Among those who accepted the invitation were four of my informants. I spoke with one of them, a daimyo descendant, while he was still on duty as a saikan, asking him whether he felt honored by the appointment.

> Yes, indeed! I could not be more grateful. I wondered why I was picked, [because] my grandfather was a chōteki. [But] my uncle served the emperor as minister of the imperial household, and that's the reason I was assigned to this task. I am thankful whole-heartedly. This is the greatest moment of my sixty-year life. At long last I feel able to stand up in front of my late parents [*kao-muke dekiru*]. You might call it *ikigai* [meaning of life]. Having had no chance to go to war, I find myself for the first and last time able to dedicate myself to His Majesty. My life has thus turned out to be worthwhile. . . . [When I was nominated] my siblings were all delighted. The other day, when I returned to my hometown, I found many local people also happy about my appointment. We still live in that kind of feeling.

Another younger informant of kuge origin echoed the above sentiment but added his usual reflective flavor:

> Emperor Shōwa, I think, was a great human being, in his human quality, be it warmth toward everyone around or firmness in

making decisions. Probably he will be remembered as an outstanding emperor. It is therefore an extraordinarily serious responsibility to serve him at this very end of his life as his soul
makes its way back to the kami world. We all consider it a great
honor and also are very tense with this heavy responsibility. . . .

None of us is a professional priest. We ordinary people rely on
the service of professionals when death occurs, but the imperial
funeral calls for no priest. Selection is made from those who
waited on the emperor or from among former kazoku, and these
laymen assume all the responsibility for the funeral. It is as if my
friends were to recite sutras or norito prayers when I die. I think
this style may have existed prior to the rise of a religion. . . . I
think the imperial family has preserved a funeral style older than
Shinto. I am not saying this in order to evade the constitutional
dispute. The whole thing is a reversion to the ancient era [*kodai-
gaeri*], a retrieval of the stored memory, a sort of computerized
memory. The imperial house is carrying its own memory, independent of the constitutional issue.

This kuge descendant appeared deeply moved by the fact that he was
taking part in such timelessness, as symbolized by the imperial mortuary
rite. Overlapping with the imperial house was his own ie, which in a
previous interview he had depicted in a similar light, with his participation
serving as a link between endless past and endless future. Ironically, much
as he, an adopted son, had to study his ie's legacy from scratch, so he
and fellow saikan learned the rules of the imperial rituals under the guidance of Shinto scholar priests and Kunaichō officials. What is more, the
model for the whole mortuary rite came from that for Emperor Taishō,
not from stored memory of prehistoric origin. Indeed, it seems safe to
assume that the ancient memory, if such there is, has been constructed
and reconstructed, forgotten and then revived in a new form, throughout
history. The "timeless" tradition is thus negotiated and reformulated.

This ironic situation is not, however, contradictory. Renewal does not
defy timelessness any more than status negotiability undermined the un-
negotiably "unbroken" line of hereditary succession. One supports and
is necessitated by the other. Most symbolic of this relationship is the
alternate renewal of two replicas of the Grand Shrine of Ise (*shikinen
sengū*) every twenty years—a tradition that, supposedly started in
Empress Jito's reign (690–97), has endured with only some irregularities,
including the wartime suspension (Okada 1977, 70–71). In the very
cyclical process of planned destruction and reconstruction, one can see
the timelessness of the imperial house from the mythical past into the
endless future. Indeed, many ordinary Japanese, I believe, not just the

above kazoku saikan, find in this ritual the timelessness of their own native identity in conjunction with ancestor worship.

Emperor Shōwa's death also evoked different emotions for different generations of Japanese. One's identity is not based simply on lineal connections with one's ancestors and successors, but also on lateral links with one's contemporaries—age-mates, schoolmates, co-workers, generation peers. The compulsion to be up-to-date in everything, from owning a late-model car or fax machine to displaying current fashion in taste and knowledge, stems precisely from these lateral links. In this regard Japanese are much like Americans.

What does distinguish Japanese from Americans is the post-Meiji tradition whereby Japanese synchronize generational identities with imperial reigns. From the Meiji period on, the successive reigns from Meiji to Taishō to Shōwa initiated new calendrical cycles such that years are identified by the name of a given reign—the controversial *gengō* system. The Great Earthquake of Kantō occurred in the twelfth year of Taishō, for example, rather than 1923; the war ended in the twentieth year of Shōwa rather than 1945; Emperor Shōwa died in January of the sixty-fourth year of Shōwa, which thus marked the first year of Heisei. These reign names are so internalized by Japanese in framing their generational identities that they often categorize one another as "typical of Meiji women," "a Taishō-born man," "early Shōwa generation," and so on.

The reign-based sense of contemporaneous identity cannot go unaffected by the death of an emperor followed by a new emperor's accession with a new gengō. Emperor Shōwa's death amounted, in a sense, to the obsolescence or death of the entire Shōwa generation. Tears shed over the emperor's death are mixed with tears over the mourner's own generational death. Even though the new emperor lived for fifty-five years of Shōwa, many members of his or earlier generations may find it difficult to switch their identity to the reign of Heisei. The indifference or alienation observable among older Japanese, including some of my kazoku informants, may be explained in large part by this symbolic discontinuity of their own selves. Nostalgia is inevitable. Mixed with the nostalgia is sympathy that Emperor Shōwa's career was one of hardship and suffering, a sympathy that resonates with the self-pity of the Shōwa generation.

Nostalgia is inseparable from a sense of loss, a mourning for the social order that was. Japan today is marked by endless flux and diversification; many likely view it as unpleasantly chaotic, and react with a nostalgia for the stability and order that old Japan is believed to have enjoyed. Here again the emperor or imperial institution as a whole plays a symbolic role as an ultimate source of order.

Order is best acted out through cycles of "fixed" rituals performed both inside and outside the palace by the emperor, his surrogates, ritualists, and support groups. These rituals dramatize the imperial house as a storehouse of ancient tradition, and give the reassuring impression that "nothing has changed for two thousand years," as a palace ritualist put it. The permanence, uniformity, and orderliness highlighted by such rituals may indeed work as a symbolic compensation for the present "reality" of Japan, where the people seem to share an equally exaggerated sense of impermanence, diversity, and chaos. In nostalgic reenactments of past events, new generations of kazoku descendants may continue for a while to play ritual roles on a refurbished stage.

The new emperor, Heisei, has started his career with a strong commitment to the spirit of the democratic constitution (A. Hashimoto 1989). It remains to be seen how he will manage to combine two distinct roles—as a free, open, accessible, self-assertive, secular, cosmopolitan emperor, on the one hand, and on the other, as an embodiment of ritually loaded imperial traditions, ancestral myth, and order, guarded and staged. Both Japanese and foreigners are watching to see how Emperor Heisei will succeed in alternating between a business suit and an ancient court robe.

Notes

1. STUDYING THE ARISTOCRACY

1. Some writers categorically distinguish "nobility" from "aristocracy." Powis (1984, 3), for instance, says, "The words are not strictly synonymous . . . 'aristocracy' carries associations of authority and leadership; 'nobility' does not." I find it difficult and unnecessary to distinguish these terms, and am using them interchangeably.

2. This might be compared with the typically American success story. For the elite, however, another dimension seems added to the American myth, as suggested by the following observation: "I favor the notion that the dynasties that have particularly excited American imagination represent the logical extreme of the success myth—from rags to riches and then back to rags in the dramatic version, from bland affluence to riches and then back to comfortable, but anonymous living for several generations in the anticlimactic version. The essential point is that part of the popular appeal of dynasties is their temporarity—that their decline and decadence are just as fascinating as their rise to fabulous wealth . . . a finite cycling of American dynasties" (Marcus 1983, 254).

3. Behind the feverish popularity of nonaristocratic Kawashima Kiko as a royal bride lie apparent tensions created by dissonance that in the end must be released. In an effort to reduce such dissonance, the media focused on her good upbringing and perfect comportment; one commentator was even heard to say, "Kiko-sama looks as if she were *born* to be a princess."

4. In defining nostalgia, of course, it is difficult to distinguish Lasch's emphasis on discontinuity from the conventional stress on the desired restoration of the past.

5. Underlying such attacks is the logic of opposition: one's own view is new, antistereotypic, and thus true, while the opponent's view is old,

stereotypic, and therefore false. To sharpen this dichotomy, the argument ends up overstereotyping and thus unequivocally falsifying the alleged stereotype. It appears as if something new could be built up only on the ruins of the old, which suggests wasteful cycles of construction and destruction.

6. Dumont's theory is also empirically faulty, logically confused, and unsatisfactory in handling social dynamics, as pointed out by such South Asia specialists as Marriott (1969), Tambiah (1972), Derrett (1976), and Lynch (1977). See also chapter 2, note 15, for my critique of Dumont's notion of "encompassing."

7. These papers by Iwai and Suzuki were brought to my attention by Marius Jansen. I should also mention, regarding political views of the nobility, that Hayashi Tomoharu, professor of political science at Gakushuin University and a descendant of a noble family, strongly advised me to take the nobility as a political, "not a cultural," group.

8. Newman (1986), for instance, compares two generations of divorced American women—the Depression-era cohort and the affluent 1960s cohort—and finds interesting differences in the meanings they attach to their postdivorce experience of downward mobility.

2. CREATING THE MODERN NOBILITY

1. In addition to the historical studies cited below, I particularly benefited from personal communication with Ōkubo Toshiaki, grandson of Toshimichi, who has written much on the history of the nobility and indeed may be more knowledgeable than any other scholar on the subject.

2. As for the imperial palace, Fujitani (1986) says that its permanent settlement in Tokyo, away from Kyoto, did not occur until two decades after the Restoration. I return to his reasoning in chapter 5.

3. *Samurai*, derived from *saburau* (to attend), originally meant armed servants to noblemen; only later did it come to refer to warrior vassals and buke in general (Takayanagi and Takeuchi 1974, 411).

4. Murakami, Kumon, and Satō (1979) make a clear distinction between uji and ie, claiming that the latter were developed by the buke during the medieval ages to replace the uji. Theirs, however, is a typological construction, whereas the actual usage of *uji* and *ie*, or of their sinified renditions as *shi* and *ke* or *ka* in compound nouns, implies interchangeability. It is my hunch that both uji and ie were vaguely conceived until as late as the Meiji era when the ie became a legal unit in the house-register law and, later, in the civil code. My usage and translations of these terms will fluctuate accordingly.

5. The inclusion of foreigners or immigrants as one of the three categories of nobility is very telling of the important role they played in the

ruling class in this period. What might come to mind in this connection is the popular theory that the Yamato state was founded by horse-riding invaders from the Asiatic continent through Korea, as advocated by Egami (1967) and more or less seconded by Ledyard (1975) with a focus on Puyo in Korea. An extreme position along this line and in support of the Korean origin of Japan was taken by Covell and Covell (1984). Archeological evidence seems to contradict this theory, however (Ikawa-Smith 1980; Edwards 1983; Kidder 1985). Kidder, for example, traced signs of the presence (or absence) of riding horses through the tomb period, and concluded that "the horse-riders represent the consolidation stage of the Yamato state, not its formative stage" (1985, 123). This point of view, though empirically more solid, does not preclude the fact that there was "a steady flow of immigrants" (Edwards 1983, 291) from Korea or the likelihood that these immigrants found themselves among the elites, thanks to their cultural and technological edge over earlier settlers which served the purposes of the ruling class.

6. The two terms, indeed, are still used today—though with no clan-like organization implied—sinified as *sei* (kabane) and *shi* (uji). Both refer to the family name, with *-shi* added to an individual's name as an honorific.

7. The Fujiwara's was the first regency held by "subjects," that is, nonroyal persons. Prior to this, the regency was assumed by members of the royalty such as the crown prince, empress, or empress dowager. To understand the evolution of sesshō out of the Fujiwara's domestic government (*mandokoro*), and the difference between sesshō and kanpaku, see Ishii 1982, 148–57.

8. Arnesen (1979, 7) gives a succinct definition of shōen: "Each shōen was a body of land for which a temple, shrine, or member of the nobility had succeeded in obtaining exemption from redistribution and taxation, as well as immunity from entry by officials of the provincial government. It was, in other words, a fully immune private estate, and by the eleventh and twelfth centuries the proliferation of such estates had removed huge amounts of land from the government's tax rolls." The shōen proliferation was a result of "commendation" (*kishin*) of lands by their holders to the nobility and religious institutions in order to share the privilege of immunity.

9. Marriage politics involving the imperial house was by no means unique to the Fujiwara. The outstanding precedent before the Fujiwara era was the Soga family. Some of the buke rulers who ascended after the Fujiwara also tried the same politics but did not succeed in taking over the Fujiwara prerogative institutionally.

10. The cloister government, like the regency government and the ritsuryō system as a whole, structurally survived its loss of power well into the nineteenth century, and was reactivated from time to time. Here we

see a good example of the historical propensity of the Japanese to avoid formal elimination of institutions, no matter whether they were of illegitimate origin or in disuse. This point will be further reinforced below.

11. The four top aristocratic clans of ancient Japan are known as Gen-Pei-Tō-Kitsu, which stands for Minamoto, Taira, Fujiwara, and Tachibana. Later, the Fujiwara's power overshadowed that of the other three.

12. There were various reasons for royal-to-nonroyal demotion, such as to prevent overproduction of princes or to bring about concordance with the lowly status of the princes' mothers. The protagonist prince in *The Tale of Genji* received the Genji name not only because his mother's low status at court was a subject of malicious gossip among jealous rivals but also because his imperial father wanted to protect this favorite son from the intrigues of court politics, which would inevitably have involved the boy if he had remained a prince and thus potential heir to the throne.

13. The naidaijin, redefined under the Meiji reform and translated as the lord keeper of the privy seal, was to play a crucial role as top in-palace advisor by mediating the emperor with the outside political world (Titus 1974; also see chapter 8, below).

14. To Hideyoshi accrued legends mystifying his birth in compensation for his genealogical deficiency. For example, he was said to have been born on the New Year's Day of a monkey year, the monkey being not only his nickname but a shrine god. Also, legend has it that his mother was impregnated by the sun or by an emperor (Hayashiya 1966, 72–73).

15. It is tempting to equate this hierarchical dualism to the Hindu *varna* system, where the Brahman priesthood was distinct from and higher than the Kshatriya kingship. In the latter system, if we follow Dumont's (1980) argument further, *dharma*, represented by the priest caste, was higher than the *artha* (power) of the ruler/warrior caste; religion outranked the secular world; ideology preceded politics; therefore the pure "encompassed" the impure. This Dumontian version of the caste hierarchy contains a logical jump from outranking to encompassing, from dualism to unity. Given the intercaste distinctiveness by virtue of which the priesthood stands higher than the royalty, it is difficult to accept one as encompassing the other. Paradoxically, the Japanese case would make the logic of "encompassing" more acceptable than the Hindu case, since the Japanese emperor, though functionally distinct from his surrogate administrator, combined the descent-based *religious* value and the ultimate *political* authority. Even then, dyarchy was a constant feature, precluding a total encompassing by the imperial authority of the nonimperial rulers.

16. The civilian statesmen in the Heian court were reluctant "to inflict the death penalty or indeed any drastic punishment. Amnesties were common, and perhaps for that very reason crime flourished. . . . But the

Minamoto and the Taira (in their early days at least) had no such scruples, and were quite ready to take life in order to preserve order and to further their own interests" (Sansom 1958, 241–42).

17. This agrarian focus is reminiscent of the original meaning of *daimyo* as the term began to appear in the late Heian era: it meant the cultivator of a large area of land, to which his name was attached. This further evolved into landlord, shōen administrator, and warlord (Takayanagi and Takeuchi 1974, 585–86).

18. The Tokugawa would have been considered the wealthiest if their main house and branch houses had been put together. It is more common, however, to treat branch houses separately. The revenue of the Tokugawa main house alone was seven hundred thousand koku.

19. The seven halls were called Dairōka, Ō-hiroma, Tamari-no-ma, Teikan-no-ma, Kari-no-ma, Yanagi-no-ma, and Kiku-no-ma (KK 1966, 47). The hall assignment was determined by the house status; in turn, the hall name became a symbol of house status, often attached to the family name.

20. The term *kazoku* is said to have originated from the Seigake, a category of noble houses that ranked right below the sekke and were also called kazoku (KK 1966, 27). Now, however, it became generalized to cover all the nobility.

21. *Monzeki* is another term so variably and loosely used that the boundary between monzeki and non-monzeki temples is not clear. Many were quasi-monzeki and yet named themselves authentic monzeki.

22. The rank distribution and numbers given in table 2 may be compared with the British counterpart as of the late 1970s: 26 nonroyal dukes, 37 marquises, 197 earls, 130 viscounts, and 506 barons (Bence-Jones and Montgomery-Massingberd 1979, 25).

23. In some cases the hereditary status and merit overlap, as with the daimyo of Satsuma and Chōshū cited above. This list counts these mixed cases as kunkō, and thus includes a number of kuge as well as daimyo.

24. The above information was gleaned primarily from Ōno and Okuse 1987.

25. As for imperial princesses, *naishinnō* authenticated as such by shinnō senge, and *nyoō* (other lesser princesses), the following careers were open. Like their male counterparts, they joined the subroyal aristocracy with kabane titles or headed monzeki nunneries. For a religious career, princesses could enter not only Buddhist monzeki temples but also the Shinto Shrine of Ise (and later the Kamo Shrine as well) as head priestess (*itsuki no miya*), at least in some periods of history. Marriage was possible with a limited category of men: emperors, princes, sekke men and other high-ranking kuge, shogun, shogunal kin, and priests not bound by the celibacy rule.

26. It was quite exceptional for two sons, instead of just one, to es-

tablish marquis houses. In this case, according to an inside informant, it was possible because the two sons had different mothers, that of the younger one being a Shimazu woman. This exception to the rule is indicative of the Satsuma power in Meiji politics.

27. Having given the historical background of the kazoku, I am now in a position to say more about my interview "sample." Within the limits of accessibility (to be recalled from chapter 1, where I discussed methodological problems), I covered a diversity of informants—descendants of kuge, daimyo, new kazoku, priests, representatives of main houses, and those of branch houses. I paid special attention to all the five ranks, but again with greater emphasis on variety than typicality, which resulted in an overrepresentation of higher ranks. Not only kazoku, but also a small number of former and contemporary royal princes and princesses were met. Marginals who fall between ranks or categories, such as kazoku of royal origin, a kazoku's wife of commoner origin, and nonsuccessor men who had lost kazoku status, turned out to have more to say than those who were situated at the center of a category. Wealth also varied in both ancestral and contemporary generations. Careers ranged as widely: chamberlain, court ritualist, former military officer, businessman, professor/scholar, engineer, artist, journalist, media executive, banker, salaried worker, and many other professionals and workers, as well as "gentlemen" with no work careers. I met most informants at their homes, their workplaces, a kazoku clubhouse, restaurants, and hotel lobbies.

The 101 respondents (about one-fifth of those to whom I sent questionnaires) have the following characteristics: average age 63, with a range from 24 to 81; 93 respondents married, 5 widowed, 2 divorced, and 1 single; 5 princes, 5 marquis, 18 counts, 32 viscounts, and 40 barons (plus 1 no answer); 2 of royal descent, 19 of kuge descent, 32 daimyo, 43 meritorious, and 5 other.

3. ANCESTORS

1. These are not to be confused with the sekke Ichijō or Kujō.

2. Note the frequent use of the word segment *-ryū* (flow) among Japanese, such as in *ichiryū, ryūgi, ieryū, ryūha*. In KKT, the word *shoryū* is used to mean branches or shiryū, but *shoryū* can also mean an illegitimate line in distinction from *chakuryū* (legitimate or orthodox line).

3. The Izumo Shrine kokusōke was divided into two houses, the Senge and Kitajima, around the fourteenth century, which resulted in the head priesthood passing in turn to each house. Rivalry between the two houses, which are located virtually side by side, is a source of anguish and embarrassment for everybody involved. The separation of Shinto and Buddhism in the Meiji period was supposed to ban the hereditary succession of the Shinto priesthood, but in fact it ended up strengthening

the Senge at the expense of the Kitajima. See Senge Takamune's attempt (1968, 196–201) to legitimize the Senge's exclusive succession to the Izumo Taisha head priesthood.

4. The roster of sesshō and kanpaku does not confirm such correlations of alliance. But the sekke as a whole did cooperate with shogunal governments for centuries, and during the political turmoil of the Tokugawa-Meiji transition they tended "to side with their Tokugawa counterparts" (Jansen 1986, 72).

5. The persistence in local memory of the Aizu tragedy is suggested by the recent mayoral election of Aizuwakamatsu. The incumbent had advocated accepting the proposal by the city of Hagi, the center of former Chōshū, to end the 120-year-old enmity between the two provinces by becoming sister cities. He was defeated, and the new mayor turned down another rapprochement from Hagi (see "Vernacular Views" in the *Japan Times,* reprinted in *Hawaii Hochi* 9/1/88).

6. This is indeed remarkable given that the real victims were often people other than the lord. Both Matsudaira Katamori and Tokugawa Yoshinobu survived the Boshin War, for instance, while their vassals and followers were killed or committed suicide, as in the case of the Aizu Byakkotai (Jansen 1986, 77).

7. In 1869, some reallocation of rice revenues was carried out according to roles taken in the Restoration war. Those who contributed to the imperial cause were rewarded with additional rice stipends, called *shōtenroku,* while the Tokugawa and proshogunal "rebels" had their sources of revenue severely cut.

8. After the war, the imperial assets were disclosed as amounting to more than 3.7 billion yen, of which 3.3 billion was removed to the state treasury in taxes (Takahashi 1987, 63). Similarly, Emperor Shōwa's death occasioned the unprecedented media disclosure of the amount and kinds of imperial properties to be inherited by the surviving family.

9. We have already referred to the case of Hara Takashi in terms of rejecting kazoku status. Nishi Amane, according to a descendant, also rejected the kazoku status offered but was "forcefully" given a baronetcy on his deathbed.

4. SUCCESSORS

1. In view of the postwar civil code that has removed the ie as a legal entity, and of the change now taking place in the Japanese thinking about the ie and family, the past tense would be more appropriate. My use of the present tense here is mainly due to the analytical, rather than descriptive, emphasis, as well as to the continued survival of the old ie culture in one form or another, selectively if not as a whole, optionally if not as a mandatory imposition.

2. Befu (1962, 38) also cites Takeuchi with reference to "the practice of *kaiyōshi* ('buyer-adoptive son'), in which a man on the verge of bankruptcy sells his entire property to a total stranger who is willing to take over the family occupation and adopt and continue its name." It is interesting that "buying" in connection with adoption can thus mean two totally different things for Chinese and Japanese.

3. Within the same system fits a case where the bride, recruited from outside and married to the insider son (the ideal form of succession), may, if widowed young after giving birth to a child, be asked by her parents-in-law to stay on in the house and remarry a newly recruited outsider husband (adopted son-in-law) (see Lebra 1984).

4. Adoption is usually called yōshi, but historically three degrees of adoption were recognized: *yūshi, yōshi,* and *jisshi.* Yūshi was a nominal adoption that did not entail succession, whereas jisshi, literally meaning a real, true, natural child, could refer to a special case of adoption where the adoptee was treated like a natural child (so one can hear a paradoxical statement like "A becomes B's jisshi"). Historically, adoption was concealed for political reasons. According to Ōkubo (1973, 8–12), the Tokugawa shogunate required the kuge to report and receive shogunal approval when a son was to be adopted, whereas no such "registration" requirement existed for the birth of a natural son. In consequence, it became customary for kuge to adopt sons as jisshi. Iwakura Tomomi, a son of the Horikawa, was adopted to the Iwakura as a jisshi at age fourteen; he then married a daughter of the Iwakura who in turn had been made a jisshi of the Horikawa.

5. There are a number of such double-succession cases, implying that this type of succession was not as deviant as it might appear. In the 125-generation-long imperial dynasty, for example, two empresses were enthroned twice under different names: Empress Kōgyoku (r. 642–45) and Saimei (655–61), and Empress Kōken (749–58) and Shōtoku (764–70). The technical term for this imperial practice is *chōso.*

6. The weight of estates as an explanation for succession varied extensively within the kazoku group. See the rich/poor contrast as it applies to kazoku, discussed in chapters 3 and 5.

7. The privilege of free tuition was terminated in 1924 (Kazoku Kaikan 1933, 93), though tuition loans were provided at the same time.

8. The only exception I could see was the sekke, in that the five houses, while they carried a strong sense of kinship with common ancestry, were not organized into the main-house centered hierarchy but were more or less equal. The Konoe, though recognized as the *hittō*, the very top, of the group, did not enjoy the main-house status. Also, another anomaly is observed in some big daimyo houses. When a powerful daimyo house such as the Mōri had a number of nonsuccessor sons adopted out, the adoptive houses could become "branch houses" of the natal

house of these adoptees, who then assumed different family names. This practice, which contradicts the ie principle, throws light on the political nature of dōzoku formation, where the dominance-submission relationship supersedes the integrity of the ie.

9. A similar punishment was enjoined on Tokugawa Yoshinobu, the last shogun, by the Restoration government.

10. It was not until after the war that a Buddhist cremation was first conducted for a [former] royal prince when Prince Nashimoto Morimasa died in 1951; the cremation was according to his wish, and was reluctantly granted by the Kunaichō, the Imperial Household Agency, only in response to the family's petitions. Since then, some other princes, including Prince Chichibu, have been cremated as well (Nashimoto 1975, 273–74).

11. *Kurodo* literally means black door, and is said to have derived from firewood soot (Sakamoto 1983, 483). This is one of innumerable indications that the palace had a vocabulary of its own, often incomprehensible to outsiders.

12. Besides the o-kurodo, signs that Buddhism had penetrated to the very interior of the palace are seen in the esoteric rituals of exorcism—now also abolished—conducted for emperors by Shingon, Tendai and Taigen priests (Sakamoto 1983, 492–94).

13. Initially, the shinden was for eight gods and thus called *hasshinden* (eight-god shrine); it was this selectivity that gave rise to the pantheon dispute mentioned earlier.

14. These shrine rank names originated, like many other institutions revived at the Restoration, in the ancient ritsuryō system (Okada 1977, 82).

15. For example, Taira-no-Masakado of the Kanda Myōjin Shrine, the tenth-century rebel and self-proclaimed emperor, was removed, to be replaced by the mythological Sukunahikona-no-mikoto (Yasumaru 1979, 160–61).

16. Attempts had been made to preserve cultural antiques since the early Meiji period, but it was only after World War II that the government formulated and began to implement an overall, systematic cultural plan (Bunkachō 1988).

5. LIFE-STYLE

1. The symbolic significance of entrances and doors was noted by a student of Victorian England's aristocracy as well: "All business and trade inquiries went to the back door. The front door was opened by a servant correctly mannered and dressed to suit the status of the family. . . . In larger houses, the Servants Hall was sometimes used to hold special categories who were halfway between back and front door status, e.g., the

doctor, schoolmaster, important tradesmen or unimportant kin" (Davidoff 1973, 87).

2. It is important to note, however, that the Japanese aristocracy commanded relatively little land compared, for example, with their British counterpart, who own(ed) tens of thousands of acres. One thousand acres (over a million tsubo) would be "not much" for a British baron (Perrott 1968, 34) but would be unfathomable to a Japanese prince.

3. Likewise, the shogun and in some cases the daimyo were called "uesama," *ue* being identical with *kami*.

4. Informants were not sure of the etymology of *otsugi*. Some gave this interpretation, but some others gave a more vertical meaning as "second to the head maid."

5. Such impenetrability involved not just the person, but the residential space as a whole. Above the most impenetrable layer of cloud—or behind the "nine folds" (*kokonoe*) of fences—was the imperial house, as symbolized by the moats and high stone walls surrounding the palace ground and the five thousand–odd Kunaishō staff members and retainers serving the court. The Kunaishō registry lists its officials, employees, and affiliates at 4,749 as of 1924, and increasing to 5,817 by 1943, plus unlisted court retainers (Kunai Daijin Kanbō, 1924, 1943).

The palace has long been a focal point of spatial orientation among kazoku. Originally the shogunal castle, it has been rebuilt twice and renamed three times (from Tōkyōjō to *kyūjō* to *kōkyo*). The kōkyo consists of various complexes of buildings and chambers with different functions, demarcated, separated, or connected by gates, moats, ponds, bridges, pathways, parks, gardens, and woods. The most important buildings for our purposes are located in the western half, surrounded by inner moats. At the eastern end of this area is the Kunaichō building, and adjacent to it to the southwest is the *kyūden*, that is, *the* palace in the narrow sense of the word. To the northwest is the densely forested park called Fukiage Gyoen, within which nestles the Fukiage Gosho (or simply Gosho), the imperial residential palace. In the southwestern part of the kōkyo ground is the kyūchū sanden, the triple palace shrine.

Applying the above binary scheme of space, we find the Kunaichō, as the center of the official administration of the imperial household and part of the state government, the highest representative of the exterior (soto). Representing the front (omote) is the kyūden, where imperial ceremonies and formal receptions are held. One of its halls is where the emperor, flanked by the empress and family, appears twice a year (at New Year's and on his imperial birthday) to receive congratulatory wishes from the mass of people who gather in the palace grounds and, looking up to him as he stands behind the bullet-proof window, shout "Banzai!" In the interior of the kyūden is the imperial office room (*omote gozasho*), where the emperor attends to his daily constitutional duties, primarily signing governmental documents. The Fukiage Palace itself is a multiple residence with living quarters and bedchambers for the imperial family; it thus represents the interior (oku) par excellence.

Where is the ura? It should be pointed out that each of these structures is internally further divided into exterior and interior, front and rear, above and below, and staffed accordingly by personnel of varying rank and sex. The kyūden, for example, while characterized as the omote, has its own oku, soto, and ura subsections, including the palace kitchen and dressing rooms. It should be remembered that even single rooms are differentiated physically or symbolically by these dimensions.

This geography refers to the present layout of the imperial palace. The kyūden, sometimes called the Shōwa kyūden, was newly built in 1968 to replace the Meiji kyūden, destroyed during the May 1945 Tokyo air raid. The Meiji kyūden contained both the front palace (omote kyūden) and the interior palace (oku goten) within the same area, connected by corridors. The new layout thus shows a clearer separation between the front and interior, as if to symbolize the constitutional separation between the emperor's public office and his private life.

Another important center in the palace map is the kyūchū sanden, the threefold shrine. Situated in the inner section of the premises, the sanden is the most sacred sanctuary of the entire palace complex. Of the three juxtaposed shrines, the holiest and largest is the kashikodokoro enshrining Amaterasu, which stands in the middle. The question is whether this sanctuary, though physically distanced from the residential palace, can be regarded as part of the interior, indeed, as its sacred pole—a question that calls attention to the Meiji restoration (or invention?) of Shinto. The palace shrine, as we have seen, is a post-Restoration creation symbolizing the union of government and Shinto rites (saisei itchi), and thus dramatizing the sublimation of the cult of the imperial ancestors from a private to a state religion, or the transformation of folk belief into a centralized theology.

Prior to the Restoration, the symbol of Amaterasu—that is, the replica of the "original" mirror placed at the Ise Shrine—was kept along with the other imperial regalia, the sword and jewel, within the interior of the imperial residential palace, even in or by the imperial bedchambers. These sacred symbols were in turn guarded by high-ranking ladies-in-waiting of the *naishidokoro*, women not aloof from sexual contact with their imperial masters. (The kashikodokoro was thus also called naishidokoro; see Kodama 1978, 14–15, 96–97; and, on the naishi office, chapter 6.) In sum, the sacred and mundane were physically proximate, both merging in the natural body of the emperor.

The post-Restoration Shintoization of the palace and the state resulted in splitting the regalia: the mirror was removed to the kashikodokoro of the sanden, while the sword and jewel remained within the interior of the residential palace. This split is a remarkable expression of the double quality of the hereditary status of the emperorship: private and public. The palace shrine, separated from both the omote and oku palaces, may be best regarded as an ultimate fusion of the frontmost and innermost space. Again, however, there are further boundaries within the shrine between omote and ura, oku and soto, kami and shimo, to differentiate levels of people with access to the gods as measured by their public status and kinship to the emperor.

The interior of the kashikodokoro—an area taboo to guest attendants at rituals, who are assigned to seats along the shrine's external periphery—is further divided into three chambers ranked according to degree of interiority: *gejin* (the outer chamber), *naijin* (inner chamber), and *nainaijin* (inner-inner chamber). No one but the emperor, empress, crown prince and princess, and special ritualists is allowed into the naijin, which has a raised floor. As for the nainaijin, it is the abode of the imperial ancestor, Amaterasu. Each chamber is hidden behind curtains. Here one can see the spatial parallel between sociopolitical rank and religious rank, the latter involving the levels of "purity" acceptable to the kami.

6. This change was synchronized with the final fixation of the imperial capital site, according to Fujitani (1986), in Tokyo as late as 1889, when a new palace was completed, thus putting an end to two decades of a capital that moved back and forth between Kyoto (Saikyō, the "western capital") and Tokyo (the "eastern capital"), an impermanence that had enabled or necessitated gyōkō so many times.

7. See above, note 5, for a full discussion of the kashikodokoro. Parallels are found in kazoku experiences. The latter-day shogun, that is, the successor to the Tokugawa main line, periodically visits the Tōshōgū of Nikkō, the central shrine of his first ancestor, Tokugawa Ieyasu, for memorial rites. No one but this present head of the house is allowed to step into the innermost of the shrine to share the same space with the great ancestor-god.

8. The terms that appear in this section are more faithful to the interview data than to published information, such as KK 1976. Variation among sources may reflect terminological fluidity over time.

9. This kind of "geononymy" is common in Korea also (Lee and Harvey 1973).

10. Hina dolls (*ohinasama*) are typically modeled after the imperial couple and their retinue and hierarchically situated in a ceremonial setting of the Kyoto palace. Among kazoku women, the hina set was a favorite subject of discussion. Many were particularly attached to their own sets because of their symbolic importance: they had been inherited, for example, from their mothers or given from someone "above the clouds"; they had accompanied the women when they married as part of their trousseaux; and some dolls were miniature or even full-size replicas of real persons. Only a few such old sets survived the Tokyo air raids and

fires, and my informants discussed nostalgically who used to have what kind of ohinasama. See also chapter 8, below.

11. The same sort of standardization is reported from Victorian England: "Because these servants were seen as an extension of the household 'aura', they were deliberately depersonalized, hidden under standardised liveries and often called standardised names, e.g., Thomas and Susan, whatever their real names might be" (Davidoff 1973, 88).

12. This remark apparently reflects some truth. According to Bence-Jones and Montgomery-Massingberd (1979, 196), "throughout the centuries, there have always been those among the British aristocracy who regard sports as a full-time business rather than just a pleasant recreation."

13. Gagaku originally referred specifically to the imported music and dances under the jurisdiction of Gagakuryō, a bureau created by the Taihō Code of 701; later, however, it came to include an array of native dances and songs as well (Oshida 1984, 13). This may come as a revelation to those who believe that gagaku represents the essence of indigenous culture. According to Marius Jansen (personal communication), "Meiji Japan 'invented' gagaku, or at least archaized what was until then a live tradition."

14. These court musicians come from *gakka* (hereditary court-music houses), which trace their ancestry back to the Nara Period or even farther and have handed down their respective house repertoires. In interview one leading musician, who called himself a jige, said his house came originally from China and has served the imperial palace since the time of Prince Shōtoku (574–622), specializing in the hichiriki flute and "right-sided dance." A portion of his narrative is cited below:

> We were Hata [read also Shin, or Ch'in in Chinese], actually originating from Emperor Shikōtei of Shin [Shih Huang Ti of the Ch'in Dynasty]. So we moved to Japan. At the beginning, a group of people must have been selected from the common class to be palace musicians, as in the NHK [Japan Broadcasting Corporation] song contests today, and have become jige. They learned palace music from kuge [though eventually the teacher-pupil relationship was reversed]. In olden days, emperors themselves played instruments. In the seventh year of Meiji [1874], in compliance with the Meiji Emperor's wish for Westernization, palace musicians went out to learn Western music from the navy band. In consequence we play Western music as well as gagaku.

6. MARRIAGE

1. This generalization stems from the assumption that the life of women, more than of men, is carried on largely within or in relation to the domestic realm. From a political angle, however, quite another picture of marriage would emerge. In simple societies, or "bride-service societies," Collier and Rosaldo (1981) argue, marriage entails a sharp

break for *men,* who thereby attain adult status, which in turn brings them sexual, political, and economic privileges not enjoyed by bachelors. Women, by contrast, have no real motivation to marry, according to the authors. Because the article's purpose is to relate sex and gender to political games and organization, it is necessarily male-centered; I believe that if the woman's inner experience were focused on, a sharp transition of another kind would emerge for women even in such simple societies— something certainly implied by their reluctance to marry.

2. The classic tale "Okagami," for instance, refers to a Fujiwara man resigning from the kanpaku office upon the installation of a new emperor because he was not a kinsman.

3. Recall the case of Iwakura; see chapter 4, note 4.

4. A totally different version is given by Muramatsu (1961) in his partly fictionalized story of Prince Kuni Asaakira. Here, the cancellation of the seven-year engagement was due to the prince's own change of mind blamed on his sexual laxity and infidelity.

5. There were eight empresses regnant, two of whom reigned twice with different names.

6. Children of such unwed mothers were also given as the lord's gift and were accepted either as natural or adopted offspring. This may explain why we find cases of downward adoption, as opposed to upward adoption for entitlement. One of my informants, a baron, suspects that an aunt who appears in his genealogy as an adoptee from a marquis house that was master of his ancestors was in fact mothered by a concubine.

7. Fujiwara Miyako, Fuhito's daughter, was married to Emperor Monmu (r. 697–707) and gave birth to Emperor Shōmu (r. 724–746), whose reign marked the imperial peak of the Nara period. It was another of Fuhito's daughters, Kōmyōshi, who married Shōmu, this time assuming the unprecedented title of "empress" (kōgō) instead of that of a secondary consort. Until then, as legally stipulated, no woman but an imperial daughter could attain more than hi (or kisaki), bunin, or hin status.

8. Such multiple marriages practiced by emperors and, to a lesser degree, by nobles may be called polygynous in the common usage of the term. Technically, however, the Japanese marriage practice was not true polygyny, which, as defined by George Peter Murdock (1949, 26–27), requires perfect equality among all the co-wives. Status hierarchy between the primary wife and secondary wives, as well as distinction between wife and concubines, apparently existed among Heian court nobles: according to McCullough (1967), the word *kitanokata* (*kitanomandokoro* for sekke) was reserved only for the principal wife. A true polygyny would not recognize the category of concubines. Worldwide, Jack Goody states, Eurasia was a practitioner of concubinage whereas Africa was more genuinely polygynous; he thus distinguishes "polycoity" for the former from polygyny for the latter (1976, 42). Another source (Fukutō 1991), how-

ever, indicates that the marriage practice was close to true polygyny in ancient Japan, down to the tenth century, despite the ritsuryō stipulation for hierarchy. I use the term *polygyny* loosely in what follows.

9. The maid might not be considered a victim of seduction by a kazoku adolescent from a household that lacked a strict segregation rule. Nagayo Yoshirō recalls having been sexually stimulated when he was a young boy by *shunga* (pictures portraying copulation) owned and carelessly left visible by a middle-aged, undisciplined maid (Nagayo 1963, 26).

10. See note 8 above for the meaning of polygyny as it applies to the Japanese case.

11. Widows had their hair cut short (*kirisage*), symbolizing their sexually neutralized status, and wore *haori* coats "like a man."

12. It may be recalled that there are different degrees of adoptedness (chapter 4): nominal or metaphorical adoption involving no succession or dissociation from the natal family; successional adoption that similarly involved no relinquishment of natal identity; and becoming a natural and exclusive child of the adoptive parents.

13. I assume that my informants were overstating the lack of discrimination against a concubine's children, judging from the many stories heard about the misery of such children. In his candid autobiography, Ōkura Yūji (1985), a son of Baron Ōkura Kihachirō, writes how his character was warped by the stigma of being a concubine's child, how he had to call his mother by her name, Oyū, while she called him "Little Master," and how he had to pay special respect to the legitimate household and to half-siblings whose mothers were more respectable. The interesting question is why my informants denied discrimination. It may be that the higher the father's rank in the hereditary hierarchy, the more likely it was for the children, legitimate and illegitimate alike, to share that sense of status, as in the imperial case. The father, or the staff representing him, was in a stronger position to compel his wife to go along with his wish to integrate his illegitimate children into his legitimate household. Thus there was less discrimination against concubines' children among the elite than among commoners, and less among higher- than among lower-ranking kazoku. In addition, one should note that most of my informants were grandchildren, not children, of polygynous unions, who had been fully incorporated into the legitimate line.

14. Ladies-in-waiting, generally called tsubone or nyōbō, often assumed new names, probably to sever themselves from their natal families. Such names were called *genjina* because originally, though not later on, they were taken from the titles of the fifty-four-volume *Tale of Genji*. The genjina for Yanagiwara Naruko, for example, was Sawarabi-no-suke. The assumption of genjina came to be adopted by other kinds of women, especially those in the sex trade (NFG, 672–73).

15. Nashimoto Itsuko, another princess coming from a big daimyo house, Nabeshima, writes that the tiara alone cost twenty-some thousand

yen, at a time when the annual salary of the prime minister was less than ten thousand yen (1975, 51). On the jūnihitoe, see below, note 17.

16. The Ogasawara is a daimyo house known as the iemoto of Ogasawara-style etiquette. First adopted by the upper class, such etiquette became popularized through the prewar school curriculum for girls.

17. This attire and hairstyle are, strictly speaking, modern versions of the formal court dress that became stylistically fixed in the Heian Period and yet were wrongly understood as replicas thereof. The terms *jūnihitoe* and *ikan-sokutai* are popular, not formal, names for the entire set of accouterments that are each formally designated separately but worn together. For simplicity's sake, I follow the popular usage, although some informants insistently alerted me to its erroneousness.

18. For a similar observation regarding the American upper class, see Ostrander 1984.

19. Let it not be forgotten, however, that the inferiority complex of the married-up spouse could be converted into a sort of tyranny, as we have seen.

20. A cross-cultural survey shows love marriage to be more the exception than the rule (Stephens 1963, 200–206). Romantic love itself may be widespread, but it is not necessarily linked to marriage or incompatible with marriage, as we know from knightly love for married noblewomen in medieval Europe or from love tales of the Tokugawa era involving double suicide.

21. The priority of the ie asset over the individual's personal feelings is carried over into the contemporary elite of business families, as Hamabata (1990) tells us, for whom marriage of sons and daughters amounts to a strategic transaction to forge *keibatsu* (an affinally based clique) and so promote ie interests.

22. A dagger given to a marrying-out daughter symbolized her chastity, in that it was to be used for suicide if she was physically attacked by an assailant. Even into this century, some kazoku women, daimyo daughters or wives in particular, kept such daggers symbolically.

23. For the sexual behavior of lower-class, rural women, in contrast, see Smith and Wiswell 1982.

7. SOCIALIZATION

1. Among the British nobility, too, daughters were so secluded that many could not make a transition from home "into Society" (Davidoff 1973, 38).

2. Gakushuin had a room for servants, but not for mothers, as if no mother was expected to take an escorting responsibility. When a mother did happen to wait for her child at school, she had to stand in the unsheltered hallway—even if she happened to be a former royal princess (Senge 1990, no. 2, 197).

3. The term *outsider insider* was suggested by George Marcus (personal communication).

4. The upper classes of Victorian England were aware that servants often functioned as emulators. "It was felt that in some way their own personal behaviour would stand as examples to the working class even in the minutiae of living. Thus card playing on Sundays should be banned as it set a bad example to the servants. And, when speaking of setting an example to the lower classes, most women really meant their servants who were the only representatives of another class they saw at close quarters and whose deferential response, outwardly at least, reinforced the seeming importance of formal propriety and individual gentility" (Davidoff 1973, 40).

5. But according to Gathorne-Hardy (1972), British nannies had as much emotional impact on aristocratic children.

6. Male initiation across cultures seems to involve the removal of the initiates from the domestic world of women.

7. Fosterage was a convenient way of temporarily putting away a child whose residence was yet to be determined owing to birth out of wedlock or of a "side womb." Also, some kuge considered newborn babies too polluted to be raised at home (Yanagiwara 1928; Nagahata 1990).

8. There was, however, a well-known group of liberals at Gakushuin represented by Shirakaba, a literary circle who detested the Nogi-style martial education (Nagayo 1963).

9. The word *tozama,* originally meant for the lords of outside domains (as opposed to vassal domains) of the Tokugawa shogunate, eventually came to encompass all outsiders. At Gakushuin, therefore, it could mean new kazoku as well as non-kazoku enrollees.

10. The recent publication of the diary kept by Princess Nashimoto Itsuko, as edited and commented on by the historian Otabe Yūji, leaks a tiny trickle of evidence that there was an inner circle of royal women around Empress Nagako who could not swallow this unprecedentedly unbalanced marriage. On November 27, 1958, when the crown prince's engagement was announced, Princess Itsuko wrote about her anger and dismay, and her feeling that "Japan has come to an end at last." Otabe associates this royal reaction with the author's Gakushuin background, commenting that Itsuko was a powerful member of Tokiwakai and that her sister, Matsudaira Nobuko, was its president and a central figure in rallying patriotic groups to protest (Otabe 1991, 370–71).

8. STATUS CAREERS

1. The questionnaire was deliberately open-ended, not only because I believe a structured questionnaire would likely alienate Japanese respondents, but also because I wanted the respondents' own views of careers.

2. Curiously, each of these is split into two houses. The hereditary chief priesthood of the Izumo Shrine became divided in the fourteenth century between two families, the Senge and the Kitajima (see chapter 3, note 3, for more on the split and animosity of the two kokusō houses). The Honganji Temple was split into the West Honganji and the East Honganji as a result of Tokugawa Ieyasu's political maneuver in 1602; each branch was headed by a line of the Ōtani family, both claiming descent from Shinran (1173–1262), the founder of the Jōdo-Shin sect. All these families were ennobled to kazoku ranks—the Senge and Kitajima as barons, and two Ōtanis as counts.

3. External sources of information are equally scanty, as if the Kizokuin never attracted the attention of professional historians. I thus had to rely on chronological documentation compiled by insiders, at least for dates and numerical information. Mizuno Katsukuni, a former peer who was convinced of the positive raison d'être of the Kizokuin, thought it important to leave a record of the peers' contributions and devoted himself to archival research, organizing seminars, writing, and editing. The result was a multivolume documentary publication on the Kizokuin by the Shōyū Kurabu, a nonprofit corporation organized largely for and by former viscount peers (see references under Shōyū Kurabu).

4. On only two occasions, the emperor's strong determination overruled the precedent: in crushing the "rebel army" in the incident of February 26, 1936; and in accepting the Potsdam Declaration for Japan's surrender in August 1945. It is reported that Hirohito admitted in retrospect having overstepped his constitutional bounds on these occasions. According to a recent revelation (Shūkan Bunshun Henshūbu 1988, 194–95), during the February 26 incident the emperor tried in vain to get information on what had really happened and who the victims were. In desperation, he personally made a phone call to the Kōjimachi police station, identified himself as "Hirohito," and, naming a number of high officials likely to be targeted, asked about the fate of each. This episode was related by the policeman who had answered the phone.

5. Court attendants were organized, in adherence to the ritsuryō, into boards (*shiki*), such as *jijū shiki* for the emperor, *kōgōgū shiki* for the empress, *tōgū shiki* for the crown prince, and so on. Each board was headed by male officials (jijūchō or *daibu*), even though that for the empress, for example, was actually staffed by ladies-in-waiting (nyokan) and supervised by the nyokanchō.

6. Overall, however, I did find Cook's observations informative of my sample of military-career men in terms of both differences and similarities.

7. The number of monzeki temples cited varies from informant to informant, betraying the ambiguous boundary of the monzeki category and the fact that temples often appropriate the monzeki title illegitimately.

8. The monzeki institution took in children who had been mothered

by low-status women or who were unwanted for other reasons. Some families are said to have dedicated one daughter per generation to a temple as a token of their religious devotion (Yanagiwara 1928, 52). Like adoption and fosterage, this institution seems to have accommodated the family's need to dispose of undesired children.

9. Cook (1983) also mentions cases of ex-officers who were economically dependent on their wives.

10. Shukkō is the practice of an employee working temporarily in outside companies or government ministries while remaining on the payroll of his own company. Theoretically, the scheme is intended for employee training, but as this informant said, it actually functions as a means for gaining inside information beneficial to the company.

11. The stylistic tradition of a kuge house, later called *ieryū* (or *o-ieryū*), seems to have evolved from diaries kept by ancestors for posterity, but it was not until the Tokugawa period that such tradition became recognized as a field of systematic learning known as *yūsoku kojitsu,* the received knowledge on precedent-based rules or customary laws pertaining to rituals, ceremonies, etiquette, conduct, specialized functions, and so on. Murai (1990) interprets the development of yūsoku kojitsu as a sign of the "ritualization" or "trivialization" of kuge politics. Since kuge houses held court offices, it seems that yūsoku kojitsu originated from rules and formulas issued by the court to regulate court officials and stipulate their ranks and assignments, which, though systematically formulated by the ritsuryō, could go back as far as A.D. 603 when Prince Shōtoku issued the twelve-cap rank system (Ishimura 1987). From the medieval ages on, the buke came to duplicate the kuge practice by producing their own *buke kojitsu,* including Ogasawara-ryū (the styles of certain martial arts and etiquette, produced and transmitted by the Ogasawara, a daimyo house), in parallel with *kuge kojitsu* (Murai 1990, 110; NFG, 659).

12. Yanagiwara (1928, 135) refers to the head maid who excelled in the ieryū calligraphy of her master house, achieving a reputation among all the relatives of the house.

9. CONCLUSION

1. Disregard of the patrilineal descent rule was observed in the British nobility as well in adoptionlike practices, including son-in-law adoption, summoned to meet a "demographic crisis" that is said to have amounted to "a series of pious fictions" (Stone and Stone 1984, 127; also Powis 1984, 33). I speculate, however, that adoption was more institutionalized and more freely and openly practiced in Japan. Especially noteworthy is evidence that the British male resisted being adopted into his wife's family, which meant assuming his father-in-law's name and arms (Cooper

1976, 303; Trumbach 1978, 46). This, in my view, does not demonstrate a greater gender equality among the Japanese aristocracy, but rather a greater structural integrity of the ie that transcended gender discrimination.

2. Perrott (1968, 12) makes a similar observation about the British: "People outside and remote from the peerage seemed to conspire to keep the mystery [of the nobility] intact."

3. This point is reinforced by Tellis-Nayak (1983) in discussing the Indian domestic hierarchy. On the one hand, there is a sharp status asymmetry between the mistress (of the employer family) and her servant, to the point of one assuming proprietorship of the other. On the other hand, this verticality involves reciprocal interdependency with an exchange of deference and largesse, loyalty and trust, devotion and empathy. Some of the critical comments on this article (for instance by Joyce Pettigrew, p. 75 of Tellis-Nayak 1983) reveal the Western bias, wherein hierarchy is associated with exploitation and the possibility of vertical solidarity is ruled out.

4. At the August 10, 1945, *gozen kaigi* (conference of state leaders in the emperor's presence) Emperor Shōwa voiced his opinion in favor of accepting the Potsdam Declaration of the Allied Powers, an act made possible because Prime Minister Suzuki had solicited His Majesty's thoughts in order to break the tied vote (Kido 1966, 1223–24; Pacific War Research Society 1968, 34–35). It seems that Emperor Shōwa, refusing to be a puppet or robot, attempted to break the tacit rule of silence even against the sokkin's strong advice. Yet this episode does reveal how severely the freedom and efficacy of his right to veto were curtailed, in that the emperor had to seize this rare and final opportunity, given by the prime minister's discretion, to express himself.

5. The subculture of elites in each society, moreover, is likely to permeate the entire culture in one way or another. Such a comparative viewpoint suggests another research project, one that I hope to undertake in the future.

EPILOGUE

1. Reported by the *Japan Times,* and reprinted in the *Hawaii Hochi,* 1/5/1990.

2. *Hinkyū,* also known as *mogari no miya,* refers to a hall in the palace where the imperial coffin is placed only for the wake, which is followed by a formal funeral elsewhere. Mogari was the prehistoric practice of attending and nourishing the dead in expectation of revival, sometimes for as long as three years, until the death was determined to be irreversible. This prefuneral rite was conducted for local chieftains until it was prohibited, for all except the imperial family, in 646 as part of the Taika Reform (NFG, 372–74).

Glossary

Many of the words appearing in the glossary are prefixed in actual usage by an honorific particle such as *o-* or *go-* (e.g., *go-sanke* for *sanke*). Italicized words are listed also as main entries.

AMATERASU	The Sun Goddess, the supreme deity of Shinto worshipped as the primordial genitrix of the imperial line of descent
ASHIGARU	A foot soldier
ASOBASE	A polite verb final used in making a request or giving an order
ASON	The highest nobility title of ancient origin attainable for nonroyal persons
BAKUFU	The shogunate; military government
BANSEI IKKEI	A single, unbroken, everlasting line of descent
BE	An occupational work group of ancient Japan
BEKKAKU KANPEISHA	An extraordinary imperial shrine where an imperial loyalist hero was enshrined
BETSU	Descent; cf. *kōbetsu*
BUKE	The warrior class
BUKE DENSŌ	The office of liaison between the court and the *bakufu*
BUNKAZAI	A cultural property
BUNKE	A branch house of a *dōzoku*
BURAKU	A hamlet
BURAKUMIN	An outcaste

BUTSUDAN	A Buddhist ancestral altar
BUTSUJI	Buddhist matters
CHAKURYŪ	The main or legitimate family line
CHAKUSHI	A legitimate child; cf. *shoshi*
CHISUJI	A blood line
CHOKUSHI	An imperial messenger
CHŌNAN SŌZOKU	Succession to househeadship by the eldest son
CHŌSO	Double accession to the imperial throne
CHŌTEKI	Enemy of the imperial court
CHŪGŪ	An empress, equivalent to a *kōgō*
DAI	A genealogical generation
DAIGAKURYŌ	The Bureau of Great Learning
DAIHAI	Surrogate worship of gods at a shrine by a servant on behalf of his or her master; cf. *daisan*
DAIJŌDAIJIN	Chancellor, the top position in the *daijōkan*
DAIJŌKAN	The State Council under the *ritsuryō*
DAIMYO	A feudal domain lord
DAINAGON	Senior counselor in the *daijōkan*
DAISAN	Surrogate visit to a Buddhist temple and ancestral cemetery by a servant on behalf of his or her master; cf. *daihai*
DANKA	Registered Buddhist temple parishioner
DANSHAKU	A baron; see *shaku*
DENJŌBITO	A court noble (literally, the class of people allowed into the interior of the imperial palace); cf. *tōshō*
DOGEZA	Prostrate on the ground to show respect and awe
DŌZOKU	A lineage group consisting of the main house and its branch houses
ENGUMI	The matching of two parties for marriage or adoption
FUDAI	A hereditary vassal
FŪFU-YŌSHI	Adoption of a married couple
GAGAKU	Court music
GAIBETSU	Foreign descent

GAKUSHUIN	A multicampus school system that used to be primarily for royal and aristocratic children
GENRŌ	Senior statesmen of the Meiji period
GENZOKU	Being laicized
GOGAKUMONJO	The palace school specially installed for the crown prince
GOGAKUYŪ	A classmate, in particular reference to a *Gakushuin* classmate or intimate friend of a royal prince or princess
GOKASHIKIN	An imperial gift of money
GONDAINAGON	Deputy senior counselor in the *daijōkan*
GONGEN	A Buddha incarnate, as Tokugawa Ieyasu was called
GORYŌRIN	Imperial forests
GOSEKKE	The five *sesshō* houses, also called *sekke* or *sekkanke*
GOSHO	An imperial or noble palace or the master residing therein
GOYŌKIKI	A house-calling sales clerk
GŌZOKU	A locally based kin group of power
GYŌKŌ	An imperial visit outside the palace
HAIETSU	An imperial audience
HAIHAN CHIKEN	The replacement of feudal domains with modern prefectures
HAKAMA	A pleated long pair of trousers
HAKAMORI	A graveyard custodian
HAKUSHAKU	Count; see *shaku*
HAN	A daimyo domain under the Tokugawa *bakufu*
HANPEI	The bulwark protecting the imperial house
HANSEKI HŌKAN	The reverential return of feudal domains to the imperial court
HANSHI	A daimyo's vassal in the Tokugawa period
HANSHU	Lord of a *han,* or *daimyo*
HARA	A womb, as synonymous with woman, mother, wife, or consort

HATAMOTO	A Tokugawa shogun's vassal
HEIMIN	A commoner; cf. *shizoku* and *kazoku*
HINA	Decorative figurines and paraphernalia displayed on Girls' Day
HINKYŪ	The temporary shrine installed for the wake of a deceased emperor
HIRAKUGE	A rank-and-file noble
HOKKE	Northern house of the Fujiwara
HON	A rank for *shinnō*
HONNE	Inner feeling
HONRYŪ	The main family line
HOTOKE	Buddha; a dead person deified in the Buddhist ritual
I	A court rank
IE	A household; an elementary stem family unit
IEMOTO	A traditional school of art such as tea ceremony or flower arrangement, or its headmaster
IERYŪ	A style of art, etiquette, or ritual evolved in and handed down by a *kuge* house
IHAI	A mortuary tablet inscribed with a Buddhist title
IKAN-SOKUTAI	A set of court dress, headgear, and footwear for men; cf. *jūnihitoe*
INKYO	Retirement from householdship or office
INSEI	Government under retired and tonsured emperors
ISSHI SŌDEN	One-child succession
JIGE	A nonnoble retainer of the imperial palace (literally "down on the ground," in contradistinction to *denjōbito*)
JIJŪCHŌ	Grand chamberlain
JIKAKU	Temple status
JINRIKISHA	A rickshaw
JISSHI	Literally, a natural child, referring to an adoptee treated as one's real child
JŌHIN	Genteel

JŪBUN	Abbreviation of *jūyō bunkazai,* an important cultural property, meaning the officially designated status of a selected treasure
JUGOI	The minor fifth court rank
JŪNIHITOE	The multilayered court dress for women originated in the Heian period, comparable to *ikan-sokutai* for men
JŪSHIN	A senior vassal
KABANE	The hereditary aristocratic title of an *uji*
KAFU	A deputy house manager, next to *karei*
KAIMYŌ	A posthumous Buddhist name for the dead
KAJŪ	The lowest level of house management staff; see *karei*
KAKAKU	House status
KAMI	Top, above, upper, etc., meaning variously god, emperor, governor, upper area, and so on
KAMI-JOCHŪ	An upper maid attending to the master family
KAMIDANA	A Shinto altar for gods
KAMISHIMO	A ceremonial outer garment for high-ranking samurai
KAN	An office rank juxtaposed with *i*
KANGUN	Imperial army
KANPAKU	Senior regent or top advisor for the emperor; see *sesshō*
KAREI	Head manager of the master's household (a modern version of *karō*), followed by *kafu* and *kajū*
KARŌ	A daimyo's chief vassal-administrator
KASHIKODOKORO	The holiest of the three palace shrines (*kyūchū sanden*), containing the sacred mirror, symbol of *Amaterasu*
KATOKU	The authority of the househead
KAZOKU	"Flowery Lineage," that is, the nobility
KAZOKUREI	The imperial ordinance installing the *kazoku*
KEIBATSU	A political, economic clique built on affinal networks

KEIGO	Honorifics
KENKYŪKAI	The "Study Group" formed by viscount-peers as a political faction of *Kizokuin;* cf. *Kōseikai*
KERAI	A vassal or retainer
KIGENSETSU	The national foundation anniversary
KIGURAI	Status-based self-esteem
KINSHIN	Voluntary retirement from office to show penitence
KISHU	Noble species or noble origin
KIZOKUIN	The House of Peers; cf. *Shūgiin*
KŌBETSU	Imperial lineages claiming descent from emperors
KŌBUGATTAI	Union of the imperial court and the *bakufu*
KŌGŌ	An empress
KŌHAI	A junior member or graduate; cf. *senpai*
KOKU	Rice measurement by volume (approx. 180 liters or 164 quarts), indicating a daimyo's revenue and power
KOKUSŌ(KE)	*Kuni-no-miyatsuko* sinified, referring to the so-titled hereditary shrine houses
KOKUTAI	Essence of the state
KŌKYO	The entire area of the imperial palace
KŌKYŪ	The rear palace, that is, the imperial harem
KŌREIDEN	One of the three palace shrines, this being for all imperial ancestors
KŌSEIKAI	The "Justice Group" created by baron-peers to challenge the dominant *Kenkyūkai*
KOSEKI	The mandatory house register
KŌSHAKU	A nonroyal prince or marquis; see *shaku*
KŌSHITSU	The Imperial House
KŌTAIGŌ	Empress dowager
KŌZOKU	The imperial lineage
KUGE	The pre-Meiji court nobility
KUNAICHŌ	The Imperial Household Agency, the downgraded postwar version of *Kunaishō*
KUNAISHŌ	The Ministry of the Imperial Household

KUNI(MOTO)	The province of ancestral origin
KUNI-NO-MIYATSUKO	A provincial governor under the Yamato court, the office being reduced to ritual functions after the Taika reform of the latter half of the seventh century
KUNKŌ-KAZOKU	The nobility of merit
KYŪCHŪ SANDEN	The triple-shrine structure in the palace consisting of *kashikodokoro, kōreiden,* and *shinden*
KYŪCHŪ SEKIJI	Seating order employed in palace receptions
KYŪDEN	The main building complex in the *kōkyo* which is sometimes equated to the imperial palace itself in its narrow sense
KYŪSHIN	A former vassal, or a vassal's descendant
MIAI	Arranged marriage; introduction to a prospective spouse
MIDAI(DOKORO)	The principal wife of a *shogun*
MIKOSHI	A portable shrine
MIYAKE	A royal collateral
MIYASAMA	A royal prince or princess; Your (His/Her) Highness
MONZEKI	A royal (or *sekke*) temple which was once an imperial residence, or the chief resident priest or priestess in the temple
NAIDAIJIN	The minister of the interior to manage State Council affairs; in the modern government, lord keeper of the seal
NAIFU	Office of *naidaijin*
NAISHINNŌ	An imperial princess of the blood; cf. *shinnō*
NAISHŌTEN	A female counterpart to *shōten,* whose main duty is to offer food daily at *kashikodokoro* and *kōreiden,* leaving *shinden* to *shōten,* and who is closest to *Amaterasu* as her personal servant
NARIKIN	A nouveau riche
NIHONKAN	A Japanese-style house
NORITO	A Shinto prayer
NYŌGO	An imperial consort formally ranking below but practically comparable to an empress
NYOKAN	A female palace attendant or lady-in-waiting

OAITE	The humble playmate of a superior's child
OBOSHIMESHI	Imperial benevolence
OHARASAN	A uterine consort or concubine
OHIKIZURI	A woman's Japanese-style outer garment with train
OKU	The interior of the house
OMOTE	Front
Ō-OKU	The shogunal harem of the Tokugawa
OSHIRUSHI	An emblem given a child to be attached to his or her possessions for identification
OTSUGI	A maidservant or lady-in-waiting
OTSUKI	A maid serving one master around the clock
RITSURYŌ	A body of penal (ritsu) and administrative (ryō) codes issued from the late seventh through the early eighth century
RŌJO	Head maid
ROKUMEIKAN	A Western-style reception hall built to bring foreign and native dignitaries together that became an infamous symbol of shallow Westernism
RYŪGAKUSEI	A student overseas
SADAIJIN	Minister of the left in the *daijōkan*
SANGI	An advisor in the court government
SANKE	The three primary branch houses of the Tokugawa
SANKYŌ	The three secondary branch houses of the Tokugawa
SATCHŌ	Label for two most powerful domains, Satsuma and Chōshū, combined
SATONAGARE	An unretrieved foster child, much like shichinagare, or forfeited pawn
SEIBO	A natural mother
SEIGUN	The western army, referring to the *kangun* led by the *Satchō* forces; cf. *tōgun*
SEISHITSU	The legitimate, principal wife, in contrast to *sokushitsu*
SEKKANKE	*Sesshō-kanpaku* houses; see *sekke*

SEKKE	*Sesshō* houses, referring to the five houses of Fujiwara descent—Konoe, Kujō, Ichijō, Nijō, and Takatsukasa—which took turns in the offices of imperial regency—*sesshō* and *kanpaku*—until these were abolished; also called *gosekke* or *sekkanke*
SENDO	The highest court office attainable by a house as a hereditary right
SENPAI	A senior member or graduate; cf. *kōhai*
SESSHŌ	The office of regent initially created as a private position outside the ryō code (see *ritsuryō*) by the Fujiwara to exercise the imperial authority in surrogacy by virtue of their kinship status as maternal grandfathers or uncles of minor emperors. The imperial surrogacy was further expanded by creation of the *kanpaku,* the office above sesshō
SHAKU	The five ranks of the modern nobility, or *kazoku,* corresponding with prince, marquis, count, viscount, and baron. In Japanese these are *kōshaku, kōshaku, hakushaku, shishaku,* and *danshaku* (the first two being homonyms)
SHIKIBUKAN	A member of the Board of Ceremonies in the *Kunaishō* (and *Kunaichō*)
SHIMO	Lower area or domain, or servants occupying the area, as distinguished from *kami*
SHINBETSU	Godly descent; deity lineages whose ancestors were gods of the mythological ages; cf. *kōbetsu*
SHINBUTSU BUNRI	The Meiji-mandated separation of Shinto and Buddhism
SHINDEN	One of the three palace shrines for the Shinto pantheon
SHIN-HEIMIN	"New commoners," a name used for a former outcaste group
SHINKA	A subject, as distinguished from the royalty
SHIN-KAZOKU	The new nobility, also called *kunkō-kazoku*
SHINNŌ	An imperial prince of the blood
SHINNŌKE	A house with the hereditary title of *shinnō* established by the Tokugawa shogunate

SHINNŌ SENGE	The imperial decree designating a prince a *shinnō*
SHINPAN	The *han* headed by Tokugawa kinsmen
SHINSEKI KŌKA	The descent of royalty to the status of a subject (by marriage, adoption, or branching)
SHINSEN SHŌJIROKU	The newly compiled register of noble lineages
SHINTAI	A god-body; a symbol of a god
SHIRYŪ	A branch family line
SHISEKI	A historical landmark
SHISHAKU	Viscount; see *shaku*
SHISHINDEN	Official Ceremonial Hall of the Kyoto imperial palace
SHISSO	Austerity
SHITAMACHI	The downtown area of urban Tokyo; cf. *yamanote*
SHITSUJI	Head manager (equivalent of *karei*)
SHIZOKU	Gentry; the class made up largely of former samurai vassals and ranking below the *kazoku*
SHODAI	The first-generation ancestor
SHŌEN (OR SHŌ)	A privatized, tax-exempt estate
SHOGUN	Military ruler and head of the *bakufu*, originally derived from the court office called *seii-tai-shōgun* (generalissimo to subjugate barbarians)
SHŌGUN SENGE	The imperial decree authenticating the title of shogun for the *bakufu* nominee
SHOSEI	A male student-servant
SHOSHI	An illegitimate child; cf. *chakushi*
SHŌTEN	An imperial-palace male ritualist who assists the emperor, his surrogate, or other royal personages in the conducting of rituals at the *kyū-chū sanden;* see *naishōten*
SHŪGIIN	The House of Representatives; cf. *Kizokuin*
SŌCHITSURYŌ	An office created in the *Kunaishō* as an agency to supervise the royalty and nobility with respect to status maintenance

SODACHI	Upbringing
SOKKIN	A close entourage
SOKUSHITSU	A "side consort," that is, concubine; cf. *sei-shitsu*
SOTO	Exterior, outside
TAIMEN	Honor; face
TAIREIFUKU	The Western-style, decorated court attire worn by men on ceremonial occasions for palace attendance
TAISEI HŌKAN	The reverential return of the shogunal government to the imperial court
TANIN GYŌGI	Well mannered, as between strangers
TATEMAE	The outward posture or enunciated principle; cf. *honne*
TENCHŌSETSU	The reigning emperor's birthday
TENJI	Naishi-no-suke, a *nyokan* in the central office of the imperial *kōkyū*
TŌGŪ	Crown prince
TŌGUN	Eastern army, the northeastern pro-Tokugawa forces, defeated by the *seigun*
TOMOMACHI-BEYA	The room reserved for servants waiting for their masters to be escorted
TONOSAMA	Lord; Your (His) Highness
TŌSHŌ	Literally, "in-palace," meaning court nobles who were allowed into the emperor's living quarters, i.e., *kuge* and *denjōbito*
TOZAMA	A *han* outside the inner group of the Tokugawa's hereditary-vassal domains (*fudai*), or its *daimyō*
TSUBO	A unit of area 6 ft. by 6 ft., or 3.3 square meters
TSUKIAI	Social interaction
UCHI	Interior, inside
UDAIJIN	Minister of the right in the *daijōkan*
UJI	A clan or lineage group of prehistoric origin
URA	Rear

URAMI	Rancor
UTAKAI	The imperial poetry party
WAKATONO	Junior or young lord
WAKON-YŌSAI	The wedding of Japanese spirit and Western technology
YABUSAME	Ritual performance of archery from a galloping horse
YAMANOTE	The hillside area of Tokyo; cf. *shitamachi*
YOBISUTE	Calling a person without the minimal honorific -*san* in disrespectful address
YŌJO	The practice of daughter adoption; an adopted daughter
YŌKAN	A Western-style house
YŌSHI	Adoption; an adopted son or an adopted son-in-law
YŪSHI	Nominal adoption without entailing succession of the househeadship
ZAIBATSU	A family-based business group of huge scale
ZOKUGUN	Rebel army

References

ABBREVIATIONS

GHHI (Gakushuin Hyakunenshi Hensan Iinkai)

KK (Kasumi Kaikan)

KKT (*Kazoku kakei taisei;* see Kasumi Kaikan 1982–84)

KRR (*Kazoku ruibetsu roku;* see *Kazoku seido shiryōshū*, 166–84)

KSS (*Kazoku seido shiryōshū;* see Kasumi Kaikan 1985)

NFG (Nihon Fūzokushi Gakkai)

SK (Shōyū Kurabu)

TDSH (Tōkyō Daigaku Shiryō Hensanjo)

WORKS CITED

Aishinkakura Hirō. 1984. *"Ruten no ōhi" no Shōwa shi.* Tokyo: Shufu to
   Seikatsusha.
Aoki, Michiko Y. 1974. *Ancient Myths and Early History of Japan: A Cultural
   Foundation.* New York: Exposition Press.
Andō Teru. 1927a. *Okoi monogatari.* Tokyo: Fukunaga Shoten.
———. 1927b. *Zoku Okoi monogatari.* Tokyo: Fukunaga Shoten.
Apparadurai, Arjun. 1986. "Is Homo Hierarchicus?" *American Ethnologist*
   13:745–61.
Arnesen, Peter Judd. 1979. *The Medieval Japanese Daimyo: The Ouchi Family's
   Rule of Suo and Nagato.* New Haven: Yale University Press.
Asai, Torao. 1985. *Nyokan tsūkai.* Tokyo: Kōdansha.
Bachnik, Jane M. 1983. "Recruitment Strategies for Household Succession: Re-
   thinking Japanese Household Organisation." *Man* 18:160–82.
Bargen, Doris G. 1988. "Spirit Possession in the Context of Dramatic Expressions
   of Gender Conflict: The Aoi Episode of the *Genji monogatari.*" *Harvard
   Journal of Asiatic Studies* 48:95–130.

Barnes, Gina L. 1988. *Protohistoric Yamato: Archaeology of the First Japanese State*. Ann Arbor: University of Michigan Center for Japanese Studies.

Bartlett, Frederic C. 1967. *Remembering: A Study in Experimental and Social Psychology*. Cambridge: Cambridge University Press.

Bateson, Gregory. 1972. *Steps to an Ecology of Mind*. New York: Ballantine Books.

Befu, Harumi. 1962. "Corporate Emphasis and Patterns of Descent in the Japanese Family." In *Japanese Culture: Its Development and Characteristics*, edited by R. J. Smith and R. K. Beardsley. Chicago: Aldine.

Bence-Jones, Mark, and Hugh Montgomery-Massingberd. 1979. *The British Aristocracy*. London: Constable.

Bernstein, Basil. 1971. *Class, Codes, and Control*. Vol. 1: *Theoretical Studies Towards a Sociology of Language*. London: Routledge & Kegan Paul.

Berry, Mary Elizabeth. 1982. *Hideyoshi*. Cambridge, Mass.: Harvard University Press.

Bestor, Theodore C. 1989. *Neighborhood Tokyo*. Stanford: Stanford University Press.

Bolitho, Harold. 1974. *Treasures Among Men: The Fudai Daimyo in Tokugawa Japan*. New Haven: Yale University Press.

Bourdieu, Pierre. 1977. *Outline of a Theory of Practice*. Cambridge: Cambridge University Press.

———. 1984. *Distinction: A Social Critique of the Judgement of Taste*. Translated by R. Nice. London: Routledge & Kegan Paul.

Brown, Keith. 1966. "Dōzoku and the Ideology of Descent in Rural Japan." *American Anthropologist* 68:1129–51.

Bruner, Edward M. 1986. "Ethnography as Narrative." In *The Anthropology of Experience*, edited by V. W. Turner and E. M. Bruner. Urbana: University of Illinois Press.

Bunkachō (Agency for Cultural Affairs). 1985. *Waga kuni no bunka gyōsei*. Tokyo: Bunkachō.

———. 1988. *Waga kuni no bunka to bunka gyōsei*. Tokyo: Bunkachō.

Bush, M. L. 1984. *The English Aristocracy: A Comparative Synthesis*. Manchester: Manchester University Press.

Cancian, Frank. 1976. "Social Stratification." *Annual Review of Anthropology* 5:227–48.

Clifford, James. 1980. "Fieldwork, Reciprocity, and the Making of Ethnographic Texts: The Example of Maurice Leenhardt." *Man* 15:518–32.

Clifford, James, and George Marcus, eds. 1986. *Writing Culture: The Poetics and Politics of Ethnography*. Berkeley and Los Angeles: University of California Press.

Cohen, Abner. 1974. *Two-dimensional Man: An Essay on the Anthropology of Power and Symbolism in Complex Society*. Berkeley and Los Angeles: University of California Press.

Collcutt, Martin. 1986. "Buddhism: The Threat of Eradication." In *Japan in Transition: From Tokugawa to Meiji*, edited by M. B. Jansen and G. Rozman. Princeton: Princeton University Press.

Collier, Jane F., and Michelle Z. Rosaldo. 1981. "Politics and Gender in Simple Societies." In *Sexual Meanings: The Cultural Construction of Gender and Sexuality*, edited by S. B. Ortner and H. Whitehead. Cambridge: Cambridge University Press.

Cook, Theodore F., Jr. 1983. "Cataclysm and Career Rebirth: The Imperial Military Elite." In *Work and Lifecourse in Japan,* edited by D. W. Plath. Albany: State University of New York Press.

Cooper, J. P. 1976. "Patterns of Inheritance and Settlement by Great Landowners from the Fifteenth to the Eighteenth Centuries." In *Family and Inheritance: Rural Society in Western Europe, 1200–1800,* edited by J. Goody, J. Thirsk, and E. P. Thompson. Cambridge: Cambridge University Press.

Covell, Jon Carter, and Alan Covell. 1984. *Korean Impact on Japanese Culture: Japan's Hidden History.* Elizabeth, N.J., and Seoul: Hollym International.

Craig, Albert M. 1986. "The Central Government." In *Japan in Transition: From Tokugawa to Meiji,* edited by M. B. Jansen and G. Rozman. Princeton: Princeton University Press.

Crapanzano, Vincent. 1980. *Tuhami: Portrait of a Moroccan.* Chicago: University of Chicago Press.

———. 1984. "Life Histories." *American Anthropologist* 86:953–60.

Dalby, Liza. 1983. *Geisha.* Berkeley and Los Angeles: University of California Press.

Davidoff, Leonore. 1973. *The Best Circle: Women and Society in Victorian England.* Totowa, N.J.: Rowman & Littlefield.

Derrett, J. Duncan M. 1976. "Rajadharma." *Journal of Asian Studies* 35:597–609.

De Vos, George, and Hiroshi Wagatsuma. 1967. *Japan's Invisible Race: Caste in Culture and Personality.* Berkeley and Los Angeles: University of California Press.

Dore, R. P. 1958. *City Life in Japan: A Study of a Tokyo Ward.* Berkeley and Los Angeles: University of California Press.

———. 1965. *Education in Tokugawa Japan.* Berkeley and Los Angeles: University of California Press.

———. 1973. *British Factory—Japanese Factory.* Berkeley and Los Angeles: University of California Press.

Douglas, Mary. 1970. *Natural Symbols: Explorations in Cosmology.* New York: Vintage Books.

———. 1975. *Implicit Meanings: Essays in Anthropology.* London: Routledge & Kegan Paul.

Dumont, Louis. 1970. *Homo Hierarchicus: The Caste System and Its Implications.* Rev. ed. Chicago: University of Chicago Press.

Edwards, Walter. 1983. "Event and Process in the Founding of Japan: The Horserider Theory in Archaeological Perspective." *Journal of Japanese Studies* 9:265–95.

———. 1991. "Buried Discourse: The Toro Archaeological Site and Japanese National Identity in the Early Postwar Period." *Journal of Japanese Studies* 17:1–23.

Egami Namio. 1967. *Kiba minzoku kokka: Nihon kodaishi e no apurōchi.* Tokyo: Chūōkōronsha.

Elias, Norbert. 1978. *The Civilizing Process.* Vol. 1: *The History of Manners.* New York: Pantheon Books.

———. 1982. *The Civilizing Process.* Vol. 2: *Power and Civility.* New York: Pantheon Books.

Ema Shuichi. 1983. *Chichibu-no-miya hi Setsuko.* Tokyo: Yamatoshobō.

Embree, John F. 1939. *Suye Mura: A Japanese Village.* Chicago: University of Chicago Press.

Fujishima Taisuke. 1965. *Nippon no jōryū shakai.* Tokyo: Kōbunsha.

————. 1987. *Tōkyō yamanote no hitobito.* Tokyo: Sankei Shuppan.

Fujitani, Takashi. 1986. "Japan's Modern National Ceremonies: A Historical Ethnography, 1868–1912." Ph.D. diss., University of California, Berkeley.

Fukutō Sanae. 1991. *Heianchō no haha to ko: kizoku to shomin no kazoku seikatsu-shi.* Tokyo: Chūōkōronsha.

Fuse, Toyomasa. 1972. "The Kazoku—A Vanishing Caste? A Study of the Japanese Nobility." *Asia Quarterly* 2:125–55.

Gakushuin, ed. 1978. *Gakushuin no hyakunen.* Tokyo: Gakushuin.

Gakushuin Hyakunenshi Hensan Iinkai (GHHI), ed. 1981–87. *Gakushuin hyakunenshi.* 3 vols. Tokyo: Gakushuin.

Galtung, Johan. 1971. "Social Structure, Education Structure, and Lifelong Education: The Case of Japan." In *Reviews of National Policy for Education: Japan,* 347–73. Paris: OECD.

Gathorne-Hardy, Jonathan. 1972. *The Rise and Fall of the British Nanny.* London: Hudder and Stoughton.

Geertz, Clifford. 1973. "Thick Description: Toward an Interpretive Theory of Culture." In *The Interpretation of Cultures,* 3–30. New York: Basic Books.

Geertz, Hildred, and Clifford Geertz. 1968. "Teknonymy in Bali: Parenthood, Age-Grading, and Genealogical Amnesia." In *Marriage, Family, and Residence,* edited by P. Bohannan and J. Middleton. American Museum Sourcebooks in Anthropology. Garden City, N.Y.: Natural History Press.

Gluck, Carol. 1985. *Japan's Modern Myths: Ideology in the Late Meiji Period.* Princeton: Princeton University Press.

Goodenough, Ruth Gallagher. 1970. "Adoption on Romonum, Truk." In *Adoption in Eastern Oceania,* edited by V. Carroll. Honolulu: University of Hawaii Press.

Goody, Jack. 1976. *Production and Reproduction: A Comparative Study of the Domestic Domain.* Cambridge: Cambridge University Press.

Gouldner, Alvin W. 1960. "The Norm of Reciprocity: A Preliminary Statement." *American Sociological Review* 25:161–78.

Hall, Edward T. 1959. *The Silent Language.* Garden City, N.Y.: Doubleday.

————. 1969. *The Hidden Dimension.* Garden City, N.Y.: Doubleday.

Hall, John Whitney. 1966. *Government and Local Power in Japan, 500–1700: A Study Based on Bizen Province.* Princeton: Princeton University Press.

————. 1973. "A Monarch for Modern Japan." In *Political Development in Modern Japan,* edited by R. E. Ward. Princeton: Princeton University Press.

————. 1974a. "Kyoto as Historical Background." In *Medieval Japan: Essays in Institutional History,* edited by J. W. Hall and J. P. Mass. New Haven: Yale University Press.

————. 1974b. "Rule by Status in Tokugawa Japan." *Journal of Japanese Studies* 1:39–49.

Hamabata, Matthews Masayuki. 1990. *Crested Kimono: Power and Love in the Japanese Business Family.* Ithaca: Cornell University Press.

Han, Woo-keun. 1970. *The History of Korea.* Translated by Lee Kyung-shik; edited by G. K. Mintz. Honolulu: East-West Center Press.

Handler, Richard, and Daniel A. Segal. 1985. "Hierarchies of Choice: The Social Construction of Rank in Jane Austen." *American Ethnologist* 12:691–706.

Hane, Mikiso. 1982. *Emperor Hirohito and His Chief Aide-de-Camp: The Honjo Diary, 1933–36*. Translated and with an introduction by M. Hane. Tokyo: University of Tokyo Press.

Hansen, Edward C., and Timothy C. Parrish. 1983. "Elite Versus the State: Toward an Anthropological Contribution to the Study of Hegemonic Power in Capitalist Society." In *Elites: Ethnological Issues*, edited by G. E. Marcus. Albuquerque: University of New Mexico Press.

Hardacre, Helen. 1986. "Creating State Shinto: The Great Promulgation Campaign and the New Religions." *Journal of Japanese Studies* 12:29–63.

———. 1989. *Shinto and the State, 1868–1988*. Princeton: Princeton University Press.

Hashimoto Akira. 1989. *Heisei no tennō*. Tokyo: Bungeishunjū.

Hashimoto Yoshihiko. 1976. *Heian kizoku shakai no kenkyū*. Tokyo: Yoshikawa Kōbunkan.

———. 1978. "Kyūchū nyokan no seido to hensen." In *Tennō: Nihonshi shōhyakka 8*, edited by Kodama Kōta. Tokyo: Kondō Shuppansha.

Hayakawa Takashi. 1983. *Nippon no jōryū shakai to keibatsu*. Tokyo: Kadokawa Shoten.

Hayashida, Cullen Tadao. 1976. "Identity, Race, and the Blood Ideology of Japan." Ph.D. diss., University of Washington.

Hayashiya Tatsusaburō. 1966. *Tenka ittō*. Nippon no Rekishi, vol. 12. Tokyo: Chūōkōronsha.

Hayden, Ilse. 1987. *Symbol and Privilege: The Ritual Context of British Royalty*. Tucson: University of Arizona Press.

Hendry, Joy. 1990. "Humidity, Hygiene, or Ritual Care: Some Thoughts on Wrapping as a Social Phenomenon." In *Unwrapping Japan*, edited by E. Ben-Ari, B. Moeran, and J. Valentine. Honolulu: University of Hawaii Press.

Hirayama Toshijirō. 1980. *Nihon chūsei kazoku no kenkyū*. Tokyo: Hōsei Daigaku Shuppankyoku.

Hobsbawm, Eric, and Terrence Ranger, eds. 1983. *The Invention of Tradition*. Cambridge: Cambridge University Press.

Howard, Alan, Robert H. Heighton, Jr., Cathie E. Jordan, and Ronald G. Gallimore. 1970. "The Traditional and Modern Adoption Patterns in Hawaii." In *Adoption in Eastern Oceania*, edited by V. Carroll. Honolulu: University of Hawaii Press.

Hozumi, Nobushige. 1912. *Ancestor Worship and Japanese Law*. Tokyo: Maruzen Kabushiki Kaisha.

Hurst, G. Cameron, III. 1974a. "The Structure of the Heian Court: Some Thoughts on the Nature of 'Familial Authority' in Heian Japan." In *Medieval Japan: Essays in Institutional History*, edited by J. W. Hall and J. P. Mass. New Haven: Yale University Press.

———. 1974b. "The Development of the *Insei*: A Problem in Japanese History and Historiography." In *Medieval Japan: Essays in Institutional History*, edited by J. W. Hall and J. P. Mass. New Haven: Yale University Press.

Ikawa-Smith, Fumiko. 1980. "Current Issues in Japanese Archaeology." *American Scientist* 88:134–45.

Inose Naoki. 1991. *Mikado no shōzō: purinsu hoteru no nazo*. Tokyo: Shōgakkan.

Inukai Tomoko. 1989. *Tomoko no nihon suteki sengen*. Tokyo: Jōhō Sentā Shuppankyoku.

Irie Sukemasa. 1989. *Tennōsama no kanreki*. Tokyo: Asahi Shinbunsha.

———, ed. 1979. *Kyūchū saijiki*. Tokyo: TBS Buritanika.

———, ed. 1980. *Kyūchū jijū monogatari*. Tokyo: TBS Buritanika.

Irokawa, Daikichi. 1975. "The Survival Struggle of the Japanese Community." *Japan Interpreter* 9:466–94.

Ishii Ryōsuke. 1982. *Tennō: Tennō no seisei oyobi fushinsei no dentō*. Tokyo: Yamakawa Shuppansha.

Ishimoto Noriko, ed. 1990. *Jitsugetsu: Aoyama no jūnen*. Tokyo: Jitsugetsukai.

Ishimoto, Baroness Shidzue. 1984. *Facing Two Ways: The Story of My Life*. Stanford: Stanford University Press.

Ishimura Teikichi. 1987. *Yūsoku kojitsu*. 2 vols. Tokyo: Kōdansha.

Ishinshi Shiryō Hensankai, ed. [1929] 1976. *Kazoku fuyō*. Tokyo: Shinseisha.

Ivy, Marilyn Jeanette. 1988. "Discourses of the Vanishing in Contemporary Japan." Ph.D. diss., Cornell University.

Iwai Tadakuma. 1980. "Seiritsuki kindai tennōsei to mibunsei: kashizoku seido o chūshin to shite." *Nihonshi kenkyū*, no. 211: 5–26.

Jansen, Marius B. 1986. "The Ruling Class." In *Japan in Transition: From Tokugawa to Meiji*, edited by M. B. Jansen and G. Rozman. Princeton: Princeton University Press.

Jansen, Marius B., and Gilbert Rozman, eds. 1986. *Japan in Transition: From Tokugawa to Meiji*. Princeton: Princeton University Press.

Jichishō Gyōseikyoku, ed. 1984. *Zenkoku jinkō: Setaisū hyō, jinkō dōtai hyō*. Tokyo: Kokudo Chiri Kyōkai.

Jinji Kōshinjo. 1985. *Jinji kōshinroku*. 33d ed. Tokyo: Jinji Kōshinjo.

Kanazawa Makoto, Kawakita Yōtarō, and Yuasa Yasuo, eds. 1968. *Kazoku: Meiji hyakunen no sokumen-shi*. Tokyo: Kōdansha.

Kasumi Kaikan (KK), ed. 1966. *Kazoku Kaikan shi*. Tokyo: Kashima Kenkyūjo Shuppankai.

———, ed. 1976. *Kuge bunka shiryō tenji mokuroku*. Tokyo: Kasumi Kaikan.

———, ed. 1982–84. *Kazoku kakei taisei (KKT)*. 2 vols. Tokyo: Yoshikawa Kōbunkan.

———, ed. 1985. *Kazoku seido shiryōshū (KSS)*. Tokyo: Kasumi Kaikan.

Kasumi Kaikan Shiryō Tenji Iinkai, ed. 1980. *Kaigai ni okeru kuge daimyo ten: Daiikkai ishin ten*. Tokyo: Kasumi Kaikan.

Kawahara Toshiaki. 1983. *Tennō Hirohito no Shōwa shi*. Tokyo: Bungeishunjū.

———. 1987. *Michikohi*. Tokyo: Kōdansha.

Kazoku Kaikan. 1933. *Kazoku yōran*. Tokyo: Iai Masahiro.

Keesing, Roger M. 1985. "Kwaio Women Speak: The Micropolitics of Autobiography in a Solomon Island Society." *American Anthropologist* 87:27–39.

———. 1987. "Anthropology as Interpretive Quest." *Current Anthropology* 28:161–76.

Kelly, William W. 1986. "Rationalization and Nostalgia: Cultural Dynamics of New Middle-Class Japan." *American Ethnologist* 13:603–18.

Kendall, Laurel. 1988. *The Life and Hard Times of a Korean Shaman: Of Tales and the Telling of Tales*. Honolulu: University of Hawaii Press.

Kidder, J. Edward, Jr. 1985. "The Archaeology of the Early Horse-Riders in Japan." *Transactions of the Asiatic Society of Japan*, 3d ser., 20: 89–123.

Kido Kōichi. 1966. *Kido Kōichi nikki*. 2 vols. Tokyo: Tōkyō Daigaku Shuppan-kai.

Kiley, Cornelius J. 1973. "State and Dynasty in Archaic Yamato." *Journal of Asian Studies* 33:25–49.

————. 1974. "Estate and Property in the Late Heian Period." In *Medieval Japan: Essays in Institutional History*, ed. J. W. Hall and J. P. Mass. New Haven and London: Yale University Press.

————. 1983. "Uji-Kabane System." In *Encyclopedia of Japan* 8:131–37. Tokyo: Kōdansha.

Kirby, R. J. 1908. "An Essay by Dazai Jun." Translated by R. J. Kirby. *Transactions of the Asiatic Society of Japan* 36, pt. 1: 96–135.

Kitagawa, Hiroshi, and Bruce T. Tsunoda. 1975. *The Tale of the Heike*. 2 vols. Tokyo: University of Tokyo Press.

Kitaoji, Hironobu. 1971. "The Structure of the Japanese Family." *American Anthropologist* 73:1036–57.

Kizokuin Jimukyoku, ed. 1947. *Kizokuin yōran, hei*. Exp. ed. Tokyo: Kizokuin Jimukyoku.

Kōbata Yoshiko. 1984. *Akasaka monogatari*. Tokyo: Aki Shobō.

Kodama Kōta, ed. 1978. *Tennō: Nihonshi shōhyakka 8*. Tokyo: Kondō Shuppan-sha.

Kojima Jō. 1981. *Tennō*. 5 vols. Tokyo: Bungeishunjū.

Kunai Daijin Kanbō. Annually. *Shokuinroku*. Tokyo: Kunai Daijin Kanbō.

Kuwata Tadachika. 1972. *Momoyama jidai no josei*. Tokyo: Yoshikawa Kōbunkan.

Langness, L. L., and Gelya Frank. 1981. *Lives: An Anthropological Approach to Biography*. Novato, Calif.: Chandler & Sharp.

Lasch, Christopher. 1989. "The Politics of Nostalgia: Losing History on the Mists of Ideology." *Harper's*, November, 65–70.

Lasswell, Harold D., and Abraham Kaplan. 1950. *Power and Society: A Frame for Political Inquiry*. New Haven: Yale University Press.

Lebra, Takie Sugiyama. 1976. *Japanese Patterns of Behavior*. Honolulu: University of Hawaii Press.

————. 1984. *Japanese Women: Constraint and Fulfillment*. Honolulu: University of Hawaii Press.

————. 1989. "Adoption Among the Hereditary Elite of Japan: Status Preservation Through Mobility." *Ethnology* 28:185–218.

————. 1990. "The Socialization of Aristocratic Children by Commoners: Recalled Experiences of the Hereditary Elite in Modern Japan." *Cultural Anthropology* 5:78–100.

————. 1991. "Resurrecting Ancestral Charisma: Aristocratic Descendants in Contemporary Japan." *Journal of Japanese Studies* 17:59–78.

Lebra, William P. 1966. *Okinawan Religion: Belief, Ritual, and Social Structure*. Honolulu: University of Hawaii Press.

Ledyard, Gari. 1975. "Galloping Along with the Horseriders: Looking for the Founders of Japan." *Journal of Japanese Studies* 1:217–54.

Lee, Changsoo, and George De Vos, eds. 1981. *Koreans in Japan: Ethnic Conflict and Accommodation*. Berkeley and Los Angeles: University of California Press.

Lee, Kwang-Kyu, and Youngsook Kim Harvey. 1973. "Teknonymy and Geononymy in Korean Kinship Terminology." *Ethnology* 12:31–46.

Linhart, Sepp. 1988. "From Industrial to Postindustrial Society: Changes in Japanese Leisure-related Values and Behavior." *Journal of Japanese Studies* 14:271–307.

Luhrmann, T. M. 1989. "The Magic of Secrecy: The 1986 Stirling Award Essay." *Ethos* 17:131–65.

Lynch, Owen M. 1977. "Method and Theory in the Sociology of Louis Dumont: A Reply." In *The New Wind: Changing Identities in South Asia,* edited by K. David. The Hague: Mouton.

McCullough, William H. 1967. "Japanese Marriage Institutions in the Heian Period." *Harvard Journal of Asiatic Studies* 27:103–67.

Marcus, George E. 1979. "Ethnographic Research Among Elites in the Kingdom of Tonga: Some Methodological Considerations." *Anthropological Quarterly* 52:135–51.

———. 1983. "The Fiduciary Role in American Family Dynasties and Their Institutional Legacy: From the Law of Trusts to Trust in the Establishment." In *Elites: Ethnographic Issues,* edited by G. E. Marcus. Albuquerque: University of New Mexico Press.

Marriott, McKim. 1969. Review of *Homo Hierarchicus,* by Louis Dumont. *American Anthropologist* 71:1166–75.

Matsuura Rei. 1975. *Tokugawa Yoshinobu.* Tokyo: Chūōkōronsha.

Mencher, Joan. 1974. "The Caste System Upside Down, or the Not-So-Mysterious East." *Current Anthropology* 15:469–93.

Miller, Richard J. 1974. *Ancient Japanese Nobility: The Kabane Ranking System.* Berkeley and Los Angeles: University of California Press.

———. 1976. "Ancestors and Nobility in Ancient Japan." In *Ancestors,* edited by W. H. Newell. The Hague: Mouton.

———. 1978. *Japan's First Bureaucracy: A Study of Eighth-Century Government.* Ithaca: Cornell University, China-Japan Program.

Miyoshi, Masao. 1974. *Accomplices of Silence.* Berkeley and Los Angeles: University of California Press.

Moore, Ray A. 1970. "Adoption and Samurai Mobility in Tokugawa Japan." *Journal of Asian Studies* 29:617–32.

Morioka, Kiyomi. 1967. "Life Cycle Patterns in Japan, China, and the United States." *Journal of Marriage and the Family* 29:595–606.

Morris, Ivan. 1975. *The Nobility of Failure: Tragic Heroes in the History of Japan.* New York: Holt, Rinehart & Winston.

Murai Yasuhiko. 1990. *Ōchō kizoku.* Tokyo: Shōgakkan.

Murakami Shigeyoshi. 1977. *Tennō no saishi.* Tokyo: Iwanami Shoten.

Murakami Yasusuke, Kumon Shunpei, and Satō Seizaburō. 1979. *Bunmei to shite no ie shakai.* Tokyo: Chūōkōronsha.

Muramatsu Shōfū. 1961. *Shōsetsu denka.* Tokyo: Shinchōsha.

Murdock, George Peter. 1949. *Social Structure.* New York: Macmillan.

Nagahata Michiko. 1990. *Koi no hana, Byakuren jiken.* Tokyo: Bungeishunjū.

Nagayo Yoshirō. 1963. *Waga kokoro no henreki.* Tokyo: Chikuma Shobō.

Nakane Chie. 1967a. *Tate shakai no ningen kankei.* Tokyo: Kōdansha.

————. 1967b. *Kinship and Economic Organization in Rural Japan*. London: Athlone Press.

————. 1969. *Kazoku no kōzō: Shakai jinruigaku-teki bunseki*. Tokyo: Tōkyō Daigaku Tōyō Bunka Kenkyūjo Hōkoku.

Nakano Takashi. 1968. *Ie to dōzoku-dan no riron*. Tokyo: Miraisha.

Nanbu Toshihide and Maeda Toshitatsu. 1978. "Tonosama ōini kataru: Taidan." *Tabi* 1:122–27.

Nashimoto Itsuko. 1975. *Sandai no tennō to watakushi*. Tokyo: Kōdansha.

Newman, Katherine S. 1986. "Symbolic Dialects and Generations of Women: Variation in the Meaning of Post-Divorce Downward Mobility." *American Ethnologist* 13:230–52.

NHK Yoron Chōsabu, ed. 1984. *Nihonjin no shūkyo ishiki*. Tokyo: NHK.

Nihon Fūzokushi Gakkai (NFG), ed. 1979. *Nihon fūzoku shi jiten*. Tokyo: Kōbundō.

Nomura Tadao. 1978. *Kōkyū to nyokan*. Tokyo: Kyōikusha.

Ōdaira Shin'ichi. 1984. *Saigo no naidaijin Kido Kōichi*. Tokyo: Kōbunsha.

Okada Yoneo. 1966. "Jingū jinja sōken shi." In *Meiji ishin: Shintō hyakunen shi*, vol. 2, edited by Matsuyama Yoshio. Tokyo: Shintō Bunkakai.

————. 1977. *Jinja: Nihonshi shōhyakka 1*. Tokyo: Kondō Shuppansha.

Ōkubo Toshiaki. 1973. *Iwakura Tomomi*. Tokyo: Chūōkōronsha.

————. 1979. "Meiji kazoku no tanjō." *Rekishi to jinbutsu*, March, 42–49.

————. 1982. "Dentō kazoku to Meiji kazoku." In *Kensei kinenkan no junen*, edited by Shūgiin Kensei Kinen Kaikan. Tokyo: Shūgiin Kensei Kinen Kaikan.

Ōkura Yūji. 1985. *Gyakkō kazoku: Chichi Ōkura Kihachirō to watakushi*. Tokyo: Bungeishunjū.

Ōno Kōshi and Okuse Isao. 1987. "Tokushū jiten: Miyake sōran." *Bessatsu rekishi dokuhon* 12, no. 3: 201–31.

Ortner, Sherry B. 1973. "On Key Symbols." *American Anthropologist* 75:1338–46.

Oshida Yoshihisa. 1984. *Gagaku e no shōtai*. Tokyo: Kyōdō Tsūshinsha.

Ostrander, Susan A. 1984. *Women of the Upper Class*. Philadelphia: Temple University Press.

Ota Toshiho. 1973. *Nanbu ishinki*. Tokyo: Yamato Shobō.

Otabe Yūji. 1991. *Nashimoto no miya Itsuko hi no nikki*. Tokyo: Shōgakkan.

Pacific War Research Society, ed. 1968. *Japan's Longest Day*. Tokyo: Kōdansha International.

Parsons, Talcott. 1951. *The Social System*. Glencoe, Ill.: Free Press.

————. 1954. "A Revised Analytical Approach to the Theory of Social Stratification." In *Essays in Sociological Theory*. Rev. ed. Glencoe, Ill.: Free Press.

————. 1961. "An Outline of the Social System." In *Theories of Society: Foundations of Modern Sociological Theory*, edited by T. Parsons, K. D. Naegele, and J. R. Pitts, 1:30–79. New York: Free Press.

Pelzel, John C. 1970. "Japanese Kinship: A Comparison." In *Family and Kinship in Chinese Society*, edited by M. Freedman. Stanford: Stanford University Press.

Perrott, Roy. 1968. *The Aristocrats: A Portrait of Britain's Nobility and Their Way of Life Today*. London: Weidenfeld & Nicolson.

Pharr, Susan J. 1990. *Losing Face: Status Politics in Japan*. Berkeley and Los Angeles: University of California Press.

Philippi, Donald L. 1968. *Kojiki*. Tokyo: University of Tokyo Press.

Plath, David W. 1964. "Where the Family of God . . . Is the Family: The Role of the Dead in Japanese Households." *American Anthropologist* 66:300–317.

———. 1980. *Long Engagements: Maturity in Modern Japan*. Stanford: Stanford University Press.

Ponsonby Fane, R.A.B. 1936. "Kōhi: Imperial Consorts in Japan." *Transactions and Proceedings of the Japan Society* (London) 33:111–58.

Powis, Jonathan. 1984. *Aristocracy*. Oxford: Basil Blackwell.

Reid, David. 1989. "Japanese Christians and the Ancestors." *Japanese Journal of Religious Studies* 16:259–83.

Reischauer, Haru Matsukata. 1986. *Samurai and Silk: A Japanese and American Heritage*. Cambridge, Mass.: Harvard University Press.

Ri (Yi) Masako. 1973. *Sugita saigetsu*. Seoul: N.p.

Robertson, Jennifer. 1991. *Native and Newcomer: Making and Remaking a Japanese City*. Berkeley and Los Angeles: University of California Press.

Rohlen, Thomas P. 1983. *Japan's High Schools*. Berkeley and Los Angeles: University of California Press.

Rundquist, Angela. 1987. "Presentation at Court: A Corporate Female Ritual of Transition in Sweden, 1850–1962." *Anthropology Today* 3(6):2–6.

Russell, John. 1991. "Race and Reflexivity: The Black Other in Contemporary Japanese Mass Culture." *Cultural Anthropology* 6:3–25.

Sahlins, Marshall. 1976. *Culture and Practical Reason*. Chicago: University of Chicago Press.

Saigō Jūkō. 1981. *Gensui Saigō Jūdō den*. Tokyo: Fuyō Shobō.

Saiki Kazuma. 1946. "Tokugawa shōgun seibo narabi ni saishō-kō." In *Rekishi to jinbutsu*, edited by Nihon Rekishi Gakkai. Tokyo: Chūōkōronsha.

Sakai Miiko. 1982. *Aru kazoku no Shōwa shi*. Tokyo: Shufu to Seikatsusha.

Sakamaki Yoshio. 1987. *Kazoku seido no kenkyū: Arishi hi no kazoku seido*. Tokyo: Kasumi Kaikan.

Sakamoto Ken'ichi. 1983. *Meiji Shintō shi no kenkyū*. Tokyo: Kokusho Kankō-kai.

Sangren, P. Steven. 1988. "Rhetoric and the Authority of Ethnography: 'Postmodernism' and the Social Reproduction of Texts." *Current Anthropology* 29:405–35.

Sansom, George. 1958. *A History of Japan to 1334*. Stanford: Stanford University Press.

Satō Tomoyasu. 1987. *Monbatsu: Kyū kazoku kaisō no fukken*. Tokyo: Rippū Shobō.

Schwartz, Barry. 1981. *Vertical Classification: A Study in Structuralism and the Sociology of Knowledge*. Chicago: University of Chicago Press.

Seidensticker, Edward. 1983. *Low City, High City: Tokyo from Edo to the Earthquake*. New York: Knopf.

Senge Norihiko. 1990–91. "Izumo kami no yakata nisennen no chi." *Shinchō* 45, nos. 1 (Aug. 1990): 196–216; 2 (Sept. 1990): 184–207; 3 (Oct. 1990): 126–46; 4 (Nov. 1990): 186–202; 5 (Dec. 1990): 212–30; 6 (Feb. 1991): 196–215.

Senge Takamune. 1968. *Izumo taisha*. Tokyo: Gakuseisha.

Shigeno, An'eki. 1887. "The Evils of Abdication, Heirship, and Adoption." *Transactions of the Asiatic Society of Japan* 15:72–82.

Shils, Edward. 1981. *Tradition*. Chicago: University of Chicago Press.

Shimazu Shuppankai. 1978. *Shirayuki*. Tokyo: Shimazu Shuppankai.

Shimohashi Yukiosa (narrator) and Hagura Keishō (recorder and commentator). 1979. *Bakumatsu no kyūtei*. Tokyo: Heibonsha.

Shin Jinbutsu Ōraisha. 1987. "Tennōke to Nippon no meizoku." *Bessatsu rekishi dokuhon,* no. 45.

———. 1988a. "Who's Who no. 3: Tennō no soshiki to jinmyaku." *Bessatsu rekishi dokuhon,* Winter.

———. 1988b. "Who's Who no. 4: Nippon no meimon senke." *Bessatsu rekishi dokuhon,* Spring.

Shively, Donald H. 1971. "The Japanization of the Middle Meiji." In *Tradition and Modernization in Japanese Culture,* edited by D. H. Shively. Princeton: Princeton University Press.

Shōyū Kurabu (SK), ed. 1980. *Kizokuin no kaiha kenkyūshi: Meiji Taishō hen.* Tokyo: Shōyū Kurabu.

———. 1982a. *Kizokuin seiji nenpyō.* Tokyo: Shōyū Kurabu.

———. 1982b. *Kizokuin no kaiha kenkyū shi: Shōwa hen.* Tokyo: Shōyū Kurabu.

———. 1984. *Kizokuin no seiji dantai to kaiha.* Tokyo: Shōyū Kurabu.

Shūkan Bunshun Henshūbu, ed. 1988. "Tennō no shomin taiken." In "Tennō Hirohito," an issue of *Kawade jinbutsu dokuhon*. Tokyo: Kawade Shobō Shinsha.

Shūkan Yomiuri Henshūbu, ed. 1987. *Nippon no meika*. Tokyo: Yomiuri Shinbunsha.

Sievers, Sharon L. 1983. *Flowers in Salt: The Beginning of Feminist Consciousness in Modern Japan*. Stanford: Stanford University Press.

Sinclair, Andrew. 1969. *The Last of the Best: The Aristocracy of Europe in the Twentieth Century*. New York: Macmillan.

Smith, Robert J. 1972. "Small Families, Small Households, and Residential Instability: Town and City in 'Pre-modern' Japan." In *Household and Family in Past Time,* edited by P. Laslett. Cambridge: Cambridge University Press.

———. 1974. *Ancestor Worship in Contemporary Japan*. Stanford: Stanford University Press.

———. 1983. *Japanese Society*. Cambridge: Cambridge University Press.

Smith, Robert J., and Ella Lury Wiswell. 1982. *The Women of Suye Mura*. Chicago: University of Chicago Press.

Smith, Valene L., ed. 1989. *Hosts and Guests: The Anthropology of Tourism.* 2d ed. Philadelphia: University of Pennsylvania Press.

Soviak, Eugene. 1971. "On the Nature of Western Progress: The Journal of the Iwakura Embassy." In *Tradition and Modernization in Japanese Culture,* edited by D. H. Shively. Princeton: Princeton University Press.

Steiner, Kurt. 1987. "The Occupation and the Reform of the Japanese Civil Code." In *Democratizing Japan: The Allied Occupation,* edited by R. E. Ward and Sakamoto Yoshikazu. Honolulu: University of Hawaii Press.

Stephens, William N. 1963. *The Family in Cross-cultural Perspective*. New York: Holt, Rinehart & Winston.

Stone, Lawrence, and Jeanne C. Fawtier Stone. 1984. *An Open Elite? England, 1540–1800.* Oxford: Clarendon Press.

Strayer, Joseph R. 1968. "The Tokugawa Period and Japanese Feudalism." In *Studies in the Institutional History of Early Modern Japan,* edited by J. W. Hall and M. B. Jansen. Princeton: Princeton University Press.

Suzuki Masayuki. 1980. "Kazokusei o meguru jakkan no mondai." *Nihon shi kenkyū,* no. 211: 27–53.

"Symposium on Ie Society." 1985. *Journal of Japanese Studies* 11:1–69.

Takahashi Hiroshi. 1987. *Shōchō tennō.* Tokyo: Iwanami Shoten.

Takahashi Hiroshi and Suzuki Kunihiko. 1989. *Tennōke no misshitachi: Senryō to kōshitsu.* Tokyo: Bungeishunjū.

Takane Masaaki. 1976. *Nippon no seiji erīto.* Tokyo: Chūōkōronsha.

Takayanagi Kaneyoshi. 1965. *Edojō ō-oku no seikatsu.* Tokyo: Yūsankaku.

Takayanagi Mitsuhisa and Takeuchi Rizō, eds. 1974. *Kadokawa nihon shi jiten.* 2d ed. Tokyo: Kadokawa Shoten.

Takeda Tsuneyoshi. 1987. *Kumo no ue shita: Omoide-banashi.* Tokyo: Tokyo Shinbun Shuppankyoku.

Taki Kōji. 1988. *Tennō no shōzō.* Tokyo: Iwanami Shoten.

Tambiah, S. J. 1972. Review of *Homo Hierarchicus,* by Louis Dumont. *American Anthropologist* 74:832–35.

Tellis-Nayak, V. 1983. "Power and Solidarity: Clientage in Domestic Service." *Current Anthropology* 24:67–79.

"Tennō Hirohito." 1988. An issue of *Kawade jinbutsu dokuhon.* Tokyo: Kawade Shobō Shinsha.

Titus, David A. 1974. *Palace and Politics in Prewar Japan.* New York: Columbia University Press.

Togashi Junji. 1977. *Tennō to tomo ni gojūnen: Kunai kisha no me.* Tokyo: Mainichi Shinbunsha.

Tokugawa Motoko. 1983. *Tōi uta.* Tokyo: Kōdansha.

Tōkyō Daigaku Shiryō Hensanjo (TDSH), ed. 1966. *Dokushi biyō.* Tokyo: Kōdansha.

Torio Tae. 1985. *Watakushi no ashioto ga kikoeru.* Tokyo: Bungeishunjū.

Toyoda Takeshi. 1978. *Kakei.* Tokyo: Kondō Shuppansha.

Trumbach, Randolph. 1978. *The Rise of the Egalitarian Family: Aristocratic Kinship and Domestic Relations in Eighteenth-Century England.* New York: Academic Press.

Umegaki, Michio. 1986. "From Domain to Prefecture." In *Japan in Transition,* edited by M. B. Jansen and G. Rozman. Princeton: Princeton University Press.

Urai Masaaki. 1983. *Mō hitotsu no Tokugawa monogatari.* Tokyo: Seibundō Shinkōsha.

Usukine Kashin. 1988. "Mōri hakubutsukan: Sono rekishi to denrai bunkazai." Bōfu, Yamaguchi-ken: Bōfu Mōri Hōkokai.

Varley, H. Paul. 1984. *Japanese Culture.* 3d edition. Honolulu: University of Hawaii Press.

Wada Hidematsu. 1983. *Kanshoku yōkai.* Tokyo: Kōdansha.

Wakita Haruko. 1990. "Nōgaku to tennō, Shinto." *Bungei Bessatsu (Tennōsei—rekishi, ōken, daijōsai),* November, 126–32.

Warner, W. Lloyd, Marchia Meeker, and Kenneth Eells. 1960. *Social Class in America: A Manual of Procedure for the Measurement of Social Status.* New York: Harper & Bros.

Watanabe, Yozo. 1963. "The Family and the Law: The Individualistic Premise and Modern Japanese Family Law." In *Law in Japan: The Legal Order in a Changing Society,* edited by A. T. von Mehren. Cambridge, Mass.: Harvard University Press.

Watson, James L. 1975. "Agnates and Outsiders: Adoption in a Chinese Lineage." *Man* 10:293–306.

Webb, Herschel. 1968. *The Japanese Imperial Institution in the Tokugawa Period.* New York: Columbia University Press.

Weber, Max. 1947. *The Theory of Social and Economic Organization.* Translated by A. M. Henderson and T. Parsons. Glencoe, Ill.: Free Press.

Yamaguchi Aisen. 1932. *Yoko kara mita kazoku monogatari.* Tokyo: Isshinsha.

Yanagisako, Sylvia Junko. 1985. *Transforming the Past: Tradition and Kinship Among Japanese Americans.* Stanford: Stanford University Press.

Yanagiwara Akiko. 1928. *Ibara no mi.* Tokyo: Shinchōsha.

Yasumaru Yoshio. 1979. *Kami gami no Meiji ishin.* Tokyo: Iwanami Shoten.

Index

Adoption: adoptees as political pawns, 124; in America, 125; compatibility with blood continuity, 126–29; in China, 107, 110, 126; and compliance, 122–23; as cultural strategy, 116; degrees of, 370n.4, 377n.12; *dōzoku* adoption, 127; falsification of, 198; frequency of, 113; husband adoption, 126; of imperial consorts' children, 219–22; among *kazoku*, 112, 116, 118–19, 123, 124, 131; of kin, 126; in Korea, 107; of married couples (*fūfu-yōshi*), 111, 112, 123; and Meiji civil code, 107; modes of, 113–17; naturalization of, 131; of nonkin, 126–27; of nonsuccessor sons, 121–22; in Oceania (Truk/Hawaii), 125; parent-child relations in, 125; and patrilineal descent model, 107; for positional succession, 125; among samurai, 122; serial adoption, 127; socialization for, 124; of son-in-law (*muko-yōshi*), 116, 123, 126, 196; for status preservation, 122, 124; for 68succession, 107–25; in Tokugawa period, 107, 108; Tokugawa control of, 198; and upper classes, 108; (*yōshi-*)*engumi*, 122, 123. *See also* Blood; *Ie; Kazoku*

Adoption, daughter, 211–14, 336–37; arranged by Sōchitsuryō, 212; of emperors' wives, 213; to gain status fitness, 212, 240–41, 336–37; as metaphorical/ritual, 213–14; to protect family honor, 337; of Tokugawa shogun's wives, 213; *yōjo,* 212, 213. *See also* Adoption; Consorts; Marriage; Status negotiability

Aishinkakura Hiro, 201

Aizu, 52, 85, 92, 349; Aizu Club, 95; and enmity with Chōshū, 369n.5; and indignation toward Satchō, 95. *See also* Matsudaira

Amae, 245, 260

Amaterasu, 34, 40; *naishōten* as servants of, 311; state shrines for, 138; symbol of, 373n.5, 374n.5. *See also* Genealogy; Ise Shrine; *Kojiki;* Shinto

Ame-no-hohi, 81

Ame-no-koyane-no-mikoto, 34, 40, 80. *See also* Fujiwara

Ame-no-michine, 80

Ancestor careers: and ambivalence toward commercialization, 329–30; and court dressing, 327; and courtly arts, 331–33; daimyo/samurai reenactments, 328–31; and genealogical validation, 324–25; and own identity, 324, 330;

Compositor:	Impressions, A Division
	of Edwards Brothers, Inc.
Text:	10/13 Galliard
Display:	Galliard
Printer:	Edwards Brothers, Inc.
Binder:	Edwards Brothers, Inc.